THE Seuss
THE WHOLE Seuss
AND NOTHING BUT THE Seuss

A Visual Biography of Theodor Seuss Geisel

THE FIRST FLOWER OF SPRING

THE Seuss
THE WHOLE Seuss
AND NOTHING BUT THE Seuss

A Visual Biography of Theodor Seuss Geisel

by Charles D. Cohen

RANDOM HOUSE 🏠 NEW YORK

To my family,
Who indulged, encouraged, and enabled my imagination
Rather than limiting me.

And to my wife,
Who sacrificed creature comforts
For Seussian creatures
In the pursuit of knowledge
And the support of a dream.

I would have liked for my father,
The best soul I've ever known,
To have had a chance to read this book.
I hope it would have made him proud.

Contents

Introduction

I never met Ted Geisel, nor did I formally interview people who knew him. I learned about the man almost exclusively from an intensive study of his work as it appeared in original sources. So this book is really his story as told through his own words and pictures—a visual biography rather than a traditional one.

I was born into one of the fortunate generations that grew up reading Dr. Seuss. I was particularly fond of *And to Think That I Saw It on Mulberry Street* and *On Beyond Zebra!,* which extolled the value of the imagination, and *The Sneetches* and *Horton Hears a Who!,* which urged tolerance. More than anything else, however, Dr. Seuss's books instilled in me a powerful sense of wonder and curiosity. As a result, my life has been a series of independent-study courses. I start out with a casual interest in something, and before I know it, my inquisitive nature has taken over and I'm doing research. My science background no doubt fuels my hunger (which my editors will tell you is more like an obsession) for accurate information and detail, and I am propelled forward. I never know when one of these little adventures will start, what its subject will be, or where it will lead me. I simply go where it takes me.

For example, while working as a busboy one summer, I lost the harmonica I had been teaching myself to play, so I took up guitar instead, asking anyone who owned one to teach me a little of what they knew. When I developed an interest in wines, I sampled about six hundred of them at various tastings during a single year. I learned to make jewelry, developed an idiosyncratic painting and photography style, and fabricated artwork from found objects. A question about the worst hitters in the history of

Major League Baseball precipitated a scrutiny of late-nineteenth- and early-twentieth-century baseball cards and led to a subsequent hunt for those featuring Bill Bergen, who held the dubious distinction of being the very worst. I learned the rudiments of filmmaking at my local public-television station and audited film noir courses at Amherst College while working with my brother to compile a database and rating system for the thousands of movies we've seen.

Most of these amusements lasted about a year, but my fascination with Ted has persisted; I can't seem to satisfy my curiosity about him. It all started when I went to see "Dr. Seuss from Then to Now," a museum exhibition that toured the United States for a few years starting in 1986. The show got me wondering about the work Ted Geisel did outside of children's books. Unfortunately, as I started trying to learn about this other work, I found that there was surprisingly little information available. Yet the more I delved, the more frustrated I became. Not only was there a dearth of information, but much of what was available turned out to be simply wrong.

As I began collecting Seuss-related data and artifacts, a powerful sense of responsibility overtook me. Someone had to set the record straight. More importantly, someone had to preserve Ted Geisel's early work. I found myself on a mission.

Please join me in this consideration of the life and work of Dr. Seuss; let me share the many delights I've discovered and explain some of what I've learned along the way.

Charles D. Cohen
November 2003

CHAPTER 1
An Elephant's
Faithful . . . Sometimes

One of the questions most often posed to Ted Geisel was "Where do you get your ideas?" His stock "Dr. Seuss" answer for two decades was "In a little town near Zybliknov, where I spend an occasional weekend."[1] Later in life, he preferred to explain, "I get my ideas in Switzerland near the Forka Pass. There is a little town called Gletch, and two thousand feet up above Gletch there is a smaller hamlet called Über Gletch. I go there on the fourth of August every summer to get my cuckoo clock repaired. While the cuckoo is in the hospital, I wander around and talk to the people in the streets. They are very strange people, and I get my ideas from them."[2]

Either answer suited amiable journalists. The fact is that when faced with Greatness, few people truly expect a good explanation of how it works. One doesn't listen to interviews with legendary athletes expecting the revelation of why they are better than anyone else in their sports. We don't believe that Genius can be explained and, much as with an illusion performed by a master magician, we aren't really sure that we want to know how it's done anyway. The mystique is part of our enjoyment, part of what we respect. A clever answer or a good anecdote is sufficient.[3]

Dr. Seuss, ever the storyteller, usually had both. An example of the latter—equally self-effacing but more intimate and revealing in tone than the Zybliknov quip—is

One part Geisel, one part Cat, all parts genius: **Ted Geisel's** *Cat in the Hat*–**infused self-portrait appeared in the** *Saturday Evening Post,* **July 6, 1957.**

1

the tale that he often told about how *Horton Hatches the Egg* was originally conceived. Thrilled to have a good story to tell, journalists faithfully reported the account as it was told to them over the years. Inevitably, one reporter would take the previous reporter's article as gospel and accordingly would paraphrase from it.

Unfortunately, the anecdote revealed approximately as much about the true workings of Ted Geisel's mind as a search for Über Gletch would have uncovered. Ted liked a good story—often more than he liked the truth. Unless the original pieces are examined, much of what we learn about his work is no more than myth.

The story Ted told of Horton's own hatching developed over almost a 40-year period:

With the publication of both *The Cat in the Hat* and *How the Grinch Stole Christmas!* in 1957, Ted found himself courted by the media, which made him very uncomfortable. It isn't surprising that he relied on his storytelling ability to amuse and placate interviewers.

Which came first, the elephant or the egg? The infamous tree, the innocuous egg (this page), and the pachyderm who happens upon it (opposite page) in Horton Hatches the Egg.

That summer, a few months after *The Cat in the Hat* was published, an article on Ted reported, "Many of his books, he confesses, have had their start by accident. *Horton Hatches the Egg* came about because Geisel inadvertently superimposed an elephant over the branches of a small tree he had drawn earlier. So he worked for days trying to figure out how Horton could have got into the tree."[4]

Three years later, Ted added a few details to this account, clarifying how the superimposition had occurred: "I was just sitting doodling on some transparent paper. I had drawn a tree, and I had drawn an elephant. When one paper lighted on top of the other, it looked as if the elephant were sitting in the tree. That's how Horton was born."[5]

An article later that year reiterated the original story that "he chanced to sketch an elephant on an old pad of tracing paper" and then "afterward, he saw that he had superimposed the animal on a previously doodled tree. . . ."[6] However, much like Marco's story in *And to Think That I Saw It on Mulberry Street*, Ted's tale grew with each retelling. Playing the role with more gusto, Ted added, "I stopped, dumfounded. . . . I said to myself, 'That's a hell of a situation. An elephant in a tree! What's he doing there?' I brooded over it for three or four weeks, and finally I said to myself, 'Of course! He's hatching an egg!'"[7] With his more colorful reactions and the increase from mere "days" to "three or four weeks" that he had to work on the dilemma of what Horton was doing in the tree, the story was becoming quite a colorful one.

The interviewer, E. J. Kahn, was insightful enough to comment, "This is his conscious recollection of the genesis of 'Horton Hatches the Egg,' but his subconscious might demur, since he had done a cartoon for *Judge,* years before, showing a whale in a tree."[8] Although the line of progression from a whale in a tree to the story of Horton hatching an egg seems like a tenuous one, Kahn was at least aware that there might be more to the Horton story than Ted was acknowledging.

By 1965, Ted was no longer satisfied with this story. The randomness of the event was apparently not palpable enough yet. So he improved the scenario, explaining that he "was doodling around with drawings . . . and a sketch of an elephant on some fairly transparent paper happened to fall on top of a sketch of a tree . . . ,"[9] rather than saying that he had made the sketch accidentally on top of another one or inadvertently superimposed one transparent page atop another.

After seven more years, the element of chance was again sounding insufficiently fortuitous to Ted. In 1972, the story being told was now that "one June morning the Doc was standing at his drawing board searching for an idea when a gust of wind wafted the picture of an earnest-looking, flop-

eared elephant onto the top of a drawing of a discouraged-looking tree. Geisel picked up the two pictures, studied them for a moment, and *Horton Hatches the Egg* was born. ('I have been leaving windows open ever since,' says Dr. Seuss, 'and all that happens is that I catch colds.')"[10, 11]

The genesis of the idea was no longer tied directly to Ted at all. He didn't make one sketch on top of another. He didn't accidentally drop a sketch atop the other one. It was a gust of wind that was responsible for putting Horton in the tree. And once that happened,

Ted didn't spend days or weeks figuring it out—just a moment of studying the two pictures was all that was necessary. The fact that for its October release, the Horton book would then have had to be conceptualized, written, illustrated, edited, printed, distributed, and released a scant four months after this incident was supposed to have occurred didn't seem to bother anyone at the time.

Ted stuck with a similar story for the next decade and a half.[12] Almost 40 years after the original story, Ted made a few final changes for his biographers, Judith and Neil Morgan. Instead of the window being open on a warm morning in June, the incident was alleged to have taken place in early January. In this final version, "On the day after New Year's in 1940 Ted was back at his drawing board overlooking Park Avenue, doodling in pencil on tracing paper in search of an idea. . . . When Ted took a break for coffee and one of his frequent brisk strolls, he left the window open. . . ."[13]

Drawing "drawing board" inferences: **The National Motor Boat Show complimentary ticket, 1940 (top), is more likely the stuff that Geisel's drawing board bore that wintry day than the wind-blown papers he claimed conspired to fashion *Horton Hatches the Egg* (bottom).**

It seems much more likely that "on the day after New Year's in 1940" Ted would have been busy with preparations for the National Motor Boat Show at Grand Central Palace that was opening three days later, since the Essomarine booth on

the third floor contained two Seuss ships, a mermaid, and a fine sea menagerie of Ted's design. Visitors could pilot a boat called the *Nellie Bellie Blurtz* through the Associated Demons of the Deep, be deemed a commodore, and receive a newspaper with a personalized headline.

And for what it's worth, on January 2, 1940, temperatures on the street outside Ted's window ranged from -15°F to 8°F with the wind chill, with a decidedly "brisk" mean of -5°F.[14]

It is, of course, possible that an incident like this one occurred in one form or another back in 1940. Or the story could have been a complete fabrication, much like Ted's canard about Escorobus, a modern painter Ted invented to make a point to a friend who thought of himself as a savvy art collector. In that case, Ted went about painting the Escorobus canon and contended that Escorobus had asked him to be his agent.

So what really did happen in the case of Horton? In fact, the story about the superimposition of the images means very little. The real story can be found in the work that Ted published long before 1940, and requires only a bit of investigative work.

But only if the original works are still available. Most readers are familiar with the books published by Theodor Seuss Geisel under the pseudonyms Dr. Seuss, Theo. LeSieg, and Rosetta Stone. These popular books, produced on a large scale and periodically reprinted, will endure for as long as there are readers to revel in them. But a treasure trove of his other work in paper ephemera and childhood toys continues to be lost over time.

The periodicals in which Geisel's work appeared were generally printed only once, and most people threw each issue away when the next one arrived. Still more were thrown out over the years as they took up too much space in people's homes, or when a new generation inherited the previous one's collections but not an equivalent interest in them. In the paper drives during World War II, vast amounts of this paper ephemera were recycled. Many of the remaining periodicals yellowed and cracked with age, because of the acidity in the pulp of the paper on which they were printed.

Similarly, many of the three-dimensional items that were created from the works of Dr. Seuss have been discarded as the detritus of childhoods and as remnants of history. They have been replaced by more modern wares, destined themselves to become obsolete.

Discovering, locating, procuring, chronicling, and refurbishing this work, and making it available publicly, is the only way to ensure that the complete legacy of Dr. Seuss survives for the entertainment and education of future generations. This book is intended to provide a glimpse into the larger world of Dr. Seuss that is available to us if we care enough to preserve it.

CHAPTER 2

Forensics—Stalking the Elephant

Two months after he arrived in New York in the autumn of 1927, Ted began a cartoon feature for *Judge* magazine called "Boids and Beasties." The first set of drawings in this series dealt with turtles. The next week's feature was devoted to elephants. One of the segments (entitled "Who Is This Morose Little Rascal?") told the sad story of an elephant named Randolph and a bird named Lucie.

Who Is This Morose Little Rascal?

> For five years Randolph had been an inseparable pal and companion to Lucie, the skylark from across the avenue. Together and hand in hand they took long, pleasant walks in the country, sang expurgated kindergarten ditties, roller-skated down the boulevards and played at poker dice. One day Randolph suspected Lucie of ringing in a pair of loaded dice. In a burst of anger, he buffeted her on the button. She died, leaving three eggs.[1]

Birds (and elephants) on the brain: This 1927 *Judge* magazine cartoon illustrates Ted's penchant for pairing birds and elephants— apparently the first of many such couplings.

Thirteen years before the Seusspicious gust of wind, Ted put an elephant and a bird together in a way that left the reader with the dangling question of what becomes of an elephant and the eggs that a bird leaves behind. Randolph and Lucie elicit emotions from the reader that are the opposite of

6

those that Horton and Mayzie would later engender. It would take a good deal more than a blustery day in New York for *Horton Hatches the Egg* to develop from these meager beginnings into a book so well loved that it is still the only book Warner Bros. ever made into a cartoon.

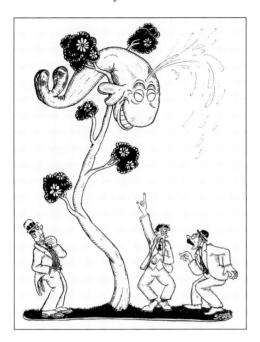

A few weeks later, "Boids and Beasties" dealt with whales and included the piece to which E. J. Kahn made reference when questioning Ted Geisel's account of how Horton developed. In "Hieronomo Is Drunk Again!"[2] Ted told the tale of Mr. Willis's whale, Hieronomo, who passes out in a tall catalpa tree. It is an early example of a very large animal out of its element, balanced precariously in a tree. However, Hieronomo the whale is no more sympathetic a character than is Randolph the elephant.

Two years later, in *Life* magazine, Ted unconsciously began to attempt to place a more sympathetic character in this situation.

Animals awry: **Other early examples of Geisel's tendency to turn the animal kingdom on its ear—a whale perched in a treetop (top left) first appeared in this late 1927** *Judge* **cartoon; a 1929** *Life* **cartoon showed a considerate dachshund bringing aid to a stork (bottom right); a 1931** *Judge* **cartoon featured a nesting walrus (bottom left).**

In the German installment of his "Life's Little Educational Charts" series, Ted drew an Obersch—"an obliging Dachshund who hatches eggs for storks"[3] atop the highest chimney in town. This cartoon introduced the concept of a cross-species surrogate who hatches bird eggs.

The idea continued to metamorphose. Two years later, an issue of *Judge* contained an illustration of a walrus perched in a tree trying to hatch the eggs in a bird's nest. However, nine years before *Horton Hatches the Egg* would be published, Ted did not think of hatching someone else's eggs as noble. The walrus was one of the pets in "The Truly-Dumb Animal Shoppe."[4]

Der "OBERSCH"
(An obliging Dachshund who hatches eggs for storks)

But if cross-species hatching were successful, what would the resulting animal look like? Flying elephants were on Ted's mind at least ten years before Horton. In 1930, they appeared to Noah's "dissolute brother, Goah," who brought two of each of the Delirium Tremens beasts on *his* ark, including a pair of airborne elephants. The following year, in *Vanity Fair*, Ted's opening illustration for John Riddell's article "The Science of Everything" was of "an early cow bird" being milked by a man suspended on a board underneath the flying beast. "Dairying . . . was a hazardous hobby"[5] back then.

AN EARLY COW BIRD
DAIRYING THEN WAS A HAZARDOUS HOBBY

Elephants became airborne (top) in the July 4, 1930, edition of *Life*, and a "cow bird" (bottom), another precursor to the trademark Seussian hybrid, made an appearance in *Vanity Fair* the next year.

Three years later, Ted began a three-part series entitled "The Facts of Life." In a timeline, he noted (for 998,000 BC), "Elephant eggs prove impractical."[6] The accompanying illustration depicted an elephant poised indelicately over an egg that has cracked under its weight. Ted was still getting

998,000 B.C. Elephant eggs prove impractical.

mileage out of cross-species egg hatching, and he was continuing to find the prospect humorously ridiculous. But—six years prior to Horton—he had finally locked in on the idea of an elephant hatching the eggs.

In 1937, Ted provided the illustrations for Albert Deane's book *Spelling Bees: The Oldest and the Newest Rage.* "For years, scientists have tried to cross the spelling bee with the ele-

Ovo-lution: Ted honed his fondness for the crossbred surrogate. Over time, it took shape and flight, as shown in *Life* magazine, 1934 (left), and in a 1937 harbinger of *Horton* from Deane's *Spelling Bees* (middle right) that bears a remarkable resemblance to Horton's hatchling (bottom right).

phant . . . who never forgets,"[7] read the caption below an image of a flying baby elephant-bee, which would be startlingly familiar to anyone acquainted with the elephant-bird that hatched three years later in the Horton book.

The real gem in this clear chain of evidence appeared in *Judge.* "Matilda, the Elephant with a Mother Complex,"[8] is quite similar to the Horton saga, but the outcome is exactly the opposite. Just two years before Horton, Ted still found Matilda the Elephant's attempts to hatch a bird egg to be as foolish as those of the walrus in "The Truly-Dumb Animal Shoppe" seven years earlier.

To place this story in the proper context, Ted's first book, *And to Think That I Saw It on Mulberry Street,* had been published just seven months earlier, and his second book, *The 500 Hats of Bartholomew Cubbins,* was still three months away from being released.

Early in 1939, Ted did an advertisement for NBC Radio that appeared in several publications and formats. It pictured an elephant cage fashioned from sticks lashed together,[9] prefiguring the cage in which Horton would be transported. Like Horton, this

Matilda, the Elephant with a Mother Complex
A Dr. Seuss Fable

ONCE upon a time, a herd of elephants decided to move from their old home jungle to a new and better jungle far over the mountains. In this herd there was an Old Maid Elephant named Matilda.

Like most individuals who own no children, Matilda was very, very envious. She would not walk with the others . . . but a little behind them, always watching the happy family groups through an eye that was dim and misty with tears.

One morning, while the herd was en route, Matilda, wandering sadly along by herself, caught a glimpse of something that made her heart surge. At the edge of the trail lay a tiny egg! A chickadee's egg . . . deserted and motherless.

"Good gracious!" gasped Matilda. "This egg is an orphan!" Down in Matilda's soul, something indescribable turned over and over.

"Yoo-hoo, folks!" she called to the others in a voice that shook and flub-bered with emotion. "Go on without me. My maternal instinct dictates that here I remain."

Wheeling about, the elephants witnessed the most amazing sight they had ever beheld. Very slowly and gently, Matilda was lowering her hind quarters down and down until they rested, ever so lightly, right on the egg.

"Why, girl, you're insane!" shouted the president of the herd. "Elephants don't hatch chickadee eggs!"

"Well here's one that does," retorted Matilda hotly. "Now bustle along." And when the president of the herd looked into her eyes, he saw that she meant it.

"We must leave her," he said gravely, turning to the herd. And silently the elephants lumbered down the trail and faded from view in the haze of the jungle. The Old Maid Elephant was alone with her egg.

Hour after hour Matilda sat and she sat, saying over and over to herself, "I *shall* have a wee one." By the end of the third day, her cramped stance began to pain her intensely. Soon she had eaten the last of the berries that grew within trunk-reach. But rather than risk moving, she sat still and went hungry. Small sarcastic animals came out of the jungle and twitted her unmercifully. But Matilda ignored them and stuck to her vigil.

Twenty-five days and nights of torture . . . and at four o'clock on the morning of the twenty-sixth, as Matilda crouched faint and shivering in a tropical downpour, she felt something stirring. Her heart stood still! There came a tiny sound of cracking, was followed by a *"peep"*!

"Eureka!" trumpeted Matilda. "My foster child is hatched!" Her joints creaked as she lurched to her feet, and she bent over to caress her new baby chickadee. But the chickadee, confronted by an elephant, cried out in terror. Shaking the eggshells out of his feathers, he spread his little wings and flapped off frantically over the tree tops.

Matilda never laid eyes on him again. Nor was she ever able to locate her herd. Today she roams the jungle, alone and friendless . . . a woebegone creature, with nothing at all to show for her pains but a very bad case of lumbago.

Moral: Don't go around hatching other folks' eggs.

A forerunner to Horton: This early "Dr. Seuss Fable" told a slightly twisted version of Horton's tale.

Dr. Seuss

elephant had been captured by a big-game hunter and bound with rope, looking very much like the lovable elephant unloaded from the boat in *Horton Hatches the Egg,* which was subsequently published on October 12, 1940.

Ted had found the sympathetic look for his elephant at last and discovered how to rearrange the pieces he had been mulling over for 13 years. The only window that had opened was one of opportunity.

Horton finds a form: Ted's ad-man day job proved to be a revealing testing ground. These ads for NBC Radio from 1939 (top left, bottom right) virtually herald the 1940 publication of *Horton Hatches the Egg* (bottom left, top right).

CHAPTER 3

My Book About Me

The true story of how Horton developed reveals a piece of information about the way Ted Geisel's mind worked that is more important than his comfort with confabulation or his predilection for practical jokes. If the adage that an elephant never forgets holds any truth, the real elephant in the preceding story is Ted himself. Ted's brain held on to ideas and images with a peculiar tenacity. This unusual trait—almost an inability to put things out of his mind—ties Ted's work to his biography more closely than is the case for most other writers and artists.

Ted's story can be traced back to at least 1650, when Joseph Geissel married Catharina Loth in the German territory of Baden, along the Enz River, in the town of Mülhausen.[1] These appear to have been Ted's paternal great-great-great-great-great-great-grandparents. Three generations later in Mülhausen, Gebhard Geisel dropped an "s" from his last name. Further down the line, Theodor Geisel (Ted's grandfather) married Christine Schmaelzle and brought the Geisel family name from Germany to America.

In 1876, the immigrant Theodor Geisel, formerly a jeweler, made a career change. He and apprentice brewer Christian Kalmbach purchased a brewing plant along Boston Road in Springfield, Massachusetts, half a mile east of Winchester Park and beyond the eastern end of the horse-car line. The plant had been built seven years earlier by Oscar Rocke and had a 1,000-barrel-per-year capacity.

The Kalmbach & Geisel Springfield Brewery Company grew quickly, as did junior partner Geisel's family. Theodor had come from a relatively large clan: His parents, Conrad Geisel and Elisabeth Frey, had 11 children, although three of them died in infancy. Theodor lost a daughter of his own—Christine Elise—less than two months after her birth in 1873. But two other daughters (seven-year-old Bertha Josephine and her younger sister, Emma Louise—Ted's aunts) were alive in 1879, when their first brother was born. The new arrival was Theodor Robert Geisel (Ted's father). Two more additions followed rapidly: brick ice vaults for the brewery in 1880, and a son, Adolph A. Geisel (Ted's uncle), in 1881. By 1884, the brewery's grounds covered ten acres, on which grandfather Theodor, his brother Robert M. Geisel, and their families were living. The brewery's capacity had burgeoned to 40,000 barrels per year.

Building blocks: Ted seamlessly wove family history into his work. A 1931 Judge *cartoon harks back to the icehouses of the Kalmbach & Geisel Springfield Brewery Company.*

These seemingly esoteric events that occurred before Ted was even born are much more than just a personal family history of who begat whom. For example, the ice that Kalmbach & Geisel harvested from nearby waterways in the winter and stored in those new brick icehouses would show up in one of Ted's *Judge* magazine cartoons 51 years after they were built.[2] The fact that his family was so intimately involved with the growth of brewing in western Massachusetts is reflected in the constant allusions to drinking in Ted's early work—from his first professionally published poem[3] to the wild menagerie of beasts that began as creatures seen by drunkards in the throes of the D.T.'s.

"Cripes! And she promised to marry me after the very first thaw!"

In 1888, Christine Cornelia Geisel (Ted's aunt) was born, and the five-story Kalmbach & Geisel plant was torn down and replaced with a new three-story brick building. In 1890, son George Alexander was born, but he died after just six months.

In 1895, Kalmbach & Geisel incorporated as the Highland Brewing Company, the largest brewery in New England, located on what would become the site of the Massachusetts Mutual Life Insurance headquarters. Grandfather Theodor was the president and treasurer of the company, which

Tools of the brewing trade: Two Kalmbach & Geisel beer bottles and one from Highland Brewing Company (top left, from left to right); a 1908 Springfield Breweries' Hampden Pale Ale bottle (top middle); and an 1870s Kalmbach & Geisel ad (top right).

employed his brothers Adolph and Robert and, in 1898, Theodor Robert Geisel—Ted's father.

In March 1899, with the new century approaching, the major breweries in Springfield—the Highland Brewing Company, the Springfield Brewing Company, and the Hampden Brewing Company—joined to form the Springfield Breweries Company. Grandfather Theodor became the manager of the Highland branch, and Ted's father became the assistant treasurer for the whole company.

In 1901, Kalmbach and Geisel organized a new brewery called the Liberty Brewing Company. Ted's grandfather was the manager, and Ted's father was appointed secretary and treasurer. He married Henrietta A. "Nettie" Seuss the same year. Like her husband, Nettie had a sister Bertha and had had a brother named George who died in infancy. Nettie's father, George J. Seuss, died in the winter of the year that she was married. The fol-

Family affair: Postcard ad for the Liberty Brewing Company (left), the brewery co-owned by the Geisels at the turn of the twentieth century. A sample of the Liberty Brewing Company's beer bottle (right).

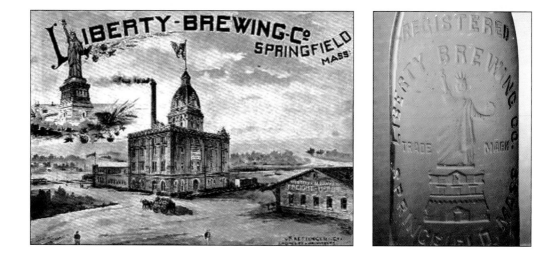

lowing year, Theodor and Henrietta named their first child Margaretha Christine Geisel (Ted's sister Marnie) after Nettie's mother, Margaretha Greim.

Two years later, on Wednesday, March 2, 1904, the future Dr. Seuss—Theodor "Ted" Seuss Geisel— began his life at 22 Howard Street in downtown Springfield, next door to buildings that give the vague sense of the castles Bartholomew Cubbins inhabited. Ted would have a sister, Henrietta, two years later, but she died within 18 months. By the time Ted was four years old, the Geisels had moved to 74 Fairfield Street near Forest Park, close to the famous crossing of streets known locally as "the X," where he lived until he left for college.

When the Liberty Brewing Company also merged with the Springfield Breweries Company, Ted's father was named manager of the Liberty branch, and he then moved on to become manager of the Hampden branch. In January 1920, he became president of the entire company.

A 1910 image of the Massachusetts State Armory on Howard Street near Ted's birthplace (top left).

74 Fairfield Street: Where Ted lived (middle right) from age four until he left for Dartmouth.

Unfortunately, Prohibition began almost immediately afterward when, on January 16, 1920, the 18th Amendment became effective, prohibiting the manufacture, sale, or transportation of intoxicating liquors. Bartholomew Cubbins would later experience something that Ted learned at an early age—that those in power can cause bad things to happen to people, seemingly at random, even to people who are working responsibly and trying to do the right thing. Despite attempts to market low-alcohol "non-intoxicating" beer as Prohibition neared, it was "last call" for the Springfield Breweries Company and Ted's familial association with the brewing industry.

Fore-and-aft drafts: In 1896, Extra Tivoli Beer was renamed when it won the competition in Baden-Baden, Germany (middle left). But with Prohibition approaching, even the recipe for the Gold Medal winner was altered to lower the alcohol content below the level considered "intoxicating" (bottom left).

* * *

What did the world's foremost children's author read when he was a child?

Hilaire Belloc, who became a Christian historian of note, wrote several books that Ted read, including *The Bad Child's Book of Beasts* (1896), *More Beasts for Worse Children* (1897), and *Cautionary Tales for Children* (1907).

These stories were illustrated by B.T.B. (Lord Ian Basil Temple Blackwood), and both the prose and the illustrations left their marks on Seuss's work.

The fact that Ted's father served as Springfield's superintendent of parks, and that those parks included the zoo at Forest Park, near his home, has led to the supposition that the zoo may have been the genesis for the Seussian menagerie. But Ted's father didn't take that job until Ted was 26 years old and living in New York City. Ted's first real exposure to animals and imaginary beasts was through Blackwood's illustrations.[4]

There was nothing in particular about Blackwood's style that stayed with Ted—just the content of the images. Ted's "persistence of memory" concerning Blackwood's images (to use the phrase popularized by Salvador Dalí, born the same year as Ted) can be readily seen in the example of the chamois from *More Beasts for Worse Children*. The image of this goatlike animal atop a peak appears in Seuss's work repeatedly for more than 55 years. Curiously, the one time he referred to a chamois by that name (in Ted's case, it was the Nelp, or Welsh Chamois), he did not use the familiar image.

Belloc's text exerted an influence quite opposite to that of Blackwood's illustrations—it was the style, more than the content, that remained with Ted. Belloc is reported to have said that children's books must have "terseness, simplicity, improbability and finality as to theme, strongly emphasized lilt—

Toddler Ted:
Photo of Ted in the backyard of 74 Fairfield Street, ca. 1908.

something indelible for the memory," an apt description of the rhymes that Dr. Seuss would later produce.

Cautionary Tales for Children, Designed for the Admonition of Children Between the Ages of Eight and Fourteen Years (1907), published when Ted was three years old, is peopled by characters with names like Godolphin, Algernon, Hildebrand, and Charles Augustus Fortescue, a list on which a name like Bartholomew Cubbins would have been right at home.

As that title suggests, Belloc's stories were intended to teach children obedience. Marco, Ted's Mulberry Street denizen with the overactive imagination, had his counterpart in *Cautionary Tales'* Matilda:

> Matilda told such Dreadful Lies,
> It made one Gasp and Stretch one's Eyes;
> Her Aunt, who, from her Earliest Youth,
> Had kept a Strict Regard for Truth,
> Attempted to Believe Matilda:
> The effort very nearly killed her.

But Belloc's world was very different from Seuss's *And to Think That I Saw It on Mulberry Street.* In Belloc's books, a "good" child does not tell stories of the sort spun by Marco, and no one finds Matilda's lies charming. After Matilda calls the fire department to report a nonexistent fire, the townspeople will no longer believe anything she says. Consequently, when she cries out for help during a real emergency:

> Every time She shouted "Fire!"
> They only answered "Little Liar!"
> And therefore when her Aunt returned,
> Matilda, and the House, were Burned.

The rhymes no doubt appealed to young Ted, but the disciplinarian behind the rhymes appears to have imparted a far different effect than the one intended. Ted's books championed the creativity of a child's mind. While Matilda's lies receive scorn from adults and cause her own death, Marco's fabrications reveal a lack of understanding in adults and cause only his own amusement.

Getting Ted's goats: The chamois (top left) young Ted encountered as an avid reader of Hilaire Belloc's *More Beasts for Worse Children* compositionally informed Ted's work for years to come. The goat made many appearances in his various magazine contributions to *Life* (top right), *College Humor* (bottom right), *Judge* (bottom middle and bottom left), and the *Jack-O-Lantern,* Dartmouth's literary-arts magazine (middle left and middle).

William Tell shot an arrow through an apple while standing on his son's head.

"WUNDERBAR! SIE SOLLTEN SIE IN DIE MOVIES GEHEN!"

Gnawing at Our Life Line

RUSSIA

PROPAGANDA ATTEMPTS TO CUT US APART

OVER THE HILLS

?MILES TO WHERE

"*** Just so long as we are traveling on the right road, it does not make much difference if occasionally we hit a 'thank-ye-ma'am.'"—President Roosevelt.

FINANCIAL NOTE—Goat's Milk is higher than ever.

Oh say can you Say?
By Dr. Seuss
說話繞口令
文・圖 蘇斯博士
譯 曾陽晴

And who do you think drew the horns on these goats?

The goat cavalcade marches on: Whether illustrating books for adults (top left), magazine cartoons (top right and middle right), children's books (bottom right and bottom middle), or political cartoons (bottom left and middle left), Ted continued to showcase the goat on the mountain peak.

19

In another story from *Cautionary Tales,* Jim transgresses by leaving his nurse's side while at the zoo and is promptly pounced upon by a lion that gobbles him up.

Notable among the victims of the ruthless march of science is the now extinct Nelp, or Welsh Chamois. For centuries herds of Nelp were raised for their slender horn, which cooks employed to jab into cakes to see when they were done. Then came August, 1427, and the Invention of the Broom! By furnishing our cooks broom-straws instead, we now save thousands of dollars yearly . . . but the Nelp is gone, and our forests are the poorer for his passing.

Now just imagine how it feels
When first your toes and then your heels,
And then by gradual degrees,
Your shins and ankles, calves and knees,
Are slowly eaten, bit by bit.
No wonder Jim detested it! . . .
The Lion having reached his Head,
The Miserable Boy was dead!
When Nurse informed his Parents, they
Were more Concerned than I can say:—
His Mother, as She dried her eyes,
Said, "Well—it gives me no surprise,
He would not do as he was told!"
His Father, who was self-controlled,
Bade all the children round attend
To James' miserable end.

Dr. Seuss's lions don't chew children—they lick lollipops[5]—and present no danger to the likes of little Lola Lopp in *Dr. Seuss's ABC.* Ted absorbed neither the fear of independence nor the fear of lions. His character Gerald McGrew, from *If I Ran the Zoo,* is not scared of "lions and tigers and that

The single chamois: **This illustration (above) from *Life* marked the only appearance of the goatlike antelope in Ted's work, intriguingly not situated high in the hills.**

Benign lions from *Dr. Seuss's ABC* (bottom left) and *If I Ran the Zoo* (bottom right).

kind of stuff." For him, in fact, those animals "are not quite good enough." Instead, he fantasizes:

> So I'd open each cage. I'd unlock every pen,
> Let the animals go, and start over again. . . .
> A *four*-footed lion's not much of a beast.
> The one in my zoo will have *ten* feet, at least!
> Five legs on the left and five more on the right.
> Then people will stare and they'll say, "What a sight!
> This Zoo Keeper, New Keeper Gerald's quite keen.
> That's the gol-darndest lion I ever have seen!"[6]

Belloc had a tendency to misspell words just for the fun of it or to make up names in order to finish a rhyme. For example, in *Cautionary Tales'* "Lord Lundy," he wrote about Lundy's aunt, referring to her as "His father's Elder Sister, who/Was married to a Parvenoo."[7] And when Charles Augustus Fortescue grows up, he marries "Fifi, Only Child/Of Bunyan, First Lord Aberfylde." Belloc's

books obviously left their mark on Ted, who raised the technique to an art form. The rhyme and the images stayed with him, and even though he rebelled against the morals of the stories themselves, the concept that a children's story should have an instructive role was one that Ted adopted too. He also took from Belloc the idea of a book structured on the

By the sea: **Approximately three-year-old Ted at play on the beach with his father and sister, Marnie (right), ca. 1907, and in a more tranquil pose with his father several years later (left).**

A manual of manners:
Popular during Ted's
youth, these books
were veritable guides
to too-good-to-be-true
behavior. Perhaps the
Goops' lesson about
treating a piano with
respect struck a
chord with Ted, who
turned the tables in
*The 5000 Fingers of
Dr. T* (top). In the film,
the piano becomes an
instrument of torment
for 500 unfortunate
children.

alphabet. Belloc's *A Moral Alphabet: In Words of from One to Seven Syllables* (1899) can easily be seen as a model for an early ABC book that Ted failed to publish and for the successfully realized *Dr. Seuss's ABC* and *The Cat in the Hat Beginner Book Dictionary*, both published in the 1960s.

Among the children's books of the time that taught lessons similar to Belloc's, the Goops books—including *More Goops and How Not to Be Them: A Manual of Manners for Impolite Infants* (1903)—also interested Ted. Gelett Burgess's book contains a story called "Piano Torture," the intention of which was to instruct children that pianos are not toys on which to bang and make a ruckus; they are fine instruments to be cared for and respected. Fifty years after the publication of *More Goops,* the cinematic world saw a very different version of piano torture, as envisioned by an older Ted Geisel. In *The 5000 Fingers of Dr. T,* it is the piano that tortures the children with the tedious scale-playing regimen, not the children torturing the piano with their playfulness.

Ted and a feline friend: Ted, with lion cub, possibly at the Forest Park Zoo (bottom). Like Gerald McGrew in *If I Ran the Zoo,* Geisel was fond of felines.

Not all the children's literature of the time was so puritanical in tone. Ted was also exposed to some very creative children's books, like those of Peter Newell. *The Hole Book* was published when Ted was four years old. An actual hole runs through the entire book, and each page tracks the passage of the bullet that makes the hole. Newell also wrote books like *Topsys & Turvys* (1893), in which the image on each page shows a second scene or interpretation when held upside down, and *The Slant Book* (1910), which follows a runaway baby carriage through pages cut on a diagonal.

Newell's books appear to have influenced Ted thematically. Unlike the children who stray in Belloc's books, Newell's Bobby in *The Slant Book* has a great time in his barreling buggy. Newell also challenged the limitations of accepted formats, such as what the traditional hardcover book was supposed to look like. In *On Beyond Zebra!* (1955), Ted would later challenge the restrictions of the very alphabet with which books are written.

Lastly, it seems unlikely that Ted missed Alice Raiker's *The Tootle Bird and the Brontos* (1907). Published when he was three years old, *The Tootle Bird* contains beasts like the Whiffle-Grub, the Snook, and the Rigglerok, along with others that bear a resemblance to future Seussian creatures in both name and look. During college, a 20-year-old Ted penned a short piece called "Our Own Natural History: The Woozle Bird." Woozles are genetically hampered—they are born with broken left wings, "and therefore cannot turn to the right while flying":

> The bird flies always in circles, and for that reason is fast dying out. The natives wait for the bird to become dizzy and fall to the ground, at which time they approach cautiously and put salt on its tail. The bird is then unduly weighted down behind and has to fly upward in circles. At length the bird reaches the upper strata of air where the oxygen is scarce and finally suffocates and falls to the earth, where the natives gather them up in large quantities. . . . The main commercial value of the bird lies in a secretion in the right foot, which is boiled out of the bird and used to make glue for postage stamps. This glue gives the stamps their delightful flavor. The males are generally black with white stripes, and the females white with black stripes, and when resting in flocks are nearly invisible due to their resemblance to a modernistic painting.[8]

The phonic similarities between the Woozle Bird and the Tootle-Bird might pass for coincidence, if it were not for the Panifh. Half a year earlier, the *Jack-O-Lantern* (the literary-arts magazine of Dartmouth College, which Ted attended) had contained the very first appearance of unusual beasts in Ted's work—the debut of the Seussian menagerie. Among those pictured was the Panifh, a six-foot-three bird whose cleats and truncated beak are its only noticeable visual departures from the Tootle-Bird.

The Tootle Bird also contains a grasshopper-like animal called a Hopper-grass—another precursor, this time for the Hippocrass, of whom Ted did a series of sketches in 1927. The story of the Hippocrass is an unfinished work apparently intended as an anti-Prohibition piece. The Hippocrass was an imaginary beast come to life—a product of delirium tremens inhabiting the real world. Although the story was never fully realized, the character of the Hippocrass crops up throughout Ted's early magazine work, as we will soon see.

From Tootle to Woozle . . . by way of Panifh: **This Tootle-Bird (right) from the early 1900s may very well have set an example for Ted. His essay on Woozles, 1924, and the illustration of one of his first uncommon creatures, the Panifh, 1923 (left), point to the shape of Seussian things to come.**

CHAPTER 4

I Can Write!

At Central High School, Ted began submitting work to the student newspaper, the *Central Recorder*, and developed the habit of assuming pseudonyms shortly thereafter. His work for the *Recorder* as a "live wire" and later as a "boys' news editor" ranged from mundane reports about the debate club to creative fare that gives us an early view of his skills as a poet and illustrator.

One of his first published pieces was "O Latin," a parody of the Whitman poem "O Captain! My Captain!" It appeared in the February 7, 1919,

Central High School, Springfield, Massachusetts: Ted's first submissions, both written and illustrated, were printed in the school newspaper.

issue of the *Recorder* and proves that 14-year-old Ted had both wit and a skill with words and rhythm. The poem was credited to "Theodore Geisel." During his high school years, he published variously under many permutations of his

O LATIN[1]

O Latin! my Latin! that study hour is done
My brain has weathered every verb, the translation now is won,
The time is near, the bell I hear, the pupils all revolting,
While follow eyes the unforeseen, a "comp" test grim and scarring.
    But O heart! heart! heart!
    The wrong lesson I have read,
    And at the desk the teacher sits,
    My lord, what she has said!

O Latin! my Latin! O when will ring that bell?
Rise up! rise up! for you are next—ye gods, but this is—,
For you bad marks and scarlet "D's", for you a failing waiting,
For you she calls, the teacher dear, her dark green eyes are gleaming.
    O trot! dear trot!
    The time is almost sped.
    It would be fine if on the desk
    The teacher would fall dead.

I surely cannot answer, my lips are tight and still,
My teacher looks so wild and bold, she gives me now a chill,
My classmates snicker, now they grin, a murmur starts to run.
A fearful class! I'll never pass! my lessons are not done.
Walk out, O class, when rings the bell!
    But I with mournful tread
    Go to the room at her request
    And come out almost dead.

name and other invented ones, including Theo S. Geisel, Ted Geisel, T. Geisel, Geisel, T. S. Geisel, T.S.G., T. G., Pete the Pessimist, Ole the Optimist, and T. S. Lesieg.

O CAPTAIN! MY CAPTAIN![2]

O Captain! my Captain! our fearful trip is done,
The ship has weathered every rack, the prize we sought is won,
The port is near, the bells I hear, the people all exulting,
While follow eyes the steady keel, the vessel grim and daring;
    But O heart! heart! heart!
       O the bleeding drops of red,
    Where on the deck my Captain lies,
    Fallen cold and dead.

O Captain! my Captain! rise up and hear the bells;
Rise up—for you the flag is flung—for you the bugle trills,
For you bouquets and ribbon'd wreaths—for you the shores a-crowding.
For you they call, the swaying mass, their eager faces turning;
    Here Captain! dear father!
    The arm beneath your head!
    It is some dream that on the deck,
    You've fallen cold and dead.

My Captain does not answer, his lips are pale and still.
My father does not feel my arm, he has no pulse nor will.
The ship is anchor'd safe and sound, its voyage closed and done,
From fearful trip the victor ship comes in with object won;
    Exult O shores, and ring O bells!
       But I with mournful tread,
    Walk the deck my Captain lies,
       Fallen cold and dead.

Ted turned his sense of humor and a penchant for puns to as much of the material as possible. Although news reports were, of necessity, somewhat dry, Ted managed to perk up even an announcement for the banjo club:

BANJO CLUB! The famous Central Banjo club is now being reorganized. It is predicted that this year will be a great success under the leadership of W. Sturtevant. He who plays, or thinks he plays, a banjo, should give his name immediately to T. Geisel, Room 13.[3]

As Pete the Pessimist, Ted turned out one-line jokes, called grinds, often directed toward the classical part of his education:

It'll be just our luck to be in Latin Class when they turn back the clocks.[4]

School days: **Whether he was covering club announcements or opining about the drudgery of Latin class, Ted marked his days at Springfield's Central High School, all the while sharpening his wordsmith chops.**

These days, such a joke seems routine, but Daylight Savings Time had been instituted in the United States only two years earlier. At the time Ted penned this joke, DST had been repealed on the federal level but Massachusetts had decided to keep it on a state level, so it was a relevant topic in Ted's neck of the woods.

"It's a fake!" growled Pete the Pessimist, after trying for two hours to translate his Cicero by the aid of a "Ouija Board."[5]

History tells us that a few words from Caesar would turn his army into a frenzied warlike mass. I'm not surprised in the least. Many is the Latin class that has been driven crazy by the same words.[6]

At little more than 15 years old, about nine months after the first citywide general strike in United States history had taken place in Seattle, Ted proposed the tongue-in-cheek notion of unionizing the students of the school to strike:

CALENDAR · 1917
CENTRAL HIGH SCHOOL
SPRINGFIELD · MASSACHUSETTS

"Day displaces day and new moons hasten onward but to fade."

A PUPIL'S UNION[7]

We, the undersigned downtrodden pupils of Central, hereby establish a Pupil's Union. We intend to gain the Student body as a whole in this organization and strike until we gain the following objects:
1. A two day week, a three hour day, and extra pay for homework.
2. Easy chairs in Rooms 1–36 inclusive.
3. Entertainment, as dancing and movies, in all study rooms.

He took a slightly more highbrow approach to the time-honored tradition of making fun of classmates:

A PLAY—IN ONE GULP[8]

Time—2 a.m.
Place—Otis Rice's bed room

A gentle noise like a sick alarm clock is heard.
'Tis Otis snoring. Noise continues for five minutes.
Suddenly a large crash breaks through the clear night air.
Racket continues. (Stage hands beat on tin boilers.) O. R. stirs, yawns, and slides onto floor (feet first). Disappears into gloom. A key is heard turning in its lock. O. R. returns, climbs into bed, and murmurs dreamily, "I thought I had locked up those loud striped socks last night."

CURTAIN.

Ted's early illustrations were not as promising. His first illustration, "'Frawncis' Blinn graduates," appeared in the January 21, 1920, issue of the

Ted's early forays into cartooning did not show quite the same degree of promise as his writing. This 1920 contribution to the *Central Recorder* bore little resemblance to his future fanciful illustrations.

Room to grow: Ted continued to hone his cartooning skills in these *Recorder* contributions.

Recorder, accompanying a piece, written by another student, called "To Come to This!" The Blinn in Ted's cartoon is a student in a class ahead of Ted's who was already in his fifth year of high school.

Cartoons in the *Recorder* were not always given attribution, and it appears that some uncredited illustrations that have been attributed to Ted in the past were more likely done by other student artists such as N. K. Fuller. Ted's illustration of Blinn is crude at best, and the other illustrations published before his graduation showed only rudimentary improvement.

Ted's final high school illustration depicts a rainy weeklong field trip to Washington, D.C., that included a meeting with recently elected Republican president Warren G. Harding (elected November 2, 1920), a visit to the National Museum, and some late-night shenanigans back at the hotel. The figure in the upper right corner, playing a ukulele in The New Varnum Hotel[9] window at 3:30 a.m. to the dismay of the guest on the floor beneath, is likely a self-portrait of Ted.

By contrast, Ted did develop better command of his writing style during his high school years. The *Recorder* provides us with one of Ted's earliest attempts at the short story. Continuing his use of pseudonyms, Ted attributed it to T. S. LESIEG. Lesieg is "Geisel" spelled backward, and Ted would later use "Theo. LeSieg" as a nom de plume in his professional career whenever he wrote the text of a book for which someone else did the illustrations. "A Pupil's Nightmare" was the first piece to carry the name:

Illustration of a simple device, the invention of Professor Keepem Workin, designed to enable members of the football squad to study while practising.

A PUPIL'S NIGHTMARE[10]

A gentle shaking awoke me from my dreams. It was Alfonse, the butler. I yawned, stretched and then lay back down again.

"What's the time, Al?" I murmured, with my eyes closed.

"Eleven-thirty, sir."

"Have you completed my homework for today?" I asked from the blankets.

"Yes, sir. Your lessons are done for the next three days."

"Fine! Have James drive me down to school at one o'clock." I turned over and slept again.

At twelve I arose and dressed, partook of a light repast of steak and mushrooms, put on my coat and left the house. My Rolls-Royce being painted, I descended to drive down in one of the little Packards. Luckily I was not seen in this disgraceful machine.

About two minutes later, I rode up before the institution. My coat and hat were carried to my dressing room by

When Theo met Warren: His final Recorder cartoon, a study of his Washington, D.C., class trip, depicted a meeting with President Harding. Note the familiar ukulele player in the upper right-hand corner.

the porter, to whom I gave the usual tip, five dollars. He glared at me and muttered something which sounded like "Piker!" I turned away ashamed of my limited finances, two hundred per month.

As I entered the room, to my surprise, I saw no one but the teacher. She informed me that it was the birthday of one of the pupils, and so school would not meet that day. Being vexed at not being properly informed, I went to the office. Upon arriving, I saw that I had come at an opportune time. The school board was meeting. I entered, and demanded the discharge of that teacher, which was immediately given, as I threatened to leave school myself.

There being nothing else to do, I left the building and rode slowly, about 80 per, down to my club. Suddenly, while I was seated comfortably in a cushioned easy chair, a well-known sound broke on my ears. I felt myself rudely grasped and was violently shaken. A shudder ran down my back, as I heard the sound. "John, ain't you ever goin' tuh git up tuh-day? It's quarter tuh eight!"

Near graduation a year later, Ted's creativity had blossomed, and he was willing to take credit under his real name (as T. S. Geisel) when asked to write the traditional "Prophecy on the Prophets" for the Central High School yearbook:

From the time of Olympus, when the half-witted soothsayers received their divinations from the gods, unto the present day, when the psychic parlor pests are favored with messages from ouija, coming events have been foretold in numerous ways. Not even the underworld visit of Aeneas, however, could have been so strange or unique as the manner in which the prophecy on prophets was delivered to the class.

Some weeks ago it came about that I was forced to undergo a serious operation at the hospital, namely the removal of a freckle from my nose. Eight surgeons

consulted, and then decided that the most powerful
anaesthetic obtainable should be used. Consequently,
I was administered several buckets of lazterp, a Russian
drug. . . . After the very first swallow of this concoction,
which was forced down my throat by means of a garden
hose, queer sights began to flash before my eyes. . . .[11]

It may seem odd that Ted was facetiously attributing the products of his creativity to hallucinogenic experiences with drugs, and that he would soon substitute alcohol as the hypothetical agent of his imagination. But he was now 17 years old, and these were much-discussed subjects at the time. While the unathletically inclined Ted was serving as soccer coach, the 18th Amendment to the United States Constitution was passed, beginning Prohibition, which must have made for some interesting dinner conversation in the brewer's son's home.

It was a historic period and an influential one upon Ted's development. His German heritage had become a sensitive subject two months after Ted started his freshman year of high school, when the United States declared war on Germany. Before the summer of his sophomore year, the upsurge of anti-German sentiment caused Congress to repeal the charter of the two-million-member National German-American Alliance. The Iowa city of Berlin changed its name to Lincoln. American orchestras refused to play works by German composers.

Less than two weeks after Ted started his junior year, school was closed for seven weeks due to an outbreak of influenza that proved to be the deadliest in history, infecting 28 percent of Americans and killing 675,000 of them—six times the number that would die in World War I.

Meanwhile, Ted was testing the water between the sexes—taking girls to Jensen's for ice cream, and serving on the Social Committee, the Prom Committee, and as assistant manager of Friday Night Dances, at a time when the 19th Amendment had only recently given women the right to vote.

By the time he graduated, Ted's quick mind had left a mark on Central High School. In the yearbook, he was voted both "class artist" and "class wit." He became an assistant editor for the *Recorder* and the grind-and-joke editor of the yearbook. He served on a committee that discussed whether yearbook contributions should go to the war effort. Although his aversion to public speaking was noted in later years, he was not as limited during high school: He served as secretary of the house for the debating club, acted in both *The Mikado* and *Twelfth Night*, gave mandolin and banjo performances at class assemblies, and performed in the dance orchestra. (He did, according to a report in his yearbook, look "very solemn and scared" during one mandolin performance when he was 14 years old.) Outside school, he volunteered to shovel snow to clear city streets during one storm, and he worked as an usher at the Court Square Theatre.

His last and largest high school contribution came in the form of a minstrel show that he wrote. Set in a hotel, the one-act comedy was called *Chicopee Surprised*. Ted also performed in the piece—as part of an instrumental quintet and for two solo songs ("Sweet Marimba" and "Dummy Practise").

When the *Recorder* published its description of the perfect high school boy, Ted was one of the chosen few:

THE IDEAL BOY AT CENTRAL MUST HAVE[12]

Arthur Lanciaux's eyes,
Don Benson's grin,
Ralph Walsh's build,
Dayton Phillips's oratorical powers,
Ted Geisel's wit,
Morris Brown's voice,
Max Savitzky's art of bluffing,
Dave Daly's ability in athletics,
Treen Hare's "shimmy."

The witty boy:
Ted's official senior photograph, as it appears on page 12 of the *Pnalka.*

CHAPTER 5

"I Am a Fellow o' th' Strangest Mind i' th' World . . ."[1]

On September 22, 1921, Dartmouth College's newspaper welcomed the class of 1925.

> Annually . . . hundreds of freshmen seek out Hanover and . . . embark upon . . . details of registration, the quest for a mattress, and a hundred other items of apparently vexatious character. . . . Problems that will look trifling in retrospect loom menacingly this morning . . . but among these hundreds are heroes of the athletic field and wizards of the book. . . . We are certain that theirs will be a substantial contribution to the College.[2]

Welcome to Hanover: College life afforded Ted a blank slate upon which to scrawl to his heart's delight. He provided this illustration for Dartmouth's literary-arts magazine, the *Jack-O-Lantern.*

Among those hundreds was a 17-year-old freshman who would prove their hopeful speculations to be understated, and who would become one of the most recognizable alumni in any college's history. For $160, Ted moved into 418 Topliff Hall, a 158-square-foot room that he had all to himself, overlooking East Wheelock Street toward the Dartmouth College Green. Directly across the hall from him lived upperclassman L. Bronner, Jr. Freshman roommates Cornelius Kurtz (from Buffalo) and Herbert Franklin Abrams lived diagonally across from Ted.

The dormitory floor plan serves to demonstrate once again the strange tenacity of Ted's memory. Six years after

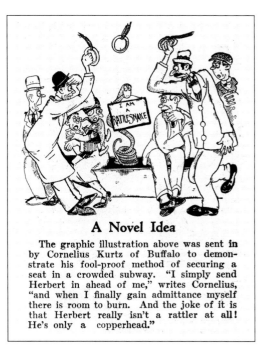

A Novel Idea

The graphic illustration above was sent in by Cornelius Kurtz of Buffalo to demonstrate his fool-proof method of securing a seat in a crowded subway. "I simply send Herbert in ahead of me," writes Cornelius, "and when I finally gain admittance myself there is room to burn. And the joke of it is that Herbert really isn't a rattler at all! He's only a copperhead."

meeting the students across the hall from him, Ted did a cartoon called "A Novel Idea," in which a pet snake poses as a rattlesnake to get its owner a seat on a subway. The passenger's name in the cartoon: Cornelius Kurtz. The setting: Buffalo. The snake's name: Herbert.

Appropriately, just nine months earlier, playing the role of Sir Andrew Aguecheek in his high school's production of *Twelfth Night,* Ted had pronounced, "I am a fellow o' th' strangest mind i' th' world."[3]

Persistence of collegiate memories: Even after graduation, Ted continued to cull his college memories. This 1928 *Judge* cartoon (top left) refers to Ted's freshman year dormmates, Cornelius Kurtz and Herbert Franklin Abrams.

Fresh(man) out of the gate: The first *Jack-O-Lantern* issue of the 1921–22 school year showcased these four pieces (middle left, middle right, bottom left, and bottom right) by freshman Ted.

Ted's closest neighbor, L. Bronner, Jr., was a member of the literary staff of Dartmouth's literary-arts magazine, the *Jack-O-Lantern,* to which Ted began submitting work immediately. Although the first issue of the year was

The Pied Piper

Soc-cer!

Two Arguments Against Matrimony

published within a month of his arrival on campus, it contained four of Ted's cartoons. They exhibit a youth's enjoyment of poking fun, a fondness for sophomoric wordplay, and—from the very beginning—images of the animal that would later become inextricably linked to his Dr. Seuss alter ego: the cat.

Also in the first two months of college, Ted was elected class treasurer and was one of two freshmen chosen as art editors of the only freshman publication—the 170-page *Green Book,* with pictures of the 537 freshman members of the class of 1925. After he'd acquired these two sets of responsibilities, his submissions to the *Jack-O-Lantern* tailed off. Despite having had four illustrations in the first issue, Ted had only four more published during the rest of the school year. However, he went on to become a prolific contributor to the *Jack-O-Lantern,* a member of its art staff and literary staff, and eventually its editor-in-chief.

He may also have managed a brief musical foray in his first month. At the Dartmouth clubs' third annual specialty acts/vaudeville Saturday night, according to the college newspaper, the *Dartmouth,* "an unannounced act was . . . slipped in. This number was a clever banjo syncopation by a freshman." There were no banjo players listed for the Mandolin Club, during whose performance the piece took place. If the unidentified person was either mandolinist Thomas Kennedy Gedge or guitarist E. M. Torbert, the only string-playing freshman members of the Mandolin Club, it would seem odd that the performance was unannounced. That leaves open the possibility that it was high school banjo player Ted Geisel who popped in for this impromptu appearance.

Ted worked to develop his illustrating skills during his years at Dartmouth. Initially, he appears to have drawn on some of his memories. An early cartoon of his that played on the popular expression "For the love o' Mike" may also have stemmed from a play of that name that had been performed in Springfield when Ted was 13 years old. On November 15, 1917, the Court Square Theatre, where Ted would become an usher during his high school years, hosted the New York production of Jerome Kern's musical *Love o' Mike,* which, while little remembered now, had been running for nearly a year in the city. Ted's father's brewery advertised in the program for that show.

Covering new ground with some old terrain: Another freshman-year illustration may very well stem from Ted's recollection of a play he saw in Springfield in 1917.

"For the Love o' Mike"

For another cartoon, "Jazz," Ted appears to have been unconsciously echoing an illustration he'd seen while working for the *Recorder,* his high school paper:

Our Jazz Band

JAZZ!

A crash! A pause!
Breaking all laws
Of music,
A wail, a moan
Of a saxophone,
A grunt, a groan
Of a mute trombone
Is JAZZ!

Minor chords
Condemned by lords
Of music,
Twangs soft and slow
Of a big banjo,
A violin's shriek
In a run unique
Is JAZZ!

Reverberation: Ted's 1922 homage to jazz (top right) may have been inspired by an illustration he encountered in his high school newspaper (top left).

Gams, games, and gin: Ted's *Jack-O-Lantern* contributions included the less cerebral but perennially popular subjects of women (bottom left and right), gambling (opposite page, top left), and drinking (opposite page, top right).

Mostly, Ted turned to puns. He drew a cartoon of perplexed students looking at pages of complicated equations in "Aftermath!!" In another, one bored duck asks another if he wants to go tease a hunter, to which the second duck responds, "I'm game." Ted spoofed the title of a popular instrumental song, intended to sound like a cat running on a piano, by depicting "Kitten on the Keys" as a rigid-backed society woman at a piano. He also provided the all-male college with a few puns that involved the popular (but somewhat risqué) subject of women.

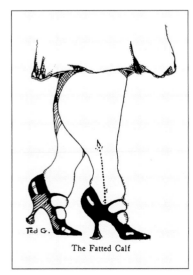

The Fatted Calf

O, clerk, there's something the matter with the keyhole in the door to my room.
That so? I'll look into that tonight.

Ted soon turned his attention to the other popular college pastimes of gambling and drinking, employing "Fish" as the first of many pseudonyms.

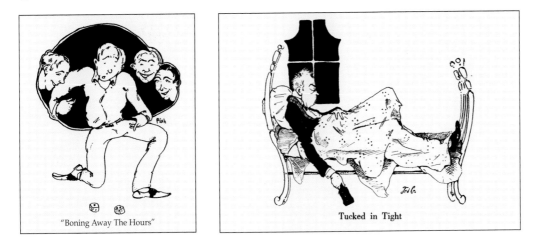

"Boning Away The Hours"

Tucked in Tight

But his education was not spent purely on the pursuit of wine, women, and wagers. Ted had done battle with the classics in high school, and as his knowledge grew, he continued the tradition at Dartmouth. In Tennyson's "The Passing of Arthur" from *Idylls of the King,* the knight Sir Bedivere sees that, with Arthur's death, an era of heroism and great deeds is ending. Arthur's dying words assure Bedivere that even the destruction of the Round Table has a purpose in God's plan:

> The old order changeth,
> Yielding place to new;
> And God fulfils himself in many ways,
> Lest one good custom should corrupt the world. . . .[4]

Classical riffs: Ted still found occasion to remark on the poets whose work was ever-present during his student days, like Tennyson (below) and Keats (next page, top).

In Ted's "The Old Order Changeth, Giving Place To The New," the change is not nearly as grand—just a switch in the order made by a diner patron. A "toast side" was Ted's frugal order at Scotty's, the local late-night hangout. It consisted of a couple of pieces of toast with a side pile of peanut butter.

The objects of Keats's awe in "On Seeing the Elgin Marbles for the First Time" were magnificent works of art—parts of the western pediment

"The Old Order Changeth, Giving Place To The New"

Expanding stylistic horizons: During his tenure on the *Jack-O-Lantern* art staff, Ted experimented with different styles and mediums, like watercolors (middle), working class character studies (bottom left and right), and airier compositions with smoother lines (opposite page, top and middle).

Mr. John Keats sees the Elgin Marbles for the first time.

"Pity the poor sailors on a night like this."

Bo-Bobians abound: The lineage of the peculiar creatures populating Ted's children's books extends back to these four 1923 *Jack-O-Lantern* works (opposite page, bottom).

A Woman's A Woman; But A Cigar's a Good Smoke

of the Parthenon in Athens that depicted a quarrel between the gods Athena and Poseidon. When Keats sees the Elgin Marbles for the first time in Ted's cartoon, they're aggies, allies, chalkies, clearies, immies, milkies.

As a member of the art staff of the *Jack-O-Lantern*, Ted also began to experiment with new themes and artistic styles. He ventured away from simple pen-and-ink sketches with an early attempt at watercolor, which reproduced poorly in the black-and-white magazine.

He continued to explore new ground, leaving Dartmouth themes and delving into somewhat more serious studies of people (misquoting Kipling's line from "The Betrothed": "A woman is only a woman, but a good cigar is a smoke").

Ted then left these more complex illustrations and tried simpler line drawings for a while—airier pieces that reflected vaudevillian humor.

"Did you have a local anaesthetic?"
"No. I went to a hospital in Boston."

In the most significant of these branching ventures, the *Jack-O-Lantern* provides the first glimpses into the strange beasts that would later become such an integral part of Ted's children's books. The Bo-Bobians are the founding members of the Seuss menagerie. Among the animals on the island of Bo-Bo are the Heumkia—the moron of the animal kingdom—which is a cow-like animal with a checkerboard coat that drools Prohibition-appropriate "near beer." Also populating the island are the Panifh (a six-foot-three bird in cleats), the Dinglebläder (a seal-like animal in a bow tie with halitosis and hoof-and-mouth disease), and the Side Hill Galloper (a goatlike animal that circumnavigates mountains solely from east to west, making it easy prey for hunters pursuing it from west to east). Other island-dwelling oddities include the Blvgk (a web-footed animal with an umbrella for a tail) and the Pseukeh Snake (a messenger snake bound to a roller skate with a bell on its tail, known for its use as a duck decoy and its ability to impersonate a pretzel). For

added faux authenticity, Ted credits the picture of the Dinglebläder to Lyman Howe, the largest producer of travelogue films in the country at the time.

41

Why is it when one sees animals like this one never has a gun along?

One particular item seems to have caught Ted's eye and precipitated the creation of more of these odd animals. In his junior year, an advertisement appeared in the college newspaper that pictured a dogfish and a catbird. These images may have set off memories of the illustrations done by Basil T. Blackwood for *The Bad Child's Book of Beasts*. In the first issue of

Jacko (as the *Jack-O-Lantern* was known on campus) to appear after the *Dartmouth* ran the Rogers Peet Company advertisement captioned "A catbird isn't kin to a cat, nor a dogfish to a dog," Ted extended his burgeoning menagerie with similar syntheses of animals, starting with a variation on the dogfish. Ted also displayed a very early version of stacked animals with hats that would recur more than 30 years later in *The Cat in the Hat Comes Back.*

Igniting the spark:
A Rogers Peet ad in the *Dartmouth* featuring odd animal hybrids (top left) and the childhood memory of *The Bad Child's Book of Beasts* (bottom left) may have influenced Ted's 1924 cartoon featuring an unusual animal tableau (top right). Of particular note is the early appearance of an animal balancing act, which would later resurface in *The Cat in the Hat Comes Back* (middle right).

ILLUSTRATED BY B. T. B.

THE BAD CHILD'S
BOOK OF BEASTS

* * *

Since written materials were not identified by author in publications such as the *Jack-O-Lantern*, it can be difficult to determine which jokes and articles in these issues really sprang from the mind and hand of Ted. Sometimes the authorship of the pieces is revealed in later issues, and occasionally the authorship is mentioned in other publications writing about the *Jack-O-Lantern*. Other times the determination can only be made based on stylistic flourishes and knowledge of Ted's history.

As a member of the literary staff, Ted had running gags about the Zimkowitzes and the Zilches (sometimes the Zilsches or the Zylsches). Ted reworked a Zimkowitz baseball gag in a 1928 issue of *Judge*. In the latter story, every single member of both the Harvard and Oahpse High School football teams is named Seuss—folks like Flossglouscester Seuss, Capt. "Whoobub" Seuss, and Hasslerig Seuss—although none are related.

Ted's running joke about the Zimkowitz and Zilch families in the *Jack-O-Lantern* is an early indication of his fondness for florid names.

Zimkowitz 14—Zimkowitz 10

Zimkowitzes Win in Annual Family Game

Lebanon, N. H. At their yearly family get-together here to-day the East Lebanon Zimkowitzes outplayed their West Leb. relations in a spectacular contest. The game was featured by the snappy playing of Zeke Zimkowitz (East) who, by the way, has been mentioned three consecutive seasons for the famous All-Zimkowitz team.

The score:

ZIMKOWITZ (EAST)	R.	H.	E.	ZIMKOWITZ (WEST)	R.	H.	E.
Zimkowitz 3b	0	0	0	Zimkowitz 3b	0	0	0
Zimkowitz rf	1	9	1	Zimkowitz rf	10	6	9
Zimkowitz cf	2	8	2	Zimkowitz cf	0	9	2
Zimkowitz c	3	7	3	Zimkowitz c	0	0	0
Zimkowitz ss	2	6	4	Zimkowitz ss	0	0	0
Zimkowitz 2b	1	5	5	Zimkowitz 2b	0	1	9
Zimkowitz lf	2	4	6	Zimkowitz lf	0	0	0
Zimkowitz 1b	1	3	7	Zimkowitz 1b	0	4	2
Zimkowitz p	2	2	8	Zimkowitz p	0	0	74
Zimkowitz*	0	0	0				

*Batted for Zimkowitz in the ninth

Home run—Zimkowitz, 2 base hits—Zimkowitz, double play—Zimkowitz to Zimkowitz to Zimkowitz, bases on balls—off Zimkowitz 0, off Zimkowitz 54, hit by pitched ball—Zimkowitz (by Zimkowitz), batteries—Zimkowitz and Zimkowitz, Zimkowitz and Zimkowitz. Umpire—Kelly.

After the game the families contended in their customary 40-man rope pull. Line-up will be sent on request.

While the juxtaposition of "Advertising: As It Is Done by the Greeks" and Ted's fencing cartoon on the same *Jacko* page doesn't necessarily mean that he was responsible for this satiric look at the "Greek" fraternity system, we know that in his freshman year, Ted was disappointed not to have been approached by any fraternities. A short time before this issue of the *Jack-O-Lantern* was published in his sophomore year, Ted had become a member of Sigma Phi Epsilon, and he would also join the honorary journalism fraternity Pi Delta Epsilon, so the timing would have been perfect for Ted's observations of the pledge-week phenomenon. Ted was taking a psychology of advertising course at the time, so the parallel between the two subjects would have been easily drawn in an amusing depiction of the process of "chinning," in which each fraternity's top one or two suave personalities try to persuade desirable students to join their fraternity (it was known as "sinking" them). Certainly names like Tappa Whosis and Hezikiah K. Whiffledinger are clearly of the type that would later be termed "Seussian." The phrase "for the love of Mike" also makes a return appearance. Ultimately, the key clue to identifying this parody as one of Ted's pieces is the presence of another Zilsch.

ADVERTISING: AS IT IS DONE BY THE GREEKS[5]

"Mr. Zilsch? I am glad to meet you I am sure. Do you smoke? . . . . . . You don't? Maybe you would like a stick of gum. I have seen you around the gym a lot lately, haven't I? . . . . . . Oh, you have been in the hospital for three months. You said you just came over from the Tappa Whosis house. What a bunch of plumbers! You must be hungry. . . . . . . What? They gave you ice cream? Jim, go out in back and see if ours is still there. As I was saying, they are an awful bunch of yeggs. . . . . . You liked them very much? Oh yes, they are a fine gang of boys only they quarrel among themselves and you know their Sophomore delegation doesn't amount to much around college this year. . . . . . Why? Well you see all but one of them flunked out. . . . . . They said that about us? Well, it's just like them. We don't believe in mud-slinging in this house. How do you like our gang here? . . . . . . That man with the pimples over there? Oh, he's a Freshman. I don't know how he got in. You see that picture on the wall up here? That's Hezikiah K. Whiffledinger. . . . . . Yes, he signed it himself. Who was he? Do you mean to say you never heard of him? Hey, Bill, here is a guy that never heard of Whiffledinger. Ha, ha. . . . . . Speaking of Whiffledinger, have you seen our new Victrola? . . . . . . O yes, it plays. Bill, where is the record? Bill says the record

"So you've taken up fencing?"
"Oh, I make a stab at it."

is lost, we'll have to get another. This furniture came from New York. It's worth . . . . . . Oh, I see. You say your father is in the furniture business? Well it's worth quite a lot. . . . . . That man over there in the sweat shirt? That's the janitor. These janitors are all terribly clubby. Excuse me just a moment." . . . . . . *Aside.* ("Bill! For the love of Mike get that dizzy wheat out of here. . . . . . What? You say the other one is back again? Good Lord, how am I going to land this freshman with that pair in the house?") "Sorry to have neglected you, Zilsch. I just told Bill to send that janitor home. He's worked hard all day—the furnace leaks. . . . . . What? You are going to the Trita Boxum house now? You had better hang onto your watch. Fine bunch of boys over there, but they don't rate a thing around the campus—awful knockers, too. So long, gladuvmetcha, 'm sure."

Ted bet that he could write about anything, considering the writing style to be more important than the subject matter. He did a comic piece on a fictional tic-tac-toe championship, complete with charts to analyze the "chuckers" between George A. Sanskrit and H. Hermann Haddock. He even wrote a book report about the B&M train schedule for a writing class and reproduced it in *Jacko*.

> *The Boston and Maine Timetable* . . . For as long as we can remember, the anonymous author of this work has

Jabs and jibes: This cartoon of Ted's appeared above an unattributed satirical piece that had all the earmarks of Ted's style.

yearly added one more installment to his great serial story, the B. and M. Railroad. And this year's offering, Form A 2435-X, adds still another bit of plush to the throne of its prolific perpetrator.

The main object of this novel is iconoclastic, in that it attacks without mercy the folly of blind faith. Page after page the author militates against the popular fallacy that "seeing is believing." And he quotes countless incidents . . . where people who believed what they were told have been left waiting in the end. It is a good point and well made.

But even the *B. and M. Timetable* is not without its faults. . . . Take for instance Chapter 17 which is entitled "Boston to Haverhill, Mass." In itself this chapter is all right—he tells his little story admirably. But when the reader reaches the end and starts in on Chapter 18 he will immediately, if not trainsick, realize that something is being pulled over his eyes. Chapter 18 is word for word exactly the same as Chapter 17, only it is run backwards. He has merely changed the title around backwards to read "Haverhill, Mass., to Boston," turned the story back side to, and expects us to swallow it. . . . It really is too bad when a capable author cheapens his product merely for the sake of quantity, and tries to get by on his reputation.

The only other bad feature of the book is found in Chapter 14, "Springfield, Greenfield, and White River." This is well written, to be sure, but horribly slow in moving, especially from Brattleboro on. . . .[6]

Although Ted was not much of an athlete himself, sporting events were on the minds of students in October of his junior year. The Dartmouth football team was undefeated, having outscored its first three opponents 130–0 (beating Norwich, McGill, and Vermont 40–0, 52–0, and 38–0, respectively). Joining the excitement, Ted drove to Cambridge with his friend Whitney "Whit" Campbell to see Dartmouth play Harvard. Upon returning from Dartmouth's victory, the two editors-in-chief scheduled a football game of their own, pitting Ted's magazine staff against Whit's newspaper staff. According to the victorious newspaper's account, "the event was Hallowe'en eve, the birthday of *Jacko*. So, befitting the occasion, president Geisel, playing a stellar game at left tackle, made a brilliant wrestle for the final play of the game. He dove for the fleet legs of Cliff Randall, quarterback for the *Dartmouth,* and found that he had those of Sleepy Jones, his own art director."[7]

On the slightly more intellectual side, French literature proved to be fertile ground for Ted's humor:

ALL FOR THE LOVE
(A piece in the manner French)

THE CHARACTERS
Gaston, soldier ordinary in the army French
Yvette, a girl of joy, his mistress
Raoul, a young man amorous of Yvette

Scene—Room of dinner to the home of Raoul.
Time—Eight hours of the evening.

Raoul—Wish you something to eat, my dearie?
Yvette—But yes, my angel, for example.
Raoul—We have of soup, of the fish, of the meat, and, for
the dessert, of peaches ripe and of the white eat.
Yvette—Me, I do not desire except of the fruit.
Raoul—Ah well, my god, what is it that you have then, my
well loved?
Yvette—Alas, my little cauliflower, I have bad to
the teeth.
Raoul—Let us go, now; I will be for you mister
the medicine.
Yvette—Thanks well, my friend. *(They each other kiss.
Enter* Gaston *by the door of the rear.)*
Gaston—Hold now, what is that which passes itself here
now for example?

Raoul and Yvette (together)—Nothing of all.

Gaston—Hey? Nothing of all? Ah well, I see that me. I have committed a grand fault irreparable. Let us go to drink.

Raoul—That goes well, I you swear.

Gaston (with the solemnity)—John has three pencils, Marie of them has six. Name of a name of a pipe, let us go to the Saloon of the Peace on the corner of the street of the Peace and the Place of the Opera. There we shall take a glass of the beer and, well possibly, a little tart of the ham. *(All the world makes the exit in a manner friendly.)*

CURTAIN

Signed,

J. B. Molière

H. K. N. Racine

P. St. V. Corneille

A. Z. Dumas son.[8]

In his "Helpful Hints for Textbook Writers,"[9] the fun with French continues, along with one of the earlier amusing takes on drinking during Prohibition that would mark Ted's cartoons for years to come, as Ted conjugates a hangover:

French liquids are easy to handle. Thence transition is simple to the verbs, thus:

Je vin	*Nous chartreuse*
Il vin blanc	*Vous benedictine*
Elle vermouth	*Ils sont absinthe*

After a few cracks about dentistry involving gumdrops and molar bears, Ted gets around to his theory of poetry, explaining, "Poetry—that is, really good poetry is supposed to rhyme. But . . . you'll find a lot of words that won't rhyme and are therefore . . . no good to poetry and poets." His solution is to provide some rhymes for difficult words, and the words that Ted Geisel creates are perfect examples of those that Dr. Seuss would later utilize:

48

Gargle—Bargle (to swat flies on an old male lion)
Silver—Pilver (to pelt with collar buttons)
Market—Darket (a small trunk to keep bats in)
Spectacle—Nectacle (one who holds hands in a niche)
Pantry—Fantry (a young woman who plays a cello in a bathtub)

In addition to the fun he might have been having with all of this word-play, Ted had a somewhat subversive goal in mind by the time he was elected editor-in-chief. His view of his regime at *Jacko* was displayed clearly when he learned that the magazine had been banned at a particular girls' school:

Jacko . . . just received news . . . of a Connecticut
Finishing School for girls that had anathematized
his magazine, and forbade its distribution in the
dormitories. . . . His monthly anthology of foul anecdotes is
locked up in the head-mistress' bureau drawer, and kept
from the addressee until the end of the semester; at which
time the matron passes the entire accumulation over to the
girl, advising her *not* to read them on the train ride home.
　　Jacko is wholly in accord with this system. He writes
his paper only for the extreme left wing of college
student[s], for the man of moral perversity. And assuredly
not for the pure-minded daughters of Connecticut
Aristocracy. . . .[10]

The aristocracy would be the butt of many of Ted's jokes once he began working professionally as a cartoonist, and bucking authority would be a theme that would carry through to his children's books. Of course, "moral perversity" didn't always carry the same connotations that it does now. In the issue in which Ted explained about writing for the extreme left wing, "Jacko's Additions to 'Etiquette'" proved risqué for suggesting that "a man should not sit down before a lady. It is, however, advisable to violate this rule if the lady expects to sit on his lap."[11]

But there were times when Ted's attitude did show through in ways that are surprising to those who know him only as Dr. Seuss:

"THE OLD CHIVALRIC FAITH—"

Some time ago Jacko was greatly worried,—worried for fear the College was becoming too gentlemanly. As a sworn enemy of Culture, Jacko from his grimy office viewed with displeasure the spread of Courtesy, Good Manners and Respect for Women. It almost seemed that the loud-mouthed swashbuckling braggart was gone forever, and that individuality was being stifled by decorum.

But today Jacko is happy, for he knows that culture has not as yet made undesirables of us all. (He writes this the morning after returning from the Thanksgiving recess.) It was balm to his heart last night, on the return train from Springfield, to watch those five Juniors tease those Prep School girls to tears. Some of the cleverest bits of insult Jacko has ever heard came to his ears last night. For what is more pleasant than to see five husky college men make some silly girls realize how insignificant and helpless they are? And so subtly, too. It is nothing short of genius to be able to sit back and whisper remarks that one has learned in the wash-room at the American House. (You know those hoarse whispers that can be heard all over the car.)

Jacko is certainly happy, for he knows that the prep school spirit is not yet dead. And he sincerely hopes he will be able to come back on the train with the same jolly Juniors after the Christmas vacation.[12]

Although this may come across as sarcasm aimed at the crass comments of the men on the train, the support for that behavior is too consistent with the view that Ted put forward during his editorship, and however odd it seems in retrospect, it dovetails with the slightly misogynistic view reflected in his cartoon "A Woman's A Woman; But A Cigar's a Good Smoke."

This was a very different time period, after all. The Marx Brothers had recently made it to Broadway and would be getting laughs there in *The Cocoanuts* (which would open on December 8, 1925, at the Lyric Theatre in New York City and run for 375 performances) with ungentlemanly interactions like this one, where Groucho, as Mr. Hammer, cuddles up to Mrs. Potter:

> *Hammer:* Did anyone ever tell you that you look like the Prince of Wales? I don't mean the present Prince of Wales— one of the old Wales. And, believe me, when I say Wales, I mean Wales—I know a whale when I see one. . . . What I meant was, uh, you're going to be here all winter and I'm stuck with the hotel anyhow—why don't you grab me until you can make other arrangements?
> *Mrs. Potter:* My dear Mr. Hammer, I shall never get married before my daughter.
> *Hammer:* You did once! Oh, but I love you, I love you. Can't you see how I'm pining for you?
> *Mrs. Potter:* What in the world is the matter with you?
> *Hammer:* Oh, I, I'm not myself tonight. I don't know who I am. One false move and I'm yours. I love you. I love you anyhow.
> *Mrs. Potter:* I don't think you'd love me if I were poor.
> *Hammer:* I might, but I'd keep my mouth shut.
> *Mrs. Potter:* I'll not stay here any longer and be insulted this way!
> *Hammer:* Oh, don't go away and leave me here alone. You stay here and I'll go away.
> *Mrs. Potter:* I don't know what to say.
> *Hammer:* Well, say that you'll be truly mine, or truly yours, or yours truly. . . . I'll meet you tonight under the moon. Oh, I can see you now—you and the moon. You wear a necktie so I'll know you.[13]

In that time period, at that age, in an all-male school, the view of women was unlikely to be any more gentlemanly.

Also like Groucho Marx, Ted was always ready to poke fun at the elite classes and the stuffy pretenders. Ted defined "intelligentsia" by breaking it down into Latinate roots: "'in'—a negation, 'telli'—to tell, 'gents'—gentlemen, 'ia'—a case ending. Literally: 'You can't tell these guys anything.'" For "cognoscenti," however, he returned to the increasingly popular Prohibition drinking jokes: "Derived from Cognac, a town in France. First applied to the natives of Cognac. Thence 'One who knows his hootch.'"[14]

On his editorial page in the first *Jack-O-Lantern* issue of 1925, Ted took space to comment, "Jacko takes delight in announcing that Mr. Anderson of the Anderson Anti-Saloon League is once again within the clutches of the law."[15] But Ted's attitude toward drinking would soon meet a rather serious and unexpected challenge.

The caption on this cartoon is Ted-ese for "This is the noisiest party I've ever been at." Later in college, such a party would lead Ted to a brush with scandal. When he dashed off this sketch during an auction some 60 years later, he apparently was forgetting his original "noisy potty."

CHAPTER 6

Theodor Grows a Welt

In the spring, there was an upsurge in the amount of attention that was paid on campus to the behavior and attitudes of Dartmouth students, and opinions were expressed about how they related to their generation as a whole. Ted had been elected to the editorial staff of the *Dartmouth* in late March, where he worked with friends like Curtis Abel, an established member of the *Dartmouth*'s business staff, and Whit Campbell, an associate editor. A couple of weeks into Ted's time on the magazine, the following editorial appeared, seemingly in marked contrast to the attitude Ted displayed as head of the *Jack-O-Lantern*. While Ted was not sole author, he may have contributed.

This Generation of Ours[1]

We are the froth of the post-war wave. Restraint cast aside, our generation rides the crest of freedom. But propriety and necessity [are] about to break the wave. The fringe of our generation will feel the downward sweep into the trough, where youth best listens.

This generation of ours had been painted a gin-drinking, thrill seeking group. As a matter of fact, the pennywise novelists have not produced accurate pictures. They have portrayed the minority who seek extremes. They have painted us as carousing with Bacchus and toying with Venus. But we do none of these as a generation. The weak among us have thus fallen victims to the freedom brought by the war. But our generation has not taken liberty for license as a unit.

This generation of ours, instead, has taken freedom to mean freedom from the duty of application. We have abused freedom until we are victims of laziness. We talk and dance and cultivate languor, but we do not work.

This generation of ours has perverted freedom as a means of escaping obligation. We ignore our duties and cast adrift our loyalties.

This generation of ours has lost appreciation. We have denied ourselves the sweet of gratitude. We have dulled the polish of sentiment, by not acknowledging our debt to the home.

This generation of ours has lost respect. Bound up in ourselves, we respect nothing that transcends us.

This generation of ours has lost humility. We do not recognize our own insignificance. We take the present as ours, instead of preparing for our heritage of the future. We assume the superman demeanor, to veil callow minds beneath.

This generation of ours is intolerant. Pretending benign tolerance, we shame the tolerant spirit by our pettiness.

This generation of ours has lost reverence. We are blind to the beauties of simplicity and faith. We scorn the virtues exalted by our elders. We bitterly arraign our elders for their sincerity. We profane beauty, because it cannot always stand the cold test of reason.

This generation of ours is stereotyped. We have confused individualism with eccentricity. In trying to be different, we have wandered from the worthy individualism which is based on valid conclusions concerning life.

This generation of ours is complacently smug. We have lost ambition and energy. We are fish outside the water of life.

This generation of ours is cowardly. We do not face life with courage, but try to escape. We flutter under the illusion of forgetting. We dodge the questions of life. We do not play square, because we are afraid to stake ourselves against life.

This generation of ours is ignorant. We expect the world to acclaim us. We do not dare to study reality, lest it show us our true unimportance. We relinquish the joy of hoping for the vanity of expectation. We are going to be surprised.

A few days later, on April 13, 1925, a similarly themed editorial entitled "The Unworthy Attitude" appeared in the *Dartmouth,* again discussing the problems with Dartmouth students—this time on the front page. But when that weekend came, Ted and his friend Curtis Abel were among a group of ten students whose Saturday-night partying became too raucous in the room that Ted shared with Robert Sharp at the Randall House, causing complaints from the proprietor and a visit from the police. Although there were certain "understandings" that were in place during Prohibition, this incident was received particularly poorly because the next morning was Easter Sunday.

Max Rudin, in the article "Beer and America" in *American Heritage,* contends that before Prohibition, there was a movement away from strong alcohol and spirits toward the less-intoxicating beer, and that, in effect, Prohibition had the paradoxical effect of reversing that trend. He quotes Samuel Eliot Morison as recalling that "college students who before Prohibition would have a keg of beer and sit around singing 'The Dartmouth Stein Song' . . . now got drunk quickly on bathtub gin, and could manage no lyric more complicated than 'How Dry Am I!'"[2]

The results of Ted's gin game were a bit more dire. Initially, the students involved were required to write letters to their parents, explaining what happened. Ted's father, who had not yet found a full-time job since Prohibition had closed the family breweries, wrote back to tell Ted, "While I do not object to your taking a drink, I do object to your taking one in Hanover, while in college, if the rules of the college do not permit it. . . . Abide by the decision of the authorities . . . and . . . serve your full sentence conscientiously.

Theodor Geisel: **Sober student or party animal?**

While . . . you are soon to graduate, make an attempt the next few weeks to eradicate this blot from your good record."[3]

The *Dartmouth* did not report the incident, but five days after it occurred, in announcing the release of the current issue of *Jacko,* the paper also announced that elections would be held the following week for a new executive staff for the final two issues of the magazine. The newspaper did promote a creative piece of Ted's that would appear in the new issue of *Jacko,* but unlike the other works it previewed, Ted's was the only one whose author was not named. By the time those elections were held, Ted's name no longer appeared as an associate editor for the *Dartmouth* either, and ten days after his mishap, Ted was replaced as editor-in-chief of the *Jack-O-Lantern.*

Attempts were made to show the changes at *Jacko* in as good a light as possible. When the day for the elections came, the April 28, 1925, issue of the *Dartmouth* described the premature election and the change of leadership as a switch to the plan that the *Dartmouth* had already adopted, "which brings the election earlier in the year to give the new officers a chance to prove their worth." The rationale appeared a bit thin, as no reason was given for why "the election of the business, advertising, and circulation managers will be held about a month from now." Presumably, they weren't at the party in Ted's room.

Literary staff member C. H. Frankenberg, class of 1926, was elected to replace Ted. The day after the elections, it was reported that "the new board will take charge immediately. There will be two more issues of the *Jacko* this year, the House Parties issue, which is at press now, and the Commencement issue, which will be put out by the new board under the direction of the retiring staff."[4] The newspaper went on to specify that "work for the Commencement issue will be credited." The pretense seems to have been that the old guard would be overseeing the new executive staff, even though no mention was made of Ted or the other outgoing staff members.

The day that the new executive staff was elected, the *Dartmouth* also reported that "what worries the President of Dartmouth College is not the immorality nor the irreligion of his students, but their 'unwillingness to subject themselves to or accept discipline in any form,' and their 'failure to think.'"[5] The paper also quoted Victor M. Cutter, president of the United Fruit Company and a 1903 Dartmouth graduate, as having said that "not a great percentage of campus leaders have shown up as successes. Many of them are unknown after graduation. Lack of seriousness and application to studies explains it. . . . After the many sensations of the war there has been an attitude of carelessness among college men."[6]

It isn't clear why Ted's drinking partner Curtis Abel continued in his position as business editor on the newspaper until graduation, whereas Ted was removed from his editorship positions on both the magazine and the newspaper. The administration appears to have been much more severe with Ted than it was with the other participants. It has been reported that his banishment from the magazine gave rise to Ted's use of pseudonyms, under which he was able to continue to publish despite the sharp punishments he'd received. However, this claim is a misstatement of the facts.

Ted had used several pseudonyms in high school. Earlier in college, he'd used many others, including Oo-La-La McCarty, Joe Liberalism, James P. Mikado, Florence Nightingale, A. A. Hennessey, Calvin Chumley, and Al Dumas on prose pieces, as well as Fish and Felix on illustrations. In the issue of the *Jack-O-Lantern* that came out more than three weeks *before* the drinking incident, Ted wrote one article as Jean Jean and signed one illustration as L. Burbank (contrary to the accounts that cite this cartoon as being published after he was removed from the magazine). There was no compelling reason for secrecy at that time; Ted's purpose was to make his work more enjoyable by employing clever references and allusions that imbued his cartoons with an extra layer of complexity.

"L. Burbank" was a reference to Luther Burbank—a horticulturist famous for his experiments with crossbreeding and hybridization, which produced plumcots, spineless cacti, and hundreds of other new plants. Ted presumably learned about him in the botany course he took at Dartmouth. He had previously written that the odd animals on Bo-Bo were "an assemblage of hybrids that would paint Luther Burbank green with envy."[7] Bovine hybridizations like the flying cow (an idea that Ted would continue to develop in his later work) and Bo-Bo's Heumkia may or may not have been the products of gin visions, but the drinking incident at the Randall House occurred too late to be factored into this cartoon.

Pseudonymous homage: **This 1925 cartoon of a cow in flight is attributed to a horticulturist known for crossbreeding experiments—an example of Ted's penchant for clever noms de plume.**

Six days after the drinking incident, the next issue of *Jacko* was released, indicating that the issue had already been at the printer when the trouble occurred. The timing is such that the party may actually have been a celebration for having completed the issue. As swift as his punishment was, Ted wasn't even replaced as editor-in-chief until several days after that issue was already for sale in bookstores. Consequently, although his work in the new issue appeared exclusively under pseudonyms, the conclusion cannot be drawn that the drinking fiasco was responsible. It should be pointed out that in the issue prior to the drinking incident, Ted had not simply used a couple of pseudonyms; he had already almost entirely stopped identifying himself directly. The closest he came to using his real name as identification in that issue came in a cartoon done by Wendell C. Jones, where "Ted Jones" signified that the caption and the idea for the illustration were not strictly Jones's own. Most likely, the move away from crediting his pieces in *Jacko* was aimed at avoiding the appearance of impropriety and favoritism; since he was the editor-in-chief, Ted had been trying to remove his name from almost all of his works, and he continued the process in this new issue of *Jacko*.

As with the flying cow that he credited to L. Burbank, Ted attributed his next drawing of a cow to L. Pasteur, the man responsible for the pasteurization of cow's milk. A comic about two jailed prisoners was signed Thos. Mott Osborne, the man known for his self-help programs for prisoners. Osborne had been warden of Sing Sing prison from 1914 to 1916. He had a Mutual Welfare League that functioned under the idea that inmates would be trustworthy if they were given trust.

Additional aliases: This cartoon of a milk cow (left) is credited to L. Pasteur; the jailed fellows (right) are credited to an individual who promoted self-help programs for prisoners; and the beleaguered fisherman (opposite page, left) was supposedly drawn by D. G. Rossetti, who would have figured prominently in Ted's fine-art studies.

"Sure is a tight jail, this."
"There's no getting out of it."

Unfortunately, Superintendent of Prisons John B. Riley claimed that Osborne's ideas amounted to "coddling prisoners," thereby destroying prison discipline and encouraging crime. Osborne received a grand jury indictment in December 1915 and resigned in 1916. Ted's use of Osborne's name, given Osborne's anti-authoritarian viewpoint and his resignation, turns out to be an interesting coincidence under the circumstances. But it carries no more hidden meaning than, for example, the fact that the new editor-in-chief was, like Ted, a banjo player.

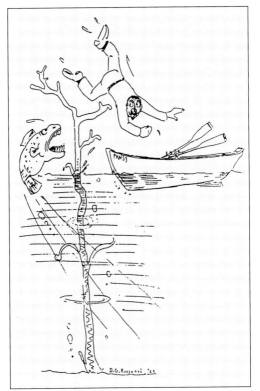

The other pseudonyms adopted in that issue of *Jacko* appear to have come from Ted's art studies. "Anton Lang" was probably a reference to the German sculptor and potter (1875–1938). "D. G. Rossetti" refers to Dante Gabriel Rossetti, one of the three founding members of the Pre-Raphaelite Brotherhood—artists rebelling against the "perfection" of Raphael's paintings, opting for more realistic scenes and people based on real models with non-idealized proportions. Ted, who had referred to the Brotherhood in the previous issue of *Jacko* as well, chose to assign the reality-seeking Rossetti's name to an image of Baron Münchausen escaping from a 40-foot smoked herring by spreading seeds underwater that instantly sprouted into pineapple trees.

By far the most significant pseudonym that appeared in this issue was Seuss. This was the first time that Ted had ever used his middle name—his mother's maiden name—to identify any of his works. In this April 25, 1925, issue, "Financial Note: Goat Milk is Higher than Ever" (part of the goat-on-the-mountaintop series illustrated earlier) was credited to T. Seuss, while "Kiss Me" was simply signed Seuss. These were not only the first cartoons credited to Seuss but

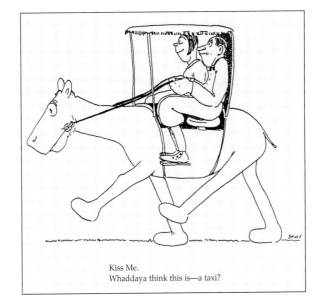

Assuming Seuss: This is the first time that Ted used the name Seuss in his credit line (bottom).

Kiss Me.
Whaddaya think this is—a taxi?

they were also the last credited cartoons of Ted's college career.

It is quite clear that this flurry of pseudonyms started in the issue that came out before the drinking incident, and that it burgeoned in the one that was already at press during the time of the notorious affair. Contrary to other reports, it was not through the use of pseudonyms that Ted was published after his removal from the magazine. In fact, he did not use a single pseudonym once he left his position with the *Jack-O-Lantern*. Rather, every one of his pieces that appeared in the next issue was completely uncredited. It is likely that the new rule, specifying that works would be credited for the final issue of the year, came as a result of Ted's use of uncredited anonymity as a loophole after he'd been removed from office.

When the penultimate issue of Ted's senior year was released nine days after the new elections, there was a note that read, "With this issue *Jack'O* goes into the hands of receivers." Prominently placed above that note, the following poem appeared:

AN INVOCATION
Being the Swan-Song of a College Wit

> If what I write at any time
>   Should make me out a dope,
> My readers fond will blame the rime
>   And judge me right, I hope.
>
> Though I may write that I have been
>   A devil of a fellow,
> My person still is free from sin,—
>   Outside my verse,—I bellow.
>
> My verse may fluently affirm
>   That I'm a thorough bounder,
> But than my will none is more firm,
>   No moral ever sounder.
>
> What I have sung, betimes, and writ
>   Is false and I abhor it.

But you've enjoyed my vicious wit,
    And paid good money for it.

And if I'd sung of virtues mild
    And wasted breath on truth,
You probably would not have smiled,
    And I'd have starved, forsooth.[8]

(At the time, students made money from the sale of these publications.)

In addition to this valedictory ditty, Ted also had several other uncredited pieces in this issue. It is heartening to see that even his embarrassing difficulties could not dim Ted's love of a good pun.

Still not completely chastened, Ted included (without credit) a story about drunken Lord Ravensoak, who comes home with a woman around his neck. She claims to be the daughter of an earl, but Ravensoak's butler, Cholmondeley, cleverly catches her concealing the accent of the lower classes in Soho and determines that she is a woman of easy virtue trying to trap herself a nobleman by getting pregnant. Ted's final words to appear in the *Jack-O-Lantern* during his time in college are those of Cholmondeley's sexual warning to the woman: "It is more blessed to forbid than to conceive."

1st Chimney-sweep: "Shall I go down first?"
2nd Chimney-sweep: "Soot yourself."

The new rules were effective—the final issue of the year does not appear to contain any of Ted's work. As interesting as the famed drinking incident may be, it occurred just two months before Ted graduated; so, however traumatic it might have been, it didn't affect him for very long. Four months after it occurred, he was on his way to England for postgraduate studies.

Reviewing his time in college as a whole, it is surprising to see that, even in his senior year, Ted's artwork had not developed to a point where a future livelihood as an illustrator and cartoonist seemed likely. On the other hand, his writing skills had developed considerably. And there were hints of

Unascribed scribe: **Even after his removal from *Jack-O-Lantern*, Ted contributed without credit.**

something else that seemed to come to Ted instinctually—an aptitude for salesmanship that would first see success in the advertising business and then be utilized in getting children to read. It didn't come from the course in the psychology of advertising that he took during his sophomore year. As he had demonstrated in his review of the *B. and M. Timetable*, Ted understood that a good presentation could make almost anything appealing. Here he applied this approach in joking fashion to educating lazy Dartmouth students:

> The average undergraduate mind broadcasted nothing
> but static. . . . That the average undergraduate was
> mentally null-and-void we were certain. . . . To make the
> undergraduate think he is being amused, and unbeknownst
> to him force learning on him at the same time would be our
> purpose. . . . The knowledge-detesting student will read
> our pages through joyfully. And then, at the last page,
> it will suddenly dawn upon him that he has been slyly
> educated. "Well, well," he will say, if he is any sort of a
> fellow at all, "education isn't so cut and dried at that."
> And he will then buy books and read them. . . . This
> then . . . is an intellectual Bromo Seltzer. Drink it before
> it stops buzzing.[9]

Even then Ted had the notion of getting people to read, despite themselves, by amusing them. There was, after all, method to the madness of "the strangest mind in the world."

Ted designed this flying cow for a membership list of the Pleiad(e), an honorary society at Dartmouth College.

CHAPTER 7

"From There to Here and Here to There"

Two weeks after graduation, Ted was back home and reporting to work for a summer job at the *Springfield Union* and the *Springfield Sunday Republican* newspapers. He filled in for columnist "R.P.M.," whose column, "On the Firing Line," was a staple in the *Springfield Union*, tossing out bits of politics, puns, and poesy. So began Ted's first foray into professional journalism. He was introduced unceremoniously in the last sentence of the column the day before he took over: "And now, dear readers, we leave you to the tender mercy of a substitute while we frolic through two weeks of vacation."[1]

In his first column, Ted quoted a piece of news from the *Union* that reported, "A salute of 21 guns was fired as the President went up to the right side of the vessel." Ted's response to this tidbit was, "Any man who has had a steam yacht at his disposal for over two years should be expected to come to the right side of it without being commended. This pampering of presidents is really being carried too far."[2]

This willful misreading of headlines and stories provided some of Ted's best comic pieces during his brief stint with the newspaper. When someone wrote to the *Youngstown Telegram* asking, "How can chewing gum be removed from a carpet?" Ted's response was "Don't take chances, is our advice. A new package will only set you back a nickel."[3]

"On the Firing Line" required that he provide pithy commentary on a wide variety of subjects. On the heels of his recent run-in with drinking and the law, Ted knew that Prohibition was still a hot topic. Accordingly, he noted: "A correspondent to the *Detroit Free Press* states that 'a person should not be regarded as drunk as long as he can hit the ground with his hat.' This test, of course, is invalidated if his head happens to be in the hat."[4]

Ted experimented with some verse early on, and experiencing a degree of success, he continued with bits of playful verse sporadically thereafter. He cited a ditty in the *Lowell Courier-Citizen* that read:

"In the name of our Republic,
    Together with our love,
We extend felicitations
    To Alvin Fuller, Gov."

Ted added, under the pun-title "Extending Felicitations":

"We'll go you just one better,
    (The *Springfield Union* says.)
And wish a happy birthday*
    To Calvin Coolidge, Pres."
(*Five days late, to be sure,
but the spirit is there anyway.)[5]

In another column, Ted quoted several examples of tombstone humor:

Upon my stone this legend write:
"He never said, 'Well, nighty-night.'"
    [*Akron Beacon-Journal*]

And on my stone, let this be chipped:
"He never wore his moustache clipped."
    [*Houston Post-Dispatch*]

And say, when weeping at my bier:
"He hardly ever said, 'Old dear.'"
    [*Youngstown Telegram*]

May this console my mourni'g widdy:
"He never called his child a 'kiddie.'"
    [*Cleveland Plain Dealer*]

Then he responded with the following couplet of his own:

> But when I'm gone no one can laugh:
> "That fool wrote his own epitaph."[6]

There were more serious subjects to cover as well. Ted continued to criticize the hypocrisy of moralistic pretense, as he had done in the *Jack-O-Lantern*:

> Maxwell Bodenheim was . . . charged with having
> published an indecent novel, *Replenishing Jessica*. Every
> once and so often these novelists will forget themselves
> and substitute letters for the dashes in "d—n."[7]

Ted also quoted the *Baltimore Sun* headline "Santa Barbara Quake 24 Hours of Hades, Says Woman," commenting, "It could have been worse. They say that the San Francisco quake was Hell."[8]

On the day that the Scopes Trial began, pitting Clarence Darrow and the theory of evolution versus William Jennings Bryan and creationism, Ted made direct commentary and, more amusingly, some observations of his own on the reaction that people have toward advances in science:

> "For the purpose of eliminating street noises, an inventor
> has perfected a tiny plastic ball that will fit any ear without
> danger of injury to the drum." Ah, that's the thing! We,
> also of an inventive nature, have devised a most delightful
> set of blinders that will fit over any eyes without the
> slightest damage to the lashes, and now besides not
> hearing the street cars, you won't even have to look at the
> nasty things. Just don these two contrivances and a pair
> of roller skates and have a friend drag you around, and
> you'll appreciate what science can do for the human race.[9]

A Bostonian had offered to contribute $10,000 to a fund to build "Bryan University, a school of fundamentalism." Reaching back to an idea he'd had during Dartmouth's undefeated season of 1924, Ted quipped, "The curriculum of this university will . . . be rigidly classical. Even the football team will call its signals in Roman numerals."[10]

After the regular columnist returned from his vacation, Ted tried his hand at theater reviews. Of Stark Young's play *The Saint,* Ted observed that "mysticism, a sensuous and ecstatic mysticism of religious fervor transcending itself, is the keynote of this four act play. . . . Without the stage directions and the author's foreword, the note of mysticism cannot hope to be conveyed to the audience, and the story stands merely as melodrama— mediocre melodrama."[11]

With those words, Ted's short time with the paper ended.

As summer drew to a close, Ted left for England to pursue graduate work in English at Oxford's Lincoln College. He did not have much success there, preferring travels and exploration to actual studies. Four months after arriving, Ted spent Christmas vacation traveling in France with Joseph Sagmaster, Donald Bartlett, and Philip Blair Rice—friends he'd made at school. These sorts of events had more meaning for Ted than his quest to become an English professor. The travel companions would remain close friends; it was to Sagmaster, Bartlett, and their families that *Yertle the Turtle and Other Stories* would later be dedicated.

Joseph Sagmaster further endeared himself to Ted by bringing him together with Helen Marion Palmer, an American woman who had spoken briefly to Ted in a class that they shared. It was by far the best thing that happened to him during his time in Europe. When Easter vacation came, Ted traveled to France again, but this time with Helen and her mother. On their first night in Paris, after knowing each other for only a few months, Helen and Ted broke the news of their engagement to her surprised mother. It was perhaps as controversial an Easter as the one he'd had the previous year at college, but it involved fewer policemen.

Ted's parents and his sister, Marnie, joined him in England that summer, with plans for travel and concerns about his fiancée, whom they'd never met. Although Ted's time there had fizzled to an end, Helen remained to finish her studies at Oxford. The Geisels traveled together, visiting the towns of their ancestors in Germany and Bavaria, including tiny Mülhausen, where Gebhard had misplaced one of the *s*'s in "Geissel." After his family left, Ted spent the rest of the summer and the early fall living the artistic life in Paris. The excited 22-year-old claimed to have run into Ernest Hemingway writing notes in a café a month before *The Sun Also Rises* was published and to have encountered Theodore Dreiser a year after *An American Tragedy* was released.

Later that fall, he traveled to meet Helen in Vienna, where he made a tentative change of plans to study German drama at the University of Vienna. However, he soon discarded that idea and returned to Paris, where he looked just as briefly into the possibility of studying at the Sorbonne. Finally, he met up with Helen and her mother in Florence at the beginning of Christmas vaca-

Classical inspiration: Ted's exposure to classical culture during his travels abroad is evident in this 1926 piece entitled "Gobelin"— a name synonymous with tapestry making since the sixteenth century.

tion. Helen opted to return to the States to start looking for work, and Ted stayed on in Italy for another month, visiting Rome and studying the artwork of European masters, which led to a few imitations and several more parodies.

Many of the pieces Ted appears to have worked on during this period have classical themes. In "Gobelin," while it may look as if the young woman and animals are running from a supernatural being like a goblin, the reference is actually to the fact that "Gobelin" is a particular type of stitch used in tapestries that Ted no doubt saw in the European museums, particularly during his time in Italy at the end of his European adventure.

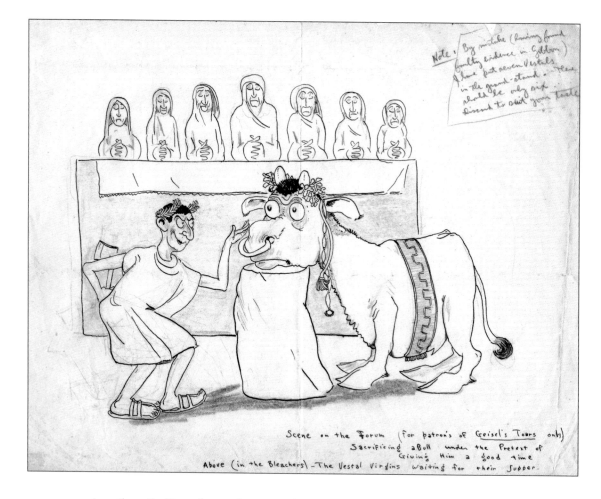

Scene on the Forum (for patron's of Geisel's Tours only)
Sacrificing a Bull under the Pretext of Giving Him a good time
Above (in the Bleachers) - The Vestal Virgins waiting for their Supper.

Another Italian-themed piece from this period is the "Scene on the Forum (for Patrons of Geisel's Tours Only)." The vestal virgins to whom Ted refers in the caption were the six priestesses of the Roman hearth-fire goddess Vesta, who were thought to ensure the luck of Rome by keeping the fire in the public hearth going. If it were to go out, it was believed that great harm would come to Rome. They served 30-year terms as virgin priestesses, after which time they could leave to marry. Traditionally, on May 15, the vestal virgins threw straw figures called Argei into the Tiber River. Interestingly, May 15 was also the day Ted was elected editor-in-chief of Dartmouth's *Jack-O-Lantern*, and at least three of his books mention this specific day. *The Seven Lady Godivas* commences, "On the fifteenth of May in the year of 1066, Lord Godiva, Earl of all Coventry, summoned his daughters to appear before him. . . ." *Horton Hears a Who!* begins, "On the fifteenth of May, in the Jungle of Nool. . . ." And in *If I Ran the Zoo*, the tizzle-topped Tufted Mazurka is described as:

A kind of canary with quite a tall throat.
His neck is so long, if he swallows an oat
For his breakfast the first day of April, they say
It has to go down such a very long way
That it gets to his stomach the fifteenth of May.[12]

During the June Vestalia festival, women brought offerings to the Roman Forum. It was usually closed to the public, reserved instead for the vestal virgins, whose Temple of Vesta was located in the southwest corner of the Forum. Apparently patrons of "Geisel's Tours" were treated to a demonstration of these offerings but had the added bonus of an extra virgin—a seventh vestal priestess whose presence he blamed on a mistake he found in Edward Gibbon's *Decline and Fall of the Roman Empire*.

In addition to working from art that he saw and history that he learned, Ted also derived inspiration from the literature he had studied. In one of Tennyson's poems, Enoch Arden, who has been shipwrecked and missing for eleven and a half years, returns to find his love, Annie Lee, wedded to her childhood suitor, Philip Ray. Ted depicts Enoch staring in the window of his old home at Annie and Philip as they admire their newborn baby.

By the middle of February, Ted was back home in Springfield, a mere year and a half after he had begun his European odyssey. Three schools had not brought him any closer to a career, but his other experiences had. He returned with a new career path; Helen Palmer and Joseph Sagmaster had steered Ted away from his halfhearted studies in Europe and directed him toward following and developing his love of drawing. Ted was certainly putting both his formal training and his informal education through travel to good use, but just how would his work be received back in the States?

ENOCH ARDEN

Once again, Ted parodied the classics in this sketch of vestal virgins as Forum spectators (opposite page, top).

Liberal artist: An allusion to a character in a Tennyson poem (this page) shows that Ted made *some* use of his college education.

CHAPTER 8

Destiny Blinx

With Helen teaching in New Jersey, Ted took a trip down to New York City and showed his portfolio around without much success. He spent the summer back in Springfield submitting cartoons to periodicals in the hopes of getting published. Drawing on his recent adventures in Europe, he planned to propose a series to *Life* magazine on "Eminent Europeans," including some clever observations about the lives of a stolid croupier and an out-of-touch palace guide. A letter to his friend Alexander Laing, to whom he had previously sent an idea for a series about the Hippocrass, reflects Ted's early, anxious attempts to get his cartoons published:

Eminent Europeans: Inspired by his trip abroad, Ted returned to the States with the idea for a series featuring two European archetypes—the impassive croupier (this page and opposite page, top) and the dense palace guide (opposite page, bottom).

> Not having received any checks, letters of praise or telegrams of disaproval [*sic*], I take it that the Hippocrass has not been housebroken. Be that as it may. I now burn with a new series—this time something for, say, *Life,* and if not for *Life* for someone else. This is a series of *Emminent* [*sic*] *Europeans,* to appear every week, and to consist of one (or sometimes two) sketches, and a verse of eight, nine, ten or eleven lines. . . ."[1]

The Croupier, as everyone knows, is the gentleman with the long rake. He is found to thrive in Monte Carlo, Nice, Cannes, Deauville and Biarritz. We are to play up on his complete detatchment [*sic*] from worry, his placid

indifference to whatever happens. If you win he is a disinterested bastard. If you commit suicide he is the same. (See sketch A.)[2]

Turning to sketch B we see him at home, where he is likewise immune from care or anxiety. . . .[3]

As for the members of his family using croupier rakes to aid their eating operations I suggest some such allusion; (very rough draft)

> And when they eat there's no such speech
> As "pass the bread" or "kindly reach
> And grab me off that hunk of steak"—
> Each member has his separate rake.[4]

Turn to sketch C. Here we find the Palace Guide. His shortcoming is this: He does not have his finger on the

American pulse. He does not know how to be selective. For, as the picture tries to show, he spends hours lecturing on the beauties of uninteresting picayunities—in this case the picayunity is a miniature statue of Napoleon astride his

steed. This statue has led the tiresome man into longwinded explanations of who made it . . . that it is not historically perfect in that the bridle shown is of a type that was not invented until three years after Nap's death. All this rot, while only two rooms away is the bedchamber in which Louis 14 dallied away his nights and his strength with Mme. Pomp or who you will. . . .[5]

Now, Sketch D is entitled I am not quite sure what. Perhaps "The Quack in the Baptistry." Perhaps "The Charlatan." . . . The scene is in the Baptistry at

Pisa. . . . Italy is full of chapels that have remarkable echoes. . . . This one is a fake. It is discovered by Mr. Abraham Nirenstein, of Brooklyn, N.Y. . . . He has paid the guide ten lira to hear the echo. The last line of your poem might read, "He got the liras back."[6]

What do you think of this as an idea for the summer months, when the tourists are in full swing. If you think it's rotten, say so and ship the bloody things back. If you think it'll pass in some sheet, no matter what, say the word and I'll turn out a half a dozen more sketches . . . post haste. I am sick and tired of being a Springfield Boy.[7]

Sketch D: **Another piece featuring the palace guide.**

The July 16, 1927, *Saturday Evening Post* contains Ted's first nationally published cartoon. In 1927, Lawrence of Arabia was a popular topic. Lowell Thomas had been showing his slide show about Thomas Edward Lawrence, called "The Last Crusade—With Allenby in Palestine and Lawrence in Arabia," and, in 1924, had published the book *With Lawrence in Arabia.* Two years later, T. E. Lawrence published his own reminiscences of his Arabian adventures in *The Seven Pillars of Wisdom,* a tiny edition of 211 copies, which was abridged and published in 1927 as *Revolt in the Desert.* This abbreviated version sold unusually well for Jonathan Cape & George H. Doran. Two months before Ted's cartoon appeared, the book was already in its fifth printing. Cape & Doran also brought out Robert Graves's *Lawrence and the Arabs*

that year, and Lowell Thomas published *The Boys' Life of Colonel Lawrence*. Ted's cartoon of two riders on camelback in the desert is reminiscent of an etching by James McBey, called "Strange Signals." McBey sketched and painted T. E. Lawrence, and his etching may have been the exact piece that Ted had in mind when he parodied the new popularity among the American upper middle class of Lawrence's swashbuckling adventures.

Encouraged by this single $25 sale (and obviously anxious to leave Springfield), Ted moved to New York within a month to try to make his way as a cartoonist. He moved in at first with former *Jack-O-Lantern* art staff member

"I Am So Thrilled, My Dear! At Last I Can Understand The Ecstasy Lawrence Experienced When He Raced Posthaste Across The Sands of Arabia in Pursuit of the Fleeting Arab."

John Clarke Rose. Change was in the air. On the last day of September, Babe Ruth became the first person in history to hit 60 home runs in a season. During the first week of October, the first successful talking picture debuted, starring Al Jolson. Ted's career began officially later that month when his second nationally published cartoon appeared in the October 22, 1927, issue of *Judge* magazine and he began his stint working on the staff of *Judge*. As premature as his move to New York might have been, Ted was convinced that he would now have a stable income, and he married Helen Palmer the following month.

These first two cartoons were credited to "Seuss," continuing a tradition Ted started with the last credited illustration he did in college. As he began his career of weekly cartoons, Ted also looked back to his college days for inspiration. The

DISSATISFIED WIFE—*And to think that today I could have been the wife of a six-day bike racer—if I hadn't listened to your rot about Higher Art!*

One-two punch: Ted's first nationally published cartoon (top), appearing in the Saturday Evening Post, tapped into the growing popularity of T. E. Lawrence's exploits in Arabia. His second nationally published piece (bottom) appeared in Judge.

"Mr. Elman, you fool, you're off the key!"
"There, there, Professor Bach, don't fly off the Händel."

"Curse you, Mr. Whitmann, once more you are off your Beethoven!"
"And again, my dear Gershwitz, you have flown off the Händel."

At *Judge* (middle), Ted continued to fine-tune cartoons with earlier *Jack-O-Lantern* themes (top).

The Dr. is in: This piece in *Judge* (right) marks the first appearance in print of the name "Dr. Seuss."

musical puns in his second cartoon for *Judge* were a thematic return to his senior year at Dartmouth.

Ted's mighty memory would not let him forget about his friends; he would often make references to them in his early cartoons. Dartmouth buddy Whit Campbell was shown using his pet elephant's trunk as an ashtray. Two weeks after Ted married Helen, Lincoln College matchmaker Joseph Sagmaster was pictured using his knowledge of psychology to hunt reindeer in a Santa Claus suit. There was an account of classmate Paul Jerman's Dartmouth fraternity initiation, in which he had to hunt a 50-foot whale with a hat pin and a collapsible boat. *Jacko* staff member John Rose was shown blackmailing millionaires by phone with the help of his pet snake Tecumseh, and Dartmouth dormmate Cornelius Kurtz used *his* pet snake to hold a seat for him on the subway. Thomas Phelps Carpenter, who belonged to the Casque and Gauntlet club with Ted at Dartmouth, successfully crossbred a deer with a dachshund. Vacation companion Philip Rice traveled to England, where he discovered that they feed their pet sea lions from across the table with a slingshot. Included with all of these personal allusions were references to the places where those people were living at the time as they continued their studies and careers, showing that Ted had kept in touch with them all.

Ted's first organized production was the creation of "Boids and Beasties," the first of several series that he would illustrate for various periodicals in the years to come. Along with the mock turtles in his first installment, Ted added some mock authority to the series by crediting it to Dr. Theophrastus Seuss. (Theophrastus was

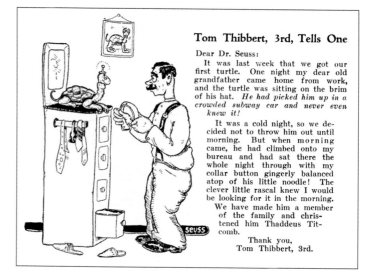

Tom Thibbert, 3rd, Tells One

Dear Dr. Seuss:
It was last week that we got our first turtle. One night my dear old grandfather came home from work, and the turtle was sitting on the brim of his hat. *He had picked him up in a crowded subway car and never even knew it!*

It was a cold night, so we decided not to throw him out until morning. But when morning came, he had climbed onto my bureau and had sat there the whole night through with my collar button gingerly balanced atop of his little noodle! The clever little rascal knew I would be looking for it in the morning. We have made him a member of the family and christened him Thaddeus Tittcomb.

Thank you,
Tom Thibbert, 3rd.

the name that Ted gave to a toy dog that he kept with him from childhood.) The segment in which Tom Thibbert, 3rd, addresses his letter to "Dr. Seuss" marks the first time that the name appears in that form in print.

As Ted's confidence grew, his characters began to develop a particular style. The pairing of animals and alcohol began to shape Ted's menagerie. In the early world of Dr. Seuss, a sober elephant can strap on roller skates and leap three men, but if he's drunk, he's liable to see serpents with little elephantine heads.

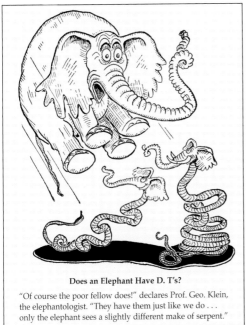

Does an Elephant Have D. T's?

"Of course the poor fellow does!" declares Prof. Geo. Klein, the elephantologist. "They have them just like we do . . . only the elephant sees a slightly different make of serpent."

An Infallible Test of Sobriety

How often people ask, "When has an elephant had enough? And "How shall I know when to refuse him another drink?" The test, friends, is very, very simple indeed. Simply put the doubtful beast on roller skates—and so long as he is able to hurdle three men he is still quite sober.

The full credit used for Ted's first periodical series, "Dr. Theophrastus Seuss," paid tribute to a childhood toy dog (top).

Intoxicating mix: The combination of animals and alcohol was recurrent in Ted's work (middle left and right).

Along with Luther Burbank's ideas of hybridization, "drunk" was the concept that—at least initially—made Dr. Seuss possible. His impossible beasts were not as implausible to the altered perception of someone in an alcoholic stupor. Ted often visited the images that one sees when suffering from the d.t.'s (delirium tremens) as a place to unleash his imagination. "The Waiting Room at Dang-Dang" is where, Ted theorized, the animals of alcohol congregate when they aren't haunting hangover hallucinations—the place where Mr. Fronk takes orders for the Beasts of Delirium Tremens, Inc. For a

The Hippocrass about town:
With this alcoholic hallucination come to life, Ted expressed his anti-Prohibition stance. Welcomed by the mayor of New York and sought by the press (this page, top and bottom), the Hippocrass made its way around town in a manner befitting an inebriated imaginary animal (first four images on opposite page).

gin party on Christopher Street in New York, he sends a carload of purple hippos with pink neckties. An absinthe orgy in San Francisco requires some flaming flamingos. A magenta puppy listens as a polar bear plays Beethoven's Fifth on his bass viol. When Fronk is stumped as to what to send for someone drinking fusel oil, a beige elephant smoking a cigar volunteers, stipulating that he'll take the job "under the condition, of course, that if I like it, I'll get all the fusel oil jobs in the future."[8]

Ted's friend Alexander Laing was working at the *New Yorker,* but Ted had been unable to interest the magazine in the story of the Hippocrass, an alcoholic hallucination come to life. It was one of the very first ideas he had for publication. In the "devolution yarn"[9] Ted envisioned, the Hippocrass is the embodiment of anti-Prohibition merriment and, as such, is imprisoned upon his arrival on Ellis Island. But flamboyant New York City mayor James Walker, who opposed nationwide Prohibition, rescues the Hippocrass and

gives him the key to the city. Once free, the Hippocrass becomes a favorite of the tabloids as he happily goes about getting drunk, leering at women, and generally championing the free spirit of the Roaring Twenties, while also studying humankind. President Coolidge, who enforced Prohibition, is depicted as a sourpuss in a sombrero emblazoned with a swastika—a symbol that the Nazi Party had adopted as its official emblem seven years earlier. A spokesman does the talking for Coolidge. Laing did write some verse for "The Hippocrass and the Tabloids" and "The Hippocrass Meets Calvin Coolidge & a Spokesman," but the series was never published.

In that series, there was another sketch in which the Hippocrass, with

playbill in hand, is the sole audience member at a play called *Asbestos.* An angry guard approaches with a lock and chain someone has taken off. The relevance of this particular sketch to the rest of the Hippocrass's adventures is unclear, but the problem of asbestos was being discovered at the time Ted did the sketch.[10] Ted may have been planning to use the Hippocrass in future sketches as a happy-go-lucky foil to expose humankind's foibles and follies and to comment on the more serious issues of the day if the idea was accepted by *Life* or some other periodical.

Ted also used the Hippocrass to comment on the scourge of asbestos (this page, bottom).

In 1957, Ted would use the Grinch to demonstrate the power of the Christmas spirit. However, in 1927, Ted abandoned his larger project and introduced the Hippocrass in *Judge* to demonstrate the effects of an altogether different kind of Christmas spirit. Incidentally, hippocras (or hippocrase) was a variant of the oldest alcoholic drink. Long before wine was made by fermenting the sugar in grapes, mead was made from the fermentation of honey. One variation was called pyment, which added grape juice to the honey-and-water recipe of "dry mead." Hippocras was produced by adding spices to pyment. It could be red or white and was served with either the main course or dessert. The name was apparently derived from the linen bag through which the mead was filtered, which was thought to resemble the sleeve of Hippocrates—the Greek physician after whom medicine's Hippocratic oath is named. As a matter of fact, Greek and Roman physicians made medicinal drinks by brewing hippocras with different spices.

The first prose piece ever credited to "Dr. Seuss" was "The Origin of Contract Bridge." His biographers reported that Ted and his wife spent their first anniversary in La Jolla, California, and returned with a resolve to conserve their income in order to purchase a home there.

Christmas Spirits And Their Effects

Orange Blossoms

"The Geisels cut out all-night partying and took up contract bridge, a new card game that was the rage. . . . Never wasting an idea, Ted satirized the game in *Judge*."[11] However, the satire was actually published more than nine months before their first anniversary, when Ted's job with *Judge,* which had started with cartoons, expanded to include lengthier pieces, such as this:

The Hippocrass had another incarnation in these 1927 *Judge* cartoons, depicting the effects of too much holiday "cheer."

It was all more or less an accident, so
I take very little credit for the discovery
myself. My brother's son, Anatole, . . .
was down in the cellar of our London
home not long ago making pop corn
for my birthday party, when all at once
the cellar caved in. Anatole, poor tot,
woke up in a nasty pile of rubbish in
a vast dark cavern some thirty feet
below the level of the cellar. . . .

Champagne

For three days the lad's curiosity led him hither and thither in the endless network of subterranean chambers. . . . Anatole forgot all about my birthday party, so absorbed was he in the rare relics he was discovering. He wandered over thirty-seven miles underground before he finally emerged through a muskrat hole on the banks of the Thames. . . .

Among the things he picked up were . . . knives with which the Druids sacrificed dingo dogs to their gods in 25 BC, an ossified doughnut, . . . and a Roman coin which without the shadow of a doubt fell from the pocket of Julius Caesar when he visited the Druids in the autumn of 52. But most important by far was a musty parchment manuscript . . . with . . . the vivid and breath-taking description of the *first game of bridge*! . . .

It seems that one balmy May afternoon in 12 AD, three fun-loving Druids, Aethelstan, Beowulf and Flloyd-Jones, found time heavy on their hands and invented bridge just as you see them doing in the picture.[12]

HOW THE GAME WAS FIRST PLAYED
Aethelstan has just bid three diamonds. Beowulf is just about to take him out in his strongest suit, or Smekyd-Skirmyt, as it was then called.

After eight installments of "Boids and Beasties," Ted created a second series for *Judge* called "Ye Knyghts of Ye Table Round," which was described as "Being ye Inside Dope on King Arthur's Court." In the first of these, the reader learns how a drunken fishing expedition led to the legend of the sword Excalibur.

The Round Table stories that followed included revealing segments about Sir Galahad, who, while the other knights are at war in France, stays behind and pushes through legislation banning alcohol. When the knights return, "ye taverns and ye inns were all be-padlocked and ye seven score breweries of Sir Budweiser were making fudge."[13] Fortunately, King Arthur has Merlin whip up an illicit still in the cellar for him.

This 1928 *Judge* cartoon, accompanying the first written piece attributed to "Dr. Seuss," satirizes contract bridge, a popular card game that the newly wedded Geisels would soon play.

JUD

How Kyng Arthur *Really* Got His Sword, Excalibur

*"When Spring doth come to Camelot
The Knights go forth and neck a lot."*

*S*O sing the bards, and they do say a mouthful. One bright spring day (not long ago) the sun was warm and all the birdies were a-chirping. It was a day when all the Knights had doffed their iron shirts and gone a-wooing. A balmy day. The daffydills did send their pleasant perfume forth to Arthur's royal snout, and it did itch for kisses.

"Methinks that I have It," thought Arthur to himself, and seeking out a comely chambermaid, did pet her upon the battlements and made the countryside resound with good substantial kisses. A jolly sport it was . . . while yet it lasted. But Artie has no luck in matters such as this. His ugly Queen, the sour-faced Gwenevere, perchanced to catch him at it. And he caught helle for fair.

Some moments after, I did chance to come upon the kyng. He hung, dejected, o'er the balustrade.

"Thy beak is red, m'lord," quoth I. "Perchance the Queen hath tweaked it."

*Ye Knyghts of Ye
Being ye Inside Dope*

*Translated from M
By
Doctor Theoph*

Ye Knyghts of Ye Table Round
*Reading from Lefte to Ryghte
Sir Bedevere, Sir Kay, Sir Gawain,
Kyng Arthur, Merlin, Sir Lavaine,
Sir Percival*

The kyng and good Sir Kay were catching fish.

Ye Faerie Queene

"She has, forsooth," spake he. "And I am mightily fed up upon her hooie. The Queen to me is so much badde news. Good Merlin, let us hence and get most primely drunk."

"Thy word is law to me, thou sage," spake I, and forthwith we did don our drinking clothes. We hiked off to the Hot Dog Inn, and there did stow away a shott or two of Gordonne Gynn.

It came to pass that after seven more, Kyng Arthur lost his crown. And while he was a-searching for it underneath the table, he ran into Sir Kay, his noble Seneschal.

'Fancy meeting you here!" quoth Arthur, greatly pleased. "I left thee here beneath this very table full a month ago. Hast thou been under ever since?"

I did chance to come upon the Kyng. He hung, dejected, o'er the balustrade.

*Ye Knyghts
of Ye Table
Round,
another of
Ted's series
to appear
in Judge,
depicted
men whose
behavior
was not
entirely
courtly
yet was
somehow
supremely
Seussian.*

G E

e Table Round
n King Arthur's Court

erlin's Memoirs

astus Seuss.

"Indeed. I have been here since Candle-mass," quoth Kay. "It is a new world's record." "Then we must celebrate," spake Arthur. We did, and soon it came to pass that I passed out.

When I came to myself again, I found me in the bow of Arthur's fishing smack, "Ye Faerie Queen." The kyng and good sir Kay were catching fish.

"One drink each time you make a catch," suggested I, the tipsy Merlin.

"That shall we do forsooth," cried Art, and straightaway he pulled up eight and fifty herring. We drank to each . . . and soon the welkin rang with song . . . and how! Then Arthur caught another fish, a fish of wondrous hue and captivating personality. A talking fish it seemed to be, and it did tell us many wondrous jests until our sides did ache. The kyng was mightily amused and fell into the lake.

"Long lave the kyng!" bawled ever gallant Kay, and threw himself in after. And long the twain did gambol like sportive whales.

"My word!" quoth Arthur when he at last had swum ashore. "I have bedrenched mine only ermine coat. And what is more, mine iron drawers are all with rust. Shrewd Merlin, how shall I escape the guff of sour-jowled Gwen, the Queen."

So I did think upon a noble gag. I knew a gent who ran the most resplendent Pawne Shoppe in the realm, and we did go to him beneath his gilded three-ball sign. A wondrous sword we purchased there for twenty shillings tupence.

It was forsooth a wow, and cheap at twice the price. And after that, I steered the kyng back to the drawbridge of his castle. The queen espied him coming with the sword.

"Thou sot!" spake Gwen to him. "Thou art all wet! Hast thou been bestewed with wine again?"

"Not so, m'love," lied he, though he was boiled as any owl. " 'Tis true . . . hic . . . hic . . . that I am dripping moist. But 'twas because a goddess made me swim to fetch this sword. The Lady of the Lake gave me this won'ful blade. 'Tis called Excal'b'r, m'love."

And Gwen, the stupid gal, got taken in, as did the knights and ladies of the court and all the yokels of the land.

"The Lady of the Lake gave me this won'ful blade. 'Tis called Excal'b'r!"

"I have forgot mine spectacles"

In another installment, Sir Launcelot circulates a rumor that a pack of dragons has been stealing women from the kingdom. When the knights ride out to slay the dragons, Launcelot seeks out King Arthur and says, "Oh, gee, m'Lord! I have forgotten mine spectacles, without which I cannot tell a dragon from an Airedale. I'll dash right home and fetch 'em."[14] While the knights spend 30 days searching for the nonexistent dragons, Launcelot has a month in which to make "goo-goo eyes at Arthur's wife, the queen, without the least disturbance."[15]

Ted's first nationally published poem was "To My Grandmother, My 'Buddy,'" and it provides the first glimpse of a more recognizable "Dr. Seuss" experience. Ted manages to be funny and lively while carefully adhering to a formal meter. The illustration is whimsical and wild, and the characters have odd Seussian names, including the Hippocrass-inspired Blinx. The subject matter, however, is still Prohibition. Ted also mentions the two competing brands of bug spray at the time—Flytox and Flit—one of which would soon carry him into the next big phase of his career. (Note that both of Ted's real grandmothers—Christine Schmaelzle Geisel and Margaretha Greim Seuss—died before he entered high school.)

The legend continues: **More Arthurian absurdity (left). Note the randy writing on the pennant.**

Ted's first published poem carried all the stock Seuss earmarks—carefully metered and inventive wordplay accompanied by a drawing featuring a bizarre beastie in the Hippocrass mode (right).

To My Grandmother, My "Buddy"

One thing that I like about Grandmother Squeers
Is the fact that she's modern in spite of her years.
She doesn't take stock in this talk about Hell
And her flask is as deep as the Bottomless Well,
And as to the contents, she cares not a bit,
Be they cocktails of Flytox or highballs of Flit.

Granny Squeers has a hound-sort of a beast called a Blinx.
You don't call him by whistling; you merely take drinks,
And when he appears we just get up astride
And he takes us right out for a heavenly ride.
We cling to his back just as long as we're able,
Then he gently deposits us under the table.

And therefore I say with a slight touch of pride
You can search the whole world, you can search far and wide,
But better companions will never be found
Than my darling old Grandmother Squeers and her hound.[16]

Providential product placement: According to Ted, two *Judge* cartoons with references to Flit garnered him the attention of advertising executives and ultimately a contract to create Flit advertisements.

Although Ted's impulsivity had gotten him into a few difficulties over the past few years, the pendulum of providence had begun to take a very long and steady swing back in Ted's favor. He had known Helen for only a few months when they had gotten engaged. He had changed his career plans completely and yet, after only a few months of effort, he had gotten a cartoon published. He'd moved to New York based on a $25 sale. Within two months, he had a job with *Judge*, and he married Helen the following month.

MEDIÆVAL TENANT—*Darn it all, another Dragon. And just after I'd sprayed the whole castle with Flit!*

Ted's fortune continued apace. Two months after getting married, Ted made a decision regarding the punch line of one of his *Judge* cartoons, choosing the insecticide Flit over its competitor, Flytox. A Flit spray gun was the focus of another cartoon two months later, and these cartoons were brought to the attention of Lincoln Cleaves, the McCann-Erickson advertising executive handling the Flit account of Standard Oil of New Jersey.

The anecdote that Ted told his biographers was that as luck would have it, Cleaves's wife thought that Flit should utilize Ted's talents. "Grace . . .

The exterminator-man forgets himself at the flea-circus.

83

"Don't worry, Papa, Willie just swallowed a bug, and I'm having him gargle with Flit."   Advt.

Cleaves . . . saw his cartoon at a hairdresser's and urged her husband to call the artist and sign him up."[17] They offered him a contract with Flit, and in the May 31, 1928, issue of *Life* magazine, Ted's first advertisement for Flit appeared. It wasn't Grandmother Squeers but little Willie who had a mouthful of Flit this time.

No doubt luck played a great part in the matter, but Ted had an active role as well. During this period, he used many brand names in his cartoons, perhaps initially as his normal use of familiar items, but then for more calculated reasons. Three weeks after the first mention of Flit, Ted referred to Gomulgene antiseptic. The next week, he used White Rock soda in the punch line of a cartoon about gin, and the company sent him 48 bottles of its product. In two issues following that windfall, Ted mentioned White Rock soda again, used Gordon's gin twice, and also made reference to Bacardi rum, Budweiser beer, and Old Crow bourbon. He also drew attention to Ostermoor beds, Lux soap, and Singer sewing machines and made his second reference to Flit during this time. Whether looking for more free products or an endorsement contract, the timing suggests that Ted was trolling the commercial waters when "luck" intervened.

Ted may also have employed some subtle negotiation through his work in *Judge* when, three weeks after this second mention of Flit, his poem about Grandmother Squeers referred to both of the competing bug sprays. It was the first time that he'd mentioned Flytox in his work. Ted's first Flit advertisement was published just five weeks later. As a matter of fact, while he was doing the Flit ads in 1934, the story he told an interviewer failed to mention Mrs. Cleaves at all. At that time, Ted said, "I . . . drew a knight in armor lying in a big bed with a huge dragon about 40 feet tall sticking his head under the canopy of the bed. I made up a caption about Flit. I tossed a coin to see whether I should send the picture to Flit or another manufacturer of the same kind of product. It came out Flit, so I submitted it. About a week later I received a letter from

Ted's first Flit ad was published within months after product references appeared in the *Judge* pieces.

Standard Oil . . . and then a contract to do a series of ads for them. That toss of a coin determined my whole career."[18]

The cartoon was published in *Judge,* so whether Ted sent it to Standard Oil or Mrs. Cleaves brought it to their attention, whether it was an ad exec's wife under a hair dryer or the random flip of a coin that got Ted's work to the proper channels at Standard Oil, it was the start of an extremely successful advertising campaign that has been acknowledged in several sources as one of the first to use humor to sell a product. It introduced "Quick, Henry, the Flit!"—a catchphrase so well known that a song was written about it. The advertisements themselves became so popular over the next two years that, by September 1929, a collection of them was printed—the first publication of exclusively "Seuss" material. Over the years, Ted became financially secure with the money he earned doing this advertising work. Just seven months after moving to New York, he had hit pay dirt.

A successful collection: **The Flit campaign proved so popular that, within two years, a compilation of Flit ads was published.**

CHAPTER 9

You Can Book a *Judge* by Its Cover

The Flit campaign had just started, and no one realized that there would be more than 125 cartoons still to come. So Ted's work for *Judge* continued. The first artwork that Ted Geisel ever signed as "Dr. Seuss" appeared six months into his time with *Judge*. That honor goes to the Makaraskiijip and the Bvorlyjk, two beasts that assist the stork in delivering Japanese and Eskimo babies, respectively.

The first artwork signed by "Dr. Seuss" appeared in these 1928 *Judge* cartoons (this page). Ted continued to try on his new moniker for size, whether showcasing Yertle-esque tiered turtles (opposite page, top) or playfully illustrating divorce proceedings (opposite page, bottom).

In Blossom-Scented Japan

"Any childlen today?" inquires the Japanese Makaraskiijip as he goes on his rounds every Thursday. And he argues so well that the almond-eyed ladies find it hard to say no.

SUPRISE!

In the Frozen North

Up in the North Pole and vicinity it is too cold to have storks, so they have the Bvorlyjk instead. Note the expression of joy on the Eskimo mother's face. To her, life is just full of happy surprises.

It was not yet a consistent change, but the Dr. Seuss signature did show up on some interesting pieces, like Ted's earliest version of turtle-stacking, which would one day lead him to *Yertle the Turtle*. The tiered turtles here are part of a hieroglyph for an unspecified four-syllable word.

Ted's imagination ran wild. He wrote increasingly longer prose pieces and touched on subjects that most of us don't associate with Dr. Seuss. In a piece called "The Cutting of the Wedding Cnouth," Ted discussed divorce. Ever playful, he focused on the Druids, explaining:

> There was one particular period
> in the era of the Druids when those
> good fellows worshipped Sulky Dogs.
> At other periods, of course, they worshipped different
> things, for they were very versatile. At first it was pine-
> needles; then it was an old bit of whale bone out of a corset
> that had washed ashore after a French excursion boat had
> gone on the rocks; after this they worshipped echoes; while
> at still another time it was buttered popcorn with lots of
> salt. But at this particular period the Druids would bow
> down to nothing but Sulky
> Dogs.[1]

The Sulky Dogs cast a pall on the populace and the divorce rate sky-rocketed. A special ceremony was invented that involved the two parties each donning an end of the cere-monial hat known as the Wedding Cnouth while standing by the Bowl of the Sacred Soap and Water, in which they symbolically washed their

His divorce having been refused him because of insufficient grounds, the Unscrupulous Ventriloquist pulls a fast one on his wife and her attorney.

Another divorce discourse showed Ted's witty take on a subject not normally associated with Dr. Seuss.

hands of the whole affair. In another cartoon about divorce, Ted used a ventriloquist's dummy to obfuscate the court proceedings.

At the same time that Ted was indulging his imagination in New York, surrealism was growing in Europe by extolling the magnificence of the imagination. The surrealist movement had its official beginning on October 15, 1924, when André Breton published the first *Manifeste du surréalisme.* The manifesto suggested that surrealism was a way of combining conscious and unconscious experiences so that the fantasy of dreams and the logic of the waking world resolved "into a kind of absolute reality, a *surreality.* . . ."[2] Breton defined surrealism as "thought's dictation, in the absence of any control exercised by reason, outside any esthetic or moral concerns."[3] He claimed, "Imagination alone offers me some intimation of what *can be.* . . ."[4] He went on to add:

> The mind which plunges into Surrealism relives with
> glowing excitement the best part of its childhood. . . .
> It is perhaps childhood that comes closest to one's "real
> life." . . . Thanks to Surrealism, it seems that opportunity
> knocks a second time. . . . Here are "the elephants with the
> heads of women and the flying lions."[5]

In 1929, Breton published the second *Manifeste du surréalisme.* While surrealists were juxtaposing incongruous items in their paintings, Ted's sense of the absurd led him to continue to juxtapose such things in his own work. In one prose piece called "Sex and the Sea God," Babe Ruth meets the sea god Neptune, who explains that a mermaid once tempted him. "She had been eating oysters, and her mouth was still chock full of pearls, which sparkled mischievously when she smiled."[6] Neptune gave in to the temptation, which explains why the sea is full of "urchins."

Research reveals an interesting tidbit from this period. In April 1928, the *Strand* magazine published Arthur Conan Doyle's novella *When the World*

Screamed, in which Professor George Edward Challenger posits that "the world upon which we live is itself a living organism, endowed, as I believe, with a circulation, a respiration, and a nervous system of its own."[7] To demonstrate his theory to Peerless Jones, Challenger utilizes a sea urchin, remarking that "it is roughly circular, but flattened at the poles."[8] Challenger reasons that the urchin would be no more aware of tiny insects crawling on its hardened exterior than the earth would be of humans inhabiting its outer crust. But if one of the "parasites" living on the external surface of either the urchin or the earth wanted to be noticed, the creature could "sink a hole in its shell and so stimulate its sensory apparatus"[9] at its core. This notion leads Challenger to the idea of digging a hole through the center of the earth. Four months later, when Ted would

THE HEIGHT OF DECEPTION
Taking advantage of his Best Girl's Astigmatism.

have had time to read the story, *Judge* published his prose pieces "Sex and the Sea God" (in which the punch line deals with sea urchins) and "Gustaav Schleswigh, 3rd, 'Hops Off'" (in which a hole for a subway is dug through the earth from Uleaborg, Finland, to Shanghai, China). Only a mind like Ted's would believe that the idea of the earth as a living organism could be improved with the addition of Babe Ruth, Neptune, a mermaid, and an intercontinental subway.

Ted's artwork also began to incorporate even odder elements, including a bouquet of fish and a xylophone made of cats. It is interesting to note that when Disney's film *Steamboat Willie* debuted four months after Ted's cat xylophone, Minnie Mouse used a cat as a musical instrument as well.

A fish by any other name: Ted's penchant for the outlandish began to appear more frequently in his work, as evidenced by this 1928 fish bouquet (top).

Kitty cacophony: Another example of Ted embracing the peculiar—a xylophone that was, quite literally, the cats' meow (bottom).

Showing musician Fritz Rynolds, the first man to design a Xylophone made entirely out of cats. (The auxiliary kitten in the foreground jumps into the place of any cat fainting during a concert.)

89

In another of Ted's pieces, Jacques Pommefritte competes against a valiant clam and a hungry cat in "The Great Diet Derby." Cheering on Aethelstan the Clam, the crowd chants:

> "Sturdy Clam, we're all behind you!
> Keep it up! Let nothing blind you
> To your great inspired ambition!
> Fight, Clam, FIGHT, unto perdition!"[10]

Unfortunately, Baumgrass the Cat breaks the first rule of the dieting competition by eating Aethelstan. Pommefritte is named victor by default. Adding to the general strangeness of this piece is the fact that the winner of the diet

Cartoons were the perfect venue in which to try out some odd pairings—firemen bobbing for pineapples (left); the proper way to doff a hat, as demonstrated with fish (right); and a tailor who sews buttons on ice cream (opposite page).

Bobbing for Pineapples

A Hallowe'en diversion for firemen who suffer from ennui.

Young men appearing socially for the first time are always harassed by the problem, "How high shall I doff my hat, and at precisely what angle?" In Finland, therefore, parents always send their sons to hat-doffing schools. As the Finns are notoriously poor mathematicians, the measurements and angles are graphically demonstrated in terms of well-known fish.

derby is a contestant whose name translates as "Jack French Fry." And the clam's name is a reference to the great warrior king who ruled England from 925 to 939—quite a noble lineage for a clam.

A Few Subtle Pleasures

Devised for Those Who Have Wearied of the Commonplace

By Dr. Seuss

For Seamsters in Retirement

When sewing on cloth has begun to lose its enchantment, what you need is a change. Amuse yourself by sewing brown trouser buttons on to a vanilla ice-cream cone.

In "A Few Subtle Pleasures,"[11] Ted depicted novel ways to stave off boredom—retired tailors sewing brown trouser buttons onto vanilla ice cream cones, and bored firemen bobbing for pineapples, buffeted by a fire hose. He explained that in Finland the correct angles and heights at which to doff different types of hats were "graphically demonstrated in terms of well-known fish."[12]

Ted also began satirizing linguistics and terminology. In "Ough! Ough! Or Why I Believe in Simplified Spelling," Ted writes:

> It was forty-five years ago, when I first came to America as a young Roumanian student of divinity, that I first met the evils of the *"ough words."* Strolling one day in the country with my fellow students, I saw a tough, coughing as he ploughed a field which (being quite nearsighted) I mistook for pie dough.
>
> Assuming that all *ough words* were pronounced the same, I casually remarked, "The tuff cuffs as he pluffs the duff!"
>
> "Sacrilege!" shrieked my devout companions. "He is cursing in Roumanian!" I was expelled from the school. . . .[13]

In chastising people for misusing phrases like "I'm agog" and "I'm befuddled," Ted explained that "there's not a Gog in America. . . . A Gog is a sentimental Swiss who collects mountain-goat tears in a brown paper bag. Unless you are one of these, you should never use the term."[14] Furthermore, "fuddling" was a game in the 1890s, the purpose of which "was to pop suddenly out of the bushes and slap a fop smartly across the nose with your 'fuddle' (a durable kind of boloney). The fop whose nose was slapped was considered 'befuddled.' Anyone claiming 'befuddlement' today is talking through his hat."[15]

Ted also investigated the phrase "left in the lurch" and reported that it had different meanings around the country. In the West, "'A lurch,' says Simon Whistlebooster, the famous traveler, 'is a *de luxe* accommodation aboard a speedy transcontinental lawn-mower. In passing over the foothills of Nebraska, it often happens that the engineers desert their posts and go native. The passenger, then, is left in the lurch.'"[16] However, in the South, "'A lurch,' writes Annabelle Choochoocubb of Lexington, Ky., 'is a sag in the back of a lady's gown. In the old days, at tiddle-de-winks tournaments, the winks were forever going astray and popping into some damsel's lurch. And as all men were gentlemen in that era, nothing was done about it. The tiddle-de-winks were left in the lurch.'"[17]

And, of course, drinking continued to be a popular topic, with the Hippocrass making repeat appearances and new beasts arriving to help transport the besotted. These remained a staple of Ted's cartoons for many years and, in fact, became the subject for which he was most appreciated among college students.

Wordplay:
Ted's affinity for deconstructing language (this page, top and bottom) brought about some interesting "investigations." Per Ted, the definition of "lurch" differed according to geography.

Boozers and the beasts:
The notion of drunkard-bearing beasts continued to preoccupy Ted, as evidenced in these magazine cartoons (opposite page and following three pages).

The Lurch in the West

The Lurch in the South

92

FORGOTTEN EVENTS OF HISTORY.

Noah's dissolute brother, Goah, preserves the D. T. beasts of his day for posterity.

"Saved at last—here

come the St. Bernards!"

A study of the unusual systems of transportation running between "Zelli's" and the "Dead Rat" in the Montmartre District of Paris.

The Flit campaign
marches on
(opposite page).

Flit bug spray pumped up Ted's profile. By 1929, one of his Flit cartoons was cited in Bart Publications' *The Sho Card Cartoonist* as an example of how a good cartoon will leave an indelible memory upon a reader far more effectively than many pages of text. Ted's images certainly had that effect, and they would continue to be fixtures in periodicals for many years to come, bolstering

"Fear not, comrade! I've killed worse ones than this with my Flit!" —*Advt.*

The Chairman—"Gentlemen, it's our last and only hope! We must tie a warning bell on every single Flit Gun in the country!"

The suicide.

The Flit Gun Wedding © 1931 Stanco Inc.

NIGHTMARE VICTIM—*Good Gosh! And not a drop of Flit in the house.*—ADVT.

his popularity and name recognition—a fact that was not lost on his employers at *Judge*.

Since the cover is the only part of a magazine that a reader can see at a distance, without having to pick up the magazine and page through it, it often determines how well a particular issue will sell. The more popular the cover is, the better the sales. The *Saturday Evening Post* had Norman Rockwell and J. C. Leyendecker. *Liberty* had Leslie Thrasher. *Sports Illustrated* had Cheryl Tiegs. In 1928, *Judge* had booked popular artists like Ruth Eastman, Jefferson Machamer, Guy Hoff, Nate Collier, and Don Herold for its covers. But with the growing popularity of the Flit advertisements, Ted had developed enough prestige that a new opportunity was opened up to him. The March 23, 1929, issue of *Judge* contains the first cover illustration of Ted's career. It was also the very first illustration of his to be published in full color. It was an event that underscored the fact that he was joining the upper echelon of the illustrators of his day. "Dr. Seuss" could now sell magazines.[18]

CHAPTER 10

"Time, a Maniac Scattering Dust"[1]

Ted's advertisements—along with his cartoons, illustrations, and articles, as well as the articles that were beginning to be written about him—continued to appear in a growing number of magazines. During the 1930s, you could find Seuss material in at least 60 different periodicals and more than a thousand newspapers. This increased popularity brought Ted more interesting opportunities. He created several privately commissioned paintings and murals early in 1930, including a four-wall installation in the home of Harkness Edwards, Sr., in Kentucky and "The Rape of the Sabine Woman" for the Dartmouth Club on 37th Street in New York. For the latter, Ted parodied Giovanni da Bologna's 1583 sculpture. Rather than the famous "serpentine" arrangement of figures that spirals up to the woman held dramatically aloft, Ted's canvas has a serpent looking at a man carrying a woman in a much less graceful position.

The rape of the Sabine women is a mythological event supposed to have taken place just after the founding of Rome in the eighth century BC, when the Sabine tribe was invited to the city to celebrate the Consualia, a religious ritual coupled with athletic contests in honor of Neptune. Rome had expanded by granting citizenship to criminals, which helped it in its wars but left the city with a dearth of women. At a signal from the Roman king, Romulus, the Romans are said to have carried off the Sabine women from the festival.[2] Ted's canvas depicts a place more likely to remind viewers of the Garden of Eden than of Roman temples. Although the Sabine woman doesn't look pleased and one set of animals looks on aghast, most of the other characters appear to be enjoying the scene.

Ted made mention that year of "a few oil murals that I have succeeded in plastering on some of the local walls,"[3] so it is impossible to identify "The Rape of the Sabine Woman" as Ted's first oil painting, but it is certainly one of his earliest.[4] Although it was termed a "mural," the existing painting is a single large (roughly five-and-a-half-feet square) canvas. It has been speculated that the painting was done as a study for a mural. The painting hung in the Dartmouth Club until the club changed locations, at which time it was stored in an alumnus's basement in New Jersey, where it remained for over 30 years. (Ted's Dartmouth classmate Alexander Laing compared the canvas's consignment to storage to the 1934 removal of Diego Rivera's mural "Man at the Crossroads" from a wall in New York City's Rockefeller Center. In Laing's eyes, whether it was the abduction of a nude woman or Vladimir Ilyich Lenin uniting workers of different nationalities and ethnicities, an artwork that found disfavor could simply be removed without regard for artistic considerations.[5]) In 1964, Ted's painting was presented to Ernest Martin Hopkins, who willed it to Dartmouth College before he died later that year.[6] The painting was cleaned and repaired for Ted's fiftieth reunion in 1975 and has been stored in the basement of the college's Hood Museum since that time, with hopes of a future restoration of the canvas.

In contrast to the single canvas of "Sabine Woman," Ted's mural in the Lexington, Kentucky, home of Harkness Edwards, Sr., was a major work covering all four walls of a room. The room has been described elsewhere as both the taproom and the children's playroom, but in fact was a room of no particular function (situated next to the taproom). At Christmas each year, a large train set was erected in the Seuss room, which may account for the erroneous report about its being a playroom—the children's playroom was actually upstairs.

The real taproom was known by the Edwards family as the "ship room," as it was a duplicate of Harkness's boat, including portholes for windows. Next to it was a room of approximately 40 feet by 20 feet, in which the Dr. Seuss installation was constructed. At the end of the rectangular room farthest from the entrance, along one of the shorter walls, there was a large mirror that Ted adorned with two floor-to-ceiling flamingo-like birds facing each other, holding a sash between them above the mirror. The left side of the wall was taken up by an enormous flying insect that looked like a Flit bug grown to nightmare proportions.

"The Rape of the Sabine Woman": Ted put his own spin on the mythological tale. This mural (opposite page), which hung in the Dartmouth Club, is one of Ted's first oil paintings.

On the long wall to the right, a bird flew above a large flower. Farther down the wall, an odd-looking beast splashed an arc of water behind him as he kicked up his multiple-jointed back legs. To the right of him was another mirror that Ted had framed with two large rabbit-like animals; a duck walked across the lintel above the mirror. At the end of that wall, directly across from the room's entrance, hovered a slender flying creature—a hybrid leaning more toward bird than insect.

Opposite the wall with the flamingos, fish leapt toward a hoop that encircled the room's only window. To the right of the window was an elephant balancing its front feet on a stand. On the final wall, to the left of the entrance, a Hippocrass-like animal ate leaves from a plant growing down from above the doorway.

Ogden Edwards was born in 1934 and grew up in the house with his brother, Harkness, Jr., and his sister, Mary. He has only a vague memory of seeing the murals. He recalls that one side of the house was prone to extensive flooding, and that the mural was water-damaged early on. The house was rented for a few years in the early 1950s to FDR's daughter and sold to a family by the name of Marx in the mid-1950s, and Sotheby's auctioned the

Ted worked on all four walls for this privately commissioned mural. Among the featured animals were flamingo-like birds, a Flit-ish bug, and a multijointed beast kicking up his heels.

contents in the late 1980s. The property is now the Kentucky Horse Park. Shortly after Ogden Edwards became old enough to remember seeing the mural (by his estimate, around 1940), it was already gone. Construction of the house was completed in 1930, so the best estimate is that the mural was in place for perhaps a decade.[7]

There is mention of a second mural that Ted did in New York prior to December 1931, but no specific information about such a piece has been found and it may have been a misstatement, as a later publication using almost the exact same wording omits the reference to a second New York mural. Or this work may have been the painting that Ted did for the Pilots' Club speakeasy with friends Abner Dean and Hugh Troy.

The summer of 1930 brought more change for Ted. He and Helen vacationed in Mexico City and, upon their return, lived at the Roosevelt Hotel on Madison Avenue while they were changing apartments. He began a correspondence with Dartmouth's assistant librarian, Harold Goddard Rugg, who had apparently heard about an exhibition of Ted's work and wanted to know if it could be brought to Dartmouth. Ted explained that there had been no

Another view of the room shows more Seussian animals—rabbits, a duck, and fish leaping through hoops. Note the Hippocrass-like animal reflected in the mirror.

such exhibition but that he'd be interested in doing one at Dartmouth. It seems that Ted's work for the predominantly monochromatic magazines was no longer satisfying, as he wrote to Rugg saying, "At present I am working on a number of oils and water colors that I think vastly superior to anything I have done in black-and-white."[8]

Most significantly, he was asked to illustrate some of the unwitting witticisms in a compilation called *Boners by Those Who Pulled Them*, which claimed to be "a Collection of Schoolboy Wisdom . . . Compiled from Classrooms and Examination Papers by Alexander Abingdon, and Illustrated by Dr. Seuss." In fact, the credited author appears to have been a fictitious one, while the person responsible for gathering most of the malapropisms remained uncredited.[9]

The Dauphin was a rare fish that used to inhabit the Arctic Circle in the middle ages.

The *Boners* series borrowed liberally from books like Colin McIlwaine's compendiums of schoolboy "howlers." *More Schoolboy Howlers*, for example, was a 20-page booklet published without illustrations in London in 1928. Three years later in New York, a better marketing strategy for *Boners* padded and stretched the text to a book-length 102 pages and enlivened it with Ted's illustrations. Unlike McIlwaine's booklet, which is now barely remembered, *Boners* was in its fourth printing just one month after it was released. In 1931, *Boners* was the fourth-best-selling nonfiction book of the year.[10] It proved to be so popular that a second book, *More Boners*, was published in April, just two months after the first *Boners* had appeared.

Its debt to McIlwaine's booklet is immediately evident in just a few examples of misguided missives from *More Schoolboy Howlers* that were appropriated for the *Boners* books:

Adolescence is the stage between puberty and adultery.

Acrimony, sometimes called holy, is another name for marriage.

Ted's illustrations (this page and opposite page) of the successful *Boners* books whetted his appetite for book publishing.

104

The Dauphin was a rare fish that used to inhabit the Arctic Circle in the middle ages.

Polonius was a mythical sausage.

Polonius was a mythical sausage.

Even when *Boners* was reprinted in 1997 as *Herrings Go About the Sea in Shawls,* "Alexander Abingdon" continued to be acknowledged for putting together the text that Ted illustrated, and the initial compiler, Colin McIlwaine, remained completely disassociated from the work.[11]

With the success of the *Boners* books, Ted saw quickly that the flat fee he was paid for his illustrations could not match the royalty income an author could earn from sales of such popular books. So in 1931, he began working on a book of his own. The road to publication was by no means smooth. He completed 23 to 26 watercolors for an animal alphabet book by January 1932. It was not, needless to say, your average ABC book. It was scheduled for publication in the summer or fall of 1932; however, in April of that year, his publisher canceled the project and Ted's agent turned the paintings over to another agency to try to find another publisher.

As a consequence, the exhibit for Dartmouth that Ted had been discussing with Harold Rugg, which was to consist of these paintings, also had to be canceled; at the time, the paintings were being sent around to Viking Press, Simon and Schuster, Bobbs-Merrill, and "ten or twelve other shoddy, gooey sorts of fellows,"[12] as Ted put it. By the following year, he'd given up on publishing the pictures in a book, and he offered 23 paintings to Dartmouth for an exhibition to be held at the Baker Library during the 1933 annual Winter Carnival. Ted gave his permission to sell them as a lot if possible, but piecemeal if necessary, and offered to give an agent's normal share to the college. In June, the exhibit moved from Dartmouth to the Hotel Duane's Book Center, a New York organization of publishers and booksellers.

The animal alphabet exhibit started arbitrarily with C for Cholmondelet, described as a "green-striped British Monster," and from there skipped around without regard to alphabetical order. Although it is not certain that the two bear any resemblance, at about the same time Ted drew a Cholmondelet for *Judge,* and he described it as "the most useless of American animals," noted for its "Look of Reproach." When one was placed on a street corner in Idaho, it decreased the divorce rate by over 14 percent.

The alphabet then jumped to our old friend the Hippocrass, which was identified as the "Spirit of an Elizabethan Drink." Following came the Escardax, a "puppy-headed snail" that was half escargot and half dachshund. An Itcutch, it was explained, smiles for an Expressionless Eyebug, while a Schimmelfritz jumps out when clouds get together. There was also a Lory-Eared Wombat and a Long-Necked Whizzleworp. The Blinket was described as a "cerise creature whose ears grow 12 inches every time he takes a drink." The

THE CHOLMONDELET

*O*F all American animals, the Cholmondelet has always been considered the most useless. Recently, however, the government decided to utilize his most outstanding characteristic . . . his Look of Reproach. As a test case, they installed a Cholmondelet at the mail-box on the corner of Thurk Street, Guimp, Idaho. In one year divorces on Thurk Street, Guimp, Idaho, decreased over 14 per cent.

Ted's planned publication of an animal alphabet book never panned out. The images remain unaccounted for, but derivations of these creatures populated Ted's work at the time. A Cholmondelet (top) and a Blinket (bottom) appeared in *Judge* and *Life*, respectively.

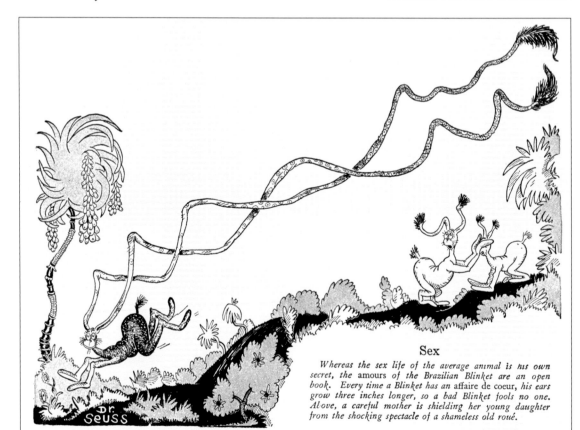

Sex

Whereas the sex life of the average animal is his own secret, the amours of the Brazilian Blinket are an open book. Every time a Blinket has an affaire de coeur, his ears grow three inches longer, so a bad Blinket fools no one. Above, a careful mother is shielding her young daughter from the shocking spectacle of a shameless old roué.

best insight into what the Blinket might have looked like comes from Ted's 1930 depiction of a Brazilian Blinket, whose ears grew three inches longer every time he had an extramarital affair. In that cartoon, the embarrassed mother Blinket, shielding her daughter's eyes from the taboo of sex, mimics the actions of the mother bear in "The Rape of the Sabine Woman."

What became of the illustrations for this ABC book is open to speculation. Somewhere there are relatives of a Bean Town man who are kicking themselves, as Ted recounted before the Dartmouth show that "a month ago I all but closed a deal, selling them to someone in Boston as decorations for a Taproom. But these pictures seem hoodoed [*sic*] . . . and like the publishers, this customer petered out at the last moment."[13] It is likely that these pieces were dispersed and no longer exist as a cohesive entity, especially since Ted did make the offer to sell them individually if enough people at the Dartmouth Winter Carnival were interested.

It has been reported that 17 publishers expressed an interest in the book, but not for publication until after the Depression was over. Unfortunately, such unrecognized pieces of Ted's legacy continue to be buried under the dust strewn by that maniac Time. If a full "Rape of the Sabine Woman" mural was ever produced, all that remains is the single canvas. It is safe, but in need of restoration. The Harkness Edwards mural appears to have been completely lost. The early alphabet book seems no longer to exist as a coherent work, likely having been scattered like the pages of da Vinci's notebooks. Any memory of another mural done in New York has vanished. The research, retrieval, and restoration of works like these must continue in order to ensure that such treasures are found, saved, and preserved.

CHAPTER 11
Standard Was Automatic

In the decade that preceded Ted's first children's book, he developed name recognition as "Dr. Seuss" simultaneously through his cartooning and through the incredible popularity of his advertisements for Flit bug spray. The success of that campaign was beneficial to both Ted and the insecticide's manufacturer, Standard Oil. A relationship developed that would link them for 25 years, involving a variety of products. Without Standard Oil, "Dr. Seuss" might never have become associated with children's books. If Ted had not made as much money as he did in advertising, he would not have had the leisure in which to experiment in other fields. He and Helen would not have been able to travel as extensively as they did. Since both time and travel were integral to the creation of *And to Think That I Saw It on Mulberry Street,* that portion of Ted's career might not have developed without his association with Standard Oil.

The idea for the Flit campaign may have had its genesis in advertising that was done for Black Flag, another insecticide, for which a series of small pamphlets was produced.[1] One of these pamphlets, *Rhymes & Riddles to Please and Tease,* which came out when Ted was 14, began with a poem and illustration about "The Wise Old Man." Given Ted's unusual memory, the similarity to one of his later Flit ads is not surprising. Presuming that a 14-year-old was more likely to look at pictures and captions than to read the advertising text of the rest of the pamphlet, the next thing young Ted would have seen was a picture of an odd beast called a Wambus standing beneath the Uggle trees, which would have fit very comfortably with the flora and fauna with which Ted would later populate the island of Bo-Bo during college. The

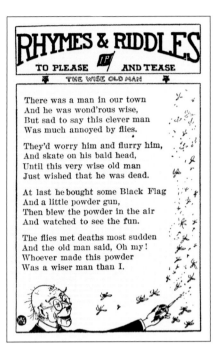

last of the memorable images from the pamphlet is of "old Wiggly Puckaroo," who "feeds on onions, beans and glue."[2] This series of offbeat illustrations by John McGrath is reminiscent of those Ted remembered from B. T. Blackwood and may well have inhabited the recesses of his brain until the opportunity for the Flit campaign arose.

The Flit campaign got its start in May 1928. In celebration of the first anniversary of Charles Lindbergh's historic flight from New York to Paris, America was abuzz with the Lindbergh craze. Accordingly, it was during that month that Mickey Mouse premiered in the Lindbergh/aviation parody *Plane Crazy*. With Prohibition still in effect, the presidential election pitted Herbert Hoover and his slogan of "a chicken in every pot, a car in every garage" against the anti-Prohibition Al Smith, who felt that the public was entitled to a different sort of buzz.

Ted's attention was focused on the buzz of flying insects, and his first Flit cartoon premiered that same month. The Flit campaign for the summer of 1928 consisted of only a half dozen advertisements, which ran every other week from May through August, when the nuisance posed by biting insects was the greatest. This was the summer that television sets, manufactured by the Daven Corporation, went on sale for the first time—during the same week in July that *Lights of New York*, the first completely talking feature-length film, premiered. There was

The Ambush

Advt.   © 1931 DR. SEUSS

This is the Wambus, strange and queer:
Just see him grin from ear to ear.
He lives in a cave by the Uggle trees
And with BLACK FLAG kills all his fleas.

This is old Wiggly Puckaroo,
He feeds on onions, beans and glue.
He hates all bugs that fly or crawl,
And with BLACK FLAG he kills 'em all.

no lack of exciting events and innovations to capture the public's fancy. But by the time the summer had ended, despite a Flit campaign encompassing only six cartoons, the advertising magazine *Printers' Ink* ran an article that proclaimed, "The most momentous theme of the summer of 1928 was not Prohibition, presidential election, aviation, or world peace. It was mosquitoes."[3]

Encouraged by the ads' success, Standard Oil began the Flit campaign right away the following year, starting in January 1929, with new ads every three weeks throughout the entire year. By the time the summer ended that year, about 12 new Flit ads had run, and Standard Oil drew on its 18 ads to print the first solo "Dr. Seuss" item in history: a pamphlet entitled *Flit Cartoons: As They Have Appeared in Magazines and Newspapers Throughout the Country.* New advertisements continued to appear every three weeks throughout 1930 and remained so popular that two more Flit booklets reprinting Ted's ads were produced.[4] That summer, color was introduced into the campaign, both in the ads that ran in periodicals and in new poster cards. Other than the March 16, 1929, cover for *Judge,* these pieces were the public's first full-color exposure to Ted's work.

"Quick, Henry, the Flit!"

When new advertisements came out, they were seen first in *Life* and then appeared the next day in *Judge.* Over the years, they appeared in many other periodicals, and when they did, they would appear in the *Saturday Evening Post* and the *New Yorker* on the same day as in *Judge,* two days later in *Time,* and a week later in *Collier's.* Initially, the ones in *Liberty* were on the same schedule as those in *Collier's,* but they later followed the schedule of the *New Yorker* and the *Saturday Evening Post.*

Buzzworthy: **Full-color ads were unveiled in 1930, adding a new dimension to Ted's popular Flit campaign.**

Ted's efforts were not the only advertisements for Flit during this period. Flit had ads in certain publications that were done by other artists and designers. One popular misconception is that Ted designed the toy soldiers that adorned the Flit pump sprayers and many of the advertisements, but the soldiers predated Ted's involvement with the company.

Ted's contribution to the Flit campaign grew more substantial in 1931. In the large-format brochure *Another Big Flit Year!*, Standard Oil reprinted some of the best ads from the previous year and revealed that the 1930 advertising campaign had involved 32 of Ted's cartoons, which had appeared around the country in 14 magazines and 3,650 newspapers, as well as theater programs in New York City.[5] The ads continued to appear every three weeks through the winter and spring of 1931, but once the summer arrived, a new one was published every week.

Another new facet of the program was the addition of an elaborate window display in 1931 in which two men, suspended on strings so that they could move when blown by a fan, parachuted downward along with a falling propeller and, of course, a huge mosquito. Full-color subway cards were produced. Most intriguingly, Ted began work on short animated movies for the summer campaign promoting Flit, which now stand among the biggest of Seuss mysteries.

Standard Oil (possibly with help from Esso producer Penola, Inc.) financed the production of *Put on the Spout* and *'Neath the Bababa Tree*, which were released by Warner Bros. on June 1, 1931.[6] Both were split-reel, three-to-five-minute, privately sponsored sound films. At least four copies of each film (one original and three duplicates) existed in New York at the time, but if any copies still remain, exhaustive research has failed to find them.[7]

Put on the Spout was a 388-foot-long, five-minute commercial (or "industrial") cartoon, for which the music was recorded on the film rather than on a separate disk. Containing only one line of dialogue,[8] it was based on a print advertisement that had run two months earlier. A reviewer at the time described it as follows:

> Fantastic cartoon in undersea locale, with the entire fish
> family beating it for cover when the warning is sounded
> that a dangerous insect is approaching. The intruder gives
> the whale a merry chase, until the cue, 'Quick, Jonah, the
> Flit,' is given by a human voice, whereupon the insect is
> sprinkled and squelched. . . .[9]

'Neath the Bababa Tree was the shorter of the two films, at 350 feet. The synchronized sound track was recorded on the film, not a disk, but it did

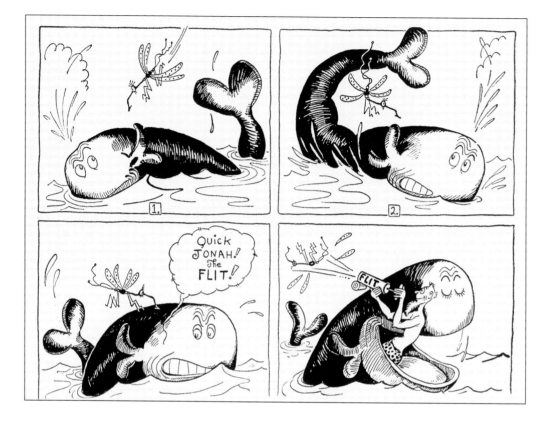

not have dialogue.[10] Little else is known about the content of this film.

Industrial short films became a significant issue in the world of cinema during the period from 1930 to 1932. While Hollywood produced most of the feature films, the commercial ones were generally produced on the East Coast. There was a quick upsurge in the amount of money that companies were willing to put into sponsoring short films, and the field grew rapidly as a result. The huge growth in this part of the industry met with resistance from the national Motion Picture Theater Owners group, which was concerned that its theaters were being turned into advertising venues and that this development would drive patrons away. Local advertisers feared competition from national brands, and newspapers were concerned about losing their ad revenues to the theaters.

Two of the leading studios in the production of industrial films in New York were Audio Cinema and Warner Bros.[11] Audio Cinema created sponsored short films for Aetna Insurance Company and New York Telephone Co., while Warner Bros. made films for Chesterfield cigarettes, A&P grocery stores, and Listerine. As the industry grew, the *Film Daily* reported, "Audio Cinema Studios promise to become one of the busiest in New York with the growing tendency toward industrial films of which this studio has made a specialty."[12] Warner Bros. announced plans to make one sponsored short per week,[13] and the *Film Daily* ran a headline predicting (with regard to commercial sponsors), "Subsidizing of Nearly All Standard Shorts Likely Within Five Years."[14]

The Motion Picture Theater Owners branches of eastern Pennsylvania, southern New Jersey, and Delaware "urged that extreme caution be used to prevent the screen from being turned into a billboard"[15] and, along with virtually all of the rest of the national group of theater owners, expressed concern over product placements within movies and implied that subliminal messages were a concern as well.

By March 1931, Warner Bros.' industrial division was operating at capacity to try to stay on schedule. It soon began expanding, but it could not keep up with the demand. The division announced plans to shut down operations for six weeks beginning in May while it erected a new studio, with only a skeleton crew remaining during that period.[16] But while the business grew, so did the debate. In April, the *Film Daily* ran a front-page editorial that explained:

> The controversey [*sic*] over paid advertising on the screen
> through the medium of sponsored pictures is getting hot.
> The relation and value of this new so-called commercial
> idea threatens to assume both major and national
> proportions. . . . The hub of the controversy around which
> the whirlwind is gathering is whether or not the revenue
> derived by the industry from national advertisers will
> offset the possible harm of alienating the good will of
> millions of picture fans by forcing them to take something
> they do not want. Those favoring the idea maintain that the
> entertainment quality of sponsored pictures will . . . always
> be as high as the conventional picture-house product of the
> hour. This, from personal contact and observation, we
> doubt. We have lately seen patrons leave their seats in
> chagrin over an advertising film of decidedly mediocre
> quality. The opponents of screen advertising, and just now
> they seem to be in the definite majority, point to the fact

that in a periodical or newspaper you can pass the ads if
you wish, and in radio you can quickly turn to another
program. Not so with the screen. . . . Personally, we would
like to see the industry as a whole take a decided stand in
the matter and keep the screens of America forever free
from this innovation that seems fraught with TNT. . . .[17]

Three of the major theater circuits (Fox, Loew, and RKO Pictures)
refused to play industrial films. In May, MGM announced that it would not
produce commercial films, and four days later, Paramount discontinued its
production and distribution of ad films. By the end of the month, just three
months after predicting that all short films would soon be sponsored, the *Film
Daily* featured a front-page headline auguring "The Death of Sponsored
Shorts."[18]

It was in this atmosphere that Ted began his work on industrial films.
On May 26, the *Film Daily* reported, "Five shorts now being made by the
Warner Bros. industrial films division will be the last sponsored pictures
produced by the company. No new contracts for productions of this type will
be accepted although . . . industrial subjects will be made upon request. Three
of the five sponsored shorts now in work are for Standard Oil."[19] Less than a
week later, on June 1, Warner Bros. released the two Flit films. Although the
studio (which was still closed while the new one was being built) did make a
few of the industrial films to which it had committed during this time, all
indications are that the Flit films were made for Warner Bros. by Audio Cinema Studios. It would not have been uncommon. In April, Universal
was making a picture at Audio Cinema Studios. Audio Cinema was also producing Paul Terry's *Terry-Toons* for Educational Pictures to release through
20th Century–Fox.[20]

The man credited with scoring the music for both Flit films is Philip A.
Scheib, who was the musical director at Audio Cinema Studios[21] in 1931 and
the man responsible for the music in *Terry-Toons*. Roy Mack and Harold Levey
held that position for Warner Bros.' Vitaphone shorts division,[22, 23] and they
were not associated with the Flit films.

Background artist Bob Little has said that his brother, animator Frank
Little, was involved with the production of *'Neath the Bababa Tree,* and at the
time these movies were made, Frank was working for Audio Cinema.[24] Also

working there was Lillian Friedman (whom Max Fleischer promoted two years later to be the first woman animator in Hollywood theatrical films). She has confirmed that her first job in the industry, working at Audio Cinema, brought her into contact with Ted Geisel:

> We were a small animation unit in a company that mostly produced documentary-type films. Studio space there was shared by Terry-Toon animation company. Now, we made a cartoon commercial advertising Listerine. Now imagine how before the times this was, with germ characters designed by Dr. Seuss. I remember he used to come and be so frustrated because even though he designed these marvelous characters, he couldn't animate. He used to try, but he couldn't. Anyway, this picture, intended for theater showing, also has no takers. Exhibitors are afraid of offending paying audiences with ads.[25]

Although no other information linking Ted to animated Listerine films has surfaced, Warner Bros. was producing them at that time. In March, for example, just three months before the Flit films were released, Warner Bros. released *Graduation Day in Bugland,* a nine-minute animated Listerine cartoon in which a little girl dreams about all of the germs that fill the air and enter the mouth. She wakes up petrified, and her mother brings her Listerine to kill the germs. That Ted might have worked on the Listerine shorts furthers the mystery surrounding this period in his life. But regardless of Ted's possible role in the Listerine films, Ms. Friedman's account does place Ted at Audio Cinema Studios during the time when the Flit films were produced, rather than at the Warner Bros. studio.

Ted Geisel's exact role in these Flit films is the subject of some speculation. The Library of Congress lists him as the animator for both films,[26] while another source credits Frank Little as the animator for *'Neath the Bababa Tree* and Ted for *Put on the Spout.*[27] Another source claims that Ted was the writer of both films,[28] while yet another one incorrectly explains that the films were based on Dr. Seuss's children's stories (the first of which wasn't published until six years after these films were made).[29] Directorship for *'Neath the Bababa Tree* has also been credited to Ted.[30] In short, there is much confusion and no one seems to have seen the films for themselves, nor can any copies be found.

Although he does not appear to have been associated with animated films before or after these Flit shorts, Irving A. Jacoby is generally credited for writing the *'Neath the Bababa Tree* story and for adapting *Put on the Spout*. The most likely scenario is that he adapted the Seuss print advertisement of Jonah and the whale for *Put on the Spout* and created an original story for *'Neath the Bababa Tree*.[31] Ted, in all likelihood, designed the look of the creatures and provided the storyboards for the films (as suggested by Ms. Friedman), which would explain why he was credited as an animator, although he is extremely unlikely to have done any of the actual animation. As Ms. Friedman pointed out, it was not one of his strengths. Producer John Bransby has also been mentioned as having collaborated with Ted on animated films for Standard Oil.[32]

Ted's involvement began after the crest of the industrial film wave, and by the time the two Flit films were cleared by the censors to be shown in New York that summer, ad films had fallen into such disfavor that the *Film Daily* was no longer reviewing them. From the summer until the end of the year, it appears that despite reviews of several hundred short sound films, *Put on the Spout* was the only industrial film reviewed. Even under those conditions, it was declared to be "fantastic" throughout—until the end, at which point "those of the audience who didn't know it before are put hep to the fact that they've had a piece of advertising inflicted upon them. No matter how good the short is, this closing revelation puts a curse on it."[33]

Despite the poor timing of the Flit short films, Ted's relationship with Standard Oil blossomed with the success of the rest of the Flit advertising campaign. The advertisements not only were successful in getting buyers interested in the product but also developed a following for themselves. In 1933, the colorful Flit window display for stores depicted a matador menaced from

Flits of every shape and size included this print ad from *Boys' Life* (this page), a popular window display (opposite page, top), and a subway card (opposite page, bottom).

either side, with a choice to make between mino-
taur and mosquito. There were also Flit billboards
released in selected areas. These locales had to be
chosen carefully because the first of the billboards
was a bit controversial. Congress had passed the
repeal of Prohibition in February, but when mosquito season had arrived by the end of June, only
nine states had ratified the repeal.[34] Ted leapt on the
issue and Standard Oil hailed, "Dr. Seuss had taken
the popular revival of beer"[35] and created a billboard poster with a German man, carrying eight
steins of beer, threatened by mosquitoes. The
Cullen-Harrison Act had made it legal to sell light
beer and wines in states that had ratified the repeal,
so there were only nine states in which Ted's new
billboards could be displayed. For the second billboard that summer, the matador from that year's

window display was used, which allowed for a wider distribution.

For most products, a successful campaign might consist of a half dozen
advertisements that bring the product to the attention of consumers in any
given season or, perhaps, a given year. Ted did Flit ads for portions of nine
consecutive years, from May 31, 1928, to August 22, 1936. He took a break
from Flit for four years when the work that he was asked to do for other Standard Oil products became too consuming. But in 1940 and 1941, when he had
finished a five-year campaign for Essomarine oil and lubricants, Ted returned

to produce more Flit advertisements, including posters for general use and for events like the March 1940 Flit Fly Hunt in Miami. Almost two decades after his first Flit advertisement, as late as 1947, the appeal of Ted's ads remained so strong that he was able to return to Standard Oil to produce new ads and colorful subway cards. Ads also ran in periodicals through 1949 and made yet another return in 1953, 25 years after they first began!

Seeing his phenomenal success in advertising early on, Standard Oil asked Ted to turn his attention to some of its other products. In 1932, Ted started with his "Greet the Boys" poster, promoting Standard gas, Atlas tires, and Koto upper motor lubrication. (Ted would also advertise Atlas fan belts in July 1936.) Up to this point in his career, if it were not for Standard Oil, the public would have seen only two full-color pieces of Ted's artwork (on the cover of *Judge* in March 1929 and January 1931). Standard Oil had printed Ted's artwork for Flit in full-color ads, poster cards, and store displays, which was yet another advantage for Ted provided by his association with Standard Oil.

Standard expansion: Ted's advertising acumen extended to other Standard Oil products, as in this 1932 poster for Koto upper motor lubrication and Standard gasoline.

He then began a campaign for Esso, a group of lubricants produced by Penola, Inc., and distributed by various local affiliates of Standard Oil.[36] In late 1932 and early 1933, a quintet of Seuss's Moto-Monsters appeared in newspapers, pamphlets, subway cards, and even a promotional jigsaw puzzle, encouraging the use of Essolube motor oil to keep one's car safe from these monsters. The Moto-Monsters are many Seuss collectors' first love. Certainly the Flit booklets came out previously, as well as many magazines with Ted's artwork and even a coaster set, but the Essolube advertisements are the most colorful and imaginative pieces from this period, and they provide some of the earliest Seuss collectibles. In particular, the *Foiled by Essolube* puzzle stands out for many enthusiasts as the first significant three-dimensional piece of Seussiana, since many of them overlook all of his earlier work in periodicals as "paper ephemera." It is also one of the earliest full-color pieces that were made available to the public as a premium.

Knowing that images clung to Ted's mind like barnacles, it is interesting to compare the first of his Moto-Monsters, the Zero-doccus, with another artist's earlier image of the Snow Bogy. Recall that in July 1927, the *Saturday*

March of the Moto-Monsters: **Another of Ted's popular Standard Oil ad campaigns featured the Essolube Moto-Monsters. They appeared in print ads (bottom right) and even promotional puzzles (top and bottom left).**

Evening Post published Ted's first cartoon. His next success came on October 22, 1927, with the publication in *Judge* of his second cartoon. During this period, we know that Ted was working diligently to get published. Surely he was reading the major periodicals of the day to see what kind of cartoons they were publishing and get an idea of what might sell. The October 22, 1927, issue of the *Saturday Evening Post* contained an advertisement for Caterpillar tractors that anthropomorphized the glitches that bedevil machines, as Ted would do in many ads during his career. The tractor ad offered a reward for capturing the Snow Bogy and gave him two aliases, exactly as Ted would do for the pests

More Moto-Monsters turned up in four-color newspaper ads (top), poster cards (middle), and pamphlets (bottom left and right).

Icy inspiration: Ted may have been influenced by this 1927 ad's villain (opposite page, top right), but the Zero-doccus (opposite page, top left) was undeniably Seuss.

Hats off: Gus, the "Happy Motoring" mascot (opposite page, bottom left).

Spot removal: This copy of the Ex-tane ad display (opposite page, bottom right) is a rare find.

in a Crosman rifle contest several years later. The gist of the allegations against the Snow Bogy was that, with his wintry pall, he made it impossible to start motors. Consequently, the Bogy was accused of everything from blocking traffic to murder (by plotting to prevent medical attendance in cases of desperate illness) and arson (by criminally hampering firefighters). Caterpillar tractors could rid communities' streets and highways of the Snow Bogy.

Once seen, the image of the Snow Bogy remained in Ted's mind until its incarnation in his work as the Zero-doccus, who was accused of similar activities: "ONE BLAST OF ARCTIC ZERO-DOCCUS BREATH AND ORDINARY MOTOR OILS JUST STIFFEN UP AND DIE. HEAVEN HELP THE CAR THAT'S UNPREPARED." However, Ted's style is the reason that the Zero-doccus is still admired 70 years after the ad campaign while no one remembers ever seeing the Snow Bogy. The Zero-doccus was also used to promote Tri-Rad antifreeze.

By 1934, Standard Oil was so pleased with Ted's work that it had him advertise its spot remover, Ex-tane.

In his work for Esso, Ted later created a character named Gus, who

appeared on a pin-back button as part of Esso's "Happy Motoring" campaign. Although the exact date has been hard to "pin" down, the button may have been distributed in 1938.

CHAPTER 12

Secrets of the Deep

In the spring of 1934, when Esso launched its line of lubricants into the boating world, the success of Ted's campaign for Esso car motor oil naturally led to a campaign for its new boat motor oil. Five years of Essomarine advertisements and the creation of the famed Seuss Navy were the result. The campaign began with a booklet called *Secrets of the Deep*. It contained more than 30 pages that were filled with Dr. Seuss illustrations and text, reputedly by "Old Captain Taylor" (though it was common knowledge that "Old

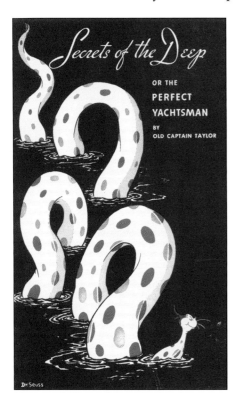

Taylor" was a popular brand of bourbon from National Distillers). Beginning in June 1934, Esso's advertisements urged people to write in and receive a free copy. In preparation for the National Motor Boat Show in January 1935, order cards for the booklet were distributed, along with advertising pamphlets bearing sample images.

The campaign picked up as the National Motor Boat Show approached. Essomarine advertisements promised "a remarkable exhibit that every skipper will want to see. Right now its details are veiled in deepest secrecy . . . but we'll let you in on this much—it will be completely new . . . entirely unusual . . . and vastly entertaining!"[1] By November 1935, full-page monthly advertisements began to appear in major boating journals like *Yachting* and *Motor Boating*

that looked like nothing else in the hefty marine periodicals. In addition to his improving artwork, some of these ads featured early experiments with rhyme.

> . . . swab me down if Essomarine
> ain't the best durned lubricants I've ever seen!
> They stand up swell when the engine's hot
> and you give 'er the gun for an extra knot.
> She starts in a jiffy, runs smooth as you please—
> keeps on turnin' in the roughest seas. . . .[2]

"Secrets" unveiled: **Sample pages from the pamphlet (opposite page, this page).**

January each year was the time for the National Motor Boat Show in New York City. After a year of growing interest in Ted's Essomarine campaign, Standard Oil wanted something special for the big show in 1936. Ted responded with an attention-grabbing display and the creation of the Seuss Navy.

> The marketers of Essomarine oils and greases increased their show space considerably . . . to present Dr. Seuss at his best. The SS *Essomarine,* Dr. Seuss' own idea of naval architecture, is the *pièce de résistance* among the goofy sea serpents, mermaids, whales and devilfish which abound in the Seuss seas. The Essomarine photographer is on the job to shoot you aboard the SS *Essomarine* in full admiral's regalia. And speaking of admirals, all motor boat

owners had best look into the new brotherhood conceived by the illustrating doctor—the Seuss Navy. Doc will make you a full-fledged admiral, with embossed commission to prove the high rank to skeptics.[3]

A big splash: **Essomarine made the 1936 show a true event by launching the Seuss Navy. Candidates for the Navy received a letter of acceptance (top) and a certificate (bottom), all designed by the "admiral-in-chief." In 1937, the Navy got its flag (middle).**

Ted illustrated a four-panel registration card for entry into the Seuss Navy. Entrants were sent a letter of acceptance from Admiral-in-Chief and Cartographer Plenipotentiary Dr. Seuss. An admiral's card was given to the recipient at his "crowning." A copy of *Secrets of the Deep* was included, along with a certificate of commission as an admiral in the Seuss Navy. The certificate commended the recipient for "nonchalance in the face of adversity" and bore the Official Seuss Navy Seal (which depicted a seal who would later be christened Nuzzlepuss), the Official Clam, and the Cousin of the Official Clam. Two different styles of the certificate were made, with the central banner reading either "Ahoy!" or "Esso."

At the beginning, enrollment was apparently limited to owners of boats with inboard motors, but the appeal spread.[4] That was the genius of Ted's latest advertising ploy—with all of the free goodies, even people who didn't own boats wanted to join the Seuss Navy.

Within two years, 75,000 copies of *Secrets of the Deep* had been distributed, and in the summer of 1936, Standard Oil continued to prime the Seuss Navy pump by publishing a sequel, *Secrets of the Deep, Vol. II.*

(By comparison, when *The King's Stilts* was published three years later, it sold fewer than 5,000 copies in its first year and tailed off to fewer than 500 in the next one. Granted, *Secrets of the Deep* was free, but the difference in distribution was enormous.) The second book was more playful than the first, continuing to impart sound advice but allowing for more humor simply to entertain its readers. *Secrets of the Deep, Vol. II* was published while Ted was first working on *And to Think That I Saw It on Mulberry Street.*

To begin the 1937 campaign, Ted drew on the popularity of the five Moto-Monsters he had created for Essolube and created six Marine Muggs for Essomarine. The series began with the Sea Going Dilemma Fish and continued with the Powerless Puffer, Carbonic Walrus, Flaming Herring, Gimlet Fish (which snitched motor oil from boats the way that the Oilio-gobelus drank motor oil from cars), and Sludge Tarpon. At the National Motor Boat Show, the official Seuss Navy flag was introduced for the first reunion of the admirals commissioned the previous year. The First Annual Manoeuvres and Target Practice Luncheon was held at the Commodore Hotel. In its first year, the Seuss Navy was already composed of admirals from "every part of the nation, and a few . . . from foreign countries."[5] Describing the Essomarine booth, one writer reported, "From the briny depths of the imagination of the famous designer, Dr. Seuss, whose murals have been a feature of Essomarine's recent Show exhibits, come a collection of the weirdest denizens of the deep ever imagined in the wildest nightmare of a skipper."[6] These were Ted's sculptures of the Marine Muggs, which another article described as "a group of sculptured fish, with expressions of phony ferocity . . . used . . . as decorations for the motor boat shows. . . ."[7]

While Ted was receiving rejection slips from publishers for his first children's book, he was receiving salary checks from Standard Oil and lots of attention for his Essomarine work.

The campaign sailed on through 1936 with this foldout pamphlet.

More marine secrets to tell: Essomarine wisely capitalized on the popularity of the Seuss Navy with the publication of *Secrets of the Deep, Vol. II* (this page and opposite page, top two images). Ted's incomparable work stood out from the typical nautical magazine fare.

Little Dramas of the Deep: The 1938 National Motor Boat Show featured a continuously performed six-act play, scribed by Ted. The play's program (opposite page, middle) showed the assorted sea monsters that plagued the vessels, like the Throgsnaggler and Sludge (opposite page, bottom two images).

Ted had figured out that trying to convince potential buyers that your company's motor oil was better than another's was a boring and fruitless endeavor. He understood that the way to increase sales was to somehow bring a lot of attention to the company, raising its profile in the communities that bought such products, thereby increasing the likelihood that customers would remember and buy the company's wares. So Ted continued to do his best to imprint the Essomarine name in sailors' minds at the annual National Motor Boat Show. He made every effort to impress in 1938, creating a real "show" for the show—a play performed continuously in the Essomarine booth. A four-page program detailed the Essomarine Players' presentation of Ted's six-act play *Little Dramas of the Deep*. The play concerned the troubles of vessels like the diesel yacht *Vesuvio* (named after the soot-belching furnace from Ted's Gilbert & Barker furnace ads two years earlier)—owned by J. Harrington Murk and run by miserable quartermaster Grimy McGuire—as well as the beleaguered boat of Mr. Eggwurth and his ex-fiancée, Mitzi. The boats were beset by the likes of a vulture named Tamberlaine, an allegorical sea monster called the Throgsnaggler (intended to represent friction), and a sea monster named Sludge. The good word about Essomarine products was spread by Ivanhoe the whale, Philomel the nightingale, and an intelligent salmon named Cholmondeley.

The impression has been given of Ted that "he suffered all his life from acute stage fright and hated speaking in public."[8] His fear is said to have started during his sophomore year of high school. The story that has been related is that Ted was the last of ten Scouts in line to receive a medal from Colonel Theodore Roosevelt, who was only given nine medals to distribute, leaving Ted stranded on the stage of Springfield's Municipal Auditorium with a perturbed former president in front of thousands of spectators. "In that pulverizing moment, Ted's wounded pride, his chagrin, and, above all, his sense of injustice overwhelmed him. He had no memory of stage fright before that hour, but within a few years, his fear of public platforms bordered on the neurotic."[9]

It is true that Ted had no stage fright before this incident. Only a month earlier, he had performed a mandolin solo at a high

Akin to the Moto-Monsters of Ted's earlier work, these Marine Muggs were kept at bay by boaters wise enough to use Essomarine.

school class assembly. But this stage fright does not appear to have taken root for quite a while. The following year, when he was a junior in high school, his position as the secretary of the house and his membership in the Mandolin Club required public interactions and performances. As a senior, he was an officer of the school debate team, which required a significant amount of confident public speaking. He did not shy away from the public eye, also becoming a soccer manager and joining the Social Committee. He worked on a production of *The Mikado*. He performed with the dance orchestra and in *Twelfth Night*. He read his "Prophecy on the Prophets" before another high school assembly. He performed in his own production of *Chicopee Surprised*.

Almost two decades later, when asked to give a speech at the New York Public Library after the publication of *And to Think That I Saw It on Mulberry Street*, Ted "got as far as the crouching stone lions at the entrance but was overwhelmed with stage fright and could not go inside."[10] And yet, that very same year, Ted's work for Essomarine products had him doing a great deal of public speaking for seven consecutive days at the National Motor Boat Show. Referring to plays Ted would create at parties during this period and his penchant for performing, his sister, Marnie, explained, "This ability of his to dress up and act has been helpful in Ted's work. . . . They have campaigns and displays for motor boat shows and Ted as an admiral, in full dress uniform, has full charge. He plans the whole show with scenery and action and then, standing on a realistic bridge, reels off a speech which combines advertising and humor."[11] Nearly 20 years after the incident in which the bigger Theodore snubbed the smaller Theodor, Ted's fear of public platforms seems to have been situation-dependent.

Ted might have been phobic about promoting himself, but his strong suit was in promoting the products of others. For each of the subsequent National Motor Boat Shows, he dreamed up new marketing tools. One of the

Grog glasses:
The Seuss Navy drinking glasses became a staple of the National Motor Boat Shows.

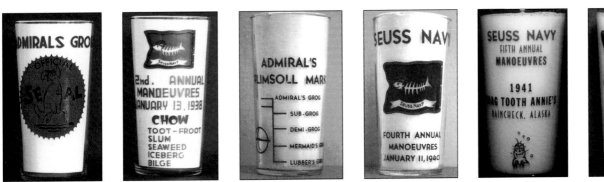

consistent features was that each year Ted created drinking glasses with new designs. In 1938, the Second Annual Manoeuvres admiral's grog glass displayed the big red Official Seuss Navy Seal, which pictured Nuzzlepuss the seal. In 1941, the Manoeuvres glass depicted the skipper of a small craft flying the lively fish carcass of the Seuss Navy flag.

Matchbooks were printed that bore the Seuss Navy flag, known as the Seuss Navy Standard. The flags may have been available by mail order. In 1938 and 1939, Ted's artwork adorned Essomarine tide-table calendars. A vote of the Seuss Navy admirals had declared Nuzzlepuss to be their mascot, and for the 1939 National Motor Boat Show, a Nuzzlepuss ashtray was unveiled. Many of these Seuss Navy promotional pieces have since become very desirable collectibles. Examples of the sculptures that Ted created during this period are extremely hard to find, but the Nuzzlepuss ashtray, by virtue of the number produced and the durability of its metal construction, represents a collector's best chance to own a Seuss-designed sculpted item.

In 1940, Essomarine prepared for 1,000 revelers at the Seuss Navy luncheon in the Hotel Astor on January 11, over which Ted presided. The Essomarine exhibit for the 1940 National Motor Boat Show displayed Ted's "Navigavarama," in which visitors navigated a boat through a sea full of islands and shoals, as well as Ted's usual unusual assortment of bizarre sea life. Included were past creatures like the Powerless Puffer and the Carbonic Walrus and new creations like the Blue-Green Funk Fish. By some accounts, the Essomarine exhibit for this show may have been the most extravagant of all:

> "Say-a-y, there's a boat I wanna ride in," shrilled Gertie Gunwale, and the maddest adventure at the current Motorboat Show was on. "Step right aboard," said Dr. Seuss, with an oily (advt.) smile, waving toward the gangplank of the good ship Nellie Bellie Blurtz. . . . You, too, can pilot the Nellie Bellie. . . . If you pilot the snubby little craft past the Associated Demons of the Deep, the two mad wags who run the exhibit hand you a special edition of an eight-page extra. In type as big as your fist, your name, with "Commodore" appended, heads the

Other popular marketing tools employed by Essomarine and designed by Ted included matchbooks bearing the Seuss Navy flag (top) and a Nuzzlepuss-bedecked ashtray (bottom).

page. . . . "Cape Monstrous, Jan. 1940—Undaunted by
nautical obstacles and sea-going terrors, clad only
in a 40-foot cruiser, this prominent American Yachtsman
rounded Cape Monstrous . . . with its rip tides, snort tides,
blizaroons and swurlpools."[12]

The special edition in question was Esso Marketers' *Sea Lawyer's Gazette*. The existing copies are four-page, tabloid-sized newspapers that look as if Ted may have produced nearly every bit of them, from the bellicose prose recounting the trip around Cape Monstrous to the ads for the abrasively funny "Off-Wid-It!" tattoo remover kit. Just as Essolube had "Foil the Zero-doccus" and "Foil the Moto-Raspus," Demons of the Deep that threaten unprotected ships, such as Sludge and Carbon, are "Foiled by Essomarine." Further illustrated with characters like Bilge Ben, the paper is a dense delight that, due to its fragility, is now extremely rare.

At the 1940 National Motor Boat Show, Essomarine booth attendees received copies of the *Sea Lawyer's Gazette,* a tabloid-esque publication that featured Ted's trademark humor throughout, from the art and stories to the tongue-in-cheek ad copy for a tattoo remover.

VOL. I.—NO. 1.   WINTER, 1940   CIRCULATION 2¾

BILGE BEN SAYS:

FOILED! Friction, Worry, Carbon, Sludge, Overheating and Blow-By —Terrifying Monsters rendered Impuissant by Esso Marine

The "Off-Wid-It" Junior Kit
(For areas of less than a dozen square feet)

The Junior Kit Treatment is simplicity itself. Only five acids, four abrasives and a googel! It's Zip! Zap! Bang! and your tattoo is gone!

Then a quick finishing touch-up with our high-grade steel wool, and your hide, to put it mildly, will *simply glow.*

At all the better Sea-going Cosmetic Saloons . . . . ($.98)

For the 1941 show, Ted created Essie Neptune, the Essomarine mermaid, and her pet whale. Visitors to the exhibit were invited to go "for a ride on the back of the Seussian mammal. Those who brave[d] the whaling excursion"[13] were rewarded by having their pictures taken with Essie, which were placed in their personal Happy Cruising passport.

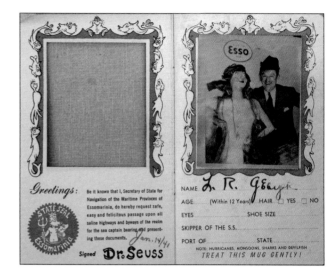

Bon voyage: **Essomarine offered booth visitors a "Happy Cruising" passport photo with a mermaid fashioned by Ted (top).**

Ted had help in producing the extravagant Essomarine exhibits. During the 1940 show, his silent partner was described as "a Bay Ridge man, who wants to remain anonymous. 'Dr. Seuss gets the brainstorms . . . and I build 'em. . . . I built the Nellie Bellie Blurtz. . . .'"[14] Ted related that "Harry Bruno, a great PR man, Ted Cook and Verne Carrier of Esso, and I cooked up the Seuss Navy."[15] Harry A. Bruno was a World War I pilot who started a public-relations firm in 1923 with fellow pilot Richard R. Blythe. They became nationally known through their work for Charles A. Lindbergh's May 1927 transatlantic flight and did a large portion of their early business promoting trade shows like the National Motor Boat Shows.[16]

"Admiral-in-Chief" Ted Geisel (left) at the 1940 National Motor Boat Show presenting a Seuss Navy certificate to "Admiral" Guy Lombardo, the beloved bandleader.

The Essomarine campaign became so time-consuming by 1936 that Ted had to stop his work for Flit until the campaign was finished. He produced more than 50 full-page monthly advertisements for Essomarine and, by the time that he "retired," Ted liked to brag that the Seuss Navy was literally the largest in the world. And why not? In *Naked Lunch*, William S. Burroughs explains that heroin is the perfect commodity because people will drag themselves through sewers and gutters to get it. Ted had managed to develop a much cleaner version of this scenario by devising a "club" to which people wanted to belong. He didn't have to sell the product; people wanted to be a part of the product. As much as he benefited for so many years from knowing that he had a guaranteed income from Standard Oil, Ted's

The Essomarine ads from the late 1930s (this page and next page) are both undeniably Ted and Essomarine—something he accomplished seamlessly throughout the campaign.

success provided the company with equally automatic benefits, including virtually guaranteed increased visibility and improved sales.

Ted's work for Standard Oil would later be a source of curiosity and amusement for his co-workers on the newspaper *PM*, the majority of whom were on the far left of the political spectrum. Fortunately, he was no longer working for Standard Oil in March 1942, when Senator Harry S. Truman charged that deals made by Standard Oil of New Jersey with Nazi Germany, and technological advances for making synthetic rubber that were withheld from the United States government by the oil company, amounted to "treasonable relations."

After World War II, 42-year-old Ted sampled a new career in Hollywood.

While he weathered its rocky start, he returned to his previously reliable stronghold to do some more work for Essomarine products. Sometime in 1947, Ted produced a booklet for Essomarine called *The Log of the Good Ship*. Since nautical publications from February 1947 refer to the availability of a free ship's log from Esso, it is possible that it was produced for the National Motor Boat Show in January. A sample entry in the booklet contains a date in July 1947. Whether it was published at the beginning of the year or at the end of that summer, it appears to predate the September 1947 publication of *McElligot's Pool*, with which it shares many images of Seussian marine life.

Regarding the demise of the Seuss Navy, Ted told a characteristically flippant story:

An interesting thing happened. I left to join the Army. And somebody said, "Thank God, Geisel's gone, he was wasting a great opportunity. He wasn't *selling* the product. We have Seuss Navy hats, and we have Seuss Navy glasses and Seuss Navy flags." He said, "These things should carry advertising on them."

They put advertising on them, and the Navy promptly died. The fun had gone out of it, and the Seuss Navy sank.[17]

As was often the case, it was a good story that didn't necessarily reflect the facts. From the first Seuss Navy products in 1934, Esso's name had appeared on most of the items to which Ted referred; they didn't wait until he left. And the Seuss Navy did not die when he "retired" in 1941, nor when he

Ted's final ad piece for Essomarine was a 1947 booklet featuring the product line.

left for the army in 1943. In 1948, seven years after it had been abandoned, the Seuss Navy was resurrected. Ted designed a new drinking glass, produced by Libbey, for which he created a bird called the Official When-Hen (as in "Say when" enough jiggers of alcohol for your drink have been poured). Like earlier glasses in the series, this one carried markers for the number of jiggers of booze to be added—this time labeled in terms of tide heights. At the National Motor Boat Show that year, the new Official Seuss Navy glasses were given to winners of the "Pick-a-Port" game featured in the Essomarine exhibit— a diversion that required no nautical skills and could be played by people of all ages. Apparently more of these glasses were later produced; unlike previous versions, this one was sold at Essomarine dealerships throughout the following year, and sets of the glasses were given to the winners of the Seuss Trophy Race at the 1949 National Motor Boat Show.

In 1958—presumably to capitalize on the popularity of *The Cat in the Hat* and *How the Grinch Stole Christmas!*, published the previous year—Ted's earlier Essomarine illustrations were used to advertise Esso oils and greases once again in periodicals like *Popular Boating*. It was a full 30 years after Standard Oil first employed his talents to promote one of its products.

Knowing when to say When-Hen: **These promotional offerings, designed by Ted post–World War II, belie his tall tale of the Seuss Navy's demise. In fact, Essomarine continued to use Ted's art for years to come.**

CHAPTER 13

What Else Can This Ted Guy Sell?

Much has been written about the strict restraints placed on Ted by his contract for Standard Oil, limiting the work he could do for other companies and in other fields of writing. But the fact is that from 1929 to 1940, Ted worked on advertising campaigns for companies other than Standard Oil in every year except 1935, when he was likely consumed with his work for the Seuss Navy.

On March 2, 1929, Ted celebrated his twenty-fifth birthday. It was a significant milestone in his life and his career. That month, his first cover illustration appeared on *Judge* magazine. There were fewer than a dozen cartoons thus far in the Flit campaign for Standard Oil, but other companies began to pay heed to their success. Research indicates that in 1929, Ted

Home Seuss home: Ted's non–Standard Oil advertising work included these postcards (circa 1929 and 1930) for L.P.C. Co. Building Contractors—a decidedly Seussian spin on home improvement.

Spring is in the Air!

The grass is growing greener . . . the birds are singing . . . and flocks of young couples are wistfully regarding vacant building lots.

Soon the mad building stampede will commence, and your hands will be more than full. In the heavy rush to please everyone at once, you'll find our ready co-opera-'tion something helpful to rely upon.

You Can't Kill an Elephant with a Popgun!

No job can be done well with inadequate equipment. That's why our company uses nothing but the best. From the pencils with which we take down your order to the trucks in which we deliver it, everything in our organization is selected with a view to serving you efficiently. Contractors who get their building materials from us are confident that the job will be done right.

YOUR NAME HERE
Your business here
Your address here   Your phone No. here

Some Men are Satisfied with Anything

But the discerning man demands the genuine product. . . . .

There is no substitute for service. If you need building materials today, you will not be satisfied with getting them tomorrow. . . . or maybe the week after. We deliver the goods whenever and wherever you want them.

YOUR NAME HERE
Your business here
Your address here   Your phone No. here

No. D 107 Card

No Matter What You Want to Build . . .

. . . . we can furnish the materials. Merely tell us what you want and how much you want of it and we'll have it over there in no time.

Speed is our password.

YOUR NAME HERE
Your business here
Your address here   Your phone No. here

No. D 106 Card

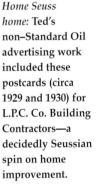

Let's Put an End to the Building Bogey!

Altogether too many people are scared stiff of the Building Bogey. Scared Stiff that the job will take too long — cost too much — and upset the routine of their lives with a hundred inconveniences.

It's up to us to convince these people that building *can* be done easily, cleanly and efficiently. Whatever job we tackle with you, you may count on our eager and thorough co-operation.

"O, Jack, I forgot to bring my skis."
"Just like a woman. What d'ye think Carnival is anyhow,—a pettin' party?"

devised a mail campaign of six postcards. Dealers were urged to send them to building contractors, architects, and city officials to promote the construction and remodeling of homes that spring. The following year, he created another set of 12 postcards.

After Ted's infamous drinking incident in college, there wasn't enough time to rectify the situation before graduation. But Ted later countered the ignominy of his final month at Dartmouth in the best way he could—he became a success in exactly the same field as the one from which he had been banned. Fewer than five years after the moratorium on the publication of Ted's illustrations at Dartmouth, his artwork returned triumphantly for the college's twentieth annual Winter Carnival in 1930. His illustrations adorned the Dartmouth Outing Club's program for the weekend, and one of the drawings was used in the program for the play being performed, *Fill the Bowl Up: An Historical Masque*. A comparison between one of these cartoons and another that Ted had done five years earlier for the *Jack-O-Lantern*, during the fifteenth annual Winter Carnival, reveals how quickly he had made enormous changes in technique and spirit. That continued

Dartmouth redux: The twentieth annual Winter Carnival at Dartmouth gave Ted a chance to showcase his artwork (middle left), a marked difference from his contribution to the Winter Carnival five years earlier (top left). He continued to draw for the Carnival over the next two years (this page, bottom left and right, and opposite page).

Carnival Committee

Dr. Seuss

improvement is evident in his Carnival contributions for the following two years, culminating in his creation of Alma, the ski-jumping cow.

In January 1936, more than a decade after leaving college, he also overcame the ban against his work appearing in the *Jack-O-Lantern*, which published a two-page spread of puzzling poetry and atypical artwork by Ted. Among the snappier of these oddities:

DON'T MISS THE SENSATION OF THE CARNIVAL!
Alma, the Ski-Jumping Cow, will attempt to break her own world's record off Bray Jump on the N. E. Slope of Balch Hill, Sunday, 3.15 a.m.

SQUARE-DANCE FOR AN AMATEUR ECHO-EATER[1]

Oh salt not the clam of old Abraham;
Post not thy bouillon by mail!
Rend not the fig from thy grandmother's wig;
For Gussie is taking the veil![2]

This improved relationship with his alma mater led to Ted's volunteering his time and creativity to help the college. Starting that summer and continuing until he joined the army, Ted contributed cartoons each year to be used by the Dartmouth Alumni Fund to solicit contributions.

By the spring of 1930, the success of the Flit ads made it clear that Ted was having no trouble selling a product that would kill bugs, so the Crosman Arms Company got him to sell a product to kill other household nuisances. The company ran a contest in which a rogues' gallery of pests were assigned various point totals. The low end of the spectrum was represented by the English sparrow (1 point), while a wolverine and a wolf were among the animals that would net a contestant the largest total (60 points). Ted illustrated six of these pests, choosing—as he had with the Flit bugs—to anthropomorphize them. John Sparrow, Adam Rat, Joseph Rabbit, Ezra Crow, Silvanus Snake, and Rufus Squirrel appeared in the pages of magazines likely to appeal to young boys, like *Open Road for Boys, Popular Science, Science and Invention,* and *Popular Mechanics.*

Among the animals for which Ted wisely chose not to provide advertisements were house cats, which were assigned 20 points, and turtles, which earned 10 points. Crosman appears to have had second thoughts about the wisdom of sending youngsters out to shoot some of these animals, and by summer, advertisements for the contest waned. It was never held again.

General Electric was the fifth organization for which Ted did work in 1930. Ted's GE campaign began with a Sherlock Holmesian murder mystery to sell the idea that GE would provide businesses with complete promotional plans to sell their electric fans. In *The Strange Case of Adlebert Blump*,[3] Watson's account begins on the evening of May 25, 1903:

> Holmes and I were seated before the electric fan in our lodgings in Baker Street betting on the blade which would stop uppermost as I flicked the current on and off. . . .
>
> "Holmes," said I, as the blade which we had numbered four again came to rest on top and Holmes pocketed my dime, "your intuition in picking the winning number is positively uncanny. . . ."
>
> Holmes yawned, placed his feet on the mantel, and toyed dreamily with his hypodermic. My last dime having fallen victim to Holmes' deductive powers, I rose and went to bed, noticing as I did so (and, I must confess, with some degree of suspicion) that Holmes unfastened his chewing gum from the back of blade number two. . . .[4]

The story develops as Inspector Botts arrives to enlist their help in the case of Adlebert Blump, a fan dealer in Uncasville, who "was murdered in cold blood. . . . The motive may have been robbery, for there was no money in the till."[5]

Proliferating pitches: Ted was extremely busy in 1930 as he applied his unique perspective to a variety of ad campaigns, including these Crosman rifle ads (this page, top left and right) and a Sherlock Holmes–themed booklet for GE electric fans (this page, bottom right, and opposite page, top left and right).

HOLMES LAY BACK IN HIS BIG EASY CHAIR BY THE FIRE
DREAMILY TOYING WITH HIS HYPODERMIC

ADELBERT BLUMP LAY IN
THE MIDDLE OF THE CEN-
TER AISLE, HIS BODY COV-
ERED WITH COBWEBS

At Blump's store, as Holmes and Watson move to the back room—where they've asked that Blump's body be placed for investigation—Sergeant Mulligan laments, "It's a shame . . . no one ever came in the store"[6] despite the fact that, as Officer O'Leary points out, Blump "stocked a good line of fans."[7] Since Blump had been lying in the main aisle of the store, Inspector Botts observes, "Nobody ever looked in this dump or they'd a seen him lying there."[8]

But Holmes interrupts the officers. "Absolutely nothing the matter with the fan business, boys,"[9] he says as he, Watson, and a revived Blump walk into the room, much to the surprise of the policemen. Holmes has deduced that Blump contracted a serious case of mercantile paralysis, which could have proved fatal if Holmes and Watson had not intervened with a GE contract and promotional plan.

Whether he was hawking wiring systems (bottom left) or lightbulbs (bottom right) for GE, Ted's humorous touch was ever present.

This very clever booklet led to other work for General Electric, and over the next two years, Ted helped to promote its convenience outlets and wiring-system contractors. In future years, he developed the "bulbsnatching" campaign to advertise its Mazda lightbulbs.

The first of five covers that Ted created for the Warren Telechron Company's in-house

BRINGING HADES UP TO DATE By Dr. Theophrastus Seuss

"Old stuff, Satan, old stuff! Why, for a few paltry dollars a General Electric Wiring System Contractor could wire all Hell and you could run this toaster by Electricity!"

1. You probably find that bulbsnatching leads to arguments in your home, even if your family never gets down to the last bulb in the house! (A sure cure is a handy supply of G-E MAZDA lamps.)

2. It may interfere with Junior's homework, through eyestrain, since bulbsnatching usually leaves the wrong size bulbs everywhere. (He needs an I.E.S. lamp with at least a 100-watt bulb in it.)

clock-industry publication, *Telechronicle,* was published in February–March 1932. It featured the
"adventures and misadventures of . . . Gus and Gussie
Guess."[10] Although largely overlooked by collectors,
this work represents half the magazine-cover illustrations that Ted did in his lifetime.

The Hygienic Cup Institute, founded in 1932,
became the Cup and Container Institute in 1933. It
approached issues like the sterilization of eating
and drinking utensils in public places as matters of
public health. This institute represented the interests of
several competing companies, including the U.S. Envelope Company (maker of Ajax cups) and the Individual Drinking Cup Company (which made Dixie
cups). Ajax cup dispensers, or "cabinets," were made
in Springfield. That fact, along with the popularity of
his Flit bugs, likely made Ted an attractive prospect. He
did a four-page pamphlet for Ajax showing insect-like
microbes that threatened the cleanliness of glassware. The style of illustration and of Ted's signature,
coupled with the timing of industry developments,
suggests that Ted did the Ajax pamphlet in the
summer of 1933.

Telling timely tales:
The adventures of
Gus and Gussie
Guess (this page)
were created for
Warren Telechron
Company's
in-house
clock-industry
publication.

Other additions
to Ted's growing
roster of ad clients
included Ajax cups
(opposite page, top
left) and Daggett &
Ramsdell (opposite
page, top right and
bottom right).

* * *

In 1934, the first interview of any significant length with Ted was held, in which he spoke with the *Dartmouth*'s Bob Warren about the beginnings of the Flit campaign. The reporter then wrote, "I looked toward the corner of the room where there stood at least two dozen cans of different colors and sizes. He pointed to them: 'Now I have to think up ideas for all those tinned propositions there.'"[11] These cans most likely contained Daggett & Ramsdell toiletries.

Ted had done an advertisement for the company's Brevo shaving cream the previous summer and was working on a general advertisement for its "Perfect" line of beauty products.

In the spring of 1936, a company from Springfield began a campaign to get customers to switch from coal-burning furnaces to oil-burning ones. Gilbert & Barker Manufacturing Company ("Gilbarco," a subsidiary of Standard Oil of New Jersey) hired Ted because they knew he could create new characters with whom consumers could identify. *Telechronicle*'s Gus and Gussie Guess were replaced by Cornelius and Cornelia Clinker. In the Gilbarco ads, the couple rationalized how much they loved their old-fashioned

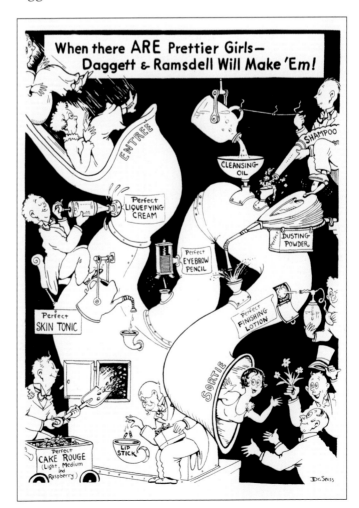

furnace—the coal mess, the fumes, the work of shoveling coal to keep it running, and the labor of maintaining the coal bin.

That same year, Benjamin Olney patented a system for improving the sound in cabinet-type loudspeakers. Stromberg-Carlson employed this new "acoustical labyrinth" in its radios from 1936 to 1950. It used Ted to promote this filtration system, which it claimed eliminated "wild tones" to produce a pure reproduction of sound in a radio broadcast. From Ted's point of view, what could be more tempting than the opportunity to draw a "Wild Tone"? The result was the charming 14-page *What Is a Wild Tone?* advertising booklet.

Ted's work in advertising campaigns like this one is more than just interesting tidbits from a celebrity artist's past. Somewhere in the wondrous landscape of Ted's mind, the images all found shelter and nested. Some, like the Stromberg-Carlson Wild Tones, would come forward to be

reincarnated in famous form. For 20 years, the question appears to have brewed in Ted's brain: What would happen if the Wild Tones got *out* of the radio? Eventually, the imps that made such a ruckus and ruined radio broadcasts became Thing One and Thing Two, who—along with the Cat in the Hat—wreaked havoc on an entire household. The images worked in both forms—selling radios to adults and books to children. Boy, could this Ted guy sell!

As winter turned to spring in 1937, Ted's first children's book, *And to Think That I Saw It on Mulberry Street*, had finally been accepted by Vanguard Press. Ted celebrated his thirty-third birthday, and soon after, his print advertisement

Ted's ability to create memorable, relatable characters like the Clinkers served him well in this 1936 Gilbert & Barker furnace ad (top).

Recalling the Wild: Did Ted evoke his 1937 advertising endeavors for Stromberg-Carlson radios when writing *The Cat in the Hat*? These "Wild Tones" (middle two images) bear a bushy resemblance to the equally untamable Thing One (bottom), pictured here without Thing Two.

for Schaefer Bock Beer was published and a poster was produced. Though he had joked about alcohol in his cartoons for so long, this was his first advertisement for an alcoholic beverage. He would go on to advertise Scotch and more beer, including a similar poster for Narragansett Bock Beer five years later.

Although some early attempts were made to put beer into cans instead of bottles, there were difficulties in producing a container that could withstand the pressure of pasteurization and in preventing the beer from reacting with the metal of the cans. During Prohibition, there was no reason to pursue the matter. But when 3.2 percent beer became legal in some states in 1933, the American Can Company resumed its attempts to convince brewers to can their product.

Apparently a test run of 2,000 cans was made late in 1933, followed by other testing of cans lined with a plastic from Union Carbide called Vinylite. The American Can Company called it "Keglined" technology. In January 1935, beer in Keglined cans went on sale for the first time from the Gottfried Krueger Brewing Company in Newark, New Jersey. Sales increased dramatically, and by the end of the year, many other breweries followed suit. In July, Pabst became the first of the major brewers to sell its beer in these Keglined cans.[12]

Two years later, the American Can Company ran an ad utilizing one of Ted's illustrations to promote its Keglined cans. Ted's ad for Schaefer Bock Beer had run the previous month. *Mulberry Street* would be published five months later.

Creative "juices": **After many liquor-themed cartoons, Ted finally landed an ad account for an alcoholic beverage with Schaefer Bock Beer (top). His work in this industry found various outlets, including this 1937 American Can Company ad (bottom).**

* * *

New York State's Westchester County had a large percentage of residents who worked within the community rather than commuting to New York City. In 1937, the local newspapers wanted to cultivate a "homey" sensibility since they carried nearly 5,000 articles and pictures of local interest each week. Ted created six advertisements with the theme "Nobody Can Resist a Mirror" for the daily and weekly Macy-Westchester Newspapers, portraying the papers as mirrors reflecting residents' daily lives. The campaign ran from July through September, stopping in the month that *And to Think That I Saw It on Mulberry Street* was published.

After *Mulberry Street* was published, Ted's advertising work continued unabated with a campaign for Chilton Wing-Flow fountain pens, distinguished by metal inlays in the body of the pens—often gold initials. As one advertising periodical quipped, "Dr. Seuss" was "a real pen name now."[13]

Ted mentioned that during this period, his contract with Standard Oil prohibited him from many types of work. As has been illustrated, the restrictions were not evident in much that he did at the time. But some support for his statement can be found in the distribution of the Chilton ads. One of the supposed limitations concerned national advertising campaigns for other companies. Accordingly, local campaigns—for newspapers restricted to Westchester County, for example—would have been allowable. Why

Reflective campaign: When Macy-Westchester Newspapers set out to woo suburban New York readers, it called on Ted to illustrate, quite literally, the papers' ability to mirror the interests and lifestyles of readers.

nobody can resist a mirror

NO. I SLOT MACHINE EGO

nobody can resist a mirror

NO. 2. MIRRORS ON THE MOVE

nobody can resist a mirror

NO. 5. UNEXPECTED PLEASURE

it was permissible for the New York–based American Can Company to use Ted to advertise in an Ohio newspaper is less clear. Even more confounding is why, in the same year, Ted could do an ad for a national brand like Schaefer beer. One theory is that this was the time when "Ted left Standard Oil to free-lance, but after a few months was back in their fold."[14] However, his output for Standard Oil was continuous during this period, so it is difficult to say. Another theory is that because these were single advertisements and not a campaign, they were not seen as conflicting with Ted's work for Standard Oil.

Still, as there were at least nine Chilton pen advertisements, they certainly represented a campaign. And a promotional poster claimed that the ads would run in *Esquire* and the *New Yorker,* both of which had national circulation. However, the ads did not run in *Esquire* at all, and although one did run in the national edition of the *New Yorker,* thereafter the ads appeared only in the New York edition. Consequently, it does appear as if the Chilton campaign was planned as a national one but may have been limited to New York due to the contractual restriction on Ted from Standard Oil.

Interviewed toward the end of 1937, Ted's sister, Marnie, confirmed that he was "designing bill boards for a western oil and refining company."[15] In 1928, Standard Oil of Indiana purchased the Utah Oil Refining Company, which owned Vico and Pep 88 stations in Utah and Idaho. Ted did at least 15 billboard advertisements for Vico motor oil and Pep 88 gasoline. The new character created for these ads, Mr. Jones, was intended to be an everyman, but unlike Ted's previous advertising characters, he never spoke. He just kept motoring along. Nothing affected him because he was protected by Vico and Pep 88 products. As a

These 1937 Chilton pen ads appear to have been run only regionally to avoid a conflict of interest with Ted's Standard Oil contract.

result, however, he failed to develop any personality and became completely forgettable in contrast to the playful characters he passed on his trips.

When the little-known Hankey Bannister distillery decided to advertise its Scotch for the first time in January 1939, it faced a problem that was unique to the liquor industry. The wording of an advertisement that might be deemed suitable in a bar would not be permissible in a liquor store or in a print ad. Ted circumvented the problem by attaching the Hankey Bird to liquor bottles:

> His display . . . didn't even mention whiskey. It was a piece of sculpture of a wistful looking scotch bird in kilts. Behind this bird was the following theory:
>
> Bartenders like to amuse their clients. The Hankey Bird is amusing. But just try to show the bird without showing the bottle! Off the bottle, the bird won't stand up.[16]

By way of introduction, Ted apparently walked into an advertising magazine's office with his bird and said simply, "There's no sense to it." But that had always been the case with Ted's brand of advertising. The secret to the success of his campaigns was not that they uniquely explained a product's

virtues. It was not the product that garnered the attention. The creatures and characters that he devised for his advertisements caught the eye, secondarily attracting attention to the product. "So there's no sense to this Hankey Bird—a cock-eyed concoction of Scotchman and flapdoodle that snaps colorfully onto the neck of a bottle of Hankey Bannister Scotch whisky with the aid of a small coil spring. . . . But it makes people laugh when a bartender sets out a bottle—gives away the bird, or sells it, as the case may be."[17] It brought attention to the Scotch—you can easily picture someone scanning the lines of bottles at a bar and being compelled to ask, "What's in that one with the bird on it?" Just as Ted managed to differentiate Esso's motor oil with the humor in his ads, he set Hankey Bannister Scotch whisky apart from its competitors with his odd bird.

Of course, once the new menagerie beast was in existence, there had to be a story to go with it. According to Ted, the Hankey Bird was developed as a carrier pigeon for the Scottish army—"a bird so distinctive that it would not be mistaken for a grouse and shot down by near-sighted American millionaires. After fifteen generations of wearing kilts, the Hankey Bird has developed sideburns."[18]

Squelching the unasked question as to why the budding children's author was advertising Scotch, Ted, speaking for the "research center" that developed the Hankey Bird, explained that the bird's "mating call is characterized by a distinct burr. Our only purpose in leasing him to Hankey Bannister is to finance further scientific effort to de-burr that mating call . . . not, I assure you, to aid the crass business of selling whisky."[19]

A search for one of those prior sideburnless generations of Hankey Birds leads to a sketch that Ted did nine years earlier for Dartmouth of a bird that puts on a cap and muffler rather than flying south for the winter. With similarly curved feet and a jaunty cap, he does appear to be a progenitor of the Hankey Bird.

* * *

Expanding horizons: These Vico motor oil and Pep 88 gasoline billboards (opposite page), featuring everyman Mr. Jones, peppered the roadways of Utah and Idaho.

The creation of the Hankey Bird sculpture piece (this page, top and bottom left) for Hankey Bannister Scotch was thoroughly Ted— it was a comical creature whose purpose was to attract attention to the product, not define it. Could this sketch from the 1930 Dartmouth Winter Carnival program (this page, top right) be a forerunner of the Hankey Bird?

149

Sellers, sell thyself:
This Snyder &
Black ad showcases
Ted's talent for
creating campaigns
for the advertising
industry (this page,
top).

Spot-on advertising:
Ted continued to be
his wonderfully
literal self when
crafting these ads
(this page, bottom,
and opposite page)
that peddled the
virtues of running
ad spots with NBC
Radio.

Snyder & Black were lithographers like Currier & Ives and other contemporaries. The New York company began printing items like maps, stock certificates, and mining certificates in 1844 and continued through the 1900s.[20]

Apparently starting in the early to mid-1910s, Snyder & Black began specializing in point-of-sale advertising, although it continued to accept requests for other kinds of printing projects.[21] The signs it printed for Coca-Cola in 1941 are an example of the type of advertising that Snyder & Black was trying to promote when it hired Ted. The company was coming up on its one-hundredth anniversary when Ted did his advertisement for it, which depicted an overdressed hunter with an ineffectual popgun—a symbolically impotent and unprepared rush forward into unfamiliar territory. The copy for the advertisement was: "Following the Barrage . . . with a POP-GUN . . . is not more futile than to launch a heavy, national newspaper-magazine-radio campaign for a product . . . and then fail to support it with point-of-sale advertising that converts your ammunition and strategy into sales—at the point-of-sale."[22] As with the NBC ads that would follow, Ted was now doing meta-advertising by creating ads to promote advertising.

January 1939 was an extremely busy time for Ted. The Vico and Pep 88 campaign seems to have just ended, but Ted was at work on the annual National Motor Boat Show for Essomarine. He'd created the Nuzzlepuss ashtray to promote boat motor oil and the Hankey Bird to promote Scotch whisky. He'd been working on his third book, *The Seven Lady Godivas*, and he had one big

idea for the upcoming World's Fair and another for the New York Toy Fair. He was doing the monthly Essomarine ads, and he was now working on monthly ads for NBC Radio.

It was an interesting twist: Ted was advertising advertising. NBC was trying to publicize the potential of ad spots on its radio shows. Ted's NBC work appeared as four-page two-color brochures and as black-and-white print ads in radio periodicals, many of which

used parts of the brochures. One of the early ones referred to Jones, as in the Vico and Pep 88 advertisements.

More campaigns would follow, but the advertisements for Standard Oil and these other companies represent more than a decade of work that established Ted's reputation in the advertising field and helped him to weather the Great Depression in relative comfort. His income from this work allowed him the freedom to travel and to experiment in other fields, as we shall soon see.

CHAPTER 14

Life, *Liberty*, and the Pursuit of Happiness

Dr. Seuss's path to fame as a children's author was wildly indirect. We have seen his career as an advertising man. But there was another world in which his reputation also flourished. From the time he joined the staff of *Judge* in October 1927 until his first children's book, *And to Think That I Saw It on Mulberry Street,* was published in September 1937, Ted produced perhaps a thousand illustrations that established him as a popular cartoonist.

Like his life in the ad trade, his career in cartooning had its instabilities. Ted worked with *Judge* for 23 months, from October 1927 through August 1929, at which time he left to work for *Life* magazine. In August 1930, after a year of work exclusively with *Life,* Ted left and returned to *Judge*. His new contract with *Judge* was not exclusive, and by the following summer, Ted was publishing weekly in *Judge,* monthly in *College Humor,* and every few months in *Vanity Fair.*

His work for *Judge* ended in April 1932, and two months later, he began a weekly series for *Liberty* that ran through the end of the year. By 1933, both *Judge* and *Life* had abandoned their weekly schedules and joined *Vanity Fair* as monthly publications. Ted published sporadically in all three, as well as in a start-up magazine called *University*. In 1934, he continued publishing monthly in *Life* until the summer, and occasionally in other magazines, but his interest in periodical work dwindled.

Ted did make two very short-lived returns to *Judge* in December 1936 and February 1938, and continued to publish in several periodicals that were new to him. But he was clearly putting the "weekly cartoonist" phase of his career behind him, moving on to support him-self through advertising work while attending to new projects and ideas for the future.

Before a career transition could take place, Ted had to establish his reputation. Ted Geisel became famous as Dr. Seuss long before children's books were in his plans. Although Dr. Seuss first gained national popularity through his Flit advertisements, he also began to have a big following for his noncommercial cartoons on college campuses. If "imitation is the sincerest form of flattery," Ted was being flattered as early as July 1929, having become popular enough to be satirized. Just as Kalm-bach & Geisel had been known to its fans as "Come Back and Guzzle," Dr. Seuss's college devotees knew him as "Dr. Souse." During Prohibition, he was seen as a wild boozer, teaching intemperance to our young, and college students loved it.

"Everyone laughed when I stepped up to the piano!"

"Quick, Henry! The Flit!"

Less than two years after he'd begun cartooning professionally, a cartoon credited to "Dr. Seosss" appeared in *College Humor,* depicting a suspiciously drunk-looking "Man Being Carried Away by His Emo-tions."[1] Before the end of the year, *College Humor* printed another parody showing a drunken man step-ping up to fight a piano, one of several appropriately signed "Dr. Souse."[2, 3] Ted's Flit ads were satirized too, first in a *Ballyhoo* cartoon on birth control signed "Dr. Souss"[4] and again the following month in a cartoon about graft.[5] *Razzberries* later devoted its centerfold to a parody of one of Ted's covers for *Judge.*[6]

As he published in different magazines, Ted's work changed and con-tinued to develop. When he left *Judge,* he began a series for *Life* magazine called "Life's Little Educational Charts," in which he began to explore lan-guage and sound, as he later would in his children's books. For several install-ments, he illustrated translations of imaginary words from different lan-guages. In French, "La Bambouliere" was a "Trysting Place for Turtles." In German, "Das Gepfeckerei" was a "Student Duel Fought with Dachshunds."

Satirizing Seuss:
Parodies of Ted's work began to turn up as early as 1929, a testament to his growing popularity. A nod to his treatment of the inebriated (top) appeared in *College Humor*. Two years later, *Ballyhoo* ran a spoof of the Flit ads (bottom).

La "BAMBOULIERE" (A Trysting Place for Turtles)

A "BLOIKUS" (A Teething-ring for quadruplets)

Das "Gepfeckerei" (A Student Duel Fought with Dachshunds)

Life "lessons":
These *Life* magazine cartoons show some of Ted's early attempts at fanciful language and wordplay— French (top left), German (bottom left), "Brooklynese" (top right), and plain old English (bottom right) all received Ted's distinctive spin.

LIFE's Little Educational Charts.
The Mediaeval Art of Catapulting.

In Brooklynese, a "Bloikus" was a "Teething-ring for quadruplets." Ted also explored real words like "catapulting" (displaying a very different attitude toward cats than would later be the case).

Ted's draftsmanship also continued to develop. One example of the maturation of his technique is the progression of his dog images. During his junior year at Dartmouth, in a cartoon perhaps drawn hastily for a deadline, his representation was rudimentary and sketchy but contained some distinctive features—the dog was wide-eyed, with an unusually extended and

pointy snout, slightly raised hindquarters, and some oddly positioned and impossibly bent joints. In a cartoon drawn four years later, when Ted had graduated and been published consistently for six months, a recognizable style developed. While the dog maintained the same basic eye, snout, and backside structure, the curves were more rounded and the proportions more balanced, with the exception of the greatly elongated ears. These ears, coupled with the fact that this dog was underwater, introduced a playfulness and sense of humor to the idea of "dog."

Two years later, Ted's dogs' eyes and ears were more pronounced, and their bodies more rounded. The dogs' faces were finally given some expression, and their haunches became even more improbable. Four years later, the playfulness developed into personality. The wide-eyed look had a gleeful element, the joints were even more rubbery and unlikely, and details like collars and hair were added.

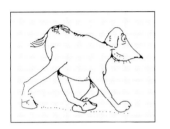

Meanwhile, Ted's bestiary continued to expand. There were Jippets, Depredatory Winklefinches, Dolmarian Whiffoxes, Buttonhole Beagles, Sargassan Gweeks, Cambrubian Cranes, Zobbels, Gwelphotami, Mellocks, and Pignolian Archipelago Walfins. He was creating new beasts all the time. One *College Humor* reader sent in an illustration of Ted's fellow contributors and staffers inspecting a Hippocrass-like beast, which ran above the caption

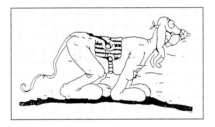

A dog drawn for the *Jack-O-Lantern* in Ted's junior year (top) would take on a progressively finer appearance four years later in *Judge* (second from top), in a 1932 GE ad (third from top), and in a 1935 Flit ad for the *New Yorker* (bottom).

"Sherwood Bundshue, a constant reader, pictures John Held, Jr., Russell Patterson, Jeff Machamer and Don Herold trying to decide whether Dr. Seuss's latest creature is bird, beast, or rodent."[7]

Inheritance of Body Markings

After six years on the Pignolian Archipelago, Dr. Hyman Blox has become the leading authority on the walfin . . . a beast whose markings are in the form of tick-tack-toe games. "A young walfin," says Blox, "inherits his mama's and papa's designs in equal proportion. If, for example, papa's games are all won by 'X's,' and on mama the 'O's are victorious, the games on their offspring are all bound to end in a draw."

In the Argentine, whenever a party begins to lag and the guests start in to fidget, the host can always save the day by starting a game of "Zobbeling." This is a game of the "problem variety," the only paraphernalia consisting of two buck Zobbels, two pieces of string, a sugar doughnut and a parasol. The idea is to get the sugar doughnut onto the other string without removing the Zobbels' horns.

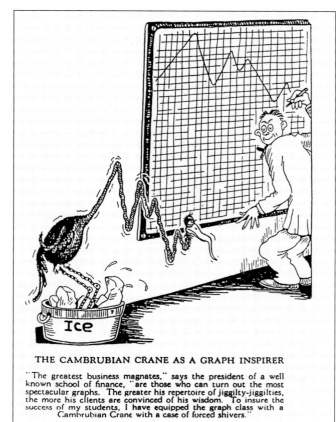

THE CAMBRUBIAN CRANE AS A GRAPH INSPIRER

"The greatest business magnates," says the president of a well known school of finance, "are those who can turn out the most spectacular graphs. The greater his repertoire of jiggilty-jiggilties, the more his clients are convinced of his wisdom. To insure the success of my students, I have equipped the graph class with a Cambrubian Crane with a case of forced shivers."

Ted later abandoned "Life's Little Educational Charts" and began a new series for *Life* dealing with forgotten events and history's unsung heroes. He drew "the cat who furnished the strings so Nero might fiddle while Rome burned"[8] and "the mule, with whose jawbone Samson slew the Philistines."[9] The change allowed him to try single full-page cartoons instead of multiple cartoons on a page. But when the summer of 1930 ended, so did his association with *Life*. His return to *Judge* was quickly rewarded—when the new year of *Judge* began, it did so with Ted's second front-cover illustration. Appropriately, Ted depicted a man waking up on New Year's Day next to one of the beasts that he encountered during the previous night's revelry. It was only Ted's second noncommercial full-color piece of artwork to appear in a periodical.

Ted created several series for *Judge,* including "Fish, Beast, and Bird: A Piscozooavistical Survey," followed by "Tardy Laurels for Forgotten Brows" and then "Some Notes on . . . ," while continuing the Doctor Theodophilus Seuss, Ph.D., I.Q., H_2SO_4 series "Animals Every Student Loves" in *College Humor*—all in the old format of multiple cartoons on one page. At the end of May 1931, Ted abandoned all of these series, starting fresh with a greater percentage of full-page, and even multipage, cartoons.

More exposure led to more opportunities. That June, Ted published his first illustrations for *Vanity Fair*. They accompanied John Riddell's text on various aspects of evolution:

> As the waters of the earth gradually receded, naturally the
> Algae on top of the water receded along with everything
> else; and slowly but surely large and strange shapes began
> to thrust themselves upward through the level of
> primordial slime. These immense prehistoric forms
> included abandoned Fords, old bed-springs, automobile
> tires, and a mammoth ichthyosaurus called Theodore

The Seuss menagerie grew with the addition of some rather bizarre beasts, including (opposite page, clockwise from top left) a Mellock, a Whiffox, some Walfins, a Cambrubian Crane, two Zobbels, and a Gwelphotamus.

This 1931 full-color cover illustration marked Ted's return to *Judge* (this page).

Dreiser, a huge and utterly impracticable species of dinosaur which emerged with bits of green Algae still clinging about its ears, under the impression they were laurel.[10]

Ted accompanied that portion with an illustration of a Dreiseropod taking a swipe at a Lewistodocus. (For those who missed the works of Theodore Dreiser in school, Woody Allen offers a quick summation in "If the Impressionists Had Been Dentists," in which a dentist runs out of anesthesia but is able to keep working on patients by reading Dreiser to them.[11])

A couple of months later, responding to "widespread criticism and dissension aroused by the recent plans for Radio City, Mr. Rockefeller's projected real-estate development," Ted and Corey Ford offered their own architectural innovations in *Vanity Fair*, including Ted's vision of jack-in-the-box gargoyles.

But 1931 was relatively rough for Ted. His mother died in March, six days after his twenty-seventh birthday. He was very busy during the spring, with the publication of *More Boners* and his work on the Flit films, on top of his contributions to various periodicals. He mentioned in a letter that he also had "a summer of legal complications," after which he "went into hiding in Yugo Slavia for seven weeks."[12] Confirming that this was not just another of Ted's tall tales, for seven weeks from mid-September until Halloween, no new material of his appeared in any periodical. Those that ran Ted's work were either printing the Flit ads done earlier or rerunning previously published pieces.

This seven-week vacation was not the foolhardy extravagance of a rich man. Ted left during the depths of the Great Depression. Food riots had broken out around the country. In March, 3,000 unemployed workers converged on a Ford Motor Company plant in Michigan and clashed with police and security guards, leaving four dead and many more injured. In September,

JACK-IN-THE-BOX PRINCIPLE APPLIED TO GARGOYLE MOTIF

Opportunities knock: Ted's increasing exposure as a cartoonist opened new doors. In 1931, he illustrated these two creature-centric pieces for *Vanity Fair.*

when Ted left for Yugoslavia, the *New York Times* reported, "Several hundred homeless unemployed women sleep nightly in Chicago's parks . . . having nowhere to sleep but in the parks, where they feared that they would be molested."[13] In December, New York's Bank of the United States would undergo the largest bank failure in American history. In New York, Ted was living among an estimated 750,000 people who depended on city relief. The need to clear his head and think about the future had to be very strong for Ted to take off as he did.

By the end of 1931, Ted's popularity as a cartoonist was such that *Vanity Fair* ran a short biography of him. A week after Al Capone's conviction ended his reign, *Vanity Fair* christened Ted the "Czar of the Insect World" for "those insecticide dramas, the Flit advertisements, which have made his name famous among cartoonists."[14] This burgeoning respect was reflected in the higher-profile positions Ted commanded in periodicals. In addition to the 1931 New Year's cover, *Judge* began 1932 with a Dr. Seuss center spread depicting the playing of New Year's Eve music on unique instruments, and the second issue of the year sported Ted's third magazine cover. Enjoying the New Year's revelry, Ted showed several shocked temperance women[15] watching a gentleman add some ice to his pitcher of illicit hooch. Don't imagine that the resemblance of the snowcapped, curving towers of the buildings to penises was accidental. Ted's first children's book was still more than five years away.

Incidental Music for a New Year's Eve Party

Taking center(fold) stage: A wild New Year's Eve party, as imagined by Ted (this page), appeared in the center spread of *Judge*'s first issue of 1932. The next issue featured his third cover illustration (next page, top), another soused celebration of the new year.

The new year brought an atmosphere of change. Surrealism came to New York City when Salvador Dalí's "The Persistence of Memory" and other works were presented in the first surrealist exhibition in the United States, which toured from the Wadsworth Atheneum in Hartford to the Julien Levy Gallery in New York. After his 1931 difficulties, Ted felt the need to branch out.

Employing the skills that had proved so successful for hawking various companies' products, Ted began advertising for himself, marketing what appear to be the first pieces of three-dimensional Seussiana. For six months, beginning in March 1932, Ted advertised a set of eight illustrated coasters in four colors, urging people to join the Society for the Prevention of Table Ruination. Mail-order enrollment in the Anti-Ring Ring cost only fifty cents per set.

In the late 1920s and early 1930s, observations about mundane phrases and quirks of human behavior were a rich source of humor for Ted. He was the Jerry Seinfeld of his day—a New Yorker observing petty annoyances and idiosyncrasies and posing ridiculous but humorous solutions or alternatives. He suggested means by which a family could take a weekend away without worrying about feeding their pet bird, how vacationers taking nighttime strolls could avoid tripping over croquet wickets, and how you could ensure that the waters you were fishing actually had fish. Of course, Ted's solutions involved tying the bird to a flat iron, buying a Horned Pomeranian, and using a hungry deep-sea-diving cat.

Starting in June 1932, *Liberty* magazine paid Ted $300 for each page of at least three cartoons. Some of that work was reproduced three decades later in *The Lost World of Dr. Seuss* and would unexpectedly land Ted in a legal battle in the late 1960s when a company produced unauthorized figurines based on some of it.

Three Summer Problems, And How to Solve Them

By DR. SEUSS

WHO-WILL-FEED-THE-CANARY PROBLEM

All canary owners know the difficulty of leaving home for a week-end. Leave the canary without food, and he starves; leave him three days' supply, and he stuffs himself to death the first day. A new device, however, solves this problem neatly. The three meals are left in three dishes, fifteen feet apart, and the canary is hitched to a flat iron. By working like blazes, the canary will get his lunch precisely at noon each day.

THE WHERE-TO-FISH PROBLEM

One thing that can spoil a fishing trip more than anything else is the absence of fish. This year the clever sportsman, instead of angling just anywhere and waiting for the fish to seek him, will be able to seek out the fish. This is done by rowing around with a hungry cat trailing on the bottom in glass diving togs. When the cat meows, that is the place to drop anchor.

THE CROQUET-WICKET PROBLEM

Of all the vacationists who spend their summer in the country, over half, statistics show, come home in wheel chairs. Although poison ivy and snake bites cause a few casualties, the majority are victims of Wicket-in-the-Dark. Croquet-wicket tripping, however, can now be avoided. Thanks to the Horned Pomeranian, the after-dark stroller can now roam his lawn without danger.

Self-promotion: Applying the same marketing skills he'd been sharpening for the various ad campaigns, Ted created a set of eight original illustrated coasters (opposite page, middle and bottom) and successfully sold them as mail-order items.

How-tos askew: Ted offered his own off-kilter insight into finding the right spot to fish, solving the problems of pet care, and avoiding croquet injuries in a 1932 *Liberty* cartoon (this page).

Liberty was more politically oriented than the periodicals to which Ted was accustomed. His cartoons appeared alongside a series by New York governor and Democratic presidential nominee Franklin Delano Roosevelt. In this different environment, Ted began addressing political and social subjects a little more frequently, although he rarely delved into serious political satire at this stage of his career. He began by suggesting that in order to improve their chances in the upcoming election, the Republicans were planning to replace

their elephant mascot with something more creative, guaranteed to overshadow the Democratic donkey. (And who better to design an animal mascot than Dr. Seuss?)

In one issue, Roosevelt earnestly addressed the problem of racketeers, claiming "the root of the racketeers' continued existence in your government lies in your own complacency. . . . As soon as the people realize that 'a little graft' in a small community is the same as 'an odious scandal' in a large community we will begin to have

Liberty's more political bent afforded Ted a chance to flex his political-cartooning muscles, as seen in his inventive update of the Republican Party mascot (this page, top).

more honesty and efficiency everywhere."[16] In the same issue, Ted's discussion of racketeering was not quite as erudite. He addressed the problem of "Love Insurance," in which a smitten young man named Looie, in love with his girlfriend, Ruth, is required to pay a gangster to prevent him from releasing blackmailing woodpeckers that will carve "Looie loves Aggie" in trees all over Central Park. In another issue—in which Franklin Delano Roosevelt's article "Why Vote Democratic?" ran against Theodore Roosevelt's "Why Vote

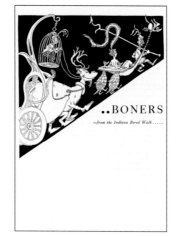

..BONERS
—*from the Indiana Bored Walk*.....

Republican?"—Ted addressed the equally portentous issue of whether a bird in the hand is really worth two in the bush.

But in his own fashion, Ted spoofed, rather than satirized, political issues of the day, like taxation (he recommended taxing bad habits, like declaring that your son is 51 months old), the Great Depression (he noted that you could boost your hatband-manufacturing business by adding catnip to the cotton, ensuring that the hatbands would need to be replaced once the kitties found them), and war and international affairs (he described heated arguments as to whether small Siamese hands or large Italian hands should be the standard for measuring the height of horses).

The multiple-images-per-page format of Ted's work for *Liberty* was balanced by the covers he did for *Telechronicle* and some wonderful new large pieces for magazines like *Ballyhoo* and *College Humor*. With increasing frequency, his work was tailored toward these longer and larger pieces. Looking at the multitude of his images in periodicals from the early years, one gets the impression that Ted drew thousands of three-inch-high cartoons. In reality, he worked in a larger format, and his pieces were reduced dramatically to fit multiple images on a single page—at perhaps a quarter of their original size—with color illustrations sometimes printed in black-and-white.[17] Even a full-page illustration was often printed at only 35 to 40 percent of its original size.[18] But as his reputation grew, so did the size at which his work was printed.

When his work for *Liberty* finished at the end of 1932, Ted returned to the now-monthly *Life* magazine in January 1933, after a hiatus of more than two years. For the first time, he was publishing concurrently in the competing magazines *Judge* and *Life*. His "Technocracy" cover for the March 1933 *Judge*

Bring 'em Buck Alive!

Ballyhoo presents the most colossal, stupendous, eye-staggering exhibit of wild animals never before captured in the history of the whole world!

GIN Buck is back from Siam! "Yes, Siam," says Gin. Ten months ago the great animal catcher sailed away with our order for one herd of long-eared Antrims, two herds of man-eating Wolgasts, one midget Zobbel, 3000 Mulcahey's Gazelles, half a dozen Vudds and a Three-toed Fepp.

Today, all these, including Mr. Buck, are on exhibition in the cellophane cages at the new Zilch Zoo at South Bookend, Minn.

Here we see Mr. Buck extracting a female Dingoe, the only living specimen, from its habitat.

A New Method of Trapping Burps

It took six months to build this Bup trap, and six months longer to catch a Bup, which later proved to be a Zop. Left—Mr. Burp, Mr. Buck's assistant, casting a spell over an adolescent Murgatroyd named Stoopnagle. Note—Mr. Burp is a notoriously poor speller; in fact he couldn't even spell "Bup."

As Ted's reputation grew, so did the size of his magazine "workspace," as evidenced by this *College Humor* spread (opposite page, bottom) and a full-page illustration from a spread in *Ballyhoo* (this page).

marked the eighth time that his work had appeared on the front of a periodical.

Life countered that month with a Dr. Seuss center spread about "The Great New Jersey Rehabilitation Plan." A year and a half earlier, the George Washington Bridge had been opened to traffic, connecting New York and New Jersey. Ted's plan was to "rehabilitate New Jersey completely—to redesign its buildings, to remould its institutions, to remodel its customs, and, finally, to undress and recostume its entire citizenry."[19] He wrote: "New Jersey . . . has color. New Jersey has quaintness. The only trouble is that so has New York State. Both states, unfortunately, are perfect examples of the *same* type of civilization. So alike are they that they offer a dearth of adventure to those who must travel between them. One might as well seek adventure in changing from one collar button to another. Contrast this to the diversity of the glamorous Balkans, where crossing each frontier treats the voyageur to a new operetta. . . ."[20]

Keeping competitors content: Ted's work was highly coveted by a growing list of publications. The solution in March 1933 was simultaneous pieces—*Judge*'s cover (this page) and a *Life* spread depicting the imaginative, Middle Eastern–tinged transformation of New Jersey (opposite page, top).

In Ted's new New Jersey, cars have been abolished so the "stench of burning oil no longer assaults the local nostrils," but the abolition of automobiles has not "thrown New Jersey back upon the horse. The horse, too, has been abolished." Instead, Ted proposes "hundreds of new and original fauna . . . no two alike. . . ."[21] He describes customizing these beasts by having them "Burbanked to order to suit the zoological preference of each and every driver"—a reference to Luther Burbank's plant hybridization experiments, which influenced Ted's animal creations beginning in college.

Ted's vision of the "rehabilitated" Plainfield, New Jersey, includes minarets atop the A&P supermarket. Sue Smith has been renamed Aeuilla Nilli Benaramb. Cohen's Market is now called the Bazaar of Illudovici. Even the panhandlers have been beautified, re-created as snake charmers with flutes and snakes provided by the state. Finally, politicians are all eliminated except for the Caliph, who is required to continually bathe himself in music to become "aesthetically purged, emotionally pristine. And, doing so, he renders laws unnecessary. His every thought a thought of harmony. . . . His subjects . . . become righteous just for his sake. For . . . who could covet his neighbor's wife, his ox or his ass, knowing that the Caliph is on a balcony bathing himself in music?"[22]

Ted's ninth cover illustration may be his most beguiling, with Seussian creatures who romp, gambol, and cavort around a water hole. It left enough of an impression on readers to be prominently parodied a few months later in *Razzberries*.

In addition to appearing on two *Judge* covers and a *Telechronicle* cover in 1933, Ted also illustrated the covers of two books and a party game that year. The deal to publish his ABC book had fallen through the year before, and it would be five

Ted's arresting ninth magazine cover (bottom left) was lampooned soon after in *Razzberries* (bottom right).

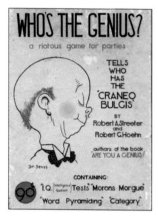

In addition to the periodical work of 1933, Ted illustrated the covers for two books (top and bottom) and the art for a party game (middle).

years before Ted got another opportunity to publish a book of his own. But he allied himself with the Frederick A. Stokes publishing company, for which he would eventually illustrate five books while waiting for his next solo effort to take flight.

Are You a Genius? Second Series was the sequel to a book of "Intelligence Tests, Brain Twisters and Other Indoor Pastimes." Ted provided six illustrations to accompany the intellectual puzzles posed by authors Robert A. Streeter and Robert G. Hoehn. Those pieces were used to illustrate 11 pages and the dust jacket, adding to his growing list of cover credits. One of the lesser-known pieces of Seussiana is a spin-off from this book—a set of cards with similar puzzles called "Who's the Genius? A Riotous Game for Parties," which had Ted's illustration of the Craneo Bulgis on its cover. Along with the Essolube puzzle and the *Judge* coaster set, "Who's the Genius?" stands as one of the earliest three-dimensional pieces of Seussiana available to collectors. Ted also provided two illustrations for the frontispiece and cover of *In One Ear . . .* , which Chico Marx called "the only book I ever borrowed that I'll be glad to return."[23] Of author Frank Sullivan, Zeppo Marx said, "The man has great talent or he could never have sold me this book."[24]

Although no one would publish Ted's animal alphabet book, he had an exhibition of its illustrations at Dartmouth during the Winter Carnival. As his twenty-ninth birthday approached, a rumor began circulating (probably started by Ted) that he was an armless artist who drew with his toes.

A new magazine called *University* started up, and for the premiere issue, at the same time that the display of his ABC illustrations was moving from Dartmouth to New York, Ted contributed a wonderful new series of drawings called "Some Mooses I Have Known." He continued to contribute to the short-lived magazine throughout the year, developing an ever-larger bestiary.

Venturing into larger and higher-profile projects, Ted's periodical work in 1934 included a three-installment series for *Life* called "The Facts of Life." Although tongue-in-cheek, it is one of the first pieces Ted wrote about educating a child. He observed that parents didn't fulfill their responsibilities in educating their children, but he wrote it from the point of view of a concerned uncle, not a parent—much as he would later educate other people's

children, though he had none of his own. He dispelled the myth of the stork and addressed birth control, mating calls, and the anatomical differences between men and women. Ted followed this series with a very colorful cover about childbirth, his tenth ever and his only one for *Life*. He even became self-referential with regard to this series—a cartoon in which two children are fascinated by "The Facts of Life" ran in *College Humor* in black-and-white and later as a colorful back cover for *Ballyhoo*.

Ted's work also appeared in new publications like *University,* where his bestiary continued to blossom (top left and right).

Sex ed by Ted: His one and only *Life* cover (bottom left) and a back cover for *Ballyhoo* (bottom right) dealt with the subject of sex.

While Ted continued to support himself with cartooning and advertising work, much of the decade would be spent pursuing new ideas. In an interview from this period, Ted claimed to be working on a musical show with "two fellows from Brooklyn; they have such terrific accents." He further explained that he was "designing the costumes. These are for pig costumes and I'm having a wicked time trying to get something that doesn't resemble a Disney pig; right now it seems impossible."[25] Disney had released *The Three Little Pigs* in May 1933, and it had won the Academy Award for short-subject cartoon in March 1934, just about the time that Ted made this statement. In theory, this may have been a show that he planned with artist friends like Abner Dean and Hugh Troy, with whom he'd worked on murals for a speakeasy's walls a few years earlier. The month before, Ted had apparently filled Hugh Troy's bathtub with Jell-O, sliced fruit, and half a dozen goldfish,[26] so they certainly were in high spirits together. However, no such musical has been uncovered, and any pig sketches from this time may have been studies for Ted's painting "Peru 4 (Angry Pig),"[27] inspired by his recent trip to Peru.

One of the many new projects that Ted was developing was something

Seuss in 3-D: Ted's vision literally leapt off the page as he explored new mediums like this sculpture (left). He even fashioned one of his trademark beasts at Dartmouth's 1931 Winter Carnival (right).

that would become known as the Seuss System of Unorthodox Taxidermy. The idea began with a visit to Dartmouth for the annual Winter Carnival. Among other things, ice sculptures were a big part of the Carnival. In February 1931, Ted participated by fabricating a cat with unusually long limbs and a tail that wrapped up onto the railing of the Phi Gamma Delta house, which he was visiting. In return, house members apparently gave Ted a pair of horns or antlers. It is believed that back in New York, perhaps invigorated and intrigued by the ice sculpture of the cat, Ted soon fashioned an animal using these horns, creating the "Blue-Green Abelard."

Ted became very interested in making the mounted heads of three-dimensional beasts, and they proliferated over the next several years. Ted had access to horns and beaks from the Forest Park Zoo back in Springfield, since his father had become the park superintendent in 1930. In the summer of 1933, Ted stopped thinking of his sculptures as individual pieces and began to think about them in terms of an Unorthodox Taxidermy, which spilled over into his work. Shaving brushes could be found not only atop Ted's Mugglesmirt and Tufted Gustard sculptures but also in his similarly themed advertisement for Brevo shaving cream, in which Ted suggested that old shaving brushes could be sold in Bavaria as hat accessories (see page 143).

By January 1934, he had completed five or six trophy heads,[28] and in the spring they were still lying around Ted and Helen's apartment, waiting to be hung on the walls "as soon as he had a chance."[29]

By 1937, his sister, Marnie, claimed that there were so many sculptures around Ted's Park Avenue home that they gave her a nightmare. "He uses them as models for his drawings . . . or else sells them as decorations for taprooms and bars. They are his main hobby. He makes them out of some pliable material which, after modeling, becomes set and hard. He picks up real horns and puts them onto heads where I am positive horns never grew before. Then he paints them all colors of the rainbow."[30]

Ted began work on yet another project in 1934. In 1929, he had been contacted by the English printing house Valentine & Sons about producing postcards or calendars from his artwork. The company was particularly interested in creating a series of "Scottish Sketches," an idea that Ted did not pursue. The Thomas D. Murphy Company was more successful, getting Ted to produce two series of 12 pictures each, which were used in promotional calendar blotters for several years. The first of Ted's series to be printed was "Seein' Things," which was apparently available in 1935, 1936, and 1941. The second series was "It's a Great World," which may have been printed only in 1937.

The pieces started as watercolor paintings on illustration board of about 12 inches by 8 inches, with Ted's captions handwritten underneath. The artwork was reduced in size almost 60 percent to 5 inches by 3½ inches, and some of the captions were changed slightly. "My Gawd! She's got on Walter!" was changed to the more socially acceptable "Good gracious! She's got on Walter!" "I wonder where my Mimi is tonight?" was changed to "I wonder where my Emma is to-night?" Two booklets of six images each, known as "progressives," were made to show the color separations.[31] Sample prints were produced on pebble-finish paper, and the salespeople used these prints to solicit orders from potential clients.

The final products were printed on blotter-type paper with each month's calendar, along with the name and contact information of the company that was purchasing the calendar. The result was some of the earliest full-color Dr. Seuss work made available to the public. Ted's work had been predominantly black-and-white, with some occasional single- or two-color printing in certain publications. These calendar pieces represented Ted's largest full-color project to this point in his career. With the exception of five covers for *Judge,* the Essolube puzzle, and a few Essolube ads in *American Weekly,* the only color Seuss pieces the public had seen were unobtainable ones in advertising campaigns, like the store displays for Flit and Ex-tane, the Flit and Essolube subway poster cards, and the Standard Oil "Greet the Boys" poster.

In 1935, there was yet another odd venture for Ted. It began when the *New York Herald Tribune Magazine,* a Sunday newspaper section that had grown in popularity for eight years, was converted into a larger, more colorful magazine called *This Week.* Early advertisements boasted future contributions from the likes of Sinclair Lewis, P. G. Wodehouse, and Emily Post. In March, Ted contributed to the second and third issues of *This Week.*[32]

But the *Herald Tribune* was not the only newspaper expanding its

Showcasing a printer's capabilities: **What is the best way to show off your printing potential? Enlist one Theodor Geisel to illustrate calendar samples (this page and opposite page) and share his extraordinary talent with prospective clients.**

"RIDE 'EM, COWBOY!"

"GOOD GRACIOUS! SHE'S GOT ON WALTER!"

"I DON'T MIND YOUR EATING PEANUTS, BUT THROW THE SHUCKS OUTSIDE"

THE FIRST FLOWER OF SPRING

"I WONDER WHERE MY EMMA IS TO-NIGHT?"

"PUT THE BLACK TEN ON THE RED JACK"

"SCRAM!"

"RIGHT NICE AUGUST WE'RE HAVING, NEIGHBOR"

FINANCIAL NOTE—
GOAT'S MILK IS HIGHER THAN EVER

"DARLING—WITH CONDITIONS AS THEY ARE, WE'VE
SIMPLY GOT TO LET THE CANARY GO!"

"SNUBBED!"

AFTER ALL REINDEER ARE SO DARNED COMMON

"BRING ON YOUR DRAGONS!"

"AW—CAN'T YOU WAIT UNTIL WE FINISH THIS RUBBER!"

"MA, I'M GETTING VERTIGO"

"IT'S OUR FIRST . . . DON'T YOU THINK IT LOOKS LIKE
GEORGE?"

"GOL DARN YA . . . QUIT STARIN AT ME!"

"WELL IF IT ISN'T WILLIAM OSBORN ESTERHAZY!
WHY, I KNEW YOU WHEN YOU WERE *THAT* HIGH!"

"F' GOSH SAKE, JULIUS . . . *UNTWINE, UNTWINE!*"

"IT AIN'T ONLY A FLAGRANT CONTEMPT OF THE LAW
. . . IT'S POSITIVELY SHOCKING!"

"THEN *YOU* BUST INTO THE CONVERSATION AND SAY,
'MY DEAR MRS. DOBBSWORTH . . . PHOOIE!"

"TALLY-HO!"

"ONE HUNDRED AND FIFTY WIVES . . . AND NOT A
CONTRACT PLAYER IN THE LOT!"

"WHAT WOULD YOU THINK OF THIS DEAR LITTLE ONE
RIGHT HERE?"

The adventures of Hejji: Ted's brief venture into the world of comic strips came courtesy of Hejji, a boy who lives in an odd world of strange creatures—not surprisingly, set in a landscape marked by typically Seussian architecture (this page and next).

entertainment sections. From the days when Ted read the Sunday comics as a kid through 1934, the color comic sections had grown from four pages to eight pages and then to 16 pages. In 1935, William Randolph Hearst's papers started a 32-page section in which most comics were given full-page treatment. This format only lasted for a couple of years, but the timing was perfect for Ted. In April, he abandoned *This Week* to begin a comic strip that ran in the *Sunday American,* the *Chicago Herald & Examiner,* and some other Hearst papers.

Twelve strips of "Hejji" were published before Ted was fired. We follow young Hejji, who arrives in the strange hidden land of Baako, where turtles gallop, goats are joined at the beard, and whales are found in the water-filled craters of volcanoes. Hejji picks an unusual flower that plays music, and he is

promptly seized by the Pale Green Guards and brought before The Mighty One. Preoccupied with learning how to blow smoke rings to please The Fair One, the girl he loves, The Mighty One orders that Hejji be thrown into the den of the Seven Deadly Wombats. Like Alice in Wonderland, Hejji jumps into a hole, hoping that it will lead somewhere. After his escape, Hejji returns to talk things over with The Mighty One. Contrite, he agrees to show Hejji around Baako, where he has 27,000 blue elephants, ponies with diamond-studded teeth, and an orchestra that plays to his poultry to make them tender.

Hejji suggests that The Mighty One bring his love a fabulous present, and the two of them set off to find the only Pitzu Bird in the world and bring back its plume tail. But an errant shot scares the Pitzu Bird off, and she leaves behind her egg, which The Mighty One is forced to sit on and hatch. (He does so five years before Horton would be

similarly engaged.) Hejji rides the rambunctious hatchling until it is overcome by volcano fumes, and then he helps The Mighty One bring the new Pitzu Bird back to The Fair One. But the bird calls for help, and birds with a toolshed's variety of beaks help it to escape, taking Hejji and The Mighty One captive, only to drop them a thousand feet to the ocean below. They are saved but buffeted by spouting whales, who subsequently blow them up a gumba tree. To get The Mighty One down, Hejji stacks turtles like stairs for him to descend (prefiguring the self-important ruler atop a stack of turtles in *Yertle the Turtle* by more than two decades).

The convoluted archways that we have come to associate with Dr. Seuss apparently made their first appearance in the Sapphire Tower of The Fair One. Lacking a Pitzu Bird, Hejji and The Mighty One set off in search of the honey found in a flower that blooms once every 700 years. Along the way, they pass a polka-dotted crocodile and cacti shaped like question marks, get chased by an enormous bearded bee, and use a crocodile like a teeter-totter. Eventually, they find themselves at the liver-colored castle of The Evil One and his henchman, Stroogo (the name that another henchman would bear 18 years later in *The 5000 Fingers of Dr. T*). Stroogo can walk up and down walls. Both he and the swift-growing mushrooms he sows look unusually phallic, particularly as the mushrooms seem to spit Hejji and The Mighty One through a nightmarish vaginal opening into a dark corridor. Whether by coincidence or design, this was the last installment of "Hejji" and Ted's last foray into comic-strip cartooning. He would return to contributing illustrations to *This Week* the following year.

The story that Ted related about the end of the "Hejji" strip was, "A telegram came from William Randolph Hearst saying fire the last three people you hired. I was one of them, so it was the end of that career."[33] Whether that story was true or apocryphal, Ted's relationship with the Hearst newspapers over the years was certainly an odd one. Despite being fired, he would return in 1939 to publish political cartoons in Hearst papers. In fact, the first time that Ted and Hearst crossed paths was more than a decade before "Hejji." During college, Ted drew an unflattering picture of a mudslinging Hearst in evaluating the 1924 presidential campaign.

Yet another of Ted's new projects during this period was a satire of the advertising business called "The Advertising Business at a Glance." In typical Seuss

Advertising inanities: Once again, Ted turned to the advertising world. These posters (opposite page) saluted and satirized staples of the advertising industry, including the slave-like copywriter, the pitfall-dodging account executive, and the "man with an idea."

fashion, these satiric pieces portray the world of advertising as one in which the "higher-ups" in their suits have no original ideas for advertisements and no understanding of what works. The underlings who produce the ideas and manufacture the campaigns are no better than slave labor. Toward that end, "The Copy Writer" is a man suspended from a hook at his typewriter, forced to slave away at his crassly commercial art until the fore-man rings the three o'clock bell to end the day. In his humiliation, he looks up at a bust of Shakespeare, on whose head sits a can of beans, reminding him of the relative unim-portance of the art of writing in his job. Only one notch up the totem pole, "The Account Executive" is depicted as a man leaping obstacle-laden hurdles while carrying a pre-carious tray of dishes and glassware as vul-tures look on, waiting for him to fall. Stroogo, from the final installment of "Hejji," lurks ahead, waiting to trip him. "The Man with an Idea" depicts a roomful of uninspired men, one of whom is resourceful enough to ask his secretary to make a suggestion. Finally, "Now Let's Really Analyze That Humorous Advertising!" surrealistically shows the futil-ity of such an endeavor, with a man making his calculations with an enormous compass at a table filled with such ineffectual analysts as a pair of dismembered legs and a man with his head literally in his hand.

By the time he began working on his first children's book, Ted was publishing his illus-trations and cartoons in periodicals as varied

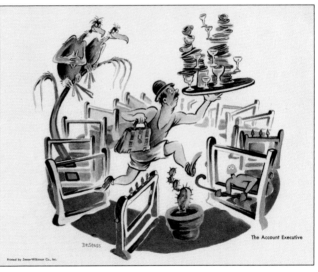

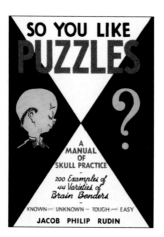

as an early sports magazine called *Sports Illustrated and the American Golfer* and a slick new fashion magazine called the *New York Woman*. In 1936 and 1937, there was a flurry of activity and experimentation, marking a truly remarkable time for him—illustrating books for one publisher and calendars for another; developing a love of sculpting; pioneering the series of posters about advertising; creating a menagerie to stock the Essomarine exhibit booth; starting a club (the Seuss Navy) that would last for several years and have a few thousand members; advertising furnaces, beer, newspapers, cans, boat motor oil, radios, and pens; and starting to write his first children's book.

While working on *And to Think That I Saw It on Mulberry Street,* Ted was still illustrating books for the Frederick A. Stokes publishing company. A new and slightly different version of the Craneo Bulgis appeared on the jacket and cover of *So You Like Puzzles?* in 1936, while the old version returned on the title page. The following year (the one in which *And to Think That I Saw It on Mulberry Street* would be published), Ted provided eight illustrations for the jacket,

cover, and 13 pages of *Spelling Bees: The Oldest and the Newest Rage.* He also provided seven illustrations for *Mystery Puzzles,* including some subject matter that fans of children's books would find *very* atypical for Dr. Seuss. The following year, he provided the dust jacket and frontispiece for one final Stokes book, *How's Tricks?*

Among the many forgotten treasures from Ted's early career are the pieces he did for the *New York Woman,* which was first published in September 1936. The next month, Ted began contributing color work to this large-format magazine. He satirized "society people"—those who were having trouble either moving up the social ladder or staying atop once there, and those who were having marital or engagement difficulties. What

176

could one do to find a butler who would impress dinner guests sufficiently, or keep one's name in the headlines if one was homebound, or ensure a successful coming-out for one's daughter at a debutante ball? How does one keep the press interested in one's engagements after nine marriages? "See Dr. Seuss for Social Publicity!" first, of course!

Ted provided testimonials from satisfied customers. Mrs. J. Brindle Packinghouse wrote to thank the Seuss Service for solving her problem with butlers who did not bring her the social recognition she craved. Although her Filipino, British, Russian, and Indian butlers had failed to make the desired impression, the centaur that Dr. Seuss sent solved the problem admirably. Arthritis had kept socialite Mrs. F. Slipweed Deitz absent from photos in the social papers. She had fallen out of the public eye until Dr. Seuss sent her escort around town with a mannequin sporting the famous Deitz diamonds to fill in for her. (Not content to let his ironic tone convey his message, Ted labeled the mannequin "Ditz" rather than "Deitz.") Nini Gherkin's coming-out party made her "the vortex of a social maelstrom"[34] once Dr. Seuss placed her in an arcade booth where young gentlemen could throw baseballs at her head. An oft-married socialite regained the press's attention by unveiling her husband in Central Park like a statue. A woman betrothed to a boring man had him brought into the engagement dinner on a platter, aflame in brandy. And a woman whose partner broke their engagement missed the wedding ceremony more than she missed the man; she was given a special ceremony to satisfy her.

Ted continued to illustrate a variety of books throughout the mid-1930s (opposite page, top, middle, and bottom left). Some dealt with decidedly mature subjects (opposite page, top and bottom right).

As his career in children's books took flight, Ted's magazine work continued to feature adult subjects—a centaur who assists a social climber (this page, left), a symbolic flipping of the bird (this page, right), and a piece regarding Santa's stopover at a sorority house (next page).

"Santa Claus Forgets Himself."

This last piece reveals a lesser known but recurrent theme in Ted's work: His final piece for an employer often contained off-color humor. The special ceremony was one in which the man who broke the engagement gave his ex-girlfriend a bird instead of a ring. The new women's magazine and its readers apparently did not miss the elaborate setup for a joke about a man "giving the bird" to his ex, a blatant euphemism for the raising of the middle finger. No more of Ted's work appeared in the *New York Woman* thereafter. His last cartoon for *University* involved sexual innuendo about Santa Claus. His last installment of "Hejji" introduced phallic images in both the character of Stroogo and his sprouting mushrooms.

Along with these thematic choices, which seem incongruous with his reputation as a children's book author, Ted experimented with his own brand of surrealism. The surrealist movement, which began in 1924 and came to Connecticut and New York in 1931, gained even greater exposure in 1937 when the Museum of Modern Art in New York hosted an exhibit called Fantastic Art, Dada, Surrealism.[35] A few months later, Ted published the most surreal of his prose-and-picture pieces, "The Phantom of El Morocco." "El Morocco" was the street name for the Fiesta Danceteria, a famous nightclub that was part of the fashionable scene on New York City's East Side.[36, 37, 38] Ted had mentioned the club half a year earlier in a cartoon for the *New York Woman*.

The "phantom" refers to a vision that the narrator sees while partying with author Frank Sullivan (whose *In One Ear . . .* sported one of Ted's dust-jacket illustrations) and an "old college chum," referred to as the Gusseteer (slang for a lecher),[39] at the El Morocco in the early-morning hours:

It was exactly two-twenty-nine. . . . The snout of every
seltzer bottle in the place was blowing green smoke rings.
They formed platoons directly above us. Then a big smoke

ring emerged from the trombone and barked a brisk order.
The platoons changed to building blocks, buckets,
locomotives, and men, pile upon pile right over our heads.
Terror curdled the roots of our hair.

"Do something!" I gasped. Sullivan offered it a potato
chip and the phantom vanished. We fled, hysterical, into
the dawn. . . .

I vowed, shuddering, never to go back, yet for the
next two weeks, every night about midnight, my feet
would march . . . back to Morocco. And at exactly two-
twenty-nine I would see it again.[40]

A taste of the surreal: This 1937 piece shows Ted's attempt at experimenting with a style of art made popular by the surrealist movement.

The narrator believes that it is the spirit of a dead Brahmin attempting to contact John Perona, the owner of the El Morocco nightclub. Shaken by the vision, he finds comfort in yoga breathing exercises and standing on his head. The illustration juxtaposes a number of disparate elements, from a waiter balancing stacks of dishes atop an elephant's ear to volcanoes blowing smoke rings. Such images, freighted with incongruity, were relegated almost exclusively to Ted's private collection of paintings, as can be seen in *The Secret Art of Dr. Seuss*. "The Phantom of El Morocco" appears to be the only one that Ted published.

In the months before the publication of his first children's book, Ted published several cartoons in *Collier's*. He produced advertisements for Schaefer Bock Beer, the American Can Company, and the Dartmouth Alumni

Fund, and created the display for the Esso-marine booth at the National Motor Boat Show. He did ads for Macy-Westchester Newspapers right up until his book came out. Afterward, without taking a break, he started a campaign for Chilton pens. His Unorthodox Taxidermy and illustrations for other authors' books also kept him very busy.

With creature sculptures, calendar sketches, and comic strips, Ted's creativity had been bursting forth in new directions. Although odd characters and visions had always inhabited his worlds, earlier in his career they were always depicted as figments of an alcohol-enhanced imagination. As Ted finally neared publication of his first children's book, the lines between his worlds grew less distinct and the work became more surreal. The path toward children's books was not always an easy one to pick out. Yet when tamed only slightly, the meeting of the fantastic and the mundane produced an imaginative world that would prove to be beguiling to young and old alike.

When worlds collide: **More and more, Ted's work centered on what happened when wild met mild. This fanciful coupling of a sea serpent and a pool toy from *Collier's* could easily fit into the fantastic worlds he would create in children's books.**

CHAPTER 15

The Annual Brat-Books

In 1936, 32-year-old Ted and his wife, Helen, boarded the Swedish American Line's MS *Kungsholm* and sailed to Europe for a vacation. Christened in March 1928, the 1,575-passenger *Kungsholm* was a luxurious ship using contemporary Swedish art and architecture in an art deco design to cater to the American market, complete with a saffron-red grand piano in the Great Lounge, a movie theater, and a Romanesque-tiled "Pompeiian swimming pool." As the promotional literature boasted, "The great social salons of the *Kungsholm* are dedicated to the pursuit of . . . carefree days and festive nights. . . . Friendly groups . . . dance to the lively tempo of a modern dance orchestra, or merely enjoy an adventure in cracked ice and tall glasses. . . ."[1]

The Seuss Navy had surrounded Ted with yachting and cruising enthusiasts, but despite the luxury and renown of the *Kungsholm,* the aspect of the ship that made the most memorable impression on Ted was the rhythm of the ship's engines. Recounting one of his adventures with "ice and tall glasses" at the American Bar, he said, "I was on a Swedish ship on the worst crossing ever, and I sat in the bar and listened to the engine's grind."[2] The *Kungsholm* prided itself on being "motordriven, therefore smokeless, dustless, and sootless,"[3] but the dum de *DUM,* dum de *DUM* of the engines bored its way into Ted's mind. Consumed by it to the point of distraction, he noticed that it had the same rhythm as the poem "The Night Before Christmas." That rhythm, or meter, is known as anapestic tetrameter. A simple anapest is a three-syllable word or phrase with the

The Geisels' 1936 trip to Europe aboard the *Kungsholm* left an impression on Ted. He later remarked that the rhythmic engine noise reminded him of a poem's scansion.

Length 608 feet · Beam 78 feet · 20,222 gross register tons · 26,700 displacement tons

THE GLEAMING WHITE DE LUXE VIKING MOTORLINER
KUNGSHOLM

emphasis placed on the last syllable, like the word "any*more*." Anapestic tetrameter has four sections of three syllables in which the last syllable is stressed in each section:

(1) 'Twas the *night* (2) before *Christ* (3) mas, when *all* (4) through the *house*

In "Punch, Brothers, Punch," Mark Twain described the "jingling rhymes" of a train conductor's ditty about punching the passengers' tickets,[4] writing that "they took instant and entire possession of me. All through breakfast they went waltzing through my brain. . . . My head kept humming . . . without peace or respite. The day's work was ruined. . . . I gave up and drifted down-town, and presently discovered that my feet were keeping time to that relentless jingle. . . ."[5] The only way he got it out of his head was to pass it on by repeating it to someone else. And that person found that the *clack-clack-clack* of the train's wheels kept time to the same jingle. For Ted, the drone of the *Kungsholm*'s engines was equally maddening, and words became similarly entwined with the beat of his transportation.

Unable to get the rhythm out of his head upon returning home, Ted tried to pass it on by beginning to write a book called *A Story That No One Can Beat*. According to Ted, "The Flit contract was 'fat,' but it precluded my doing anything else and I was going crazy. I could finish up a year's work in six months. I finally found that one thing it didn't specify I couldn't do was children's books, so I started doing that just to do something."[6]

Once again, it's an explanation that has been accepted without question for many years. It turns out that Ted's last Flit cartoon in the 1930s appeared in August 1936, just when he was working on this children's book, so the contract for Flit was not likely to have been relevant anymore.

Ted was not the most likely candidate to write a children's book. He had ten years of experience in cartooning, illustrating, and advertising. He had no children of his own, and his humor was often inappropriate for kids—and not just the references to alcohol or the surrealistic turn of his later work. On November 18, 1928, *Steamboat Willie* had premiered at the Colony Theatre in New York City; it was the first fully synchronized sound cartoon, and it provided great family entertainment. The following week, in contrast, Ted's cartoon for *Judge* was "Making Our Daughters Less Irritating," which included a

Ted's acerbic humor and adult subject matter usually resulted in work that was far from kid-friendly, as evidenced by these *Judge* cartoons concerning the disciplining of children (opposite page).

device called "The Pout Extinguisher." It did not reveal the same burning mission to entertain youngsters that Walt Disney had exhibited.

Nor did Ted's *Judge* article "Punish Your Offspring Scientifically!" In it, he illustrated the error of grabbing your son by the *nape* of the neck rather than scientifically by the *scruff* of the neck. He also depicted an argument between Mr.

and Mrs. L. Pffeff as to whether to *box* their son's ears or *cuff* them. Ted's response was that both methods were frowned upon, and he suggested that the proper method was *buffing* the ears with "the aid of a pair of old buttonhole-shears." Ted also advocated that each curse word be washed out of a child's mouth with a different kind of soap.

Once he finished *A Story That No One Can Beat,* Ted had a difficult time finding a publisher willing to take a chance with the unusual book. While he prepared for the first big Seuss Navy Manoeuvres and designed another elaborate Essomarine display for the 1937 National Motor Boat Show, he shopped his book around. Another of the interesting anecdotes about this book, which would become *And to Think That I Saw It on Mulberry Street,* is the oft-told tale about how many publishers rejected it. The figure differs depending on the source, but several specific numbers have been cited:

20 ("a score"), 25, 26, 27, 28, 29, and even 43.[7] Ted was told that neither fantasy nor verse sold well and that his story lacked a moral or lesson.[8]

Sometime in early 1937, Ted ran into a fellow who had been in the class behind him at Dartmouth. Marshall "Mike" McClintock had recently become the children's book editor of Vanguard Press. According to one source:

> On the . . . day he learned of his twenty-seventh rejection, Ted fought back frustration and anger and decided to return to his apartment, stage a ceremonial burning of the now tattered manuscript, and get back to cartooning for adults. As he walked grimly along Madison Avenue, he was hailed by Mike McClintock. . . .
>
> "What's that under your arm?" McClintock asked.
>
> "That's a book that no one will publish. I'm lugging it home to burn."
>
> McClintock smiled. Three hours earlier he had become juvenile editor of Vanguard Press. "We're standing outside my new office," he said. "Come on up and let's look at it."
>
> Half an hour later McClintock took Ted in to meet James Henle, president of Vanguard Press, and Evelyn Shrifte, an editor who later succeeded [Henle]. Henle agreed to publish the book. "But," he said, "you've got to give me a snappier title."
>
> . . . Ted said later, "If I had been going down the other side of Madison Avenue, I'd be in the dry-cleaning business today."[9]

Although some of the many coincidental details may be exaggerated, the basic story is true. The book is dedicated to "Helene McC."—Mike McClintock's wife—and the now-famous protagonist is named after their son Marco.

In September 1937, under the revised title *And to Think That I Saw It on Mulberry Street,* Ted's first children's book was published, and "Oh, the *humanity* of it!"[10] This was a book that the unsaintly could appreciate. In comparison with some of the rule-enforcing books that Ted read as a child, which taught young readers how to behave and improve their manners, this was a book that reveled in allowing a child's imagination to run wild and to remain at odds with grown-ups who would never be able to appreciate a child's sense of wonder and creativity.

Vanguard printed 15,000 of the first edition and 6,000 of the second edition a couple of years later. Even the negative reviews, like the one in the September *Booklist*—which claimed that there was only enough of a good idea for a comic strip—agreed that the idea was a great one, and they all recognized that Ted had captured the spirit of a young boy's imagination.[11]

The book draws on several aspects of Ted's childhood memories and his earlier work in periodicals. From Marco's first sight of a man riding beneath the small awning on his horse-drawn carriage, it is clear that Ted is harking back to the Springfield of his youth.

That image had stayed with Ted from his childhood and found its way into his work through the years. Early in his career, Ted drew the cart with the beer barrels that he remembered from the days of his family's brewery. Shortly thereafter, he added the awning and reduced the beer barrels to a stylized and convenient keg. During his tenure with the Warren Telechron clock company a few years later, clocks replaced the beer. For the children's book, Ted used flowerpots instead of beer barrels.

Among the many animals that fill the pages of *Mulberry Street,* the blue elephant ridden

Ted would repeatedly call upon the canopied carriages of his youth (top right) to transport various items, including beer in his earlier work for *Judge* (top left) and *Life* (bottom right) and clocks in his Warren Telechron ads (middle left). Ted remembered these carts when illustrating *Mulberry Street* (bottom left).

185

by the Rajah can be traced back most readily to the blue elephants of Baako in the first installment of "Hejji."

To prevent a traffic jam, Ted places policemen at the intersection of two streets—Mulberry and Bliss—that do not really cross in Springfield. The officers ride motorcycles that reflect the ones Ted knew on the streets of his childhood. Springfield was the home of the famous Indian Motorcycles, manufactured by the company George W. Hendee and Carl Hedstrom started in 1901. When Ted was ten years old, the 1914 Indian V-twin—one of the earliest models with an electric starter—had the same red body, white wheels, handlebar configuration, and headlight as the ones the police ride in *Mulberry Street.*

Ted continued juggling his diverse career opportunities. In time for his thirty-fourth birthday, he published in *Judge* a six-page "cartoonovelette" called "Quality." It contained ten illustrations and lots of new entries in the avian section of the Seuss menagerie. At first, the premise seems to be representative of the Dr. Seuss that the world now knows, with quality put before profit. However, like the end of "Matilda, the Elephant with a Mother Complex" (which appeared the following month), the outcome is the opposite of what one might expect. After no expense or effort is spared

Evoking modes of transportation: It's clear to see how Ted's "Hejji" work (top left) influenced his rendering of the Rajah's blue elephant (bottom left) in *Mulberry Street.* Additionally, the Indian Motorcycles produced in Springfield (top right) inspired Ted when drawing the *Mulberry* motorcycle cops (bottom right).

to track down feathers from rare birds like the Gibney Grackle, yellow-green penguin, and Andulusian Feeney Fowl in the quest to make a product of the highest possible quality, it turns out that the item is "one of those blower things that people play with at parties."[12] Although it is a fine one and the patron who buys it has a good time, the expenditure of resources is so clearly exorbitant that the reader is forced to conclude that such a quest for quality is absurd. In fact, Ted probably contributed more to the good of

humankind in an advertising campaign a decade later, when he finally gave those blowers a name, deciding that they were called "flubbel-squees."[13] At the time Ted published "Quality," the idealism with which we associate Dr. Seuss was still overshadowed by his cynicism.

Ted had an exhibition of the Seuss System of Unorthodox Taxidermy in a Fifth Avenue store in New York in the fall of 1937, and in order to promote *And to Think That I Saw It on Mulberry Street,* some of the sculptures were displayed in bookshops around the city. Adding to the menagerie that he'd been displaying at home and at the National Motor Boat Shows, Ted created more recognizable animals like red turtles, green camels, and purple elephants. The exhibits proved to be quite popular, with numerous people asking if they could buy the sculptures.

Although there is a commonly held belief that Ted shunned the merchandising of products based on his work, that opinion is probably drawn from the anticommercialization message in *How the Grinch Stole Christmas!* The fact is that, having hawked others' wares for years, Ted was very much interested in making money from some of his own merchandise, as was his publisher, Vanguard. This was, after all, still the Great Depression. Ted learned of the interest in his sculptures, and within months he and Vanguard teamed up to begin a mail-order business to sell them. Furthermore, according to the *Mulberry Street* dust jacket, he began "designing and planning to manufacture children's toys as unusual as his drawings."[14] So while Walt was continuing to charm children with the premiere of *Snow White and the Seven*

At the same time *Mulberry Street* was being lauded, Ted continued cartooning for *Judge* with a six-page "cartoonovelette" about the pursuit of quality items. In it, he introduced new birds to his aviary (top and middle). The feathers from these unfortunate fowls were eventually used to produce a silly party favor (bottom).

Dwarfs on December 21, 1937, Ted was planning his marketing strategy for Blue-Green Abelards, Tufted Gustards, and Mulberry Street Unicorns.

From the Seuss System of Unorthodox Taxidermy, the Dr. Seuss Zoo (Seussological Zoologica) was made available to the public in April 1938. Returning to the fictitious home of the first creatures in Ted's menagerie in

college, the inside back cover of that month's *Judge* announced, "DR. SEUSS RETURNS FROM THE BOBO ISLES . . . with Rare and Amazing Trophies for the Walls of your Game-Room, Nursery or Bar!" At $15, the Blue-Green Abelard was the most expensive of the trophy heads. Unlike animals that molt but once a year, "the Blue-Green Abelard changes every night for dinner. Blue-green for the hustle bustle of the day, it adopts Green-blue for the formalities of the evening."[15] A Tufted Gustard could be had for about a third of the price of an Abelard. Embarrassed by the slow development of its tuft, a Gustard will spend the first 40 years of life blushing in a whortleberry thicket until its tuft blooms. And Ted, fresh off the success of his first children's book, also offered a Mulberry Street Unicorn to the budget-minded. He wasn't sure what it did, but surmised that it was unlikely to be thinking about xylophones or zippers.

Marketing the mounted beasts: In 1938, Ted teamed up with his *Mulberry Street* publisher and offered by mail an array of wall-mounted "animals" from the Dr. Seuss Zoo.

The Unorthodox Taxidermy collection would come to encompass many beasts, often assigned different names over the years. The changes of name were akin to the shifts in Ted's story about how *Horton Hatches the Egg* originated: Over time, his incessant need to create sometimes led him to improve upon his previous inventions. For example, Ted referred to one of his beasts in the late 1930s and early 1940s as the Twin-Screw Ant Twirp. He later called it a Stuffed Ormie when it hung over the window in his La Jolla workroom in the 1970s, but its original name was the Two-Horned Drouberhannus. This name provides yet another example of Ted's peculiar memory. He first used it in a 1929 cartoon that exposed the scarcity of mistletoe on the Island of Kwafa, necessitating a law that "made it permissible to kiss a lady beneath a 1927 Wilkes-Barre, Pennsylvania, Telephone Directory, provided it is opened to the name Grimalken, Drouberhannus, Nalbner or Fepp."[16] Not only did he like the sounds of these names, but once he used them, they remained in his tenacious memory. In 1932, Norval Drouberhannus invented the Bunnyoptician, which allowed him to overcome his inability to make shadow rabbits on the wall for his son. N. Fepp showed up in an accompanying cartoon.[17] In a 1934 piece, New York City Police Commissioner J. J. Drouberhannus padlocked the Fepps in an underwater bedroom. Four days later, Mayor J. J. Grimalken unlocked the chamber.[18] In 1959, 30 years after the first appearance of "Drouberhannus," Ted received a letter from a woman whose three-year-old had stained their rug with Merthiolate and avoided punishment by suggesting that it could be cleaned with "Voom" from *The Cat in the Hat Comes Back*. Ted responded that "the transportation of 'Voom' . . . whether in liquid, solid or gaseous form, across state borders is to be discontinued immediately as a result of a Supreme Court decision (Justice Douglas dissenting) in . . . the case of Grimalken vs. Drouberhannus. . . ."[19]

Ted's later names for the Two-Horned Drouberhannus had their own stories. He called the sculpture the "Twin-Screw Ant Twirp" when he was working for Essomarine, and the boating magazines were always full of articles about boats with "twin-screw" propulsion (in which a propeller rotates in one direction on the starboard side while another rotates in the opposite direction on the port side). The similarity between "Antwerp" and "Ant Twirp" is notable, but its significance has not been determined. The Stuffed Ormie came about after Ted created a character called a Carefree Ormie in 1949,[20] and that's how he described his sculpture during a visit from an *Architectural Digest* writer in 1978.

Ted's time on the Essomarine campaigns provided more sculptures for the Seuss System of Unorthodox Taxidermy. For the 1937 National Motor Boat Show, there were the six Marine Muggs. Of the Sea Going Dilemma Fish, Ted wrote, "For piscatorial peskiness, this ornery so-and-so takes the barnacle-lined bathing suit. He's so mean he makes a tiger shark look like a minnow."[21] The Dilemma Fish sniffs out boats having engine trouble and snags them, lifting them out of the water on his antlers—leaving the boatman on the horns of a Dilemma. The Carbonic Walrus and the Gimlet Fish caused engine knocking and drank motor oil, respectively—like their car counterparts, the Karbonockus and the Oilio-gobelus. The Powerless Puffer, Flaming Herring, and Sludge Tarpon rounded out the posse of Marine Muggs.

Also in Ted's Unorthodox Taxidermy collection was the Kangaroo Bird, "so called because it carries its young in a pouch before eating them on buttered toast."[22] The Tufted Toucan became the Andalusian Grackle and then the Andulovian Grackler. The Cruel Hack-Biter "kills only when hungry: Which is very foolish because . . . it has no stomach."[23] This sawfish, likely done for the 1937 National Motor Boat Show, would become familiar to readers when Ted included it ten years later in *McElligot's Pool*. The menagerie's Goo-goo-eyed Tasmanian Wolghast[24] was temporarily renamed the Sea-Going Hornswaggle, likely for the same 1937 National Motor Boat Show; the Hornswaggle's capture was said to have led to Ted's promotion to admiral of the Seuss Navy. There was also the Flower-Pot Walrus (which loved little daisies), the Mugglesmirt—Before Moulting (which sported a shaving-brush hairdo like that of the Tufted Gustard), the Semi-Normal Green-Lidded Fawn, and an unknown number of others.[25]

With confidence in their future popularity, Vanguard promoted the Abelard, Gustard, and unicorn sculptures as "the first three," adding, "In all seriousness, we state that we confidently expect the craze for Dr. Seuss animal heads to sweep the

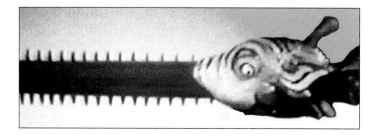

country. They are too irresistible to be less than best-sellers when they appear."[26] A picture that ran in *Look* magazine demonstrated that at least a dozen Mulberry Street Unicorns were produced for the mail-order business, but the actual number of these three beasts that were made and sold is unknown. However, the business was not nearly as successful as envisioned, and these sculptures are now highly coveted by collectors.

This was clearly Ted's most prolific sculpting phase. One curious item that has surfaced from 1938, when Ted was running his mail-order sculpture business, is a ceramic piece that appears to have been intended as a candleholder. The slumbering rabbit certainly could have appealed to consumers, although no advertisements for any such pieces have been found. It is believed that this item was intended for mail-order sales but that the idea was discarded due to concerns about breakage during shipping.

For January 1939, Ted was also preparing his Nuzzlepuss ashtray for the National Motor Boat Show and his Hankey Bird for the Hankey Bannister Scotch campaign. He even created prototypes for marionettes! Back when Ted was in college, one of the most famous puppeteer groups, Tony Sarg's Marionettes, came to Dartmouth and performed in his junior and senior years. At the same time, marionette great Sue Hastings was beginning her rise in the profession, which would lead to a company with more than 2,000 marionettes and a dozen touring groups. Hastings's repertoire included skits like "The Elephant's Child" (based on the Kipling story), "Aladdin and the Wonderful Lamp," "Abdullah and His Donkey," "Spot the Clown and His Trained Dog," and many others.

In 1936, the first National Puppetry Conference took place in Detroit, and Edith Flack Ackley published her well-known book *How to Make Marionettes: For Fun at Home, Plays at School, and Clubs and Professional Performances.* The following June, three months before *Mulberry Street* was published, the Puppeteers of America was founded and began holding its annual conventions and exhibitions. Sue Hastings likely contacted Ted after *The 500 Hats of Bartholomew Cubbins* was published in July 1938. She planned to have him make sample marionettes that her workshop would then produce. There was some effort to get them ready for a big toy fair,[27] which they failed to do. (Since 1939, the New York Toy Fair has been held in February, and this is probably the one for which they were aiming.[28]) After that, Ted got busy with

Capturing the master craftsman at work: Ted sculpting a unicorn (opposite page, top left). His handiwork yielded an amazing display, including the Goo-goo-eyed Tasmanian Wolghast (opposite page, second from top, left), the Mugglesmirt (opposite page, third from top, left), a winsome Mulberry Street Unicorn (opposite page, top right), the Kangaroo Bird (opposite page, bottom right), and the Cruel Hack-Biter (opposite page, bottom left).

Perhaps too delicate for the rough-and-tumble mail-order business Ted was pursuing, this 1938 ceramic piece (this page) apparently was not offered to the public like the Dr. Seuss Zoo figures.

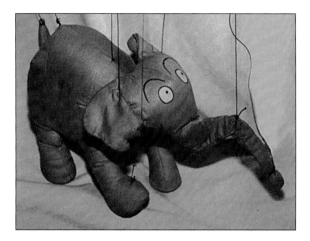

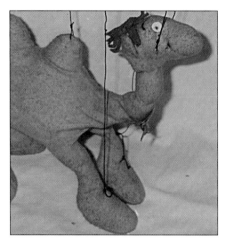

another project, called the Infantograph, but once the war in Europe escalated, both projects were abandoned.

Ted produced five marionette prototypes (and began work on a sixth that was never finished): an elephant, camel, donkey, clown, and tiger. Although *Mulberry Street* does depict elephants, it is significant that Sue Hastings's productions featured characters corresponding to most of these prototypes—Kipling's elephant, Aladdin's camel, Abdullah's donkey, and Spot the Clown.

Fortunately, sculpting did not take over Ted's life after *Mulberry Street.* A month after Superman made his debut in the premiere issue of DC Comics' *Action Comics* on June 1, 1938, the everyman from the Kingdom of Didd made his debut in *The 500 Hats of Bartholomew Cubbins,* published by Vanguard.

By the time it was written, Ted already had a substantial hat collection of his own. His sister, Marnie, reported, "Ted has another peculiar hobby. That of collecting hats of every description. Why, he must have several hundred and he is using them as the foundation of his next book. . . . I have seen him put on an impromptu show for guests, using the hats as costumes. . . . He has kept a whole party in stitches just by making up a play with kitchen knives and spoons for the actors."[29]

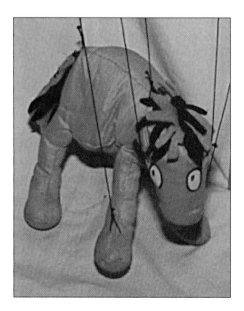

Parties may have had something to do with Ted's initial interest in hats. When he was a child, Howard R. Garis created a rheumatic rabbit named Uncle Wiggily Longears, who first appeared in the *Newark News* on January 30, 1910. More than 15,000 daily Uncle Wiggily stories would follow over the next 37 years, and their popularity soon led to books[30]

and then games. As Uncle Wiggily's fame grew, so did Ted. He was six years old at the rabbit's debut and 15 years old when a game called Put a Hat on Uncle Wiggily was released in 1919. The game was a pin-the-tail-on-the-donkey derivative produced by the Milton Bradley Company in Springfield. A two-foot-high picture of Uncle Wiggily showed him dressed and ready to go, with suitcase in hand, needing only a hat before he could leave for his trip. The object was for blindfolded players to pin a hat on Uncle Wiggily. Among the 20 hats in the game

were a top hat, bowler, tricorne, marshal's hat, straw hat, sombrero, fez, bandleader's hat, military hat, baseball cap, beanie, and fire chief's hat, plus a few more ornate and frilly numbers, including a busby—a military hat with a feather plume.

The jump from 20 hats to 500 may seem like a very large one to make, but it developed gradually as Ted wrote the book and increased Bartholomew Cubbins's burden from 48 to 135 and, finally, 500.[31] Incidentally, a party game with the goal of putting an unusual hat on an animal who wears a large red bow tie, stands erect, and carries a crutch in his right hand brings up an interesting connection: 38 years later, Ted put an unusual hat on a cat who wore a large red bow tie, stood erect, and carried an umbrella in his right hand most of the time.

Mulberry Street had reached the hearts of children who knew that many things went on in their imaginations that grown-ups would not understand. *The 500 Hats* touched another sore spot for children—trying to do the right thing and arousing an adult's anger through no fault of their own. Bartholomew naively believes that "the King can do nothing dreadful to punish me, because I really haven't done anything wrong."[32] But Ted pointed out that bad things can happen to good and innocent people, often at the whim of people in positions of power. In his experience, an ex-president of the United States could run out of medals just when he got to you, even though you'd done just as much as the people who received their medals. The government could pass legislation that suddenly made your family's business illegal. The head of your college could remove you from your position on the school literary-arts magazine. And a selfish dolt like King Derwin (who learns nothing throughout the book) could allow a child to die for a perceived sign of disrespect. If Bartholomew had not had a useless but attractive possession with

Dipping into other mediums: Ted was encouraged to create these marionettes (opposite page), but his venture into puppetry never went beyond the prototype stage.

Did this popular board game from Ted's youth (this page, top) fuel his fascination with hats and inform his work in *The 500 Hats of Bartholomew Cubbins* (this page, bottom)?

which to tempt King Derwin, the king would have allowed his nephew to push Bartholomew off a turret. *And to Think That I Saw It on Mulberry Street* and *The 500 Hats of Bartholomew Cubbins* are books for children written by an adult, but they were created by someone who had not lost his memory of the fantasies and injustices of childhood. Their magic lies in Ted's ability to honestly address the injustices while ameliorating them with the sense of wonder established by the fantasies.

Although Ted was finally beginning to publish books during this time, it was not a complete change of careers. He was continuing many projects, not the least of which was his advertising work. As a consequence, Ted's images developed across many media, as we see in the progression of the mysterious men who began as smoke ring–blowers in the comic strip "Hejji" (April 1935), transformed into the seven black-gowned, chanting magicians in *The 500 Hats of Bartholomew Cubbins* (July 1938), and then became the Assyrian choir in an NBC Radio ad (May 1939).

Just as images persisted in Ted's mind long after he had first seen them, slights and disappointments lingered long after the events that caused them had passed. His departure from Dartmouth had not gone as planned. First he had been removed from his position as editor-in-chief of the *Jack-O-Lantern.* Then he had prematurely told his father that he would be attending Oxford on a fellowship that did not materialize. When his father, feeling a need to save face, sent him to England to study anyway, Ted did not do well in his postgraduate studies and left after a year. While traveling in Europe afterward, Ted wrote "a long novel on which he placed high and unshakable hopes"[33] of making himself a respectable name in the field of literature. But as Ted would later say, "I was heavily influenced at that time by Carl Van Vechten, who often lapsed into Italian during the course of his books. Accordingly, I lapsed into Italian in my book, for pages at a time. I don't even speak Italian. . . ."[34] Consequently, that novel was abandoned. Despite his marvelous success in the fields of cartooning and advertising, Ted's Dartmouth friends and classmates established themselves in more "respectable" professions. No matter how many new fields he conquered, Ted considered his achievements to be inferior endeavors.[35]

Even children's literature seemed to be a less important type of writing than "serious" books. To his friends, he referred to a new book of his as "the annual brat-book."[36] Referring to his recent children's books and advertisements for Flit and Essomarine, Ted explained that his next book, *The Seven Lady Godivas,* was written "to escape the monotony of writing about nothing but 'men folks and children, dragons or fish.'"[37]

Although it was far from a serious work, *The Seven Lady Godivas* was aimed at a different audience. The change of subject matter accompanied a change of publishers. It was his first book for Random House, where publisher Bennett Cerf had convinced Ted that his prospects for recognition would be greater than at Vanguard due to the company's promotional abilities.

The Seven Lady Godivas is an odd book. If, as one reviewer suggested, *Mulberry Street* had only enough material for a comic strip, then perhaps *Godivas* might have been better suited for a single cartoon gag. As a result, "only twenty-five hundred copies of a first printing of ten thousand were sold."[38] Because of the growing concern about the war in Europe, one writer observed, "In 1939 America was feeling too blue to be cheered up by pictures of silly ladies with no nipples and funny knees."[39] Ted may have been aware that this book was inferior to his other work. On the inside-cover illustration, Ted depicts the book as meager drippings of sap collecting in a Bennett Cerf bucket, falling from a branch representing the offspring of the heaviest Godiva and Peeping Tom.

In his college studies of Tennyson, Ted may well have come across the 1842 poem "Godiva." During his time in England after Dartmouth, he no doubt came across the legend again. The theme of the Lady Godiva story—championing the rights of the common man—is what links this "adult" book to Ted's "children's" stories and his political cartoons. Lady Godiva was a real

The curious convocation of robed men who appeared first in the "Hejji" comic strip (opposite page, top) would resurface three years later in *The 500 Hats of Bartholomew Cubbins* (opposite page, middle) and then the following year in an NBC Radio brochure advertisement (opposite page, bottom).

person who lived in England in the eleventh century. The basic story is that she made her ride through town to try to free the populace from burdensome taxes. Her husband, Leofric, was the Earl of Mercia. The couple had moved from Shrewsbury to Coventry, becoming nouveau riche climbers of the social ladder. In 1043, they founded a Benedictine abbey, and in exchange for main-

tenance of the abbey, Leofric was given lordship over two dozen villages. Countess Godiva was a religious woman with a particular affinity for the Virgin Mary, and she is said to have had all of her gold and silver melted to make crosses and other religious decorations for the abbey.

While Leofric became more involved in governing the township and began levying taxes, Countess Godiva[40] became aware that the populace spent most of their time concerned with their basic needs of food, clothing, and shelter. The countess asked Leofric to remove some of the taxes; amused, he said that he would eliminate certain taxes if she would prove that she really believed in her cause by riding naked through Coventry:

> The countess . . . loosed her hair and let down her tresses, which covered the whole of her body like a veil, and then mounting her horse and attended by two knights, she rode through the market-place, without being seen, except her fair legs . . .[41]

Later versions of the incident added fictions born of puritanical ideology, including the notion that Godiva asked the townspeople to stay in their homes and not look at her—a request denied only by Peeping Tom, who was struck blind after daring to look at her.

Contrary to popular belief, it was not the first time that Dr. Seuss had published illustrations of topless women. There were bare-breasted cavewomen, African tribeswomen, and mermaids. Nor was it the first time he had reevaluated the Lady Godiva legend. More than ten years before *The Seven Lady Godivas*, Ted found humor in diminishing the historic ride by "discovering" that "Lady Godiva's bareback ride through the streets of Coventry was NOT so romantic as everyone thinks. . . . For THREE WHOLE DAYS before her public appearance the sly lady practiced riding on her kid brother's hobby

The growth of Godiva: **Ted was already considering Lady Godiva's curvaceous form in his own inimitable way (this page, and opposite page, top right) well before publishing** *The Seven Lady Godivas* **in 1939 (opposite page, bottom left and right).**

horse!"[42] The following year, in 1929, Ted revisited the Lady Godiva story, this time humorously suggesting that onlookers, far from moved by her nakedness, were much more concerned about her undernourished horse.

"*Shameful! Disgraceful! Godiva riding that poor old nag. Why, you can almost see his ribs!*"

These illustrations were all cartoons, of course; for more anatomical realism, one can look to Ted's version of the "Rape of the Sabine Woman." There is an interesting set of circumstances that may have linked the legends of Lady Godiva and the Sabine women in Ted's mind, beyond their nakedness. The connection lies in a piece written by Stephen Vincent Benét, whose short stories brought him fame beginning in the 1920s.

Benét published his story "The Sobbin' Women" in the November 1938 issue of the *Argosy*.[43] It is a refiguring of the rape of the Sabine women, in which seven brothers come to look for seven wives. The woman who has agreed to marry the eldest of the brothers sets rules intended to keep the brides separated from the brothers until all are overwhelmed with a need to see one another.

In 1939, Ted's *The Seven Lady Godivas* was published, in

which seven brothers are waiting to marry seven brides, whose romantic futures are determined by the eldest woman, who sets up tasks that keep the brides apart from the seven peeping brothers until they are . . . Yes, the story is somewhat familiar.

In 1938, the most prominent literary figure of the period reimagined the abduction of the Sabine women as a comedy about seven brothers and their brides. In 1939, Ted, who had focused on a Sabine woman previously, reimagined the Lady Godiva legend as a comedy involving seven brothers and seven sisters as brides and grooms.

Another project he was readying for the beginning of 1939 was a money-making enterprise, inspired by the approach of the World's Fair, which opened in Queens, New York, on April 30.[44] Almost 45 million people visited the fair, with its optimistic theme of "The World of Tomorrow."

The 1939 World's Fair looked like an art deco wonderland. The focus of the fair was creativity and the world that technology could create. The most popular exhibit was General Motors' "Futurama: A Metropolis of Tomorrow." It depicted the world as it might be in 1960, when tenement housing would be replaced by parks, and technology would allow for seven-lane roads and 100-mile-per-hour speed limits. Visitors were conveyed on a moving sidewalk. Two-seat compartments with loudspeakers moved them over a 36,000-square-foot model of the envisioned city, complete with 500,000 buildings and twice as many trees. The highways carried 50,000 little auto-mobiles. The narration explained that "the world, far from being finished, is hardly yet begun; that the job of building the future is one which will demand our best energies, our most fruitful imagination; and that with it will come greater opportunities for all." That was certainly the case for Ted, who continued to explore ever more diverse means of fulfilling his creative spirit.

For the fair, however, his goals were less noble. Eager to cash in on the influx of tourists to the fair, Ted created the Infantograph, "a camera for making humorous photographs . . . [by] simultaneously photographing on a single negative selected portions of two or more persons so aligned as to produce a composite picture which is instructive, entertaining, and amusing."[45]

He received a patent for this device a month before the fair opened. Like many of the other ideas that the fair projected into the future, the Infantograph now seems like a primitive idea. However, it can also be contended that Ted's invention, like some of the other dreamers' visions, turned out to be prescient.

A movie or television show at the beginning of the twenty-first century can manipulate photographs digitally, as in the running gag "If They Mated" on *Late Night with Conan O'Brien,* in which celebrities' faces are combined to produce horrific offspring.[46] But that technology did not exist back in 1939, when Ted had the idea that young couples would pay to see what the result

The patented plans for Ted and Ralph Warren's proposed contribution to the 1939 World's Fair reveal the Infantograph (opposite page), a camera for making humorous photographs by combining photos of two individuals.

would be if they had a child. Ted planned to lure them to his pavilion with a sign that read: IF YOU WERE TO MARRY THE PERSON YOU ARE WITH, WHAT WOULD YOUR CHILDREN LOOK LIKE? COME IN AND HAVE YOUR INFANTOGRAPH TAKEN.[47]

He and partner Ralph Warren looked at this opportunity as a business venture. They worked at creating a camera with two lenses that could superimpose one person's features over another's to create a face that would be placed on the image of a baby lying on a bearskin rug. Much work was done in creating and trying to improve the camera and the pictures. The partners even went so far as to get Norman Bel Geddes to volunteer to design their pavilion—quite a feat, considering that Bel Geddes designed General Motors' famed "Futurama" exhibit for the fair.

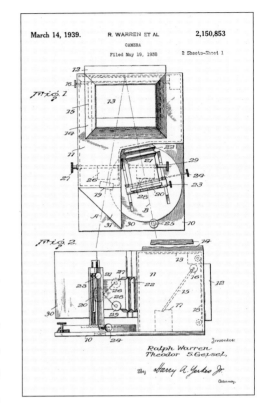

The results were very much like those on *Late Night*'s "If They Mated." However, at the time, the partners did not think that the grotesque images could be played for laughs. Ted opined that "all the babies tended to look like William Randolph Hearst,"[48] displaying a bit of prickliness about his rocky relationship with the news magnate but also revealing the basic problem with the invention. The fair began before he and Warren could work out the difficulties, so the main reason for its existence was gone. The partners persisted, but the enterprise was never completed. The death knell, according to Ted, was their inability to import special lenses from Germany due to World War II. It was one of the few ventures that did not work out for him. The Infantograph never joined the fair's visions of "The World of Tomorrow."

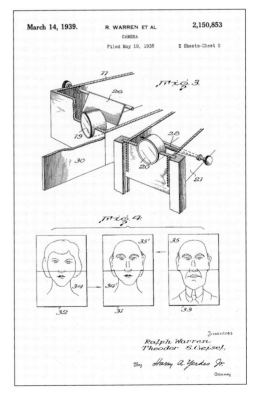

After the disappointing *Godivas*, Ted returned to writing for children. His second book for Random House was *The King's Stilts*, which came out in 1939. Unlike The Mighty One in "Hejji" or King Derwin in *The 500 Hats of Bartholomew Cubbins*, the book's titular King Birtram was a wise, conscientious, and competent ruler. He was the

first intelligent authority figure in Ted's books, and he set a good example by working hard and then having the self-confidence to enjoy himself without worrying what others might think of his behavior. This time Lord Droon was the callous and selfish authority figure who wanted everyone to conform to his way of life. He forced the forthright pageboy Eric to do something that Eric knew was wrong and dangerous. It was only by having the strength of character to rebel against this misuse of power that an average boy like Eric could help save the city. (In his "Forgotten Man" speech, FDR had reminded Ted and the rest of the nation that Napoleon had overlooked the common man, who made his armies strong. Ted worked his support for the common man into his cartoons and books in the early 1930s and would continue to do so throughout his career.)

A hint at Ted's inspiration for the Kingdom of Binn can be found in a part of the book's original dedication that was removed from later editions. The book was initially dedicated not only to "Alison Margaret Budd and Deirdre Clodagh Budd" but also to "All the Irish Cats and seagulls on the shores of Inchydoney." Inchydoney Island is located in County Cork in southern Ireland. For towns in that area, protection against flooding is one of the more important public-works issues. The Great Flood of 1853, for example, caused enormous destruction in much of County Cork. The impression one gets is that Ted was able to take a vacationer's view of cats and seagulls along the shoreline and transform it into the patrol cats protecting the seawall of Dike Trees from the Nizzards in *The King's Stilts*.

The idea for the patrol cats themselves likely came from Ted's college days, when Felix the Cat was the most popular cartoon character in the country. Felix appeared in ads in Ted's college newspaper, and the silent Felix cartoons were popular movie fare. In *Felix Revolts*,[49] Felix leads the town's cats out on strike. The regiments of patrol cats in *The King's Stilts* certainly resemble the united rows of cats coming together to organize their strike in the Felix cartoon. In other scenes, the striking cats laze around, allowing squadrons of rats to invade the town until the city leaders ask the cats to come back—just as the cats in *The King's Stilts* are needed to return to save the town of Binn from Nizzards.

The Seven Lady Godivas sold only 23 copies from June to December 1940, during its second year on sale, earning Ted just $2.55 in royalties.[50] Reviews of *The King's Stilts* were much brighter than they had been for *The Seven Lady Godivas*. One reviewer wrote, "Dr. Seuss's latest extravaganza has a meaning so good it makes its madness all the merrier. . . . This is the best Dr. Seuss so far, and that's no small praise."[51] But sales were still disappointing: 4,648 copies were sold the first year and only 394 the following year.[52] Fortunately, Ted had not forsaken his other sources of income, since he had not made a sudden, life-altering career change.

For three successive books after *And to Think That I Saw It on Mulberry Street*, Ted had left the worlds of rhyme and color, working his text in prose and his illustrations in black-and-white with single-color highlights. He returned to full color and to rhyming text in *Horton Hatches the Egg*. As illustrated earlier, the story was based on a concept that Ted had been honing for more than a decade. Two years earlier, he had told almost the exact same story in the fable "Matilda, the Elephant with a Mother Complex." Matilda was characterized as a foolish failure for her dogged and well-meaning but ridiculous efforts. But the world had changed in the two years between Matilda and Horton. Germany had invaded Poland in 1939 and would invade Norway, Denmark, Belgium, the Netherlands, France, and Luxembourg in the spring and early summer of 1940. Ted held a growing belief that the United States had to join the war in Europe, and the concept of duty became very important to him.

Like *Mulberry Street, Horton Hatches the Egg* is written in strict meter. It is a form of anapestic tetrameter, but this time, instead of the four sections of three syllables each, a syllable (or beat) is missing from the first section; thus there are 11 syllables in the four sections rather than the traditional 12. *Horton Hatches the Egg* picks up part of the theme from *The King's Stilts*. Both Horton and King Birtram are willing to work hard and remain dedicated to an important job, but they need to have some relaxation or small reward after the

Cat patterns: Ted's inspiration for the cats in The King's Stilts (opposite page) may have been the Felix the Cat cartoons that were all the rage during his college years.

work is done—one can't work nonstop in a vacuum. That theme runs through Ted's work, whether in a book about a king inspecting tree roots or an elephant hatching an egg.

Horton Hatches the Egg is an absolute delight. It is not just a welcome return but also a celebration of rollicking rhythm and playful rhyme. Instead of using poetic license to overlook the absurdity of an elephant hatching an egg, Ted approaches the subject directly with a smile. Horton is like the overweight kid who has learned to accept that he's larger than everyone else:

> "ME on your egg? Why, that doesn't make sense. . . .
> Your egg is so small, ma'am, and I'm so immense!" . . .
> "H-m-m-m . . . the first thing to do," murmured Horton,
> "Let's see . . .
> The first thing to do is to prop up this tree
> And make it much stronger. That *has* to be done
> Before I get on it. I must weigh a ton."[53]

The plot about an animal oddity brought back to civilization for display bears an obvious resemblance to *King Kong,* a movie that premiered in New York City on Ted's twenty-ninth birthday in 1933. Although Kong and Horton are similarly sympathetic figures, the unjust persecution leads Kong to a violent and tragic resolution, while Horton's patience, persistence, and dedication are eventually rewarded.

Ted's elephant went through many changes of name. One source relates, "In early drafts he was named Osmer, then Bosco, then Humphrey; finally Ted chose the name of a Dartmouth classmate, Horton Conrad. . . ."[54] Horton Conrad, from La Grange, Illinois, was the advertising manager for the *Jack-O-Lantern* when Ted was editor-in-chief. The name Osmer, in keeping with Ted's tenacious memory, was likely based on Osmer Cushing Fitts—a sophomore living on Ted's floor, next door to Ted's close friends Whit Campbell and Curt Abel, during Ted's junior year. An elephant, by any name, still never forgets.

"Bosco" tends to bring to mind "Don Bosco," the common name for St. John Bosco—a nineteenth-century Italian priest whose mission was to prevent children from falling into lives of crime, rather than trying to rehabilitate them after they had already done so. He was renowned for his endless patience, kind soul, and self-sacrifice in pursuing the goal that he had accepted—characteristics that he shared with the elephant in question. *Bosko* was also the name of the first talking cartoon from Warner Bros., which produced 20 *Bosko* cartoons in the early 1930s; that association may have led Ted to decide against using it in his book, much as he tried to keep his pigs from looking like Disney pigs after the success of *The Three Little Pigs*. The relevance of these facts lies, however, in the realm of conjecture.

In any case, the theme of fidelity, which is so strong in *Horton Hatches the Egg,* was an appropriate one for Ted at the time. Up until the previous year, his career had involved moving from one magazine to another, creating advertisements for one company after another, and moving from one book publisher to another. The only stability had been provided by Standard Oil, for which he'd worked for more than a decade. Random House had shown him loyalty by sticking with him after two books that sold poorly. He was pledging himself to a new relationship, and he would remain with Random House for the rest of his long career.

Horton Hatches the Egg sold 5,801 copies in its first year and declined to 1,645 copies in its second year. Although those numbers still did not match those posted by *Mulberry Street,* they represented an increase of nearly 25 percent in first-year sales and more than 300 percent in second-year sales compared with *The King's Stilts*. It was a return to form for Ted in the eyes of his American readers. But overseas, the book was still "rejected by seven British publishers before Hamish Hamilton issued the book in 1941, with only modest success."[55]

Horton Hatches the Egg was the last book Ted would publish for seven years. Of his move to political cartooning, Ted would later write, "On the night of June 14, 1940, while Paris was being occupied by the klanking tanks of the Nazis and I was listening on my radio, I found that I could no longer keep my mind on drawing pictures of Horton The Elephant. I found myself drawing pictures of Lindbergh The Ostrich."[56]

As usual, this comment has to be read skeptically—Ted's first Lindbergh cartoon would not be published until ten months later. In the interim, Ted would work on much less serious fare, finishing his advertising campaigns for Essomarine and NBC Radio, continuing his work for the Dartmouth Alumni Fund, returning to produce some Flit posters, and beginning new campaigns for Ajax cups and the Narragansett Brewery. But the storm of war was brewing, and Ted's ship was setting sail once again.

CHAPTER 16

Shunning His Frumious Brand of Sneetch

Most people's understanding of Ted Geisel begins with a man hovering around 50 years of age, already established as a wildly popular children's author. It was in that context that Ted published an article in 1952 in which he excoriated adults for losing a healthy sense of humor when they grew up:

> Have you ever stopped to consider what has happened to your sense of humor? When you were a kid named Willy or Mary the one thing you did better than anything else was laugh. . . . A strange thing called conditioned laughter began to take its place. . . . [It depended on] financial conditions. Political conditions. Racial, religious and social conditions. You began to laugh at people your family feared or despised—people they felt inferior to, or people they felt better than. . . . You were supposed to guffaw when someone told a story which proved that Swedes are stupid, Scots are tight, Englishmen are stuffy and the Mexicans never wash. You discovered a new form of humor based on sex. . . . Your capacity for healthy, silly, friendly laughter was smothered.[1]

This statement will appear perfectly consistent with the Ted Geisel known solely through Dr. Seuss books. It would be an act of revisionism, however, to accept this passage as an indication of what he had always believed. Ted did not come to this point of view easily or directly. In reality, the statement renounces the very same ethnic generalizations and caricatures Ted resorted to in his early cartoons and condemns the sexual jokes that dotted his early career. In fact, during his time in charge of the *Jack-O-Lantern*, he mentioned, without apology, "According to psychologists a joke should contain three different ingredients: Surprise, Sex, and Superiority."[2]

It would be a disservice to Ted to overlook his early pieces that now seem controversial, failing to address the changes that he made in his approach to humor. To do so would be to underestimate the strength of character it took for Ted to overcome the prejudices of his time and his efforts to teach future generations not to make the same mistakes. One measure of heroism lies in a person's ability to overcome such learned behavior.

Ted was not born into what today might be termed a "politically correct" atmosphere. Yet he grew up to write stories that taught generations to believe that "a person's a person, no matter how small" and that it doesn't make a difference if you have a star on your belly or not. It would be easy to look at Ted's childhood and conclude that the prejudice directed at him in school during World War I, despite the respect his German family garnered in the community and the pride they took in their heritage, caused Ted to develop a hatred of such inequitable treatment. The picture of a boy who experienced unfair stigmatization and grew up to crusade against such injustices is a satisfying one. But real life is rarely that simple. For Ted, the road to righteousness was by no means smooth.

In Ted's early years of publishing, jokes at the expense of women and various minorities were de rigueur and were not recognized as being directed at "people your family feared or despised—people they felt inferior to, or people they felt better than."[3] And the only subject getting more attention in jokes than sex might have been drinking.

The young Ted Geisel didn't frown on jokes based on the notion that "Scots are tight." During his reign as editor-in-chief, the *Jack-O-Lantern* published many such quips, like:

> "Joe seems rather tight."
> "Yes, he's under the influence of Scotch."[4]

Such bits were not identified by author, and although Ted most likely

A *"BONNIE BRRRECH"*
(A hole in a wall through which
a barber snitches free lather
from a beer stein.)

A *"BONNIE
GRROMRRH"*
(A lightning rod on a
pipe that attracts a free
light every eight or ten
years.)

penned them, it matters very little. Even if these were not examples of Ted's own "grinds," it was he who reviewed the submissions from other contributors and approved them for publication. And Ted continued to use the "cheap" premise in his professional magazine work, drawing Scotch cupids who tethered their arrows so they could retrieve and reuse them. He also depicted Scotsmen who were so niggardly that they bet a measly shilling on which of two birds would lay an egg first; after a week of watching them intently through inclement weather, the loser still wanted to make it two out of three.

In fact, every one of the seven jokes in "Life's Little Educational Charts: The Language of Scotland at a Glance" revolves around the supposed penuriousness of the Scottish people, including barbers who snitch the foam from the glasses of nearby beer drinkers to use as lather; a man who attaches a lightning rod to his pipe, hoping to attract "a free light every eight or ten years"; and a man who plays horseshoes by throwing the entire horse, shoes and all, because he "sees no need of wasting extra shoes." Far from frowning upon these jokes, a publisher in England wrote to tell Ted that he was "highly amused" by them, adding, "If you have any other Scottish Sketches of this type, we shall be pleased to see them with a view to publishing in the form of Postcards or Calendars."[5]

The fact is that during the 1920s and 1930s, Ted joined all the other humorists of the day in making the same sorts of jokes that he would begin to condemn as an older man in the 1950s. In one piece, he declared that "the national fruit of England is the Prince of Wales" before continuing a story in which monkeys attend Sinn Fein meetings and the "Free Staters" can't distinguish between the monkeys and the "Harps."[6]

Virtually all ethnic groups were the butts of Ted's jokes during this time. But this was the character of that period. It was no coincidence that Ted's series of language parodies for *Life* began four days after the Immigration Act of 1924 went into effect. The prevailing nationalist sentiment made the languages and customs of "foreigners" particularly agreeable subjects for humor.

Conspicuous by their absence from Ted's 1952 article were Jews and blacks. It is clear that Ted avoided mentioning them because the issue of prejudice against them was particularly sensitive at the time. However, neither group was given such careful treatment earlier in his career. Ted poked fun at both groups in the same issue of the *Jack-O-Lantern*. His illustration of a newly engaged Jewish couple (with the punning caption "Nice Cohen") depicts both people with the prominent proboscises that would be understood to identify them as Jewish. In the same issue, he depicted black

"Nice Cohen"

Highball Thompson wins from Kid Sambo by a shade.

boxers "Highball Thompson" and "Kid Sambo," punning that one of them won "by a shade."

As with the Scots, Ted continued to stereotype these groups in his humor pieces after college. For example, he placed Jewish merchants on the football field, where "Quarterback

Cheap shots: Ted's magazine work sometimes spoofed the stereotypically tightfisted Scot. His "bonnie" barbs were directed at a Scottish cupid recycling arrows (opposite page, top), a frugal barber (opposite page, middle), a pipe smoker (opposite page, bottom), and a horseshoe pitcher (this page, top).

Some of Ted's jabs were at the expense of Jews (middle left and bottom) and blacks (middle right).

Portrait of a perfect wife.

The lighthouse keeper's wife gets a carpet for the stairs.

The obvious and the implied: There's no ambiguity about Ted's definition of the supportive wife (top). He did, however, employ innuendo and visual cues (bottom) for sex jokes.

Mosenblum always calls out the name of a salable object, such as 'fine old trombone,' 'ten karat brooch,' or 'new set of uppers.' He then reels off the prices, and not until a first-rate bargain has been established does the center relinquish the ball. No one but an expert merchandiser could ever get wise."[7]

The view of women that he expressed was no more enlightened. In one of his columns for the Springfield newspapers shortly after college graduation, Ted observed:

> At the same time they remove the "obey" from the woman's role in the marriage ceremony, a certain church intends to shorten the Ten Commandments also. Now that a man's wife is no longer under the obligation to obey him, it is only fair that they make it O.K. for him to covet his neighbors.[8]

He continued to perpetuate this view of women and marriage in later cartoons. In one, the perfect wife is portrayed as one who will allow her husband to stand on her shoulders and peek through a harem window.

As for sex—the "taboo" subject that the older Dr. Seuss described as a matter for private snickering—his early work was peppered with allusions and innuendo to avoid censorship, but hallowed figures were not exempt. In one cartoon, Santa's reindeer peer down a sorority's chimney to see what is taking him so long to return (see page 178). Other cartoons contained direct visual references to sex—which may have passed undetected because of the odd humor—like the phallic and vaginal images in the cartoon captioned "The lighthouse keeper's wife gets a carpet for the stairs."

Ted's eventual break with the routine use of stereotypes in his work might be underappreciated without a careful examination of the humor at the expense of African and American blacks during his youth. The greatest challenge to overcome was the widespread acceptance of jokes about this group.

When Ted was growing up, Al Jolson was a supremely popular artist.

"You've got to quit knockin' your neighbors."
"I notice you roast a few yourself."

In Darkest Africa

Jolson started out as a blackface vaudeville singer around 1906. He began his Broadway career in 1911 as "a colored aristocrat" in *La Belle Paree,* singing "Paris Is a Paradise for Coons," and continued to play a series of black characters as his fame grew.

When *Robinson Crusoe Jr.* opened in 1916, Jolson was billed as "America's Greatest Entertainer." The popular show went on a national tour, and in November 1917, when Ted was 13 years old, Jolson performed at the Court Square Theatre in Springfield. From February 1918 through late 1920, Jolson starred in *Sinbad,* which he performed in blackface at the Court Square Theatre when Ted was working there as an usher during high school.

Jolson's most famous moment came in October 1927 when he appeared in blackface in the first successful talking motion picture, *The Jazz Singer.*

Of course, the use of blackface wasn't exclusive to Jolson. It was widely used at the time. As a consequence, it was this image of black people that Ted and others of his generation saw most often. At the end of high school, Ted even wrote his own minstrel show. So it is not at all surprising that his first images of blacks were based on blackface performers.

It is critical to view Ted's cartoons and jokes within the context of their time. For example, from the following list, try to separate the names of real boxers in 1923 and 1924 from the ones that Ted created in his boxing joke from that period:

Battling Siki
Young Zulu Kid
Kid Norfolk
Kid Numbers
Kid Sambo
Highball Thompson

Stylistically, Ted's early drawings of blacks in the *Jack-O-Lantern* (top left) and then *Judge* (top right) seem to draw on the popular blackface images of the times (bottom right).

209

The first four were real boxers. At the time that Ted drew the cartoon during college, a black man was involved in a title fight for the first time in seven years. Baye Phal, a Senegalese man who boxed under the name Battling Siki, had recently won an upset victory in the light-heavyweight world championship. He had signed a contract to make his American debut against Kid Norfolk, and the two black men were supposed to battle it out in Madison Square Garden. The fight was postponed for a year, and instead, a month before Ted drew the cartoon, Battling Siki fought Mike McTigue in Ireland on St. Patrick's Day for 20 rounds before losing the decision to the Irishman but leaving quite an impression.

While Battling Siki was making headlines in his weight class, Young Zulu Kid was a popular fighter in the flyweight division. Ted knew about Battling Siki, since he referred to him in another college piece, in which he made him a ski jumper, along with Young Stribling, another popular boxer at the time.

Ted's cartoon about Kid Sambo fighting Highball Thompson was consistent with newspaper headlines about Zulu Kid and Battling Siki. The name "Sambo" did not carry the stigma that it has rightfully developed since then, so the racism lay mainly in Ted's pun about winning by a "shade." But in the context of what was being written at the time, the joke was intended to be no more derisive toward blacks than the "Nice Cohen" pun was toward Jews. One or another identifiable group was used as fodder for a joke, but the humor itself was supposed to derive from the play on words. To Ted, ethnicity was just a necessary setup for the joke, just as a bar might have been a setting for a different joke. This fact becomes much clearer when Ted's cartoon is placed alongside the newspapers that called Battling Siki "Championzee." Ted's frame of mind has to be interpreted next to that of people like Battling Siki's own manager, Charlie Hellers, who said, "I used to think that if one could find an intelligent gorilla and teach him to box, one would have the world's champion. Well, that's what I found in Siki. There's much of the monkee [sic] about him."[9]

Growing up, Ted was not likely to have developed the hatred of blacks that many others had, because race relations underwent an upheaval just as animosity became directed at people of his own ethnic background. Two months after Ted entered high school, the United States declared war on his ancestral home, Germany. Three months later, there were race riots in East St.

Louis, Illinois, and the NAACP organized thousands of blacks to march down New York City's Fifth Avenue, protesting lynching and the denial of their civil rights. The following month, there was a race riot in Houston. Before the year was out, the U.S. Supreme Court struck down a Louisville, Kentucky, ordinance mandating segregated neighborhoods. It was amid this environment that, later the same month, Al Jolson came to Springfield to perform. The following summer, a wave of anti-German sentiment put once-respected German immigrants in an uncomfortable position, with Congress repealing the charter of the National German-American Alliance, a group with two million members. Later that month, there were race riots in Philadelphia. Ted's biographers, Judith and Neil Morgan, relate that since his dog, Rex, tended to favor one leg, Ted was being described in high school as "the German brewer's kid with the three-legged dog."[10] Ted's image of minorities could not have been simple in his youth, formed from such a complex mixture of information, emotions, and experiences.

Overall, Ted addressed blacks somewhat less than he did most of the other groups. One period in the late 1920s stands as an exception, reflecting the proliferation of images of blacks in the media at the time. Ted's first racially oriented material after college appeared in the April 28, 1928, issue of *Judge*. On the radio, *Amos 'n' Andy* had debuted in March 1928 and kept the subject of blacks in the mind of radio listeners six nights a week. For most listeners, the image to go with the radio voices was that of Al Jolson in *The Jazz Singer* from the previous year.

Although Jolson's *Jazz Singer* had opened the door to sound films, it was his follow-up, *The Singing Fool,* that really swung the door wide.[11] The promotional material, seen all around New York City prior to its release, pictured Jolson in blackface. Ted's second and third racially themed cartoons since the debut of *Amos 'n' Andy* flanked the movie's September 1928 opening. But behind the language now recognized as offensive, one cartoon makes as much sport of marriage as of blacks, with a wife chastising her husband for indulging in frivolity when, in fact, he's humiliating himself to earn money for his family. Like Jolson, who is reported to have refused to eat in restaurants that would not serve black performers, Ted did not necessarily intend to be disrespectful.

The theater at the time had its own blackface image. Eddie Cantor was

Even subtle childhood snubs like "the German brewer's kid with the three-legged dog" surely must have stayed with Ted and shaped his feelings about bigotry.

starring in Florenz Ziegfeld's Broadway production of *Whoopee!* He played the part of Henry Williams, who has a comic encounter with a stove that leaves him in blackface. Although Ted had done no racially themed cartoons since the opening of *The Singing Fool,* for a short period after *Whoopee!* opened in December 1928, his work in *Judge* had a high proportion of jokes at the expense of blacks.

Many of Ted's pieces were visual gags that reflected the blackface look. It is hard to look beyond these cartoon depictions to realize that Ted made people of every race and culture look equally ugly. It was just part of the humor. But the different nature of Ted's cartoons can be seen clearly when they are compared with other comics from the same period, for which the motivation was obvious derision or hatred. For example, during Ted's freshman year at college, a filibuster killed an anti-lynching bill in the U.S. Senate; a few years later, that sort of atmosphere in the country made it possible for a national magazine like *College Humor* to run a cartoon about a black man being hanged, without raising any protest. In contrast, many of Ted's comics would fall under the category of social commentary, remarking on some supposed aspect of black culture that he perceived as different from his own, like having large families or "dressing to impress."

But others are indefensible, clearly evidencing that Ted sometimes fell prey to the prejudices of the day. Among this latter group is a subset whose most troubling aspect is the imagery itself, more than the punch lines. Although all of Ted's faces during this period were clownish, his cartoons of blacks shifted from using a blackface approach to showing them with simian features.

Relative racism: Setting aside Ted's use of questionable language, the universal subjects of a no-account husband (left) and a decked-out dandy (right) were much more palatable than other period pieces like this *College Humor* cartoon (middle) by another illustrator.

SHE—*Out sportin' again, are yo', nigger? Jest wait 'til I lay hands on yo' tonight!*

" Say, boss, put that knot under my other ear. I've got a boil on this side."

"Stand aside, woman! I'se on mah way to the three hundred and fifty-second semi-annual conclave and gatherence of the Antiquated Order of Loyal and Diversified True-blue Ravens, of which organism ah am a sixty-seventh degree Mahoot, to say nothing at all of mah exalted and revered position and office as corresponding scribe and ex post facto protector and guardian of the sacred scrolls and parchments!"
"My, my, nigger, what an impression youse goin' to make when you deliver this here wash to my clients."

Religion vs. Fashion, and a Compromise

In the little jungle island of Mwammb (just off Madagascar), the turtle is considered holy, and to kill one is a capital offense. At the same time the Mwammbs are a stylish folk, and when tortoise-shell glasses became the rage, they wanted to follow the fashion. The picture shows how a local optician solved the problem without the sacrilegious taking of life.

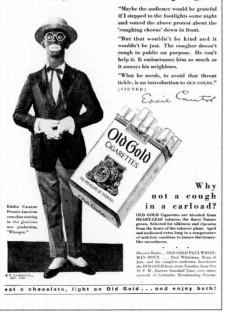

"Sorry, sister, but you can't get wholesale baptizin' rates unless you got a minimum of twelve chillun."

"Well, pawson, duck these five kids now, and give me credit for seven mo' in the very near future."

Ted's handling of black subjects ranges from the relatively innocuous blackface cartoons (top left, middle, and right), based on media images like this one of Eddie Cantor in *Whoopee!* (middle left), to his uninformed observations of black culture (middle right), to the indefensibly offensive (bottom left and right).

Disgusted Wife: "You hold a job, Worthless? Say, nigger, when you all hold a job a week, mosquitoes will brush their teeth with Flit and like it!"

Advt.

Cross-section of the World's Most Prosperous Department Store.

Odious imagery:
**While homely
human faces of
all races were
trademarks of
Ted's work, his
portrayal of blacks
occasionally took
on an insulting
simian appearance
(this page).**

**Even as Ted's most
offensive art was
being published,
other work
reflected a more
egalitarian
approach. A 1929
Flit ad (opposite
page, top) places
"his" man Friday
in charge, and an
interracial romance
(opposite page,
middle) is hinted
at in** *Life.*

Fortunately, after six months, when blackface media presentations died down, Ted's cartoons about blacks tapered off until they were proportionate with those about other groups.

So how did Ted grow from someone who participated in this behavior to the man whose books taught the concept of equality to generations of children? The seeds of dissent had been there from the start. Presumably because of the prejudice he experienced as a German American child during World War I, Ted had feelings, even from a young age, about treating all types of people with respect. During the Scopes trial, H. L. Mencken referred to the locals as "morons," "hillbillies," and "yokels." While giving a knowing wink to the evolutionists, Ted still displayed a kernel of his trademark egalitarianism. "Mr. Mencken should remember that, even though these people evolved in a way different than the rest of us, they are still American citizens and should be respected as such."[12]

Furthermore, from the beginning, Ted created cartoons that expressed his sense of fairness, including a belief in racial equality—cartoons that were published at the same time as some of those that now seem racist. A Flit ad from early 1929 shows a bedraggled Robinson Crusoe washing ashore and, from his knees, asking if he can have the honor of joining the black man on the island. The man, presumably Friday, declines unless Crusoe agrees to swim back and get some Flit to combat the flies.

This portrayal of a white man in a subservient position to a black man was not typical for this time period. Several years later, Ted published a cartoon in which a white man strides in his finery in one direction while a black woman rides sheepishly in the other direction. Labeled only "Chart No. 2," it is easily lumped in with the other derogatory cartoons of this era. However, Ted's description of the scene shows that it was radically different. He explains that the man is:

> . . . en route to visit his fiancée. The lush lady in the background is a total stranger.
>
> Now, no matter how fine a young man's character, no matter how devoted he is to his betrothed . . . sometimes

he is attracted by a new pair of eyes. This occasionally leads him into forbidden pastures.

But with his head ensconced in a Wooer's Cap, no one dares tempt him. His Wooer's Cap announces his sweetheart's monopoly. The lady in the background may be making eyes at [him] . . . but only sisterly eyes. . . .[13]

"My name's Crusoe, Robinson J. May I have the honor of joining you?"
"Not unless you swim back after some Flit, mistah. The flies on this island are fearful."—ADVT.

The description of the black woman as a "lush lady" is far from the "mammy" image that was the norm for the time. The hint at the possibility of an interracial romance also betrayed a liberal bent far ahead of its time.

The following year, 1934, Ted illustrated a tryst between an "Abyssinian Admiral" and a "Negro Mermaid." The caricature faces are still regrettably simian, but Ted had moved beyond the period's usual humor at the expense of blacks and was envisioning them in positions of power and competence, intrigue and desire. The concept of a black mermaid is probably no less foreign today than it was then, and a particular type of creativity was required to envision it in 1934, even for use in a joke. This cartoon appeared the same month that the Hollywood Film Production Code went into effect, beginning censorship in the movies. It is possible that Ted and Helen's travels and their interactions with people of other cultures helped to open their minds. This particular cartoon appeared shortly after they had traveled in Turkey and Peru and Ted had mentioned that he and Helen planned to go to Africa.[14]

But the real change for Ted came during World War II. Working for the left-wing newspaper *PM* ensured that he was surrounded by very liberal ideas in the early 1940s. The issue of racism was addressed there, and as the war progressed, one

CHART No. 2

Although Ted continued to give blacks apelike features, by 1934 he was imputing a certain authority (as a ship's admiral) and desirability (as a sea nymph) to his subjects (bottom).

Our Inexcusable Ineptitude in Amatory Nomenclature

"In touring America, lecturing on my adventures," complains an Abyssinian Admiral, "I have been horribly handicapped by the wretched limitations of your inexpressive vocabulary. I am forced to deny my audiences my very best stories, for your doltish dictionary has no noun whatever meaning a Tryst with a Negro Mermaid."

question became increasingly obvious. How could anyone, in good conscience, justify fighting overseas to protect the Jews from Nazi oppression without seeing the need to change the way that minorities—in particular, people of color—were treated in this country?

When Ted joined *PM,* he was confronted with the issue immediately. He began his work for *PM* in earnest on April 25, 1941. (His previous work for the newspaper was just one stray illustration of Italian fascist Virginio Gayda, which had been reused several times earlier in the year.) Three days later, the U.S. Supreme Court made a decision concerning the rights of black Americans on railroad trains, related to a case from four years earlier. While in Arkansas, Arthur W. Mitchell, a black Democratic congressman from Illinois, had been forced to ride in a "Jim Crow" car for blacks, even though he had a Pullman car ticket. He sued the Rock Island Railroad for $50,000, but the district court rejected his suit. The Interstate Commerce Commission upheld the railroad's right to move Mitchell to the Jim Crow car, ruling that there was not enough first-class traffic among blacks to justify the cost of accommodating them. Mitchell appealed the case to the U.S. Supreme Court, which ruled unanimously that "colored passengers who buy first-class tickets must be furnished with accommodations equal in comforts and convenience to those afforded to first-class white passengers."[15]

The following week, *PM* began pressing the issue of the disenfranchisement of black Americans. It covered the arguments made by leaders like New York mayor Fiorello La Guardia, who issued a statement "demanding that Negroes be given a larger share of employment in defense industries."[16] A banner headline quoted the 14th Amendment to the Constitution, reminding readers that all people are guaranteed equal protection under the law. A full page was devoted to a passage from Richard Wright's novel *Native Son,* explaining that the protagonist's "life was a disaster, because he was a Negro oppressed—as all his people are oppressed—by the blind misunderstanding and hostility of whites. . . ."[17]

Page after page carried sizeable articles with headlines like "No Help Wanted . . . If You're a Negro," "This Negro Is a Military Ace—But We're Not Using Him," "What Have Negroes to Fight For? Here's How People in Harlem Feel About It," and "North American Aviation Rejects Negroes, No Matter How Expert." An editorial from that issue by Tom O'Connor sums up the attitude that Ted encountered at *PM:*

The Negro people aren't sold on this war. . . .
They don't like Hitler. They don't like Fascism.

"But," they say, "why should we fight? Things
couldn't be much worse."

. . . We have given them so small a share of
democracy that the very word is a mockery. . . . We have
beaten them . . . ignored their needs, laughed at their
hurts, treated their wounds with the acid of bigotry and
prejudice.

Now, in a time of national crisis, do we recognize
our mistakes, try to correct them?

We don't. . . . We still won't let them build our
airplanes. . . . We are . . . taking a few in the army . . . but
in strictly segregated units, the very concept of which is
an insult to the Negro.

. . . Will it advance the cause of democracy to isolate
a tenth of the nation much as Hitler has isolated the Jews?

What are we going to do about it?[18]

This was Ted's new work environment. When he first arrived, however,
he focused on the issue that had caused him to get involved with *PM*—
convincing Americans of the need to enter the war. To do so, he
had to get them to look beyond themselves to understand that
other people mattered—even in other countries. In one cartoon,
Ted satirized the isolationist approach of the America First
group, aiming at the sympathy that he presumed people of all
nations felt toward innocent children.

Once Pearl Harbor was bombed on December 7, 1941, and
Germany and Italy declared war on the United States on
December 11, Ted no longer needed to get Americans interested
in going to war to help other people; our own country's security
was at stake. Ted now focused on the war effort and spent the
first few months of 1942 on fund-raising.

In time, he turned his attention to getting folks interested
in the welfare of people here at home. In June 1942, he began to
use his cartoons to address the issue of racial prejudice. Employing an image

*Tapping into Ted's
truer nature:*
**Working for PM, a
decidedly left-wing
publication,
afforded Ted the
chance to express
how he really felt.
Foremost on his
mind—ending
America's
isolationist stance
regarding the war.**

. . . and the Wolf chewed up the children
and spit out their bones . . . But those
were Foreign Children and it really
didn't matter."

that would be familiar to fans of his famous Flit advertisements, Ted began by depicting Uncle Sam with a can of "mental insecticide," with which he cleans the "racial prejudice bug" out of ordinary citizens who don't even realize that they have it. To close the month, Ted drew a "war industry" figure seated at an organ. Uncle Sam taps him on the shoulder and reminds him to use both the "black labor" *and* the "white labor" keys.

The next month found Ted reworking a couple of familiar phrases to make two powerful statements. In one cartoon, he addressed the black-labor issue by reversing an offensive racial slur. In the other cartoon, he made a dramatic statement concerning Hitler's treatment of the Jews by corrupting the Joyce Kilmer 1913 poem "Trees."

In August, he turned his attention to populist demagogue Eugene Talmadge, who was serving his third term as governor of Georgia. In 1941, Talmadge ordered that books dealing with racial integration be removed from Georgia school libraries and caused two college educators whom he accused of "promoting racial equality" to be fired.

He swore that he would "rid the state of any signs of social equality,"[19] telling a white constituent, "Before God, friend, the niggers will never go to a school which is white while I am governor."[20] These sorts of remarks led A. Philip Randolph to ask, "What have Negroes to fight for? What's the difference between Hitler and that 'cracker' Talmadge of Georgia?"[21]

Before long, Ted weighed in on issues like prejudice (top right) and the plight of black laborers (bottom right and top left). By the summer of 1942, he was, in his own peerless way, already speaking out about Hitler's treatment of the Jews (bottom left).

Ted's cartoon—which made it clear that he found Talmadge's racial hatred downright un-American[22]—came a month before the Democratic gubernatorial primary, which Talmadge lost to Attorney General Ellis Arnall. Ted contended that he could not draw people, but judging from photographs of Talmadge taken at the time, his depiction of the governor is spot-on.

A few months later, Ted enlisted in the army. The propaganda films that he wrote required him to concentrate on reasons to dislike different groups of people, including his German ancestors, and to make those reasons sound plausible to the American troops. Aspects of that job often troubled him. From that point on, it became Ted's personal quest to slay intolerance and promote equality.

In June 1951, a U.S. district court finished hearing the case of *Brown* v. *Board of Education,* in which Oliver Brown and the NAACP brought suit against the Topeka, Kansas, Board of Education for refusing to admit Brown's daughter Linda to the white elementary school seven blocks from her house. The board insisted that Linda had to walk a mile through a railroad switchyard to attend the black elementary school.

The court's decision was based on the 1892 case of *Homer Adolph Plessy* v. *The State of Louisiana,* in which Judge John Howard Ferguson found Plessy guilty of failing to leave a white train car. The appeal of Judge Ferguson's decision, known as *Plessy* v. *Ferguson,* led to an 1896 U.S. Supreme Court ruling that upheld the finding of guilt. As a consequence, a constitutional precedent for separate facilities for whites and blacks was set. The concept of "separate but equal" developed, in which many public places were allowed to be segregated as long as the all-black facilities were theoretically of equal quality.

Because the U.S. Supreme Court had not overturned the *Plessy* v. *Ferguson* decision, the district court in the 1951 case felt it had no choice but to rule in favor of the Board of Education. The case was appealed to the U.S. Supreme Court, which heard it in December 1952 but failed to reach a decision.

It would be another year until the U.S. Supreme Court heard the case again, in December 1953, but in the interim, during the summer of 1953, Ted published a three-stanza poem called "The Sneetches" in *Redbook.* It predated

Sizing up the segregationist: Ted's stance on Georgia governor Eugene Talmadge comes through loud and clear in this 1941 cartoon for PM.

the book version by eight years. With economy of language and illustration, Ted cut through all the social and legal issues that obfuscated the court case, distilling prejudice down to a rhymed couplet in which he summed up the point of view for which he would ever after be known:

> And, really, it's sort of a shame,
> For except for those stars, every Sneetch is the same.[23]

In May 1954, Chief Justice Earl Warren finally read the U.S. Supreme Court's decision in the appeal of *Brown* v. *Board of Education,* in which the Court unanimously concluded that "in the field of public education, the doctrine of 'separate but equal' has no place. Separate educational facilities are inherently unequal. . . ."[24] As a result, segregation of public schools was ruled unconstitutional. Four months earlier, Ted had already given his publisher *Horton Hears a Who!,* in which Horton—the antithesis of the Star-Bellied Sneetch—hears a cry for help and cares only that "some poor little person" is "shaking with fear."[25] Without knowing anything about the endangered being's race, religion, sex, or nationality, Horton immediately realizes:

> "I'll just have to save him. Because, after all,
> A person's a person, no matter how small."[26]

Of course, it is the smallest creature's voice that saves the Who race, proving that even one tiny voice can make a difference. Horton's persistence as the sole supporter of the tiny Whos, in the face of many others who think them so insignificant that it would mean nothing to do them harm, manages to change popular opinion in the Jungle of Nool. In the end, even the original detractors pledge to help protect the Whos, reinforcing the idea that even one voice can create change—not just on the small scale of the Whos' world, but in our world as well.

Horton Hears a Who! was released in August 1954, three months after the U.S. Supreme Court ruled against segregation in public schools. But the Court had not given a timetable for desegregation and had not addressed

The shame of prejudice is strikingly yet plainly illustrated by Ted's Sneetches in this illustration from the book *The Sneetches and Other Stories.*

segregation in other facets of public life. The boycott of the Montgomery, Alabama, bus system, which was spurred by Rosa Parks's simple act of courage—a landmark of the racial equality movement in America—would not start until December 1955. Ted's work on "The Sneetches" and *Horton Hears a Who!* during the summer and fall of 1953 was the "one-two" of the blade he had learned to wield against intolerance, and he was as much ahead of his fellow Americans as he had been in urging them to enter World War II.

Ted applied his concept of equality to humankind in general. Despite his wartime rhetoric in pieces like *Know Your Enemy: Japan,* he became somewhat of a Japanophile after the war, visiting Japan and writing a piece about the Japanese educational system called "Japan's Young Dreams."[27] *Horton Hears a Who!* was dedicated to a professor he met in Kyoto: Mitsugi Nakamura.

Ted's view of Asians had changed along with his view of other groups. As he matured, Ted understood that his earlier characterizations were inappropriate. *Mulberry Street*'s yellow-faced "Chinaman who eats with sticks" became, in later editions, a "Chinese man who eats with sticks."[28] Along the way, the offensive yellow face and the ponytail were eliminated.

The next time you're in a discussion about intolerance, see how many people cite a childhood encounter with *The Sneetches and Other Stories* or *Horton Hears a Who!* as the first time they learned about it. Ted's long maturation process helped him surmount the attitudes of his day to become a pioneer in the fight for equality, so that children would grow up already knowing what it took him several decades to recognize.

In response to David and Bob Grinch of Ridgewood, New Jersey, who wrote to Ted requesting that he change the name of his famous Christmas story because people were always teasing them about having the name of the "bad guy," Ted wrote, "Can't they understand that the Grinch in my story is the hero of Christmas? Sure . . . he starts out as a villain, but it's not how you start out that counts. It's what you are at the finish."[29]

"Come to my arms, my beamish boy!"

Ted's depiction of Asians evolved over time. A 1930 window washer (top) bears only a slight resemblance to the young man from a later edition of *Mulberry Street* (bottom).

CHAPTER 17

Changing Views

U ntil recently, most people were unaware of Ted's numerous political cartoons. Richard Minear's *Dr. Seuss Goes to War* brought Ted's work for *PM* newspaper to the attention of surprised and bemused readers. The *PM* cartoons might represent his most concentrated period of political cartooning, but the assertion that Ted's "opposition to Italian fascism led him to set pen to paper for his first editorial cartoon"[1] is somewhat misleading. While his irritation with a particular Italian propagandist was the motivation for his first *PM* cartoon, it was by no means his first *editorial* cartoon.

Judge published Ted's first professional editorial cartoon in 1932.

"What! Stop the wheel and spoil the Five-Year Plan?
No! Let him ride it out for two more years!"

Although political corruption was the subject of some of his college work, Ted's primary focus was on entertainment. His social commentary was limited to Prohibition and the foibles of the rich and famous. Occasionally he responded to political issues that were Prohibition-related, like the Wickersham Report. But he rarely editorialized until 1932, when he finally began to address political issues in *Judge,* beginning with a simple stab at Josef Stalin's second "five-year plan" for the Soviet Union.

The first five-year plan, adopted in January 1928, was successful in some respects. "Production [of goods in the U.S.S.R.] did increase, but it was at the expense of quality and . . . the standard of living of the workers."[2] But Stalin pushed to meet the objectives ahead of schedule with posters like the ones that read: "Full speed ahead for the fourth and final year of the Five-Year Plan!"[3] The resolution for the Second Five-Year Plan for the National Economy of the U.S.S.R. was adopted in February 1932, prompting Ted to respond with his first professionally published editorial cartoon, which depicted a Soviet worker with his beard stuck in an industrial fan. Rather than jeopardize production, his co-workers decide to let him be whipped around until the end of the five-year plan.

Back in the States, Congress had established the Reconstruction Finance Corporation in January 1932 as a response to our economic woes. But the RFC provided relief and security solely for large financial institutions, which angered many people. Comparing the 750,000 New Yorkers on city relief and the 130,000 more on the waiting list to the corporations aided by the RFC, Ted drew "Holding the Bag: A Projected Monument to the Great American Public."[4] Although Ted had not delved into political humor much previously, in the course of about a month, he had intriguingly drawn a parallel between the plight of the Soviet and the American worker.

From there, he went to work for *Liberty*. Rather than seriously engage the public on social and political issues, Ted chose to amuse readers while they got their dose of earnestness elsewhere in the magazine. At this point,

Crazy quilt: **In this** *Vanity Fair* **piece, Ted crammed in enough symbolism to fuel a dozen political cartoons.**

"DROPPING THE PILOT." PUCK'S FAMOUS CARTOON WHICH STARTED THE ASTOR HOUSE RIOTS

with the Great War in the past and no knowledge that another war loomed, Ted was occasionally able to belittle war and international affairs. But events would begin to change that viewpoint. In January 1933, German president Paul von Hindenburg appointed Adolf Hitler chancellor. Immediately thereafter, in *Vanity Fair,* Ted published a political cartoon overflowing with the conflict between isolationism and foreign entanglement.

The cartoon, "'Dropping the Pilot.' *Puck*'s Famous Cartoon Which Started the Astor House Riots," is an intentionally crazed mélange of symbolism and commentary, amounting to what Ted would later say was "a spoof on political cartooning in the 1890s."[5] It is crammed with references to 70 years of American history and the problems that America faced on both the domestic and foreign fronts.[6]

"The State of the World in 1931," as imagined by Ted in oils on canvas (this page).

Ted took up political cartooning again in 1937 (opposite page, top) with a piece setting forth the plight of the financially strapped everyman in a world where meat is as precious as a Wall Street commodity.

When Hitler was appointed chancellor, Ted recalled the dismissal of Otto von Bismarck from that position in 1890 by Kaiser Wilhelm II. In many people's eyes, that transition led, however indirectly, to World War I. With Hitler on the rise in the land of Ted's forefathers, it was almost as if all of the thoughts that Ted had been saving up while he drew his humorous cartoons came flooding forth in a single cathartic work. This was not the only outlet for his concerns about the greater world. A painting he did at this time betrays a growing global awareness. "The State of the World in 1931" (also known as "Tower of Babel") owes more to Bosch than Botticelli.

Ted was next moved to political commentary in 1937, but the history of this editorial cartoon began several years earlier. Addressing the nation's economic problems in April 1932, New York governor Franklin Delano Roosevelt gave a radio broadcast in Albany criticizing President Hoover's handling of the economic situation. FDR was elected president later that year, and his address became known as "The Forgotten Man" speech:

It is said that Napoleon lost the Battle of Waterloo because he forgot his infantry—he staked too much upon the more spectacular but less substantial cavalry. The present administration in Washington provides a close parallel. It has either forgotten or it does not want to remember the infantry of our economic army.

These unhappy times call for the building of plans that rest upon the forgotten, the unorganized but the indispensable units of economic power . . . that put their faith once more in the forgotten man at the bottom of the economic pyramid.

Regarding the forgotten man, who experienced foreclosures on his home or farm, FDR said, "The two-billion-dollar fund which President Hoover and the Congress have put at the disposal of the big banks, the railroads, and the corporations of the Nation is not for him." At the time, Ted was pleased to hear FDR championing the average American citizen.

But four years later, just before *Mulberry Street* was published, the cost of meat, which had peaked during World War I, rose to its highest price in eight years. Under FDR, it had risen more than 28 percent in one year and 21 percent in the previous six months, moving Ted to re-enter the realm of political cartooning. He responded with his own version of "The Forgotten Man"—a cartoon that depicted cuts of meat so expensive that they were being treated as precious commodities, under lock and key, traded on Wall Street. Earlier, when Ted had compared the previous administration's treatment of the common man to that of workers in the Soviet Union, FDR's ideas had sounded very appealing. Here, however, the reference to the speech was an obvious criticism. FDR had failed to live by his own words. He too was guilty of not doing enough to help the common man with such daily problems as putting meat on the table. Coincidentally, immediately after Ted's cartoon appeared in the *New York Sun,* meat prices dropped precipitously, reaching the previous year's levels within three months and then continuing to drop and remaining significantly lower for at least the next four years.[7]

Increasingly disillusioned by FDR's broken promises, Ted questioned the president's economic direction (this page, bottom).

On October 12, 1937, FDR gave his tenth Fireside Chat after returning from a trip across the nation, in which he observed that Americans "want the financial budget balanced. But they . . . are less concerned that every detail be immediately right than they are that the direction be right. They know that just so long as we are traveling on the right road, it does not make much difference if occasionally we hit a 'Thank you marm!' "[8]

Ted listened to the speech on his radio, and the next day the *New York Sun* ran his cartoon of FDR driving aimlessly across the country over rough roads, leaving small but essential parts of his car behind after each bump. FDR's assertion that Americans just wanted the economy to be

" * * * Just so long as we are traveling on the right road, it does not make much difference if occasionally we hit a 'thank-ye-ma'am.'"—President Roosevelt

So Say We All!

"You know . . . sometimes I wonder, are we overfeeding the canary?"

headed in the right direction and didn't mind some bumps presupposed that FDR knew in which direction the economy was heading and was aware of the damage done by each economic "bump."

In 1939, Ted resumed political cartooning. Given his new reputation as a children's author, he chose to keep his "Dr. Seuss" pseudonym out of the series of political cartoons published in such Hearst newspapers as the *New York Journal,* using "Tedd" as a pseudonym instead.

Initially, it was economic issues that set Ted off. In 1939, many Americans were already questioning the new taxes that would be necessary to accommodate the proposed budgets for federal and state relief. Ted grew even more concerned when, in February, Roosevelt declared that "an emergency now exists" and recommended to Congress that $150 million be restored to the relief bill to bring it back to the $875 million originally recommended. On the state level, it was reported that New York governor Herbert Lehman's budget contained $85 million for relief.[9] The next day, a political cartoon by Ted appeared, in which a taxpaying couple is eating birdseed while their pet canary, labeled "Taxes," grows enormous from gorging on gourmet foods provided by the couple.

He continued to question Roosevelt's economic policies, believing that they deceived the public into thinking that the nation was closer to achieving prosperity than it really was. Increasingly, Ted viewed the taxpaying American citizen as overly burdened. He termed the New Deal "goofy economics," and in comic after comic, he portrayed the American taxpayer as struggling along under inefficient and deceptive economic policies. In several cartoons, he suggested that these policies had alienated many Democrats, badly damaging Roosevelt's chances of being elected for a third term in the 1940 presidential election.

Domestic policies were not the only ones that captured Ted's attention. In March 1938, Hitler sent his army into Austria and, two days later, the German Third Reich "annexed" that nation. In October, Germany invaded Czechoslovakia. In November, Germans burned hundreds of Jewish homes, businesses, and temples, arresting and deporting 30,000 Jews, on Kristallnacht. In January 1939, the Reich Central Office for Jewish

Ted continued to turn a critical eye toward Roosevelt's economic policies of the late 1930s.

Stooging for a Sturgeon

COME ON! GET BUSY! THE CUSTOMER ORDERED CAVIAR!

Immigration was established to facilitate the "expulsion of the Jews from the living space of the German people."[10] As a child during World War I, Ted had already seen his German heritage, in which he took great pride, become a source of derision owing to the actions of German political leaders. Sensitive to this issue, he quickly grasped the growing problem in Europe.

'A Young Man's Fancy-'

What Lucky Girl Gets the Next Bouquet?

He first addressed the issue in February 1939, showing Hitler handing out bouquets of rotting fish carcasses to women representing Austria and Czechoslovakia, asking, "What Lucky Girl Gets the Next Bouquet?" But Germany's aggression was not all that caught Ted's eye. He also noticed the almost daily skirmishes between Japan and Russia over Manchuria, Mongolia, Korea, China, and other areas.[11] Since April 1939, the two countries had been engaged on the Soviet-Mongolian border. That summer, Ted addressed the effects of their muscle flexing on the rest of Asia. The expansion of Russian communism and Japanese imperialism threatened Asian nations just as Germany threatened Europe.

On August 23, 1939, the German-Soviet Nonaggression Pact was signed, prompting Ted to draw a cartoon showing the effect it would have on Europe. In Ted's cartoon, France and England, at the theater to watch a play about military arms, are surprised to find an act partnering Hitler and Stalin, since it wasn't listed in their program. Nine days later, the Germans invaded Poland, prompting British prime minister Neville Chamberlain to declare war on Germany. Two weeks later, on September 16, 1939, Soviet forces also invaded Poland, and Poland surrendered after 11 days. One of the results of the pact was that communism was now associated with Nazism, which disillusioned American communists.

Ted sensed that war was coming and that the United States was going to be drawn into it. In the political cartoons that he would draw from 1941 to 1942, Ted's stance was clear—regardless of what Americans *wanted* to do, the United States had to join the war. But in 1939, this was a controversial stance, and it is unclear whether Ted was already trying to alert Americans to get over their qualms and enter the coming war, or was just as reluctant as his fellow countrymen to see America dragged into the middle of Europe's problems. The *Journal* editorial page on which Ted's cartoons appeared began adding extended captions with isolationist messages, presenting them as if they were

Foreign affairs: Ted's first cartoon of Adolf Hitler represented the German chancellor's appropriation of the neighboring countries as a perverse courtship.

Just Warming Up

HEAVEN HELP ME WHEN THEY REACH FOR THEIR GUNS!

"Mon Dieul But It's Not On Our Program!"

'Say! Haven't We Met Before?'

The war to end wars ended no wars.

In fact, the war now being fought in Europe is but a continuation of the last war.

America foolishly got into that war twenty-two years ago.

Will America be so foolish as to get back into that same war now?

Ted's. When confronted with the cartoon version of another "war to end wars," the newspaper's interpretation was that the last one hadn't worked, so we shouldn't fall into the same trap again. But Ted's depiction of a diminutive, wounded, poorly armed, and vulnerable man representing Europe against a hulking, well-armored enemy leaves the viewer feeling distinctly uncomfortable about abandoning the former to his fate. Ironically, the editorial over which Ted's cartoon appeared begins with a quote from Charles Lindbergh and goes on to insist that the "U.S. Should Heed Col. Lindbergh's Patriotic Advice" to stay out of European wars. In his later cartoons, no one would bear the brunt of Ted's attacks as scathingly and frequently as Lindbergh.

In another cartoon, Uncle Sam is asked whether he wants to check his brains with his hat before entering the "salon of war." The characters representing "Old World Diplomacy" have done so readily. The newspaper interpreted this cartoon to mean that "Uncle Sam needs very much to 'keep his head' in these parlous warlike times. Old World Diplomacy FAILING to 'keep its head' is no example for us to follow. By 'keeping his head' Uncle Sam will keep American boys away from the battlefields of Europe."[12] A quite different interpretation is that Uncle Sam can see that European (Old World) attempts at dealing diplomatically with Hitler's aggression have left the Europeans headless before even entering the theater of war. His reaction suggests that the United States should not follow that same path. If diplomacy had failed to counter German aggression, the alternative was to go to war.

The most confusing of the cartoons from this period is one in which Uncle Sam wears earmuffs to keep from hearing the propaganda, rumors, lies, and bunk. Taken out of context, the newspaper's interpretation is convincing: "Unfortunately, Uncle Sam had laid his earmuffs aside in the years 1914 to 1917. He listened, to his distress, to war propaganda then. Today, Ulysses-like, Uncle Sam has his ears clamped down as the same old 'siren' voices are heard again."[13] However, Ted did not specify whether the propaganda being ignored was the pro- or anti-war side. The newspaper chose to believe that Uncle Sam was ignoring the pro-war propaganda, but in the context of his other cartoons from this time and his very definite pro-war position in the years to come, Ted could just as easily have been urging Uncle Sam to ignore the *anti-war* propaganda. Perhaps the final word on the subject is that after one more *Journal* cartoon, Ted published no more in that newspaper that year, suggesting that he was not comfortable with the text appended to his cartoons. The caption that was added to his final cartoon urged America to "deport all Red aliens and dissolve the Communist Party so that they may not be allowed to foist un-American doctrines upon our people."[14] But in the cartoon, the American communist that Ted drew was in the middle of giving "Stop-Hitler Speeches" in New York's Union Square—not exactly an "un-American doctrine." Evaluating all of the evidence, it appears that, contrary to the newspaper's line, Ted was of the opinion, as early as 1939, that the United States had to get into the war.

'Check Your Brains, Sir?'

Uncle Sam needs very much to "keep his head" in these parlous warlike times.
Old World Diplomacy FAILING to "keep its head" is no example for us to follow.
By "keeping his head" Uncle Sam will keep American boys away from the battlefields of Europe.

Meanwhile, despite his growing concern about events in Europe, Ted continued to work on other things. In August 1940, the Champion Recording Corporation cut the six-part LP master of *The 500 Hats of Bartholomew Cubbins*, leading to the release of Ted's first record album, which appeared on the RCA Bluebird label and later on the RCA Victor label. On October 12, 1940, *Horton Hatches the Egg* was published, and in December, the LP master for *And to Think That I Saw It on Mulberry Street* was cut.

In 1931, Rudolf F. Haffenreffer II had been approached to manage the struggling Narragansett Brewing Company. Rudolf II had an interest in Native American artifacts, assembling one of the largest private collections in the country, with an emphasis on "cigar-store Indians." He had a younger brother Rudolf Frederick "Pete" Haffenreffer III—who was in the same class as Ted at Dartmouth—as well as a younger brother Carl, who would become the company's aggressive director of marketing. Perhaps motivated by the advertisement that Ted did for Schaefer Bock Beer in March 1937 and, the following month, for the beer-canning company, American Can Company, the Haffenreffers got Ted to start an advertising campaign for the Narragansett Brewing Company. Ted capitalized on Rudolf II's interest in cigar-store Indians and created Chief 'Gansett.

The pro-isolationist opinions that appeared alongside these cartoons (this page and opposite page) for the *New York Journal* seem to contradict the spirit of Ted's own messages: that Europe is vulnerable, that "Old World Diplomacy" has failed, and that America must inevitably enter the war.

Soldiers and Sailors' Monument, Rome, (N. Y.)

This impressive triolith, or cenotaph, was presented by Leaping Owl Hoolihan, Dartmouth's first Indian graduate, to the town of his birth.

Ale to the Chief: In creating the Chief 'Gansett campaign for the Naragansett Brewing Company (bottom left and middle), Ted resurrected his affinity for Native American imagery, dating back to Dartmouth (middle left) and even, perhaps, a Springfield Halloween, circa 1911 (top left).

Use of the Native American image was not wholly new to Ted. The Dartmouth Indian was his college's mascot, and an early version of his cigar-store Indian appeared in the *Jack-O-Lantern* when Ted was editor-in-chief. Ten days after *Horton Hatches the Egg* was published, the first of Ted's advertisements for Narragansett Lager & Ale appeared in the *Boston Evening Globe*. The Chief was relaxing and pouring himself a frosty mug of Narry Ale that, according to the ever-present Seussian cat, was simply "Too Good to Miss!" The following week, it was revealed that "Boston newspapers will feature Chief 'Gansett in amusing cartoon-type advertising for the remainder of the year. Drawn by the famous Dr. Seuss, nationally famous cartoonist and creator of successful advertising campaigns of this nature—these Narragansett advertisements will attract wide attention. . . ."[15] Accompanying that advertisement was a Chief 'Gansett that presumably would serve as the prototype for the one emblazoned on the wonderful Narragansett beer tray that has become such a favorite among collectors.

For Thanksgiving, Ted reminded everyone that Narragansett beer "Goes Great Guns with TURKEY!" After Christmas, Ted took January off from the Narragansett campaign to work on the final National Motor Boat Show of his six-and-a-half-year stint with Esso-marine, after which he was able to return to do some subway ads for Flit. As 1941 began, his "Seein' Things" calendar series was available for the last time. Early in the year, he worked with the writers of *Unusual Occupations,* which produced a short film about his sculptures that was released in October 1941.

The Narragansett ads would return in February 1942, by which time Ted had penned his first submission to *PM* newspaper. It showed Italian fascist propagandist Virginio Gayda suspended in front of a typewriter, exactly as the copywriter had been positioned in Ted's series of posters on advertising (see page 175). In Ted's illustration, Gayda punches away at the keys while his enormous typewriter spews forth clouds of poisonous thought. Over the next few months, *PM* would occasionally run that image when addressing Gayda's pronouncements. Meanwhile, Ted continued to work on the Narragansett campaign. In addition to scenes of parlor games like bridge, tiddlywinks, and billiards, Ted's ads uncharacteristically addressed sports like skiing, wrestling, and baseball, trying to appeal to beer drinkers. Also, modeled on his print ads, Ted produced a Narragansett coaster, a menu insert, and a Narragansett Bock Beer poster. A common misconception holds that Ted graduated from Williams College with Rudy Haffenreffer III in 1938 and, as a favor to him, designed a beer can in 1963 for their twenty-fifth reunion. But Ted, who graduated from Dartmouth in 1925 (as did Rudy), had nothing to do with the Williams Purple Cow lager beer can.

More beer here! Ted made ads with holiday and sporting themes (top left, top right, bottom right).

Meanwhile, *PM* used its first Seuss cartoon (top middle) on several occasions.

Ted's ads inspired marketing gimmicks like a beer coaster (middle left), poster (bottom left), and tray (opposite page, bottom right).

* * *

The world owes Ted's next re-entry into political cartooning to another speech from Roosevelt. In April 1941, the president criticized Charles Lindbergh and other Americans who expressed the opinion that the German-led Axis powers would defeat Britain. *PM*'s complete edition[16] for that day contains Ted's first political cartoon for *PM,* other than the Virginio Gayda spot. It pictures Lindbergh piloting a plane trailing the banner: IT'S SMART TO SHOP AT ADOLF'S. ALL VICTORIES GUARANTEED. In the very next issue, on the day that Lindbergh resigned his post in the Army Air Corps Reserve in response to criticism from President Roosevelt, Ted's illustration of the "Lindbergh Quarter" replaced the American eagle with an ostrich. Ted had found the perfect embodiment of Lindbergh's isolationism in the ostrich—hiding its head in the ground so that it can't see danger while its massive body is left open for easy attack. For the third day in a row, Ted addressed Lindbergh's views, this time depicting the Lindy Ostrich Service handing out strap-on ostrich-head bonnets, which claimed to relieve Hitler Headaches.

These three cartoons marked Ted's return to the arena of political cartooning. On May 4, 1941, he did his first cover illustration for the newspaper; four days later, his second—and Ted's career at *PM* was up and running.

Ted attacked the line of thought held by the America First group, which believed that America had too many problems of its own to be sending its money and resources overseas to help other countries. To illustrate this point of view, Ted drew cartoons of the United States dawdling, both in sending aid to Britain and in entering the war itself, postponing the inevitable until it was too late to do any good. He satirized the people who had convinced themselves that if Hitler conquered Europe, he would leave the United States alone. He shouted down those who claimed that Roosevelt's policies were more damaging to our country than Hitler's policies would be. But he illustrated his points with the same odd menagerie of beasts that he used in his advertisements and children's books. Situated as they were in a block of newspaper text, Ted's cartoons—which looked like nothing else in the hard-news section—really grabbed readers' attention.

Ted did his last Narragansett ad of the year in the first week of May 1941, followed the next week by one for Dupont Cellophane. A week later, he signed a contract to provide *PM* with a minimum of four cartoons per week

"Since when did we swap our ego for an ostrich?"

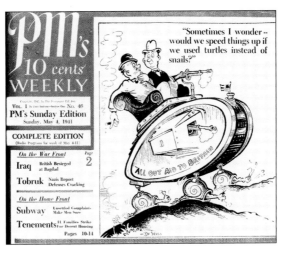

and put his advertising work on hold, perhaps in deference to *PM,* which did not accept any advertising. However, Ted did do a series of "bulbsnatching" ads for General Electric later that year and would begin a campaign for New Departure ball bearings the following year. He did not share all of the radical liberal views of many of his fellow *PM* staffers; not every corporation was evil, and earning money didn't necessarily make you selfish. His motivation for working with *PM* was primarily to pound away at the isolationists.

Being around the very liberal-minded thinkers at *PM* likely made Ted more politically aware. In September 1941, in a shortwave-radio broadcast from Berlin to South America, announcer Don Juan, speaking of the United States, said, "There are too many prominent Jews in powerful circles in the government. There are too many Jews who control the North American radio and the North American press. There are too many Jews who work in the

In the spring of 1941, Ted returned to politics full tilt. These *PM* cartoons are unadulterated Ted—Seussian characters and creatures spreading his anti-isolationist views.

Communique: "The annihilation is proceeding according to schedule."

'Remember . . . One More Lollypop, and Then You All Go Home!'

A contract with
PM afforded Ted
the opportunity to
hammer home his
conviction that
America must enter
the war (this page).

Ted pulled no
punches when
airing his
thoughts about
anti-Semitism in
America (opposite
page, top and
middle).

Ted goaded the
anti-war holdouts
with the GOPstrich
(opposite page,
bottom).

United States as newspapermen, as commentators, and as propagandists."[17] On that same night, Charles Lindbergh gave a speech at an America First rally, in which he said of Jewish Americans, "Their greatest danger to this country lies in their large ownership of and influence in our motion pictures, our press, our radio, and our government."[18] Ted responded with a cartoon of Lindbergh shoveling fetid garbage off the back of the Nazi Anti-Semite Stink Wagon.

At an America First rally later that month, Senator Gerald P. Nye supported Lindbergh. "As Lindbergh said, without being anti-Semitic, those of the Jewish faith are contributing to the cause of inter-vention. Their interest is very natural. If I were one of them, I should feel as they do towards those who have persecuted my people. But I should not try to let my natural hatred blind me to the first and best interest of my own country."[19] A few days later, *PM*'s front page carried Ted's reaction to Lindbergh and Nye, showing the American eagle in a stockade, with a note on its beak reminding readers that America is part Jewish.

In June, the Germans invaded the Soviet Union and fought their way toward major Russian cities. The sieges of Leningrad and Moscow began in September. A movement arose in Congress to repeal the American neutrality acts, or at least to revise them to allow for guns on American ships. But there were still "obstructionists" who argued against United States involvement. So Ted created the GOPstrich—the offspring of the Republican elephant and the isolationist ostrich—which, though small, squawked enough to make it seem much larger than it actually was.

Occupied with the fighting in Russia, Germany began to appear as less of an immediate threat to the United States than Japan was. In the summer of 1941, America placed an embargo on exports to Japan of crude oil and aviation gasoline. The conflict escalated rapidly that fall, as Premier Konoe Fumimaro and his cabinet, who had worked to keep Japan in peaceful nego-tiations with the United States, resigned. The new leaders appeared to be headed for war; Captain Hideo Hiraide warned, "The Imperial Japanese Navy is confident that it can oppose any force the U.S.A. might throw against it in the Pacific. . . . It is to be hoped that the U.S.A. realizes Japan's sea strength and will consequently follow a cautious policy."[20] In November, the House of Representatives voted to repeal the neutrality acts by a margin of 18 votes. Four days later, Premier Hideki Tojo and Foreign Minister Shigenori Togo addressed a special session of the Diet, voicing their intention to continue expansion into China and reiterating their ties to the Nazi regime.[21] By the end of the month, Secretary of State Cordell Hull's ultimatum to the Japanese ambassador and special peace envoy was that Japan break its Axis alliance, remove its troops from China, and end its support for the regimes it had established there.[22]

Ted did not appear to take the Japanese threat to the United States nearly as seriously as he did the one from Germany. In relation to America, Ted usually depicted Japan as a character of diminutive stature, making the type of threats that a kid makes to his much older brother. He did see Japan as a threat to less powerful countries, however, and sized his Japanese images accordingly.

Regarding his political cartoons for *PM*, Ted explained:

> I got irritated into becoming a political cartoonist by one of our nation's most irritating heroes, the late Col. Charles Augustus Lindbergh.
>
> In 1940, when Adolf Hitler was putting out the lights and bestowing terror on the people of Europe, Col. Lindbergh was bestowing defeatism and appeasement on the people of the U.S.A. . . .
>
> Lindbergh and his America Firsters and their sour-note choir leaders, Senators Burton K. Wheeler and Gerald Nye, seemed to be on the

radio or at a Madison Square Garden rally every night preaching the gospel that we must not get involved because we were licked before we started. . . .

A Gallup poll established the fact that 70 to 85% of all Americans were strongly opposed to any involvement in the war.

And so was I.

But I also believed that we had absolutely no choice in the matter and had better by God get prepared for a war that sure as hell was going to sock us.

And on the night of June 14, 1940, while Paris was being occupied by the klanking tanks of the Nazis and I was listening on my radio, I found that I could no longer keep my mind on drawing pictures of Horton The Elephant. I found myself drawing pictures of Lindbergh The Ostrich.

'Well, It Looks Like the Mighty Hunter Has Us Convinced'

The next thing I knew I was newspaper P.M.'s political cartoonist in charge of Lindbergh, Wheeler and Nye. . . .

The New Yorker magazine dismissed us as "a bunch of young fogeys." But I think we were, rather, a bunch of honest but slightly cockeyed crusaders, and I still have prideful memories of working along side . . . dozens of other hard-working souls who helped Marshall Field lose

Final Warning
"You gimme a brick to bean you with, or I'll paste you with a pie!"

Ted felt Japan's power was relative, posing little threat to the United States and England (top and middle) but proving overwhelming to less powerful nations (bottom).

"If I chew you up, honey, it's only to save you from the British!"

236

thirty million dollars backing a truly unique newspaper that refused to accept advertising.

Whatever I lacked . . . (and it was plenty) . . . as a polished practitioner of the subtle art of caricature, I did become prolifically proficient in venting my spleen.[23]

Of course, once the Japanese attacked Pearl Harbor on December 7, 1941, everything changed, literally overnight, when the United States Senate unanimously endorsed President Roosevelt's demand for a declaration of war against Japan. It was no longer necessary to get America to go to war. As Ted had been warning all along, the war had come to America.

On December 11, 1941, the United States declared war on Germany and Italy. The next day, American authorities seized the *Kungsholm*—the ship on which Ted had gotten the inspiration for *Mulberry Street*—for the transport of troops. Ted, like his ship, was redirected. On the same day that the *Kungsholm* changed jobs, the first of Ted's cartoons promoting the purchase of defense savings bonds and stamps to raise money for the military effort appeared in *PM*. He did three such cartoons in the first week alone, relying again on his success with Flit for a bug-spray parody.

When everything changed: The world-altering wake-up call of Pearl Harbor was not lost on Ted (top and middle). He soon refocused his cartooning efforts on raising funds for the war effort (bottom left and right).

"Ceiling? Heck! She's growing through the Roof!"

TO WIN THIS WAR ... MORE PEOPLE HAVE GOT TO ENJOY RIDING IN FEWER CARS

It has been reported that Ted's work was used by Nelson Rockefeller's Office of the Coordinator on Inter-American Affairs (CIAA), which reprinted his *PM* cartoons and distributed them in places like Latin America.[24] Ted also began doing work directly for the government through the Office of Emergency Management in late April, producing advertisements aimed at getting readers to reduce their driving and to carpool in order to save gas and rubber needed for the war, as well as to try to keep a cap on the cost of living.

This sort of work in the first five months of the war, mostly in periodicals but also for the government, led to a civilian War Savings Commendation for Ted on May 27, 1942. He then assisted the War Production Board with a campaign to get people to conserve resources and to salvage and recycle items like scrap metal, rubber, fat, and other materials needed for the war effort. For the Treasury Department, Ted urged people to take the money that they saved and earned through these methods and use it to buy war savings bonds and stamps.

This war called for a different mind-set. Everyday items suddenly took on more significance. A newspaper was no longer just a means of finding out the latest information about the progress of the war. Old paper was chemically reduced to pulp to make new paper and was, for example, made into cartons in which the Red Cross shipped dried human plasma. Old rags weren't for cleaning—woolen rags were shredded and the fibers rewoven into blankets and clothing for the troops, or combined with recycled paper to make roofing material. Metals of many sorts were needed but scarce. Tin, for example, was in very short supply because the Japanese-occupied countries accounted for two-thirds of the world's supply. Since "tin cans" were really made of steel with a very thin coat of tin, it was estimated that it would take 28 families, saving a can a day, an entire year to salvage the amount of tin required for just one medium tank. It was one thing to have a vague notion that there was a rubber shortage and that the government wanted you to drive less so that you wouldn't need to replace your tires as often. But it was quite different to learn that there was enough rubber in a raincoat to make a gas mask, enough zinc in a toy locomotive to make a Jeep carburetor, and enough steel in a pair of skates for seven hand grenades.[25]

In Germany, the forced emigration of Jews, at their own expense, had begun in January 1939, in order to purge them from "every sphere of life of the German people"[26] and "cleanse German living space of Jews in a legal manner."[27] On January 20, 1942, government leaders and high-ranking Nazi Party officials gathered at a villa in a wealthy section of Berlin near Wannsee Lake to discuss a course of action, euphemistically termed "The Final Solution." Reinhard Heydrich, the chief of the Reich Security Main Office, assembled officials from different Nazi agencies with the intention of working out some of the practical and bureaucratic details that would be involved in ridding Europe of its estimated 11 million Jews, including the likely assistance or resistance Germany could expect from 35 European and Asian countries in transporting their Jews to camps for extermination.

Even though Ted would not have known at the time about the secret conference, his experience at *PM* clearly made him increasingly aware of the treatment of the Jews in Germany. Ted viewed the very concept of such racial hatred as patently absurd. Although he was not yet moved to campaign against anti-Semitism, the cartoon that appeared in *PM* the day after the Wannsee Conference serendipitously shows Hitler as an infant refusing to drink milk that came from "Jewish-sounding" Holstein cows.

As the threat of Japan grew, so did the

Ted's promotion of war bonds led to work for the Office of Emergency Management (opposite page, top and middle) and the Treasury Department (opposite page, bottom).

All the while, Ted was urging Americans to ration (this page, top).

Ted's growing awareness of Hitler's anti-Semitism was evident in early 1942 (this page, bottom).

Mein Early Kampf   **by Adolf Hitler**

June 5, 1889
I reject milk from Holstein cows as Non-Aryan

stature of the Japanese images in Ted's cartoons. After Pearl Harbor, Americans were actively afraid of Japanese attempts to conquer more of the world. An invasion of the West Coast now seemed like a real possibility.

This concern over Japan rapidly expanded to include people of Japanese descent living in the United States. The growing suspicions were reflected in Ted's February 13, 1942, *PM* cartoon, in which he portrayed orderly lines of caricatured Japanese men stretching from Washington through Oregon and into California. The men are receiving packages of explosives while a man from the "honorable fifth column"[28] looks out over the Pacific Ocean with a telescope, waiting for a signal from Japan to start the domestic terrorism. Less than a week later, on February 19, 1942, U.S. Executive Order 9066 called for the relocation of Japanese Americans on the West Coast to internment camps.[29]

Ted's cartoon reveals that even those who were arguing for equal treatment of blacks and Jews in America and around the world felt threatened enough by the Japanese to accept internment camps. Ted was of German descent, and internment camps for Japanese Americans were theoretically no different from ones for German Americans. Rather than make any kind of comparison between this concentration of Japanese Americans in camps and the gathering of Jews in extermination camps in Europe, Ted, like the populace, accepted the policy. That month, an article in *Newsweek* complimented Ted's work for *PM*. A month after Pearl Harbor, fear had trumped ideology. As a result of this cartoon, the opinion has been expressed that "Dr. Seuss's campaign for civil rights and against racism and anti-Semitism had one major blind spot: Americans of Japanese descent."[30] Although this statement is reasonable when comparing this cartoon to the general view of Dr.

Far East fears:
Ted honed in on the growing threat of Japan (top) and the resulting xenophobia toward Japanese Americans (bottom).

240

Seuss as a champion for equality (derived from his children's books), it must be placed within the proper context of his work overall and, specifically, at *PM*. In truth, Ted had not yet begun his campaign against those forms of prejudice. It is true that, five months earlier, he had addressed the issue of anti-Semitism. But at that time, Ted wasn't really beginning a crusade; he was responding with his usual irritation to Charles Lindbergh, who had issued anti-Semitic statements. From April to December 1941, Ted's goal was to get Americans to realize that no matter how much we wanted to avoid doing so, our country had to enter the war. Once we entered the war, from January to April 1942, his focus changed to raising support, both monetary and moral, for the war effort. It wasn't until the period from April to July 1942 that the bulk of Ted's work addressing issues of racism and anti-Semitism appeared. So the cartoon revealing suspicions about Japanese Americans predated by several months Ted's first real focus on issues of equality.

Jokes at the expense of various ethnic groups and minorities were a matter of course for humorists, including Ted. Experiencing anti-German prejudice personally during World War I had sensitized him. Encountering many cultures during his travels had broadened his mind. But it was his involvement with *PM* that provided the true impetus for change. Soon Ted would be portraying the Japanese people in a more sympathetic light, even in the scripts he would later write for propaganda films. As of February 1942, Ted had not yet made that change. But it could be argued that reassessing his reaction as a German American to the internment of Japanese Americans may have contributed to his changing attitude. Within two months, he began a series of cartoons about anti-Semitism and racism.

But was there a particular incident that triggered this change in Ted? Although he never addressed this question directly—and, as such, it cannot be definitively answered—analysis of the work he produced and the timing involved suggests that there may have been a single defining moment. On March 26, 1942, the upcoming week's issue of the *Saturday Evening Post* appeared on newsstands with an article by Milton Mayer titled "The Case Against the Jew." Although Mayer's intention was to analyze the state of the American Jew, he was unable to hide his bias. *PM*'s leading front-page headline for the next two days concerned the *Saturday Evening Post*'s "attack" on Jews. *PM* editor Ralph Ingersoll devoted the first three pages of the March 27, 1942, issue to the matter, including his full-page editorial response:

Milton Mayer's article in the *Saturday Evening Post* . . .
is to be taken very seriously. I don't know how the Jews
will react to it. I presume that everyone with a Jewish
grandmother will be a little frightened—and hurt. I do
know how the anti-Semites will feel about it. They will
feel fine. But the article that was blazoned across the
newsstands of America yesterday was more than just
another nauseous attempt to justify Adolf Hitler's
contention that the proper place for Jews is in a ghetto
being spat on. The article, in what still is the best-known
magazine in America . . . was a glove slapped across the
American mouth. Its challenge was not alone to Jew or
Gentile—its challenge was to this country as a whole. . . .
As an American, there rose in me, while I read it, a deep
sense of indignation. In its polished cynicism, it said
there was no such concept as a government of the
people, by the people, for the people regarding their race,
color, or creed. It said this was a Gentile country of
shopkeepers without morals . . . competing only for the
privilege of exploiting one another. . . . Milton Mayer put
it this way:

"They [the Jews] know that every war since
Napoleon has been followed by collapse, and they know
that the postwar collapse will remind a bitter and
bewildered nation that 'the Jew got us into the war.'"

This statement is a bald lie. . . .

America is great . . . because of the fact that not
races or creeds, but the people themselves are what is
important. Neither the colors they come in nor the creeds
their fathers handed down to them shall be allowed to
hinder nor to help them in their pursuit of happiness. . . .
This is the American principle that is worth working and
worth dying for. Worth shouting for, with your hands
behind your back and the noose around your neck: "I
only regret that I have but one life to lose for my country."

. . . Stop plucking at our sleeve while we take aim at

PM's reply to
a piece in the
*Saturday Evening
Post* perceived
as anti-Semitic?
A scathing
full-page editorial,
accompanied by
a Seussian barb
(opposite page,
top). In less than
two weeks, Ted
followed up
with a wholesale
condemnation of
bigotry (opposite
page, bottom).

242

our enemies! We are too busy making the America that
you despise.[31]

    PM received so many requests for copies of the editorial that the paper
ran it again six days later. On the page preceding that second printing, surrounded by a selection of letters in support of *PM*'s denouncement of the
"Case Against the Jew" article, Ted's cartoon against anti-Semitism appeared,
with American Nazis trying to convince Uncle Sam to allow anti-Semitism to
lop off both his hands. Ted later would single out Ingersoll as one of the "honest but slightly cockeyed crusaders" of whom he held "prideful memories,"
and he was obviously moved by Ingersoll's response to this issue. Fewer than
two weeks later, Ted drew another cartoon concerning discrimination within
the United States. In this piece, Jewish labor is segregated and controlled by
prejudiced employers; Negro labor is relegated even further behind the Jews.

This was the beginning of the Dr. Seuss we know and
admire. The *Saturday Evening Post* had marked the
biggest break of Ted's career by publishing his first
cartoon. Nearly 15 years later, it marked the biggest
change as well. By the end of July, Ted's stand against
prejudice was firmly established.

    Ted took a break from *PM* during most of Sep-
tember, probably during the time he and Helen were
driving back from their summer on the West Coast.
When he returned, his political cartoons drew com-
pliments and proposals from the editors of the *Nation*
and *New Republic*. But despite invitations to contribute work to these publications, Ted had plans of
his own. He'd been telling people to get involved in
the war for a year and a half. He no longer felt that
this was good enough. In October, he applied for a
commission with Naval Intelligence. While the navy
did a background check on Ted, he finished his stint
at *PM*, returning to an old theme. In the House of
Representatives, Bill 860, the teenage draft bill, was
intended to lower the draft age from 20 to 18. But
Oklahoma senator Josh Lee had included a rider on

the bill that prohibited the sale of liquor in areas adjacent to military posts, and the concern was that there were few stores in the country that were not near some kind of military establishment. Some people were concerned that

The Guy Who Makes a Mock of Democracy

"I pledge allegiance
To the Flag of the United States
And to the Republic for which it
stands.
One Nation indivisible,
With Liberty and Justice for
all . . .
(Except the boys and girls
I keep down in the cellar)."

Your Nutty Aunt Carrie Is Loose Again!

Buck Bilbo Rides Again

the need to draft 18- and 19-year-olds would not be met while debate over the rider prolonged the passage of the bill. On the day that *PM* ran an article headlined "Prohibition Threat Hangs over Nation," Ted published his first anti-Prohibition cartoon in nearly a decade, with a hatchet-wielding Carrie Nation once more riding atop a crazed Prohibition beast.

The following month, one of the issues Ted addressed was the filibuster organized by Mississippi senator Theodore Gilmore Bilbo, intended to stall a bill to abolish the poll tax—a fee collected before residents were allowed to vote. The pro-poll-tax bloc was generally from southern states. The northern, liberal anti-poll-tax bloc felt that the fee was discriminatory and prevented poor residents from voting; one article cited Bilbo's Mississippi as a state "where it costs $2 to vote and less than 10 per cent of the citizens do."[32] Consequently, it was also viewed as a means for political corruption: A Virginia audit revealed deficits among 40 percent of the state's treasurers, totaling more than a million dollars, suggesting that the deficits were the result of a failure to collect poll taxes from favored citizens.[33] Bilbo intended to hold the Senate floor and talk for 30 days, or yield the floor to congressional friends who were similarly in favor of the poll tax, until the current Congress expired in January 1943.

Ted's cartoon isn't exceptionally enlightening regarding the poll tax. Nor does it take Senator Bilbo to task for his past, including a grand jury investigation into whether he had accepted graft and a 25-to-1 state legislature vote in favor of asking him to resign. Corruption, divorce, and a belief that "all Negroes should be sent to live in Africa"[34] might have been fodder for a political cartoon about Bilbo. However, Ted appears to have been much more interested in drawing a really good filibuster.

In December, while waiting to hear back from the navy, Ted marked the first anniversary of the bombing of Pearl Harbor in a cartoon showing the offspring of the union between Japan and Germany. He also provided one last warning that Hitler's ultimate legacy to the world would be racial and religious prejudice.

Ted reserved a particular distaste for French premier Pierre Laval, reaching for new ways to describe just how low a human being could descend in his estimation. In April, he had depicted Laval as a rancid rat that a Hitlerian cat had dragged back to the doorstep of French president Philippe Pétain. The following month, the rat was even smaller—low enough to walk under a dachshund's belly (with Hitler's face on the dachshund, of course). The next month, working on an even smaller scale, Ted drew a conversation between two cockroaches in which one asks the other if he thinks that Laval goes a bit too far.

Unable to get any smaller without drawing microbes, Ted switched his approach and tried to illustrate the depths to which Laval would demean himself for Hitler, showing him first as a diving board on which Hitler bounces and, the next day, as one of two dogs strapped beneath Hitler's feet (along with Mussolini), propelled forward by the "carrot" dangling in front of them. In place of the metaphorical carrot is the even more metaphorically ripe rotten fish carcass labeled "War Spoils." But even Ted's depiction of Laval as a subservient dog hoping to feed on the rotting scraps of Europe discarded in Hitler's wake did not convey fully how loathsome Laval was to Ted. In September, Ted opted for the proverbial "he'd sell his own mother" routine in a cartoon that shows Laval selling Mother France down the river to Hitler, rationalizing that she would have died soon anyway, so he might as well make some money from her while he could.

In November, Ted claimed that Laval's German allegiance was so

Married Exactly One Year Today

"Put your finger here, pal . . ."

While awaiting his military commission, Ted railed against racism (opposite page, top) and congressional confusion and corruption (opposite page, middle and bottom).

He marked the anniversary of Pearl Harbor with eloquent reminders of how the world had changed (this page).

"Crawl Out and Round Me Up Another 400,000 Frenchmen!"

Copyright 1942 Field Publication

extreme that he ate dachshund for Thanksgiving. In the cartoon, it is Laval who is on the serving platter in front of all the dachshunds. Recall that Ted traced the beginning of his involvement with *PM* to the day German tanks entered Paris. So when the BBC reported on December 16, 1942, "that Laval would offer Hitler a new French army of 200,000 Fascists to be used in France to relieve German occupational troops,"[35] Ted really had to reach down deep to convey how completely and utterly repugnant he found the Frenchman. In his cartoon published the next day, from the depths of a brooding cave, the dark lord Hitler sends forth the albino-pale, nearly sightless, slithering creature Laval to crawl into the daylight and bring him back new minions.

In the two months it took the officials to evaluate Ted's character before clearing him to enter the navy, he had already been offered a position in the army. On the last day of the year, Ted was given a temporary appointment and was soon ordered to proceed to California. On January 7, 1943, he was officially inducted into the army and was commissioned Captain, Information and Education Division, A.U.S. (Army of the United States), three days later. Although he had several more cartoons prepared for *PM*, including a wonderful dragon mobile he used to illustrate one of the problems that Hitler's forces faced on the Russian front, the last of Ted's cartoons published in

PM appeared on the day before his army induction. He'd spent nearly two years with *PM*, trying to change American views—in the process, he had himself undergone a big change.

Parting shots: Before entering the army, Ted truly outdid himself in expressing his utter contempt for French premier Laval (top). Even this unpublished piece (bottom) shows Ted in fine, fighting trim.

246

CHAPTER 18
Taxing the Axis

During World War II, 37 percent of the United States armed forces had less than a high school education.[1] General George C. Marshall, the army chief of staff, ordered a series of orientation films to explain to the troops why they were fighting. An independent Signal Corps office was set up in Hollywood, and some of the top people in the movie industry were recruited for duty,[2] including Major Frank Capra, who began his active duty with the Signal Corps in Washington, D.C., on February 15, 1942.

By the time Ted was assigned to Capra's unit in January 1943, it consisted of Hollywood directors, screenwriters, novelists, and journalists. Capra was a seasoned professional, between directorial duties for *Arsenic and Old Lace* and *It's a Wonderful Life*. In contrast, Ted was a novice who didn't know the first thing about basic movie equipment and whose writing had been limited to cartoons and children's books. When recalling his stint at the Fox studio in Hollywood ("Fort Fox," as it was called by those stationed there), Ted remembered Capra's patience as a teacher and his abilities as an editor—high praise from someone who trusted few people other than his wife, Helen, to offer advice about his children's books. Regarding one of Ted's training-film scripts, Capra is reported to have told him, "The first thing you have to do in writing is find out if you're saying anything."[3] Capra then underlined the sentences in which Ted had advanced the plot. "He taught me conciseness, and I learned a lot about the juxtaposition of words and visual images,"[4] Ted remembered.

During Capra's three years of military service, his unit

Reporting for duty:
Captain Theodor S. Geisel.

produced 17 orientation and propaganda films, a weekly compilation of war footage for the military leadership called the *Staff Film Report* (starting in 1944), and biweekly newsreels called *Army-Navy Screen Magazine.*[5] It is quite natural to want to ascribe authorship or directorship of these wartime films to specific individuals and to analyze their contributions relative to what we know of the art that they created in their civilian lives. After all, Ted was not the only future luminary toiling in Capra's unit. Among the other people who worked on scripts for these movies were John Cheever, Irving Wallace, James Hilton, William Saroyan, Irwin Shaw, Lillian Hellman, Ben Hecht, John Huston, and *Casablanca* screenwriters Julius and Philip Epstein. Attributing credit for specific contributions to these orientation and propaganda films is, however, a risky proposition and can be very misleading. As Capra wrote to those in his command, "You are working for a common cause. Your personal egos and idiosyncrasies are unimportant. There will be no personal credit for your work, either on the screen or in the press. The only press notices we are anxious to read are those of American victories!"[6]

Further complicating matters, everything had to be filtered through the government. For example, if a draft of a script portraying the Soviet Union as our ally was successful, governmental reviewers might then question whether the writer was a communist sympathizer, and the writer might be dismissed, after which a new writer would take over.

Such problems were exacerbated after the war, when many people in the film industry were called before the House Un-American Activities Committee (HUAC) to defend themselves against charges that they were communists. Moreover, once we were no longer at war, the films' portrayal of people from different cultures looked blatantly offensive. For both reasons, many people who worked on these propaganda films tried to dissociate themselves afterward.

What film-studies professor and author Charles J. Maland said about Frank Capra in relation to these films can also be applied to Ted: "If we do discover some of Capra's social vision . . . it is probably because his vision coincided with . . . American policy and not vice versa."[7] The lack of credits, the changes of personnel, and the numerous revisions to fit governmental edicts and policies all conspired to create films that are attributable primarily to the army rather than to individual participants. With that consideration, however, some of Ted's contributions are known and serve as an interesting contrast to the children's author's better-known work.

Like the other members of his unit, Ted worked at the Fox studio at 1421 Western Avenue during the day and returned home each evening. Initially judging that his talents were better suited to animation than to dramatic documentary filmmaking, Capra assigned Ted to work under Leonard Spigelgass, who supervised the production of the *Army-Navy Screen Magazine*. Ted helped create Private SNAFU, a recurring character in these newsreels.

Ted had always had a knack for selling things to people by using humor. He employed the same strategy to sell army policy and, not surprisingly, the short animated Private SNAFU cartoons quickly became favorites. Ted worked with Warner Bros. stalwarts like directors Charles M. "Chuck" Jones, Isadore "Friz" Freleng, Robert "Bob" Clampett, and Frank Tashlin to produce a series of roughly 30 episodes of the bumbling GI whose misadventures were intended to teach our servicemen how to avoid serious military mishaps, from contracting diseases to leaking classified information. Mel Blanc added a voice similar to Bugs Bunny's, and Robert C. Bruce did some narration for episodes like *THE CHOW HOUND* and *OUTPOST*. Carl W. Stalling provided the scores. Later, animation crews from UPA, Harman-Ising, and MGM worked on Private SNAFU shorts, although apparently not all of them were completed.

SNAFU does not look like a Dr. Seuss character; watching him is very much like watching Bugs Bunny or any other Warner Bros. cartoon from that period. The design was reportedly based on a model sheet done by Art Heineman and further developed by Chuck Jones. Special-effects wizard Ray Harryhausen helped design the models. According to Harryhausen, "Dr. Seuss . . . was in charge of the Snafu character."[8] Ted contributed to the storyboards, but his main influence is observable in the scripts that he wrote for many of the episodes, particularly those produced during the first six months.

The series debuted with Chuck Jones's *PRIVATE SNAFU: Coming! SNAFU!* in June 1943, which introduced the Private SNAFU character as "the goofiest soldier in the U.S. Army." He was "a patriotic, conscientious guy," but his laziness and his impatience usually resulted in disaster. Although the films' standards were relaxed for the all-male military audience, relative to those for theatrical release (even allowing for some nudity), the limitations on language could be stretched only to allow words like "hell" or "damn."

Accordingly, *Coming! SNAFU!* explains the private's acronym as Situation Normal—All *Fouled* Up, rather than using the expletive that the *F* is known to represent (a common SNAFU euphemism). When spelling it out in the cartoon, there is a prolonged pause at the *F*, which shakes before *FOULED* appears. The film closes with a view of a horse's ass, on which the words "The End" appear, while the narrator delivers the closing line, "This is SNAFU."

Ted's influence can readily be seen in the series' second entry. *PRIVATE SNAFU: "Gripes"* was released in July 1943.[9] SNAFU is on kitchen patrol—scrubbing a frying pan with his hands while peeling potatoes with his feet—vowing that he'd make changes if *he* ran the army.

The Technical Fairy arrives—a cross between SNAFU's guardian angel and fairy godfather, with a permanent five o'clock shadow, ever-present cigar, and Brooklyn accent—and grants SNAFU's wish:

> I heard you sayin' that everything stank—
> That you'd run things different if you had more rank—
> So as Technical Fairy, I've got a good notion
> To give you a chance, pal, here's a promotion.
> You're MasterSarge-SuperSarge-Hoopity-Do.
> You're boss of the works, now take over, SNAFU!

With zoot suits replacing uniforms under SNAFU's relaxed regulations, no one gets around to menial chores like cleaning the latrine. As expected, SNAFU's unit is completely unprepared when the Germans attack. The Technical Fairy concludes:

> The moral, Snafu, is: The harder you work,
> The sooner we're gonna beat Hitler, that jerk!

What could be better than a children's author teaming up with animators to educate troops about beating Hitler? How about *two* children's book authors collaborating to educate troops about beating malaria? Captain W. Munro Leaf, as well known for Ferdinand the bull as Ted was for Horton the elephant, was assigned to act as a public-relations consultant to the United States Medical Corps. Doctors there wanted to teach the troops in the tropics

Ted's touch is all over this pamphlet (opposite page) about preventing malaria.

about the dangers of that mosquito-borne disease. Technical manuals had already been distributed, but they had not done the trick. Just as Captain Geisel was doing with the SNAFU cartoons, Captain Leaf decided to put the message into a story that might be more palatable for the average soldier. He wrote the story in longhand and roughed out a presentation. Once it was approved, Ted was called in to provide the illustrations.

she's dying to *meet you*.

The result was a charming little booklet titled *This Is Ann,* which anthropomorphizes the anopheles mosquito as Ann, who forsakes drinking "whisky, gin, beer, or rum Coke" for her true passion—blood. The army's anti-malaria units had drained areas of standing or stagnant water where anopheles mosquitoes bred. They had spread poison in the areas that couldn't be drained. Still, they could not hope to eradicate all the malaria-bearing mosquitoes. It was up to the individual soldiers to protect themselves. This was pretty dry material. But in Ted's playful hands, with Leaf's informal text, suddenly it was much more engaging.

. . she drinks Blood

A few months after *This Is Ann* was first printed for the troops in August 1943, Ted wrote:

> I did the illustrations, of which I am not overly proud, in my spare time . . . between sessions on the rifle range . . . and . . . in the Army Motion Picture Studios. The booklet is interesting for one main reason. It is, to my knowledge, one of the few booklets signed by the Chief of Staff and the Adjutant General that is completely goofy and informal in style and content. . . . As an old Flit salesman, I find that I am of occasional use in doing semi-educational propaganda against the mosquito.[10]

*A*nd she stands on her head to get it.

She jabs that beak of hers in like a drill and sucks up the juice.

This Is Ann has become one of the more coveted (and costly) pieces of Seussiana. The assumption has been that few copies remain after the majority were lost or discarded in the many decades since it was published. But that line of thought fails to take into account the sheer number of booklets that were printed. A minimum of two

and don't forget that a hole this big

in your net can cook you.

Ted's sketch
betraying his
concern about his
writing abilities
(top) was all for
naught. His unique
style came through
loud and clear
(middle and
bottom) in training
films that
entertained as they
educated.

printings were done in 1943 and, according to Ted, 500,000 copies were shipped to troops by that Thanksgiving. Another printing was made in 1944. It seems that a surplus was discovered and, later that year, the government obliterated the copyright information on the inside back cover of the remaining 1943 copies by printing a negative image of one of Ted's illustrations over it. Yet another printing was done in 1944 and one—or more—in 1945. All told, with at least seven editions, there were probably more than 750,000 copies of the booklet printed.

After *This Is Ann* was published, Ted could turn his attention back to the next SNAFU installment. Some insight into the creative processes back at Fort Fox can be gained from the sketches Ted made during his time in the army. In one drawing, Ted and another man cower while two officers fence in front of them, yelling "Take it out" and "Put it in." Regarding his work on the Private SNAFU segments specifically, Ted drew a scene inside the *Army-Navy Screen Magazine* office with script pages littering the floor and a handgun sitting ominously on the desk. At first glance, it looks as if Ted is contemplating using the gun on himself, perhaps in frustration over the script. Upon close inspection, however, it is at least as likely that the image was intended to suggest that one of his superiors at the *Army-Navy Screen Magazine* may have committed suicide after reading one of Ted's scripts.

Ted's hand is evident in the August episode, *PRIVATE SNAFU: SPIES,* which follows the gradual revelation of a military secret through SNAFU's negligence. Spies are everywhere, including one disguised as a horse pulling a cart. One look at the "horse's" haunches pegs it as Ted's. Even mounted and stuffed trophy moose heads turn out to be spies.

In September, *PRIVATE SNAFU: THE GOLDBRICK* demonstrated how slacking off and faking illness hurts a soldier's preparedness, which affects his chances of survival and the army's chances for success. After two anti-German installments, this one ends with a caricatured Japanese man— short, with glasses and buckteeth—revealing himself as the person who has been encouraging SNAFU to "goldbrick," leading him to his death:

Banzai! Here lies the Goldbrick; I now go to find more.
If I find enough Goldbrick, Japan could win war!

PRIVATE SNAFU: THE INFANTRY BLUES that same month addressed SNAFU as a grumbling foot soldier trudging along, wishing that he was in an easier branch of the service. When the Technical Fairy grants his wish, SNAFU experiences the rough terrain over which the tanks rattle and soon wishes that he was in the navy. In the navy, rough waters churn his stomach and make him wish he was in the air force, where loop-the-loops nearly knock him unconscious.

During the naval segment, SNAFU rides the waves with two fish strapped to his feet—an image that Ted had used many times in his cartoons.[11] Images like this one are a clear indication that, in addition to the scripts, Ted sometimes had a hand in the design of animation for the SNAFU cartoons.

The following month, Ted worked with director Bob Clampett on *PRIVATE SNAFU: FIGHTING TOOLS*. Eighteen months earlier, Clampett's adaptation of *Horton Hatches the Egg* for Warner Bros. had been the first animated feature based on a Dr. Seuss book. Now Ted was working with the supervisor of that cartoon on one of his own. The cartoon begins with an interesting coincidence. The opening sequence contains a newspaper with the prophetic headline "Adolf Hitler Commits Suicide"—18 months before Hitler would shoot himself in the head and Eva Braun would take a cyanide pill while Russian troops battled toward their subterranean bunker.

In the cartoon, SNAFU has confidence in the superiority of the weaponry he was issued by the army, singing:

> I'm the best damn fighting machine-o.
> Them Nazis will learn what I mean-o.
> My wonderful guns
> Will murder them bums
> And I'll bury them in the latrine-o.

But in typical SNAFU fashion, he neglects to care for his armaments and pays the price.

With Thanksgiving looming, the next cartoon, released in November 1943, turned its attention homeward. *PRIVATE SNAFU: THE HOME*

Advice to Wager Makers

SEA TRAVEL FOR ALL!

The use of fish as a mode of transportation, employed in *PRIVATE SNAFU: FIGHTING TOOLS,* was nothing new. Ted had employed the imagery in his civilian work as far back as 1928 (top) and 1932 (bottom).

FRONT addresses SNAFU's notion that the folks back home have it easy while he freezes and toils overseas. He pictures his dad playing pool, his mom playing bridge, his girlfriend keeping the home fires burning with some stateside lothario, and his grandfather at a striptease show with binoculars. But the Technical Fairy shows him that his father is manufacturing tanks out of scrap metal, his mother is plowing fields to raise corn, his girlfriend Sally Lou has joined the WACs, and his grandfather is a riveter on warships. Ted's most notable contribution comes at the beginning of the film. His adult humor provides an amusing counterpoint to his children's literature when the narrator comments on the wintry conditions in Europe, quipping, "Cold? Brrrr. It's so cold, it could freeze the nuts off a Jeep." The cartoon quickly cuts to a picture of a Jeep, from which the nuts pop clean off of their bolts.

In November, with the holiday season approaching, the War Finance Division (WFD) of the Treasury Department began a campaign to try to limit unnecessary spending by civilians. The Women's Section of the WFD sponsored a campaign featuring a character called the Squander Bug, originally created by our British allies. The English Squander Bug looked a bit like a hairy peanut with swastikas on its body. It tempted people to buy things they didn't need and to be wasteful rather than lend money to the government through savings certificates to help support the war effort. Depicted in government-printed posters and British newspaper cartoons by Sidney Strube, Philip Zec, Joseph Lee, George Whitelaw, James Francis Horrabin, Victor Weisz, Neb, and others, the repetition of the image in the various media successfully left its impression on English citizens, particularly children.

Continuing his longstanding bug theme, Ted drew the American prototype, which the WFD used in posters and advertisements. Ted's Squander Bug eats money that should have gone to purchase war bonds and stamps. Like all of his work for the military, Ted did not own the copyright to the Squander Bug character. In fact, through the Schools at War program, one of the ideas was to try to popularize the bug by encouraging schoolchildren to draw their own versions or to draw a scene using Ted's bug as the centerpiece. The Squander Bug appeared in a government-printed war savings news bulletin

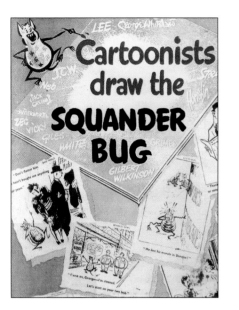

for teachers. A civilian press printed booklets for the Schools at War program showing versions of the bug that children had adapted. Private companies ran Ted's Squander Bug in their newsletters.

The WFD issued a series of Squander Bug advertisements to newspaper and magazine editors with the proviso "Your use of this feature, we believe, will not only aid in the sale of War Bonds as Christmas gifts, but will help in preventing the dread specter of inflation."[12] Among the suggested materials were 18 different Squander Bug ad samples detailing the Squander Bug's diet of dollars and his enjoyment of "dimes and quarters as side dishes." The brochure also contained a vertical Squander Bug poster on the cover and a horizontal foldout version in the centerfold. A smaller version of the horizontal poster was also produced for distribution.

These Squander Bugs were not Ted's only insect images to be made into posters at this time. While producing the Squander Bug illustrations and working on the SNAFU cartoons, Ted also continued the anti-malaria

To rein in excessive consumer spending, the United States adopted the successful British campaign featuring the Squander Bug (top left and top right). Ted's prototype (middle left) was used in school materials (bottom left) and war-bond posters (middle right and bottom right).

A vicious little insect is at the bottom of every spending spree—causing prices to soar. He's the "Squander Bug." His diet is the dollars you throw away. And he likes dimes and quarters as side dishes. The best way to give him indigestion is to hand him a big helping of War Bonds. Do your part to starve him to death—now!

Ever had your money burn in your pocket? Ever gone into a store and bought articles you didn't really need? For lack of any other name, call this unreasoning urge to throw money away the "Squander Bug." It can gobble dollars as sun melts snow. But the "Squander Bug" can't digest War Bonds. Up your bond-buying now!

The termites have a cousin, the "Squander Bug." Termites will undermine a house, gnawing at its wooden underpinnings until it's ready to topple. The "Squander Bug" uses the same system, chews your dollars until he undermines your savings, your security. But he can be exterminated. You can do it yourself—by investing all you can in War Bonds.

campaign. In the same month that the Squander Bug campaign was launched, the images from *This Is Ann* were used in two different versions of an issue of *NewsMap*. The larger of the two double-sided maps showed two of the booklet's illustrations above a map depicting the areas in which malaria was most prominent. The second, smaller version reproduced all but five of Ted's illustrations from the malaria booklet, along with a slightly altered version of Munro Leaf's text. Ted wrote, "I have done quite a few posters for use in the South West Pacific,"[13] which suggests that there may also have been other anti-malaria posters that he designed during the war. Stateside, Ted's illustrations of Ann appeared on camp billboards.

By December, one of the war-bond illustrations that Ted had done as a civilian, which had appeared in periodicals as varied as *PM* and *Big Detective Cases,* was printed anew on a limited run of envelopes.

Among these many examples of the "print" portion of Ted's service, there is also some speculation that he may have worked on a servicemen's primer on Germany. He would later write that he "spent considerable time tracking down the undistributed 'Pocket Guide to Germany' which was, for obscure reasons, hidden away in some continental warehouse. . . ."[14]

He was overseas seeking approval of his film *Your Job in Germany,* which was also the title of the first chapter of the booklet. His interest in finding the booklet, which quotes from the film nearly verbatim, suggests that Ted was more than likely involved in its creation.

Also in December, Ted's group released their next animated cartoon, *PRIVATE SNAFU: RUMORS.* In the latrine, SNAFU comments to another man that they're having nice weather, to which the man retorts sarcastically that it's nice weather for a bombing. SNAFU's imagination and paranoia take over, and soon the rumor being spread is that "They're gonna bomb us," which is quickly replaced by "They bombed us." The rumor is rapidly transformed and exaggerated into the "worst air raid of the war," then "They blasted the hell out of Brooklyn Bridge," eventually leading to "Their parachute troops landed right on the White House lawn" and "We have nothing to fight with . . . our shells are all duds."

Ted appears to have provided the rhyming dialogue, but there is also more of his influence detectable in the visual content than in other SNAFU cartoons. There are creatures that bear a noticeable resemblance to those that we associate with Dr. Seuss. Disembodied hands work to produce the flying bologna that represents the rumors—a similar winged sausage appeared in *Boners* 12 years earlier, and the image of the disembodied hands is one that Ted used often in his earlier cartoons and would factor prominently in his

Pest control: **With pen in hand, Ted fought the good fight against figurative insects like the Squander Bug (opposite page, top) and the very real malaria-carrying mosquito (opposite page, bottom).**

One of Ted's civilian war-bond pieces was adapted and printed on envelopes (this page).

movie *The 5000 Fingers of Dr. T.* There is also a bird with a trumpet for a beak, which Ted would use later in his work, and a quite Seussian beast in bed with SNAFU.

As 1943 ended and the new year began, Ted appears to have been busy with the anti-malaria campaign and other health-related projects. His contributions are not evident in the next two Private SNAFU cartoons, *PRIVATE SNAFU: BOOBY TRAPS* and *PRIVATE SNAFU: SNAFUPERMAN.* Ted joked that he was placed "in charge of malaria," and finally "promoted to syphilis. . . . They wanted me to make an anti-V.D. film . . . that the men wouldn't laugh at. It was, I believe, an impossible task. Instead of using actors, actresses and so-called real situations, we tried to get our message across by means of abstract animated figures. The film made no sense whatever. As far as I know it was never shown."[15] Private SNAFU did appear on matchbooks with messages warning against venereal diseases.

The next cartoon to which Ted seems to have contributed was *PRIVATE SNAFU: VS. MALARIA MIKE.* In reference to the anti-malaria campaign, Ted had mentioned in a Thanksgiving letter a few months earlier that he was "now completing an animated cartoon on the subject."[16] The cartoon covered the same warning points as those enumerated in *This Is Ann.* Directed by Chuck Jones, the cartoon was released in March 1944, the month that Ted turned 40 and received his promotion to the rank of major.

After his promotion, Ted continued to work on some of the SNAFU cartoons, but Colonel Capra (himself recently promoted) felt that Ted had learned enough about filmmaking to move on to bigger projects. Ted soon began work on the first of three propaganda films. He finished a version of the movie, pending approval, by October 1944. Ted's contributions to the intervening SNAFU cartoons were more sporadic.[17]

Ted appears to have been involved with Jones's cartoon, *PRIVATE SNAFU: GOING HOME,* made in May 1944. In it, SNAFU returns from the war to his home in Podunk and relaxes his guard about keeping military secrets. After getting drunk in a bar, he reveals ever more sensitive information, until he blabs details about a superbomb that destroys Japan.

PRIVATE SNAFU: GOING HOME was ready for release 15 months

before Colonel Paul Tibbets, piloting the B-29 *Enola Gay*, would drop the atomic bomb on Hiroshima. For obvious reasons, the SNAFU cartoon that Ted had written was not released. It was not the last time that Ted's "explosive" imagination would run afoul of the army

authorities. In the summer of 1945, Ted was working on "a film spurring post-war troops to help avoid a third world war. He found inspiration in a brief *New York Times* item: There was so much energy in a glass of water, scientists said, that if it could be harnessed it could blow up half the world. . . . He drafted a film treatment that warned of the potential threat of devastating explosions."[18] Colonel Paul Horgan, a Pulitzer Prize–winning historian who worked in Capra's unit with Ted and served as their Pentagon liaison, regarded Ted's work as an "extraordinary projection of the most lethal weapons" and brought it to the attention of "Vannevar Bush, head of the wartime Office of Scientific Research and Development, who telephoned within the hour, ordering the immediate destruction of Ted's storyboards and scripts on grounds of national security."[19] In Ted's version of the story, they even made him locate a copy of the *Times* article and burn it in a wastebasket. Horgan recalled it differently: "I called Ted . . . and he was devastated, since he'd put three months in on the project. He told me he got the idea from the Buck Rogers comic strip. I left for Europe for six weeks, and while I was gone the first atom bomb was dropped on Japan. When I returned, my secretary said Major Geisel had been making calls daily. . . ."[20]

Ted's contribution to the SNAFU film about rumors is easy to detect in the trumpet-beaked bird (opposite page, top) and the beast abed (opposite page, middle), the latter bearing a striking resemblance to Seussian creatures to come (opposite page, bottom).

Strike against VD! Ted's film about venereal disease never made it to the screen, even though SNAFU matchbooks with a similar theme (this page) were distributed to GIs.

The fifteenth installment in the SNAFU series appeared in June 1944. It is difficult to determine the extent of Ted's involvement in Frank Tashlin's *PRIVATE SNAFU: THE CHOW HOUND,* which was aimed at preventing the GIs' waste of food. There are some hillside trees that look quite Seussian, but the meter and type of rhymes employed in the narration suggest that *CHOW HOUND* may have been one of the films written by P. D. Eastman rather than Ted.

As the summer approached and Ted's documentary work increased, his involvement in the SNAFU cartoons tapered off. Neither Frank Tashlin's June entry, *PRIVATE SNAFU: CENSORED,* nor Jones's *PRIVATE SNAFU: OUTPOST* in August resonates with Ted's style. In July, Frank Capra flew to Hawaii for a month to organize special-coverage operations in the Pacific, so

SUNSET HOUSE

Ted was presumably left to work even harder on the documentary in his absence.

The next film that bears signs of Ted's involvement is Friz Freleng's September episode, *PRIVATE SNAFU: PAYDAY,* in which SNAFU buys useless things, gambles, drinks, and finds ways to blow his money in the Middle East, the Caribbean, and the Arctic while his excesses are reflected in scenes showing the losses to the postwar house and family he could have had. In each area of the globe, SNAFU is pulled toward responsibility by the "good" Technical Fairy of his conscience and lured toward pleasures by a porcine, gargoyle-devilish "bad" fairy. These same two characters appear in one of Ted's wartime sketches, with a determined Ted following the Technical Fairy out of the Sunset House back to work, while the bad fairy tries to lure him back into the bar. The sketched characters are virtually identical to those in the film.

Ted finished the initial version of his documentary *Your Job in Germany* the following month and then flew on assignment to Europe for several months. As a result, the next few installments of the SNAFU series have little of Ted's influence, and the time between new entries in the series slowly increased.[21] In February 1945, Ted was back in camp, filing a report on his work in the European Theater of Operations, when Chuck Jones released *PRIVATE SNAFU: IN THE ALEUTIANS—ISLES OF ENCHANTMENT (OH BROTHER!).* There are a few touches that feel like Ted's, including a game of craps that bears some resemblance to a sketch that Ted did during this period and, more importantly, the appearance of a small fish in a parachute—an image that Ted would use later in *McElligot's Pool,* his first book after leaving the army. He worked on the script of another propaganda film, *Know Your Enemy—Japan,* and the script was completed in April 1945. Consequently, there was no SNAFU episode in March, and there is nothing much of Ted to be seen in April's *PRIVATE SNAFU: A Few Quick Facts About FEAR.*

Sixteen days after *Your Job in Germany* was released, Germany surrendered, and the focus turned to Japan. Ted next began work on a third propaganda film called *Our Job in Japan.* Before turning to that script, however, he was able to play a greater role in Chuck Jones's *PRIVATE SNAFU: it's MURDER she says.* This entry was yet another anti-malaria piece, with a

Ted's self-portrait shows him being ordered about by the spirits of good and evil, which is virtually identical to a scene from *PRIVATE SNAFU: PAYDAY.*

script reportedly adapted by Majors Geisel and Leaf from their *This Is Ann* booklet. Released in May, the story picks up years later, with Ann, now a faded beauty (voiced by Marjorie Rambeau), reminiscing about the good old days before the army's efforts sent her on the run.

Ted's role in the SNAFU cartoons diminished again considerably[22] until the last episode, *PRIVATE SNAFU: Presents SEAMAN TARFU in THE NAVY*, was released in January 1946, when Ted was discharged from the army. The cartoon was directed by George Gordon at the Harman-Ising Studio, and two of Ted's personal sketches from the time suggest that he was involved with its production. In one, the phrase "We want Ising" appears. In another titled "SERVICE OF SUPPLY," a group carries boxes of Coca-Cola for "OUR FIGHTING MEN!" The men in the Service of Supply lugged to the infantrymen the food, clothing, and equipment that they needed. The relevance of the sketch lies not in the importance that is placed on Coca-Cola as an essential supply but on the character leading the supply line. Although he looks nothing at all like the sort of person Ted would have created as a Dr. Seuss character, he is clearly the same serviceman as the skirt-chasing sailor who provides the running gag in the *TARFU* cartoon.

Ted had plans for several other animated projects, including two entries at the beginning of 1945 in the *A Few Quick Facts* portion of the SNAFU series, one on "the reasons for the failure of our last occupation of Germany"[23] and another detailing "what it cost the world to defeat Germany. In terms of lives lost, homes destroyed, forests cut down. . . . The time it will take to reclaim the blasted land, to drain and save the salted fields of Holland. The amount of permanent hospitalization . . ."[24] Although they reached various states of progress, most of these projects probably never came to fruition. Tex Avery's unit is reported to have completed animation for *PRIVATE SNAFU: MOP UP* (AKA *How to Get a Fat Jap Out of a Cave*), but filming was abandoned when the war ended. Reports also exist of a "missing" episode called *PRIVATE SNAFU: SECRETS OF THE CARIBBEAN*. Like the April 1944 episode of *A Few Quick Facts* concerning diarrhea and dysentery, in which SNAFU's dirty mess kit is the cause for urgent trips to the latrine, no information about Ted's involvement has been uncovered.

This sketch is evidence of Ted's involvement in the TARFU episode in the SNAFU series.

The Private SNAFU films, the anti-malaria campaign booklet and posters, and the Squander Bug advertisements and posters all harnessed Ted's talents as a humorist and cartoonist, and some made use of his proficiency with rhyme. But they also relied on his abilities as an advertising man to "sell" ideas as well as he sold products. It was this latter skill that was exploited during the remainder of Ted's work in the army on the propaganda films.

Of the orientation films produced by Capra's unit, the seven films that comprised the *Why We Fight* series had a budget amounting to 20 percent of Capra's budget for the 1939 film *Mr. Smith Goes to Washington*.[25] So Capra decided to make the movies from existing footage found in propaganda films—from allies and enemies alike—plus newsreels, feature films, and real combat footage. Due to the patchwork nature of these films, Capra referred to himself as the executive producer rather than the director, while personnel like Ted Geisel and Anatole Litvak, who were put in charge of individual films, were known as "project officers." Ted worked on *Know Your Enemy—Japan* and was a project officer for the films *Your Job in Germany* and *Our Job in Japan*.

The process was a communal one. As described by Allen Rivkin:

> Usually two writers would work on a script at the same
> time, with one fellow writing the narration. We would
> prepare a rough outline without knowing what film we
> had available, and then production would begin on the film.
> We would try to make the bits and pieces of film fit in, and
> figure out the gaps we had to cover with animation. . . .
> Frank [Capra] was always the arbiter of what went into
> the script. . . . When we had a script, [editor] Bill Hornbeck
> would put the film together with his assistants. Frank would
> watch the rough cut and someone would read the narration
> aloud. . . .[26]

In April 1944, Ted was entrusted with the job of creating a film, dubbed Project 6010X, that would explain to American soldiers what their jobs would be when Germany surrendered and American troops remained as an occupation force to monitor and enforce the new peace.

At first, it seems strange that Ted, with his German background, should produce such strong anti-German rhetoric. But he had seen the Germans' actions in World War I through the eyes of a German American child who was subjected to the barbs of other American schoolchildren, and it had left an impression on him.

Just before joining the military, Ted drew a comic in which both Hitler and Mussolini, dressed as Santa Clauses, commiserate with each other that their citizenry may figure out who they really are; Japanese prime minister Hideki Tojo is noticeably absent. Ted's *PM* cartoons depicted the German people as being taken advantage of by Hitler but viewed the Japanese people themselves as being a threat; his propaganda movies reverse that point of view almost entirely.

Ted's PM cartoons represented the German people as being misled by their rulers, as in these 1942 pieces. His later propaganda films would blame the German people instead.

Your Job in Germany begins by explaining to troops that "just as American soldiers had to do this job 26 years ago, so other American soldiers—your sons—might have to do it again another 20-odd years from now."[27] If the German people had been deceived by corrupt rulers just once, he would have approached the issue differently. But Ted felt that a historical pattern had emerged, for which he condemned the entire nation. "You are up against German history. It isn't good. This book was written chapter by chapter. Not by one man, not by one Fuehrer; it was written by the *German people*. . . ."[28] Ted describes the German people following the first führer, Bismarck, as they built the German empire at the expense of Denmark, Austria, and France, then following the second führer, Kaiser Wilhelm, into World War I, and now a third führer—Adolf Hitler. Ted's script then explains to the troops that they are remaining as an occupation force in the defeated country to prevent history from repeating itself yet again.

The most poignant point made—and one that clearly would have the greatest effect on Ted as a writer for and educator of kids—concerned the effect that the Nazi Party had on German children. "They know no other system than the one that poisoned their minds. . . . They heard no free speech, read no free press. They were brought up on straight propaganda, products of the worst educational crime in the entire history of the world."[29] But even Ted's pity for the crimes that were perpetrated against the innocent German youth was tempered by the realization that, once trained in this manner, they were like everyone else in the country. "Some day the German people might be cured of their disease—the Super Race Disease, the World Conquest Disease. But they must prove that they have been cured beyond the shadow of a doubt, before they ever again are allowed to take their place among respectable nations."[30]

Casting the movie, Ted realized that the nearest actors were in the air force, which used the Hal Roach Studios ("Fort Roach") in Culver City for their training films. Ted requested that they send over some actors to read the narration for his film. Sergeant John Beal and Lieutenant Ronald Reagan were sent. Beal had already played the leads in *The Man Who Found Himself* and *Doctors Don't Tell,* as well as prominent roles in films like the William Powell/Myrna Loy vehicle *Double Wedding* and the Katharine Hepburn/Charles Boyer film *Break of Hearts.* Until his recent turn in *Kings Row,* Ronald Reagan had "played square romantic leads in . . . mainly routine B productions."[31] Ted later recounted with some amusement that he felt that future president Reagan "didn't seem to have the understanding, that morning, of the vital issues,"[32] and Ted chose Beal to narrate *Your Job in Germany.*[33]

In October 1944, Ted's draft of a script for *Your Job in Germany* was approved preliminarily, pending the final approval of the generals in combat. Capra's unit probably finished the original version of the film in November. Under Ted's supervision, the script for the ten-and-a-half-minute film was aided by screenwriter Anthony Veiller and "directed" in part by Anatole Litvak, with Frank Capra directing Beal's narration. The process was obviously circuitous—one of Ted's personal sketches shows Veiller and Colonel Litvak eating apples while Ted explains his idea to them using a wall chart.

Ted was then assigned to the Ardennes campaign in the Rhineland as liaison officer for the Information and Education Division in the European theater. His first assignment was to accompany Major John Boettiger in securing approval of the film from the generals in Europe. They apparently traveled to Versailles,[34] where Lieutenant General Walter Bedell Smith, the chief of staff for the Supreme Headquarters, Allied Expeditionary Force (SHAEF),[35] approved the film for release after V-E Day, whenever that might be,[36] and ordered a new version for immediate showing.

Ted developed an appreciation for the foot soldiers during his time in the European theater and came to believe that the perceived problems lay not in the soldiers themselves but in the attitude with which the war had been presented to them by their superiors. He reported, "For three years, our main information pitch has been defensive. We have fought *against* this. We have fought *against* that. We have rarely fought *for* anything. . . . If Goebbels could indoctrinate a whole nation with lies, we can indoctrinate an army with the truth. . . . Let us make it clear that the United States is not a planet revolving all by itself. . . . The soldier must realize that, from now on, everything that happens in Germany, or China, or Venezuela, or Abyssinia affects the tires on his automobile, the food on his supper table, the laundry on his clothes-line, and his wife and children and him. . . ."[37] Ted wrote the new version of *Your Job in Germany* in December 1944 in Paris and sent the script to Hollywood so that the film could be finished.

Despite the fact that General George S. Patton is reported to have "walked out on a screening of *Your Job in Germany* after giving it the one-word review . . . 'bullshit,'"[38] the film was approved for viewing by other generals. The version of *Your Job in Germany* that was completed lies somewhere between the one intended "for immediate release" and the one envisioned for release after V-E Day. In a February 1945 letter, it is clear that Ted believed his revised script had been produced in Hollywood and sent back to the front to be shown as soon as possible, but it was reworked and finally shipped to troops on April 13, 1945. It also played in some American theaters.

Neither of Ted's proposals for an "official follow-up film" to *Your Job in Germany* nor an animated piece about the "costs" of World War II were completed by the army. But the two ideas were combined and developed by Warner Bros. in 1945 into the film *Hitler Lives?* without Ted's participation. One review described it as "a sober reminder, from a motion picture, that the maniac's doctrines are still abroad in the world," a movie that takes a peek "behind the mask of a . . . 'cultural and a peace-loving Germany.'"[39]

Ted's account was that "somebody at Warner Brothers discovered a rule, which has since been rescinded, that any film done by the army could be

According to Ted, a technicality allowed Warner Bros. to reconstitute *Your Job in Germany* into the 1945 documentary film *Hitler Lives?* He did not receive credit for his wartime work on this film, even though it earned an Oscar that year.

picked up by commercial organizations if they changed the voices on the soundtrack. So they took our narrator's voice off and put theirs in and brought it out as *Hitler Lives?* And they got an Academy Award for it."[40]

His bitterness is understandable. Contrary to accounts that have Ted winning an Academy Award for *Hitler Lives?,* it was the movie that received the Oscar, not Ted. The new film quite literally followed the old one, using the same structure, sequence, images, and, for the most part, the same words. Minor edits were necessitated by the change in the target audience. Instead of being aimed at individual servicemen, it was directed to the American citizenry as a whole. Consequently, "You are up against something more than tourist scenery. You are up against German history" became "We're up against something more than tourist scenery. We're up against German history." The only section of Ted's script that could not be adapted was the part concerning the non-fraternization policy, relevant only to the troops, who were encouraged not to mingle with the locals. As it happens, that was the only part of his script that Ted was forced to include in his film. Since he did not believe in the policy, he gladly would have edited it out.

To be fair, Warner Bros. did more than just replace the narrator's voice, although it probably seemed like little else to Ted. It is true that Knox Manning's voice replaced John Beal's and that the sound track was replaced with music by William Lava. To lengthen the movie from army orientation film to Hollywood documentary, the script was padded with narrative tracts written by Saul Elkins, adding six and a half minutes to the original ten-and-a-half-minute film. But the first quarter of the film is an exact duplication of *Your Job in Germany.* No new material appears until four minutes into the movie and, when it does, interestingly, the subject matter is the hidden "costs" of the war, just as Ted had suggested it should be.

The title *Hitler Lives?* is drawn from the new ending. The final three minutes and 46 seconds of the movie address the specter of Hitler's spirit living on, perhaps even in America, through our mistreatment of our fellow man—a sentiment repeated in the Bill Crouch/Red River Dave song also called "Hitler Lives," performed by several artists, including Herman "The Hermit" Snyder. Rosalie Allen performed a version in 1947.

If Ted felt slighted by the production of *Hitler Lives?*, he was not alone. The people responsible for *Your Job in Germany* were overlooked in the credits for the latter film, as they were still in the army at the time and could not be a part of a commercial concern. Gordon Hollingshead supervised the new movie and received credit, with no mention of Frank Capra's or Anatole Litvak's earlier work.

The major change in the Hollywood film is the addition of two segments concerning Nazi war atrocities, much of it containing disturbing images from concentration camps. These sorts of images, and details of "the hobnail pleasures, the unspeakable shame of German superiority over adolescent girls, manhandled and half-stripped,"[41] are where the two films diverge.

Concentration-camp footage was not available when Ted's film was completed. Although Ted's film ostensibly took place at a time when concentration camps were emptied, United States involvement in the liberation of the camps took place in April and May 1945,[42] after production was finished. The only footage in *Your Job in Germany* purporting to be of a concentration camp looks more like a staged crowd scene of uniformed men. The fact is that when Ted returned from Europe in February 1945, the liberation of the Nazi concentration camps had not yet begun, and Ted's understanding of the extent of the carnage in the concentration camps was still very limited. Ted, like many other servicemen and civilians, was incredulous as to the stories about Nazi atrocities.

Ted would not have written about such things if his unit and its film editors didn't have footage to put in the movie. But more importantly, he, like Capra,[43] just couldn't believe that such things were going on. Whether the incredulity was general disbelief or a vestigial defense of his heritage is unclear, but based on the small amount that he had seen at two abandoned concentration camps during his two months in Europe, Ted warned:

> All men writing information to troops should be cautioned
> to steer clear of all German Atrocity Stories unless they have
> been doubly and triply checked and found *absolutely true*.

Many of these stories will backfire on us later, as did the rape of the Belgian Nuns in the last war. The backfiring of last war's over-emphasized atrocity stories did a great deal to whitewash the Germans and made us pretty cynical people about this sort of thing.

Visiting the Concentration Camps at Strudhof and Shirmek, I examined two widely-publicized "mass murder Gas Chambers."

One of them *might* have been used for this purpose. The other so-called gas chamber gives no evidence whatever of having been used as a place where people were murdered. In all likelihood, this was a room where clothes were disinfected. The hooks on which the victims were supposed to be hung would not support my weight. The room was labeled "clothes fumigation," and in the ante-room there were dozens of suits of clothes.

The crematorium is a crematorium, all right. But there are thousands of crematoriums in undertaking establishments in the states. A one-holer, this furnace could never have been used to get rid of bodies of mass-murder victims. It is connected with a very small morgue, and was undoubtedly used to cremate prisoners who died of natural causes.

The "torture table" on which hundreds of people were supposed to have been carved up alive by Nazi madmen turned out to be a conventional embalming table, attached to a mortuary.

The real atrocity about these camps was the fact that human beings actually were locked up in them. There is enough horror in that to condemn the Nazi system forever. If we overplay one detail and have to retract, our audience will be apt to disbelieve everything.[44]

Presumably, Ted's "Strudhof" was the Natzweiler-Struthof Concentration Camp in the Vosges Mountains of France. In addition to the main camp, it had 70 satellite camps, one of which was Schirmeck-Vorbrüch, probably

Ted's "Shirmek." The French army had liberated the main site on November 23, 1944, prior to Ted's arrival, so what Ted was seeing was already a somewhat sanitized version of a concentration camp. In anticipation of the liberation of the camp, many of its occupants had been either dispatched to other camps or killed.[45] Furthermore, it is reported that, unlike others, this installation was mostly a slave-labor camp. However, later reports would confirm that the gas chamber at Natzweiler-Struthof was used to supply bodies to the Strasbourg University Institute of Anatomy, which paid the gas bill.[46, 47]

Upon his return from Germany, Ted wrote a memo in which he critiqued the film work he and his unit were doing. He realized that he was "dispensing information to men I had never met, whose language I did not speak, and whose lives and problems I knew only through second-hand contacts, research reports, and stories printed in the civilian press."[48] Ted explained:

> The soldier hates with a violent passion the type of
> information that he calls "propaganda." Being remote from
> the soldier, we tend to talk down to the soldier. . . . The
> information we give him is the information he wants . . .
> but we often irritate him by the way we present it. The
> overseas soldier has his own private brand of humor.
> When we attempt to imitate it, without knowing how, we
> sound like a Sunday School Superintendent trying to be
> one-of-the-boys by saying, "Twenty-three, skidoo!" . . .
> I feel that I have been one of the prime offenders, having
> turned out quite a few films that now I would give my
> eye-teeth to get recalled.[49]

A cogent example of this behavior can be seen in the fact that, ten days after Ted made that statement, the marines invaded Iwo Jima. After eight days of bitter fighting, they finally took the summit of Mount Suribachi from the enemy, by which time nearly all 21,000 defenders of the island had died, in addition to 6,821 invading American soldiers. Six weeks later, *PRIVATE SNAFU: A Few Quick Facts About FEAR* was completed and released, in which the fight-or-flight response is explained through a childish cartoon, diagramming simple glandular and neural mechanisms. As a documentarian and a soldier who had now seen the European theater of war, Ted's new view was that, to the men who had fought so fiercely in such horrific conditions, the intended levity must have seemed very condescending. Ted realized that it was one thing for infantrymen to call themselves "dogfaces," but it was quite another when someone making cartoons in Hollywood used that term. Notice that after his European tour, Ted's approach to his documentary work shifted, as reflected in the change of titles from *Your Job in Germany* to *Our Job in Japan*.

Your Job in Germany was released to the troops the day after Roosevelt died. Had he lived another three weeks, he would have heard that the German forces laid down their arms in Italy on April 29, 1945, and that Adolf Hitler committed suicide the next day. Nine days later, he'd have learned that, under Admiral Karl Dönitz's authorization, General Alfred Jodl had signed a treaty in France at General Dwight Eisenhower's headquarters in Reims, surrendering unconditionally, which ended World War II in Europe at 11:01 p.m. (Central European Time) on May 8, 1945, leaving Japan as the remaining unvanquished enemy.

Now that Ted had successfully made the transition from cartoons to documentaries by completing *Your Job in Germany*, Frank Capra was able to rely on him more heavily. As part of a series of films called *Know Your Enemy, Know Your Ally*, Capra had started work on *Know Your Enemy—Japan* several years earlier, but production had been limping along for almost three years. While the United States fought Japan in the Battle of Midway, screenwriter Warren Duff (*Angels with Dirty Faces* and *The Fallen Sparrow*) completed the first draft for Capra in June 1942, half a year before Ted was even inducted into the army.[50] Many other famous writers had worked on versions of the script over the years, including screenwriters Carl Foreman (*High Noon* and *The Bridge on the River Kwai*), Frances Goodrich and Albert Hackett (*It's a Wonderful Life* and *Easter Parade*), Allen Rivkin (*Dead Reckoning* and *The Farmer's Daughter*), and John Huston (*The Maltese Falcon* and *The African Queen*), as well as novelist Irving Wallace (*The Chapman Report* and *The Prize*).

Many of the writers who preceded Ted had difficulty achieving the balance the army wanted regarding the apportionment of blame among the Japanese people, in good measure because the United States government and military had no defined point of view on

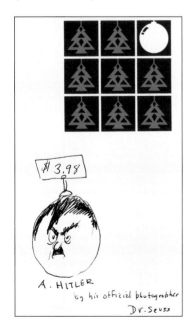

Years after the war, Ted could make light of Hitler with a proposed Christmas ornament (December 1982).

the subject. Irving Wallace "was particularly concerned about surveys under-taken by the Army showing that 58 per cent of the GIs in the European Theatre and 42 per cent in the Pacific Theatre believed peace could only be achieved by killing all Japanese."[51] However, as late as the February 1945 version of *Know Your Enemy—Japan,* the Pentagon still felt that "the script generally created 'too much sympathy for the Jap people.'"[52]

The script that Capra finished with Ted in April 1945 made the Pentagon's message clear: "Defeating this nation is as necessary as shooting down a mad dog in your neighborhood."[53] But the finished product succeeded in appearing to present a very thorough examination of Japanese culture, heritage, and history, viewed through the tinted lens of American war propa-ganda.[54] The final script worked because blame was doled out in a complex fashion. Ted's (and Capra's) wording managed to portray the Japanese citizenry both as a group with a history of warring tendencies *and* as an oppressed mass that had been misled by its leaders.

Part of the change came in the development of the script's tone. Duff's original script addressed the Japanese by saying, "We didn't bother about your way of life because it was none of our business. But now we're interested and we're going to bother quite a bit—because you're our enemy. We think we'll surprise you."[55] The final script altered that sentiment to: "We shall never completely understand the Japanese mind, but then, they don't understand ours either. . . . But we must try to understand Japan because we have become locked in the closest of all relationships—war. . . ."[56]

Ted's approach was to posit that both the Germans and the Japanese "believe that they were born to be masters—that we are inferiors, designed to be their slaves."[57] But while he viewed the Germans as a power-crazed version of normal people, he portrayed the Japanese as a different breed altogether and, as such, painted them with much more subtle brushstrokes. In *Your Job in Germany,* the only group shown any sympathy was the children, and although they were seen as having been abused by their educational system, they were still an irredeemable threat. In *Know Your Enemy—Japan,* the vast majority of the population is portrayed, at some time, with compassion. In addition to the expected sympathy for the Japanese children, Ted's script explained, "Women . . . must obey the males in all things. Even today . . . a father still has the right to sell his daughter . . . to a factory or mill. She will eat, sleep, and go to school in the factory but all her earnings will go to her father. Or, if she is a little older and he needs money, the father can sell her outright to a Geisha house, or house of prostitution. . . ."[58]

Ted also elicited sympathy for the enormous number of underprivileged laborers, pointing out that "the Jap peasant works harder, eats less, and pays more taxes than any other peasant on earth but he seldom complains, for he is carrying out the divine will of the Emperor. . . ."[59]

While depicting the Japanese "masses" as having been abused by their religious, political, and business leaders, the final version of the film contends that their own beliefs allowed that abuse to occur, effectively creating sympathy for the Japanese and undercutting it at the same time. In this way, Ted was able to successfully portray the Japanese people as being every bit the enemy that Germany was, as our government intended, while still managing to differentiate them from the Germans as potentially redeemable. Tracing the history of Japanese culture back to the 1500s, the film was able to conjure the Mongols and the ancient warlords, simultaneously offering a convincing portrayal of the Japanese people in humble pursuit of ancient mystical beliefs and as "warring, bloodthirsty people"[60] to whom "treachery, brutality, and torture are all justified if used against non-Japanese."[61]

Ted's approach to the Germans had been that they were sick—plain and simple. They had a disease—"the Super Race Disease, the World Conquest Disease."[62] Hitler was so ravaged by the disease that he'd gone insane. The Japanese motivation was portrayed as being more philosophically derived. To explain the Japanese emperor, the film describes him as a mix of the natural and the supernatural embodied in one person. "Entrust to one man the powers of the President of the United States . . . add . . . the power . . . of the Pope . . . then top it all with the divine authority of our own Son of God and you will begin to understand what Hirohito means to the Japanese, why they call him the God-Emperor. For, to the Japanese, Hirohito is a direct descendant of the Sun, and what is so high, so brilliant, and so mighty as the Sun?"[63]

As a consequence, *Know Your Enemy—Japan* posits that understanding the Shinto religion is critical to understanding the Japanese people, from their reverence for the emperor to their belief that they share their homes and their land with the spirits of all Japanese people who have died, making "each living Japanese . . . merely a link in this endless chain of ghosts."

The film's contention is that Shinto would be just "a nice quaint religion for a nice quaint people" if not for a divine command supposed to have been given to the Japanese people 2,600 years earlier. Emperor Jimmu's edict, known as Hakko Ichiu, was quoted as, "Let us extend the capital and cover the eight corners of the world under one roof." In this fashion, a religious principle became inextricably linked to sociological and political issues; as one Japanese scholar put it, "From the viewpoint of Hakko Ichiu, the Emperor of Japan is the Emperor of all the races of the world. . . . There are no seven seas. . . . All the oceans are to be recognized as the great Japanese Sea."[64]

In addition to the religious precepts that predisposed the Japanese people to be manipulated by their leaders, there were social factors as well. According to *Know Your Enemy—Japan*, for two centuries preceding the 1850s, no one was permitted to enter or leave Japan, effectively isolating them during a period of time in which the outside world advanced tremendously. Consequently, the Japanese people were "still living in the Middle Ages" when Japan was opened again to the world, and any new ideas that entered were "first tried out by the ruling classes, changed to suit their purpose, then . . . handed down to the people as divine law."

Additionally, although education is compulsory in Japan, "the Japanese school is not an institution for development of the mind. It is a government-controlled institution, designed to teach only officially selected facts and officially approved ideas. The object is to mass-produce students who all think alike. . . . Their minds absorb the official lessons like a sponge absorbs water and, like a squeezed sponge, they give back the same water. Teachers are trained only by the government and only those fanatically loyal to the Emperor are allowed to teach."[65] As a consequence, the film suggested that the Japanese people essentially were powerless to resist, which, by itself, is *not* the picture that the government wanted portrayed, nor is it the "message" that many critics have used to summarize the film.

Into "a vicious ironclad social structure, a system of regimentation so perfect, it made Hitler's mouth water"[66] stepped the emperor, the army and navy leaders, and a small number of extremely wealthy industrialists. The military leaders made sure that the businessmen had "cheap uncomplaining labor" and, in return, the businessmen provided money for the military buildup. Professional politicians, who owed their jobs and their lives to those in power, were appointed to rule the 47 Japanese provinces. To further their control and "to make sure the masses stay in their place, there are the police, the gendarmes, the Japanese Gestapo, and the billions of ghosts of dead Japanese ancestors who watch over every act of the living."

Once again, the view of the Japanese people's lot is clearly a sympathetic one. And yet the result was that they formed "a nation with a tough, seasoned, fanatic army of four million, still practically intact. A nation that can supply a million new conscripts a year, willing to die in their foxholes. A nation that believes *we* will throw in the sponge because *they* will outfight us, outlast us. A nation hell-bent to rule the world or commit national suicide."[67] The quotation used to reinforce that fact came from a Japanese colonel: "Japan is firmly determined to fight a hundred years' war to crush the United States."[68]

After Capra was discharged from the army in June 1945, Ted added the pep-rally ending to the film, citing our victories in the Pacific. He was also ordered by Assistant Secretary of War John J. McCloy to add a preliminary text screen citing the bravery of Japanese Americans during the war. Due to the many changes of personnel and the different times at which the film was compiled, the narrator's voice changes during the film, alternating among Walter Huston, John Beal, and Anthony Veiller. After three years of work and revisions to best explain to soldiers their Japanese enemy, the final version of *Know Your Enemy—Japan* was released to the troops in August 1945, on the day that the United States dropped an atomic bomb on Nagasaki. Ironically, six days after the film's release, Japan agreed to an unconditional surrender and signed the document of surrender a few weeks later. The war was over.

The exultation was diminished for Ted in several ways. After a telegram from General Douglas MacArthur pointed out that our policy regarding the occupation of Japan had changed in light of the recent events, Brigadier General Frederick Osborn ordered the hour-long film to be withdrawn from release—three years of work for three weeks of limited release, after which it was not seen commercially for more than 20 years.[69] Less than two weeks after Japan surrendered, Ted's only remaining sibling, his older sister Margaretha "Marnie" Geisel, died on September 14, 1945.

Once Japan surrendered in September 1945, American troops found themselves in the same situation they had faced earlier in Germany. These occupation forces also had to be educated about what to expect and how to behave overseas, and the army had been preparing another film for that eventuality. Ted's final propaganda film was the movie intended to explain *Our Job in Japan*.

The film begins with footage aboard the USS *Missouri* in Tokyo Bay as

Foreign Minister Mamoru Shigemitsu and General Yoshijiro Umezu signed the document of surrender on September 2, 1945, two and a half months after Frank Capra had been discharged, leaving Ted in charge of the film's production. The last film to be completed by Capra's unit, it was not finished until March 1946, two months after Ted too had returned to civilian life. However, Ted supervised most of the 18-minute film, which he wrote with Carl Foreman.

The policy in postwar Germany had been sharply defined when Ted wrote *Your Job in Germany*. Soldiers were to stay there, stolidly avoiding interactions with the German people until such time as the Germans proved through their actions that they would never again foment war. No means were given, no explanation of how or when that objective would be met. But it was made clear that, even with their leaders gone, no German citizen could be trusted, based on their history. In *Our Job in Japan*, the goals, like the enemy, were more difficult to define. But from the beginning of the movie, Ted again reinforced his view that the Japanese people were different from the Germans. These were people who were "trained to play follow-the-leader. People trained to follow blindly wherever their leaders led them. . . ."

In order to sell the idea that the actions of the Japanese were reprehensible but that they had been misled, Ted took an unusual approach—one that effectively eliminated potential prejudice based on skin color, facial features, and stereotypical images. In a strategic move that often strikes postwar viewers as particularly offensive, Ted dehumanized the Japanese people by distilling them down to their brains. The problem wasn't one of people and their culture; it was a question of how to deal with brains that had been badly programmed—brains that "like our brains can do good things or bad . . . depending on the kind of ideas that are put inside." Ted was particularly sensitive to the effects on the developing minds of the Japanese children, and one can see the development of Ted's desire to instill good ideas in children— ideas of tolerance rather than hatred.

Instead, Ted contended, Japanese leaders manipulated the Japanese brain, with its unusual mixture of the ancient and modern. "With such a brain . . . some very interesting things could be done. A brain that thought in the modern way could be taught to use the latest modern weapons. A brain that thought in the ancient way could be hopped up to fight with fanatical fury. . . ." Ted's script explained how that could be accomplished: "Steam up the emotions of the modern Japanese—that was the warlords' business. Muddle the modern Japanese mind. Hammer the ancient stuff in. Up from the barbarous bygone ages, bring back the ancient Japanese gods of war. Tell 'em of the glory of the samurai knights of old. Tell them that the soldiers of yesterday are the Japanese gods of today—that a Japanese warrior *never dies* . . . and over and over and over again, keep on telling them . . . 'The Sun Goddess Created the Japanese to Rule all the Other People of the Earth.' . . . Make him bow; make him say it. Make her bow; make her say it. Make them bow; make them say it. Everybody bow; everybody say it. . . . When they've bowed enough, when they've said it enough, when they've heard it enough, they'll begin to believe it. . . ."[70]

Unlike the situation in Germany where everyone was suspect, Ted did not have to sell a non-fraternization policy concerning Japan. In fact, soldiers were encouraged to mingle in order to demonstrate that the American way was a likable and reasonable one. Ted's version of postwar Japan was that there were plenty of Japanese who were good at heart, and once they were allowed to read and speak freely, they'd develop into peaceful people. In stark contrast to his prewar views of the German and Japanese people, as expressed in his political cartoons, these films clearly demonstrate that Ted had reversed his position. In fact, a few years after the war, he became somewhat of a Japanophile.

As it happened, *Our Job in Japan* fared no better with General MacArthur than *Know Your Enemy—Japan* had; he ordered that it not be released to the occupation troops when it was finished in March 1946, and apparently it was not released publicly either until 1982.[71]

There have been erroneous accounts that neither Ted's war propaganda films for the army nor the Hollywood reworkings of those films survived. Fortunately, that is not the case. Nearly every one of the films still exists.[72]

On January 8, 1946, Ted received the Legion of Merit award. Five days later, he was promoted from Major to Lieutenant Colonel. Two weeks after his promotion, Ted was discharged. Coincidentally, after working with Warner Bros.' personnel on most of the SNAFU films during the war, he returned to civilian life on the exact day that *Hitler Lives?* was nominated for an Academy Award. Within a few months, Ted took a job working with Warner Bros.' West Coast studios in Burbank, California.

CHAPTER 19
Moving Pictures

For Ted, this was a period of transition during which he moved from army life to civilian life, from the East Coast to the West Coast, from cartoonist to writer, and from playful youth to mature 42-year-old with a sense of mission and responsibility.

After his discharge, Ted decided to use the skills and connections he had acquired during his military service in Capra's unit and try to forge a career in Hollywood. His first experience with movie production had been the June 1931 release of the Flit films *'Neath the Bababa Tree* and *Put on the Spout,* which were well reviewed but doomed due to the change in the public's attitude toward advertising films. As early as March 1938, Ted had an interest in Hollywood. His college alumni magazine reported that "his ambition is to write, and his next venture might well be in movie scenarios."[1]

His next connection came in 1940, when *Horton Hatches the Egg* was published. Director Bob Clampett loved it and broached the idea of animating it to producer Leon Schlesinger, who in turn made an offer for the motion-picture rights relatively soon after its publication. It was the first book to be adapted by Warner Bros. for a cartoon and remains one of only two books to be licensed in Warner Bros.' history.[2] The story and animation were adapted from Ted's book by Michael Maltese and Robert McKimson, respectively. It was not nominated for an Academy Award, which would prove to be an exception to the rule for Ted.

In April 1943, while Ted's association with animation was beginning with the creation of the Private SNAFU cartoons, Paramount Pictures released George Pal's Puppetoon version of *The 500 Hats of Bartholomew Cubbins,* part of the Madcap Models series that Pal did for UM&M TV Corp. Puppetoons were the precursor to Claymation. For eight minutes of film, about 9,000 wooden figures[3] would be carved and hand-painted with colored lacquer. The artists had to paint each figure precisely because "the slightest deviation in color or line will make the figures jerk on the screen."[4] Those eight minutes of footage required about 12,000 stop-action photographs, with the figures being repositioned or new ones substituted after each ¹⁄₂₄th-second exposure. *The 500 Hats* was nominated for the Academy Award for Best Animated Short Subject, along with films from Walter Lantz, Leon Schlesinger, Dave Fleischer, and Walt Disney, but they all lost to Fred Quimby's *The Yankee Doodle Mouse.* However, George Pal won a special Academy Award for the Development of Novel Methods and Techniques in the Production of Short Subjects.

The following year, while Ted was at work on *Your Job in Germany,* Paramount released the Puppetoon version of *And to Think That I Saw It on Mulberry Street.* It too was nominated for Best Animated Short Subject, along with films by Walter Lantz, Walt Disney, Paul Terry, and Screen Gems, but it lost to another Fred Quimby film, *Mouse Trouble.*

Lieutenant Colonel Theodor S. Geisel returned to civilian life on January 27, 1946, on the same day that nominations for the eighteenth Academy Awards were announced. The awards were presented on March 7, 1946, with James Stewart and Bob Hope hosting the ceremony at Grauman's Chinese Theatre. *Hitler Lives?,* Warner Bros.' re-editing of Ted's *Your Job in Germany,* received the award for Best Documentary Short Subject. That marked three successive years in which some form of Ted's work had been nominated for an Oscar while he was in the army, getting none of the recognition in Hollywood. Three months later, Ted was working in Warner Bros.' West Coast studios in Burbank and living on Wonder View Drive in Hollywood.

During the latter half of 1946, Ted toiled away for Warner Bros. While the Dead Sea Scrolls were brought to a Bethlehem antiquities dealer in April 1947, it was becoming clear that no such magnificent finds were going to be made among Ted's script attempts for Warners, which included an early treatment of *Rebel Without a Cause.* As a creative antidote for the restrictions he experienced in the army and then in the studio system, he began working on his first children's book in seven years. He augmented his income with new jobs for Flit and Essomarine but would soon move from Warners to RKO in an attempt to approach Hollywood from a different vantage point.

Watching his works receive recognition without him was like receiving the flat fee for his illustrations in *Boners* while the royalty checks for the book went elsewhere. Ted and Helen decided to adapt Ted's other wartime propaganda film, *Our Job in Japan,* themselves, working together on the screenplay for *Design for Death.* Starting with the premise of the earlier film, they illustrated how the Japanese rulers perverted the ancient Shinto religion to manipulate the populace.

For the Geisels, the story was not particular to Japan but stood as an example of how all wars occur. According to the movie's narrator, "It was a blueprint of aggression, of the . . . racket that thrives in any country when too much power gets into the hands of too few. The same old swindle that's been . . . making murderers out of peaceful men since the beginning of time."[5] Of the film and its "thirty-two major revisions,"[6] Ted wrote to a friend:

> Confidentially, Helen and I are not too well pleased with
> the job. Simply because this industry is sort of hamstrung
> when it comes to dealing with ideas of this nature.
> Censorship forced us into straddling lots of issues that
> should have been met straight on. . . . Certain hunks of
> history are considered too hot to handle. The industry
> wants to please everyone and offend no one. That's how
> they make money. . . . But don't quote that, or I'll get
> fired out of Hollywood. ANYHOW, we think the job was
> worth doing because it's the first feature length straight
> documentary to be produced by any major Hollywood
> studio. And, for that, it's not bad. And it does manage to
> say some things strongly.[7]

In December 1947, *Design for Death* was previewed to the Academy, and it was released in January 1948. The twentieth Academy Awards were announced on February 15, 1948, and presented on March 20, 1948, at Los Angeles's Shrine Civic Auditorium. Despite Ted and Helen's qualms, *Design for Death* won for Best Feature-Length Documentary—their first official Oscar.

Later in life, Ted was convinced that the government pulled existing

prints of *Hitler Lives?* and *Design for Death,* leading some sources to conclude that "the Geisels had had a hand in two Oscars in two years. Yet neither film would survive."[8] In fact, the two films were not done in successive years—the former won for 1945 and the latter for 1947. Actually, *Design for Death* represented the fourth nomination in five years for films based on Ted's works. And far more important, both films have survived.

After *Design for Death,* Ted, writing on Columbia Pictures stationery rather than RKO, told a friend that he was working on a melodrama "based on fact, and hence semi-documentary" as a welcome break from the "historical sociological document[s]" with which he had tried to "change the course of human events or solve the universal problem of war . . . for five long years. . . ."[9] At about the same time, it was reported that Ted was "writing and directing another, shorter documentary for the Academy of Motion Picture Arts and Sciences, to be released about March" 1948.[10] Although the melodrama does not appear to have been produced, the shorter documentary may have been the 1949 RKO production of director Tholen Gladden's *The Costume Designer,* for which Ted wrote an original screenplay. Costume designer Edith Head appeared in the nine-minute piece, which may have been of interest to the Academy in demonstrating the role of one of the many behind-the-scenes contributors to a film's success.

Following this film—yet another straight documentary—Ted came full circle back to his first fledgling attempts in the movies, returning to the realm of sponsored short films. In 1949, Ted began work on animated movie shorts for the Ford Motor Company, similar to the ones that he'd done for Flit 18 years earlier. This time around, he had much more experience with moviemaking. Ford ran a series of Ted's print advertisements in May 1949 and continued in August with the series of short movies. These cartoons were made available for dealers to show in local movie theaters with personalized trailers. In 1950, some of these short advertisements ran as television commercials.

In 1947, Ted and Helen decided to rework *Our Job in Japan.* The result—*Design for Death*—received an Academy Award.

280

Ford produced 19 of these spots. Six were black-and-white case histories concerning Ford trucks, none of which involved Ted. Six color films addressed the cars' "New Ford Feel." It is not certain how many of those six films Ted worked on (if any). He was, however, responsible for the seven 40-second Technicolor movies that advertised Ford's service.

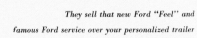

New Ford Movie Shorts!

They sell that new Ford "Feel" and famous Ford service over your personalized trailer

New Ford films in technicolor

Funny, fast and terrific—they sell famous Ford service in a new way!—page 14

These characters appear in the Dr. Seuss service trailers.

These commercials could easily have suffered the same uncertain fate as the Flit advertising shorts. But scripts and sketches have survived from these Ford commercials, as well as printed materials concerning the campaign. Fortunately, some of the Ford films are known to have survived as well. Ted scripted at least 11 potential short pieces for Ford. Four of the seven known to have been produced were *The Unicyclist, The Zither-Player, The Squeak-Squeak,* and *The Professor.*

Although they are very brief, films like *The Unicyclist* are everything a fan could desire of a Dr. Seuss commercial. *The Unicyclist* begins with a bird—one that would look at home in any favorite Seuss book—riding a unicycle until it feels threatened by an approaching car, which the bird must help to slow down. Once the car comes to a stop, the bird instructs the driver:

> If you'll kindly look down here, my friend,
> I think that you will find . . .
> That your brakes need some adjustment
> And they need to be relined.

The commercial then entreats drivers to utilize Ford service to keep their brakes in prime condition.

In *The Zither-Player,* a similar bird takes a nighttime stroll with his stringed instrument, proceeding to make such terrible music that even the full moon has to complain.

By now a seasoned filmmaker, Ted once again created short films for advertisers. His work on these Ford films is unmistakable.

You can take your good old zither
And go strolling neath the moon. . . .
But you cannot make good music
If your zither's out of tune.
You can also take your car out
In the country with the moon up. . . .
But you cannot have much fun, Bub,
If your motor needs a tune-up.

The Unicyclist (top left, middle, and right), *The Zither-Player* (middle left), and *The Squeak-Squeak* (middle right) first brought Dr. Seuss to television.

The Squeak-Squeak refers to a mustachioed bird resembling the arche-typical silent-movie villain who tethers the heroine to the railroad tracks, as in *The Perils of Pauline*. As he bounces and runs, his legs emit a mechanical *squeak-squeak,* which he brings with him as he jumps into a car's engine.

It has not yet been determined which of the other seven scripts, with

titles like *The Hypnotist* and *Weight Lifter,* were produced. Some of the scripts and storyboards described cars like the Billikan Six, the Dibble-Dorber Bubble Top ("the most modern car in the last sixty-two centuries . . . it's so modern . . . it doesn't even have wheels"),[11] the Do Me Sol Six with its musical exhaust pipes, and the Doberman Atom Splitting Roustabout ("the only car in the world that is fueled by atomic energy")[12]—none of which compared to the new 1950 Ford.

Frustratingly, the still images dis-covered from the films that *were* produced don't match any of these playful car creations. They show other characters, like a marching-band musi-cian blowing a trumpet and a rabbit pulling another rabbit out of a hat.

THESE DR. SEUSS *shorts fully animated in best Technicolor cartoon style*

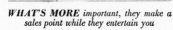

WHAT'S MORE *important, they make a sales point while they entertain you*

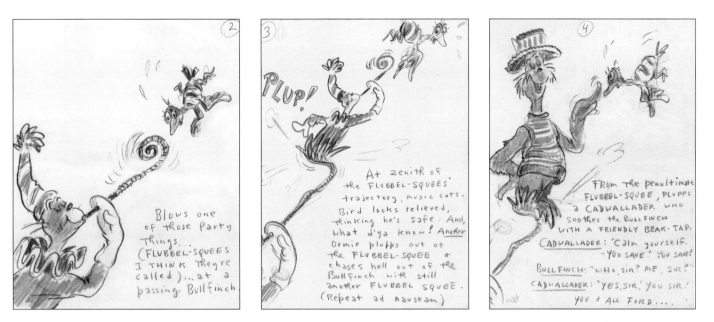

The most detailed storyboards (and, consequently, the most intriguing of these other films) involve the harassing of a bullfinch by a Carefree Ormie blowing a Flubbel-squee—a situation mediated by a Cadwallader. Whether or not this particular idea was produced as one of the three remaining "service" shorts has not yet been determined.

In 1950, Ted's Hollywood career careened off into yet another direction. A story he had sold to Capitol Records was developed into a very enjoyable record. The Great Gildersleeve, a character spun off from the *Fibber McGee and Molly* radio program, performed the story, *Gerald McBoing-Boing,*[13] concerning a boy who can make sounds but cannot speak words. Instinctively realizing that the tale was auditory in nature, Ted chose not to publish the story in written form. Consequently, the only record of how Ted pictured Gerald is his illustration for the album cover.

In Gerald McBoing Boing, Ted had spawned yet another popular character, just as he'd done with SNAFU. Although he was not directly involved with the franchise after the release of the record in early 1950, Ted's character took on a life of its own. Four *Gerald McBoing Boing* movies were made. Ted's original story was adapted by Phil Eastman and Bill Scott and made into an animated short, previewed in time to be eligible for the 1950 Academy Awards

Sketches (opposite page, second from bottom left), movie stills (opposite page, bottom left and right), and storyboards (this page, top left, middle, and right) show the creative energy behind Ted's Ford campaign. The next year, his only illustration of Gerald was on the album cover (this page, bottom).

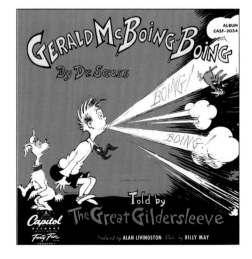

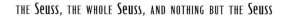

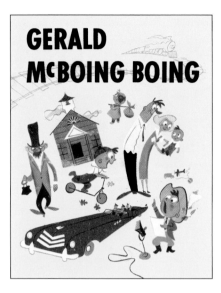

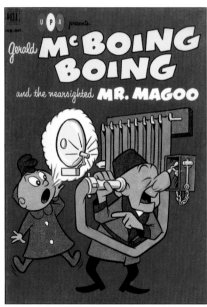

and released on January 25, 1951, to be followed by a book based on Mel Crawford's characterizations for the movie. Beginning in August 1952, Gerald became a companion of Mr. Magoo in comic books; interestingly, although both the *Gerald McBoing Boing* book and the first comic book use Mel Crawford's images and Dr. Seuss's text, the illustrations in the two versions are different. Next came the movies *Gerald McBoing Boing's Symphony* (July 1953), *Gerald McBoing Boing in How Now McBoing Boing* (September 1954), and *Gerald McBoing! Boing! On Planet Moo* (February 1956). In the 1956–57 season, CBS Television produced 13 episodes of *The Gerald McBoing Boing Show,* the first animated series ever produced for television. A short, *Magoo Meets McBoing Boing* (April 1962), followed.

Gerald's popularity continued for decades after Ted abandoned him. In 1970, 20 years after its initial release, *Gerald McBoing-Boing* was re-released on a 45-rpm record, along with *Gerald in the Wonderful Kingdom of "Oop."* Twenty years after that, a new version of Ted's story was produced with Werner Klemperer narrating. The following year, Carol Channing narrated yet another version. Nearly 50 years after Simon and Schuster and The Musson Book Company released the first book version based on the movie, Random House reintroduced a new generation to the book in 2000.

Even though Ted was not directly involved with the animated cartoon short, when *Gerald McBoing Boing* won the

1950 Academy Award for Best Animated Short Subject on March 29, 1951, it meant that projects from Geisel-based scripts had received five Academy Award nominations in the past eight years and had won three of them. Woody Allen holds the record for the most nominations in the writing category, including a run of ten in 14 years, but few other writers have had such a successful stretch. Although *Design for Death* was the only one of the five nominees with which Ted was directly involved, his incredible track record makes it easy to see why a project like *The 5000 Fingers of Dr. T* was greenlighted.

Ted's friend Elin Vanderlip confirmed, "He so desperately wanted to be a success in films."[14] Ted's cartooning, advertising, and film work had all been very successful, but none of this work gave him the personal satisfaction that he felt would have come from writing the "Great American Novel." Similarly, documentaries were not true "Hollywood" and he still held the romantic notion of making his mark in a great "major motion picture." He got his chance when, on April 27, 1951, a month after *Gerald McBoing Boing* won its Oscar, Stanley Kramer purchased the rights for Ted's project.

The major obstacle standing between Ted and the realization of his Hollywood dream can be found, ironically, in the lyrics of one of his songs from *Dr. T*. In "Dream Stuff," the plumber, August Zabladowski, explains that dreams are "ever fleeting, ever shifting" and observes how difficult it is to grasp their evanescent essence and try to "carry it right into bright blue day." Ted's fantasy world was dream stuff. The magic of Dr. Seuss is Ted's belief that our fantasies can be brought into waking life if we dare to try and, as he expressed in the song, if we don't let others take them away from us. Readers don't get the impression that Marco's vision of Mulberry Street is driven away by adults; he just hides it from them so he can hold on to it. But Ted was unable to bring the dream stuff of *The 5000 Fingers of Dr. T* into the Hollywood world and make it stay because he did not have the same control over the production of the movie as he had over his books. The difference between his conception of Dr. T's world and the practical requirements of producing that world under the constraints of the Hollywood system was simply too great.

Early in 1952, eight months into the project, Ted was so frustrated by the delays, the changes to his script, and the diminution of his vision that he announced his intention to withdraw from the movie. Although eventually

Even though Ted's creative involvement was limited to the genesis of Gerald, the character continued to take form in a picture book (opposite page, top left), comic books (opposite page, middle left), recordings (opposite page, bottom left), and film (opposite page, bottom middle and bottom right).

285

he was persuaded to stay, the abysmal audience reaction at a preview in January 1953 further tainted Ted's view of the film. Recalling a day during production in which one of the hundreds of boys seated at Dr. T's very grand piano vomited, beginning a chain reaction that caused "one after another of the boys to go queasy in the greatest mass upchuck in the history of Holly- wood," Ted quipped, "When the picture was finally released, the critics reacted in much the same manner."[15] As a result, the consensus is that Ted abhorred both the film and the experience. His biographers relate that "for years Ted grew grim at any mention of the film, and declined to list it in his official Random House biography. He called the making of *The 5000 Fingers* the greatest 'down period' of his career."[16]

Of course, what would a good Ted story be without a bit of controversy? When the movie's young star, Tommy Rettig, was told of Ted's apparent distaste for the experience in an interview, he responded, "I've heard quite the opposite. . . . Other people have talked to him, and apparently he has fond memories of it."[17] Regardless, the film itself has developed a devoted cult following over the years. No matter what criticisms can be made about the film, it remains the single best attempt to translate the two-dimensional Seussian book world into three-dimensional "reality"—to grasp that world we've been to and carry it back "into bright blue day."

The movie follows the exploits of Bart Collins, a young boy who'd rather be out playing baseball than practicing piano at the behest of his persnickety teacher, Dr. Terwilliker (Dr. T), and at the insistence of his concerned mother. The jaded plumber, Zabladowski, seems to side with Bart but does his best to isolate himself from any involvement. When Bart falls asleep during a piano lesson, he finds himself at the Institute for the Happy Finger Method, where Dr. T plans to conduct 500 boys (and their 5,000 fingers) as they play his music on an enormous double-tiered piano. Mrs. Collins has been hypnotized into assisting him with this nefarious plan while the fugitive Bart tries to enlist Zabladowski's help to free his mother and the rest of the children.

Initially, the movie must be considered in terms of its structure and background. The resemblance between the protagonist, Bart Collins, and Ted's literary everyboy, Bartholomew Cubbins, is obvious. The character comes across as two parts Dorothy Gale in *The Wizard of Oz* (with the conceit whereby the lead character transforms her family, friends, and acquaintances in a dreamland fantasy) and one part Tommy Woodry in

The Window (with the "nobody believes the kid is in danger" motif).

Additionally, in a thinly veiled parallel to Adolf Hitler, Ted depicted Dr. Terwilliker as imposing control and regimentation on the children to facilitate his mad and egomaniacal vision. Early script directions for him even include descriptions like "He stares at the ceiling in Hitlerian anguish."[18] Dr. T's indoctrination creates workers as slavishly dedicated to his Happy Finger Method as the Germans were to Nazism. Most working versions of the script even have Mrs. Collins saying, "My son, I assure you, no longer means a thing. To me, now, he's just another boy for your piano."[19, 20] As an obedient drone in the filmed version, she vows, "The work for the Happy Finger Method must go on!"—lacking only the implied "*Sieg heil!*" To complete the metaphor, Zabladowski is reluctant to get involved with other people's problems, just as Ted had depicted America prior to its entry into World War II. Although it was cut from the final production, Zabladowski was to have sung a number called "I Will Not Get Involved."

The film then comes across as a battle between good and evil—a retelling of the recent victory in the war against Hitler—and a potent diatribe against the perils and injustices of childhood, all rolled into a blockbuster musical fantasy, as seen through the remarkable eyes of Dr. Seuss.

Ted's vision is clearly present throughout the film. When Les Paul applied for his first design patent in the production of the electric guitar in July 1952, Ted had already designed a bevy of patented Seussian instruments that had been filmed for the production of *The 5000 Fingers of Dr. T*. Along with production designer Rudolph Sternad, Ted devised a marvelous array of

No one but Ted could tell a tale pitting rampant tyranny against wholesome, ordinary kids with a musical fantasy as backdrop, seen here in lobby cards for *The 5000 Fingers of Dr. T* (right) and its re-release several years later as *Crazy Music* (left).

Fanciful
instruments
(top and middle
left) and looming
stairways with
portal-like
entrances (bottom
left and right) were
the stuff of Dr. T
and Ted's world.

bizarre musical instruments. One such "instrument" consists of a man wearing a set of antlers with tiered bells that ring when someone shakes his neck. Another man wears a tuba-like instrument that wraps around his body four times, and saxophones are contoured to fit over a musician's entire mouth. There are also instruments made from fireplace bellows, mannequins, bicycle pumps, and radiators.

It isn't just the props that bring the fantasy world to life. In Woody Allen's *The Purple Rose of Cairo,* a character steps out of the movie screen into the "real" world. It feels like the opposite happens in *The 5000 Fingers of Dr. T.* The costumes—and to a far greater extent, the sets—make it seem as if the viewer is stepping through the movie screen into the world of Dr. Seuss's imagination. Shortly after Edmund Hillary and Tenzing Norgay became the first people to climb to the dangerous and dizzying summit of Mount Everest on May 29, 1953, Ted's film was released and theatergoers got to watch Bart's perilous ascent up the vertiginous red ladder that arches ever upward but ultimately leads nowhere, dangling high above the skewed archways and off-kilter parapets of Dr. T's institute. Stairways that look as appropriate for Dr. Caligari as they do for Dr. Terwilliker abound, some going nowhere and others leading to manhole-like entrances into bedrooms.[21] Even if no words were ever spoken, the visual effect alone would have endeared the movie to Ted's fans.

But there is more to the film than just the metaphors and the mise-en-scène. However memorable these external trappings, Ted wanted the

plot of the movie to be meaningful as well. Alas, it is here that the movie falters. Despite Ted's usual economy of language, a good deal of the film was apportioned to musical numbers, leaving less room for plot development. Consequently, the movie works best when songs advance the themes and the plot. In "Kids Song,"[22] Ted captured wonderfully the division between adults and children. Feeling abandoned by adults, who don't believe him, Bart sings:

> Now just because we're kids,
> Because we're sort of small,
> Because we're closer to the ground,
> And you are bigger pound by pound,
> You have no right, you have no right
> To push and shove us little kids around.
> Now just because your throat
> Has got a deeper voice
> And lots of wind to blow it out
> At little kids who don't dare shout,
> You have no right, you have no right
> To boss and beat us little kids about. . . .
> But we'll grow up someday,
> And when we do, I pray
> We won't just grow in size and sound
> And just be bigger pound by pound.
> I'd hate to grow like some I know
> Who push and shove us little kids around.[23]

The film also captures Ted's sense of the division between children and their parents and between parents and their own childhoods. He even manages to work both sides of the issue, delving a bit into the complexities of parenthood that children can't understand, as when Zabladowski comments to Bart, "If kids had their way, practically no parents would be born at all."

Some of the songs contain the rollicking rhymes and playful nonsense of Seussian poetry. The best example, "Terwilliker's Dressing Song," became one of the most popular tunes from the film. Dr. T sings to his henchmen as they dress him for his big performance:

Come on and dress me, dress me, dress me
In my peekaboo blouse
With the lovely interlining
Made of Chesapeake mouse. . . .
Come and dress me
In the blossoms of a million pink trees.
Come on and dress me up
In liverwurst and Camembert cheese. . . .

Such musical numbers limited the time for dialogue and forced editorial decisions, not all of which were bad ones. Eliminating Bart's sister, Jane, and her boyfriend, Fred, from the script was an excellent idea, for they served no useful dramatic purpose. Nor was it a great loss, given time constraints, to cut out the song by the twins, Judson and Whitney. Reducing them to mute characters lent them an air of intrigue.

Seussian song and dance: One of the more popular musical numbers was "Terwilliker's Dressing Song."

But other aspects suffered greatly. In early versions of the script, the twins were fleshed out, both as great-uncles in Bart's real world and as Dr. T's roller-skating guards who are joined at the beard in Bart's dream world. In a first draft, the camera was supposed to focus on a framed photo atop the piano at which Bart is dawdling over his practice lessons. In the photo, "two bearded gentlemen, as of 1910, are irritatingly posed playing a piano duet."[24] Bart was supposed to comment on the photo, saying, "'*The Whiskers'* were watching me. My mother's uncles . . . Judson and Whitney! I've gotta grow up to be just like *them*!" Then, mockingly, he was to have added, "Great musical talent runs in our family" and then to have held his fingers below his chin, making "goat's whiskers" to wag at his great-uncles. In the final version, this setup is reduced to quick glimpses of two unidentified men in separate photographs atop Bart's piano, blocked most of the time by Dr. Terwilliker's hat. Devoid of commentary, it is particularly hard for first-time viewers to establish the link to the roller-skating twins. It also leaves the twins' relevance to Bart completely nebulous and renders his "goat's whiskers" gesture

290

to them, in their showdown with Zabladowski, meaningless.

Gone too is the description Zabladowski gives of removing a sink according to the rules promulgated at the International Congress of Associated Sink-Taker-Outers at their annual meeting in Uleåborg, Finland, in 1907, which include adjusting the Cantalator, affixing the Grokkin, turning the Hoogle-Span, and giving half a revolution to the Oscillating Ding-Ding.[25] These are the types of details and flourishes, playfulness and humor, that might have smoothed some of the rough edges from the final production.

Instead, those scrapes are given ineffectual bandages, both figurative and literal. At the end of the movie, a final attempt to tie Bart's real world to his fantasy is made when Zabladowski notices Bart's bandaged finger and asks what happened to it. Bart says that he hurt it at the same time that Zabladowski hurt his. When the plumber finds that he too has a bandage on his thumb, he is at a loss as to how to explain it. So is the viewer, for the injury violates the logical physical separation between the two worlds. Instead of the helpful bridge that could have been made between Bart's dreaming and waking worlds by spending the same amount of time on Bart's great-uncles at the beginning, the choice was made to include this illogical and unnecessary attempt to tie the two worlds together at the end. Changes to the script also blurred the division between Mrs. Collins as Bart's doting mother and as Dr. T's assistant, who either does not recognize Bart or is actively trying to remove him from her life. For example, rather than have her burn his picture from its frame as originally conceived, the filmed version has Dr. T take the framed picture and place it facedown. When he leaves, Mrs. Collins recovers it longingly. As a result, the viewer never sees her as sufficiently changed by Dr. T to worry about her. The result of these oversights is that the production's scuffs and scrapes are more noticeable. The world doesn't need a director's cut of *Doctor Detroit* or an unedited version of *Bring Me the Head of Alfredo Garcia,* but *The 5000 Fingers of Dr. T* is the kind of movie that begs for a restored and expanded release on DVD.

As with much of Ted's work, the past and the future are brought together because of Ted's unusual memory. Among the most memorable images from the film is the bizarre one of roller-skating twins joined at the beard. However, this was an image that had amused Ted as early as the December 1931 issue of *College Humor,* in which his cartoon of the "ANNUAL

Déjà Seuss:
Although unlike anything he'd done before, *Dr. T* included images that Ted had employed earlier in his career.

Connecting bushy beards was a motif from a 1931 cartoon (this page, top left), a "Hejji" installment (this page, top middle), and even political cartoons (this page, top right) long before two beards were bridged in *Dr. T* (this page, bottom).

The disembodied hands were another recurring image in Ted's work (opposite page, top left, top right, middle left, and middle right).

The "Hejji" henchman Stroogo (opposite page, bottom left) and Dr. T's dungeon elevator operator (opposite page, bottom right) are strikingly similar.

DIRECTORS' MEETING OF THE GILLOPPY SAFETY RAZOR COMPANY" showed several men similarly conjoined. For *Liberty* the following year, Ted drew firemen who become joined at the beard accidentally during a fire. In the April 7, 1935, installment of his "Hejji" cartoon, Ted created goats joined at the beard. He used the image in two consecutive months in 1941 for *PM,* the last of these images being closest to the one that would appear in *Dr. T.*

The disembodied hands that decorate many of the sets and costumes in the movie can be traced back at least 20 years to ones used in consecutive weeks during 1932, first as props to measure the heights of horses in "Italo-Siamese Discord" and then as holders in a scientific study of the cat's cradle game. Ted used them a great deal during the 1949–50 Ford advertising campaign just before going on to *Dr. T.* Moving forward 30 years, the hand with the happy fingers on the Dr. T beanies resurfaced in hand-shaped hats that abound in Ted's book *Hunches in Bunches* (1982).

One of the odder examples of Ted's image recall concerns the characters of Stroogo and the dungeon elevator operator. In the movie, Stroogo is Dr. T's evil henchman who runs the dungeon for non-piano players. The elevator operator, who wears a distinctively shaped hood/mask, remains nameless. These two movie characters were derived from a single source from much earlier in Ted's career. In the comic strip "Hejji," Stroogo was The Evil One's henchman. He wore the same oddly shaped hood/mask and had no need for elevators, since he could walk up and down walls.

There were high hopes for *Dr. T* initially, despite the misgivings of Ted and producer Stanley Kramer. At the time, it boasted the largest merchandising campaign in cinematic history. In addition to the usual press book for the movie, a separate merchandising press book had to be printed, which advertised a prodigious

parade of products: barrettes, bracelets, brooches, pins, charms, keychains, rings, stickpins, tie clips, women's hats, children's beanies, button-down shirts, T-shirts, dungarees, handkerchiefs, suspenders, ties, puppets, lollipops, balloons, roller skates, phonographs, horns, harmonicas, accordions, concertinas, organs, player pianos with rolls

of *Dr. T* songs, clarinets, and original instruments like the wonder harp and the pick-a-tune gondolier. These items were planned 25 years before *Star Wars* wares would change movie budgets and 40 years before *Jurassic Park* paraphernalia would accustom viewers to an incredible array of movie tie-in products.

Of the first sneak preview of the film,

Dr. T spawned such memorabilia as jewelry (this page, top), musical instruments (this page, middle), record players (this page, bottom), and roller skates (opposite page, middle right), this pair missing their original cardboard hands.

Ted claimed, "At the end there were only five people left besides Kramer and our staff. It was a disaster. Careers were ruined."[26] In contrast, married stars Mary Healy (Mrs. Collins) and Peter Lind Hayes (Zabladowski) explained that "the movie passed the popcorn test. *The 5000 Fingers of Dr. T* was shown to hundreds of kiddies in a Santa Monica . . . theater. Five popcorn machines were going full blast in the lobby, and not one child left in the middle of the movie to buy a bag. This is a fairly new way to pre-test pictures for box-office appeal."[27] In the late 1980s, Tommy Rettig recalled that he and the cast went on a promotional tour for the movie that opened at the Criterion Theatre in New York, with the premiere attended by celebrities like Mickey Mantle and Whitey Ford. As far as he knew, they were supposed to "tour to open at various theaters across the country, starting with New York and coming back to L.A." As a child, he might not have been as insightful as Ted was at that time, but Rettig's memory is that "the story that went around was that [producer] Stanley Kramer and [Columbia president] Harry Cohn were having their famous fight, and Cohn pulled all support from every project that was Kramer's. . . . Suddenly the tour was cut short and the film stopped playing. . . . All I know is that it seemed very strange to me. It wasn't like it played to empty theaters or anything like that. We had crowds everywhere we went. Then suddenly they pulled the rug out from under it. . . ."[28] The film was re-released in 1958 under the title *Crazy Music.*

There is no such confusion in Rettig's recollection of his time as a child with Ted on the set of *The 5000 Fingers of Dr. T.* His account captures the joy that Ted had intended for the film:

I still have packed away somewhere my script with drawings that he would sketch in. Mostly he would sit there sketching the next set, or the next scene, showing things to the director and the cameraman about how he pictured it. . . . It was so much fun. I mean, if you can imagine being eleven years old and having a set like that to play on, and people like that to have access to. I mean, just to be able to run up to Dr. Seuss's chair and watch him draw in his script. It was really an outstanding experience.[29]

Ted, who hadn't enjoyed the lack of independence as a screenwriter at Warner Bros., nor the tinkering RKO had done with the Geisels' vision for *Design for Death,* nor the limitations placed by Columbia on *The 5000 Fingers of Dr. T,* decided to leave the Hollywood life behind and indulge his storytelling abilities more freely. For him, freedom still lay in his stories for and about children and childhood. As Zabladowski says to Bart, "People should always believe in kids. People should even believe their lies."

Although *Dr. T*'s young star (top right, with Ted) had fond recollections of being on the set, the film's failure left its mark on Ted. By the time the studio re-released it as *Crazy Music* in 1958 (top left), Ted had already returned to the world of publishing.

Dr. T's extensive publicity campaign gave rise to many colorful posters, like the American-style B half-sheet (bottom left) and the Spanish-style A herald (bottom right).

CHAPTER 20
The Missing Linnix

It would be misleading to give the impression that Ted's pursuits in Holly-wood were all-consuming endeavors. It was not a paradigm shift, as World War II had been. Although he truly wanted to make a mark in the movie industry, Ted—always easily bored—worked on many other projects during that period.

After a seven-year hiatus, he allied himself again with Standard Oil and Random House. His first projects for both companies developed along very similar lines, returning to a familiar theme. Ted had spent five years creating aquatic advertisements, seafaring sculptures, briny boating booklets, and all

Even at a young age, Ted probably knew the value of a good fish tale.

manner of marine mayhem. As he sought out his comfortable submarine world, he also summoned back the protagonist from his first book. Marco's fertile mind was the perfect one to ponder a pond and wonder what might lurk beneath, as he does in *McElligot's Pool*.[1]

The influence of Ted's previous work on his new book should not be surprising at this point. Many of the odd fish that populate McElligot's Pool share characteristics with those found in Ted's earlier work, like corkscrew snouts or parachutes. Others were fusions of two previous entities. For example, the Powerless Puffer and the Flaming Herring, both Marine Muggs, were combined to form the overheated puffer fish making their way from the Tropics to McElligot's Pool.

Ted's first new work for Essomarine after the war was a booklet called *The Log of the Good Ship*. There are overt similarities between this booklet and *McElligot's Pool*, which were published within a few months of each other at the end of the summer of 1947, with the

booklet apparently preceding the children's book.

In addition to his work for the 1948 National Motor Boat Show, Ted created the Friction Finch for New Departure ball bearings, for which he had done a series of ads in 1942.

A year after *McElligot's Pool,* Ted's seventh children's book, *Thidwick the Big-Hearted Moose,* was published. Five days later, construction began on the Geisels' new house on La Jolla's Mount Soledad, where Ted would live for the rest of his life.

The following month, just as he had returned to Marco when he needed an endlessly creative child for *McElligot's Pool,* Ted called upon the long-suffering Bartholomew Cubbins for the second time in "King Grimalken and the Wishbones," which was printed in the *Junior Catholic Messenger.* Bartholomew, of course, was Ted's human equivalent of Thidwick, always trying to please others and remain

Side by side, the similarities between Essomarine's aquatic life (top left, top third from left, and middle left) and Marco's water world (top second from left, top right, and middle right) are remarkable.

The Seuss menagerie grew on both the ad and book fronts with the birth of the Friction Finch (bottom left) and the publication of *Thidwick the Big-Hearted Moose,* who made a humorous appearance in the December 1948 issue of the *Dartmouth Alumni* (bottom right).

courteous in the face of unreasonable demands. "King Grimalken and the Wishbones" is far less recognizable. It was the first of a series of stories that are best referred to as "the lost stories." Sure, you know *The 500 Hats of Bartholomew Cubbins* and *Bartholomew and the Oobleck,* but what about "The Royal Housefly and Bartholomew Cubbins"? You loved *Horton Hatches the Egg* and *Horton Hears a Who!* But what do you know of "Horton and the Kwuggerbug"? Ted published many such short stories in several periodicals throughout the decade, some of which were later anthologized, but many of which were discarded and forgotten when the next month's issue arrived.

Ten years elapsed between Marco's 1937 amble down Mulberry Street and his musings beside McElligot's Pool in 1947. Ten years had also elapsed since Bartholomew Cubbins's previous conflict with King Derwin over his difficulty removing his hat in 1938, and the Kingdom of Didd now had a new king—Grimalken. With his elders presumed to have expired, wise man Nadd is now officially the wisest man in the kingdom. The story is told in four installments, in which readers learn that Bartholomew Cubbins is known around the castle as Wishbone Boy, for he has the duty of bringing the king an endless supply of chicken for every meal. The king is already so wealthy that he has pearls on the handle of his toothbrush and each of his hundreds of horses "had a special boy to paint his hooves with fresh gold dust every morning." But the greedy Grimalken still wants more. "The king really didn't like the taste of chicken at all. But every day he ate chicken for breakfast, chicken for lunch, chicken for dinner, and still another chicken just before he went to bed. Just so he could get his hands on those wishbones!"

Bartholomew's errant wish "that all the wishbones were gone from every chicken in the land" comes true, much to the consternation of the kingdom's chickens, and the rest of the story follows Bartholomew's quest to restore the wishbones to their rightful owners.

In the summer of 1949, Ted's latest Flit creations helped promote the seasonal upsurge in sales of the insecticide, which had been improved with the addition of DDT. He was also invited by Professor Brewster Ghiselin to lecture at a ten-day writers' conference in Salt Lake City, Utah, along with the likes of

Vladimir Nabokov, Wallace Stegner, and William Carlos Williams.[2] While Americans were contemplating "Big Brother" following the June publication of George Orwell's *1984*, Ghiselin recalled Ted relaxing and floating in a pool with Helen at the conference, calling her by the pet name "Big Boy."[3] But it wasn't all fun in the sun for Ted. The conference represented his first real opportunity to develop and expound upon his theory of writing for children.

During World War II, Ted had been struck by the generation of German and Japanese children whose lives had been devastated by the educational system to which they had been subjected—"products of the worst educational crime in the entire history of the world."[4] One of the things that the war did for Ted was to allow him to realize the importance of the education of children. These were no longer "brat books." Children's literature had an extraordinarily important place in the education of youth and, as a consequence, in the future of the world. But he was concerned that the books weren't sufficiently entertaining. He believed that children absorbed much more if they learned in a forum in which they were enjoying themselves. To illustrate this point, Ted contrasted the current state of children's literature to that of comic books. "Over *here,* we put our readers to sleep. Over *there,* they wake 'em up with action. . . . Over *here,* we bore them with grandpa's dull reminiscences of the past. Over *there,* they offer them glimpses of the future."[5] He reiterated that children "want *fun.* They want *play.* They want *nonsense.*"[6]

Ted continued to take this approach in his own work and, when John Hersey published his "Why Do Students Bog Down on the First R?" article in *Life* seven years later, Ted's message had obviously started to get through to others in the field. Hersey claimed that little boys recoiled from children's books in which a boy is "condemned to play endlessly, and with unnatural control of his manners, with two syrupy girls. . . ." He pointed out that such pap had to go up against "television, radio, movies, comic books, magazines, and sports. . . . This is hard competition because most commonplace pictures demand only the act of looking, while words, to mean anything, demand an act of imagination."[7] To get a child to make that effort to read, Hersey urged that children's books employ more imaginative text and illustrations—"drawings like those of the wonderfully imaginative geniuses among children's illustrators, Tenniel, Howard Pyle, 'Dr. Seuss,' Walt Disney. . . ."[8]

At the conference, Ted posited, "Children are thwarted people. Their idea of tragedy is when someone says you *can't* do that."[9] Ted's books succeed because he believed that children's abilities and their imaginations exceed adults' expectations. In Utah, Ted experienced an incident that reinforced this point and appears to have helped to direct the development of his career in children's literature. "Libby Childs, a Salt Lake City teacher, and her husband, Orlo, a geology professor, introduced themselves and asked what they could do to make Ted's stay happier."[10] He requested a visit to the Great Salt Lake. At the Childses' house before the drive to the lake, "their son Brad, not yet three, recited all of *Thidwick*. 'I don't write for kids that young,' Ted said as they drove on. 'How does he do it?'"[11]

Since Ted was mulling over his theory of children's literature at the writers' conference, this incident appears to have been a very meaningful one for him. It was likely the impetus for Ted to begin challenging the accepted age at which children could be reached through writing. He would carry on a crusade against word lists. Compiled by educators, word lists claimed to encompass and define the range of words that children of certain ages could learn and comprehend. Ted felt that all these lists did was limit children by placing lower expectations on them.

The importance of the incident with the Childses' son can readily be seen in *Scrambled Eggs Super!*, which Ted dedicated to the entire family. But with his fly-strip memory, Ted also used the husband's name ten years after the conference in an article that demonstrates why Ted eventually abandoned word lists and used "any word that had to do with a child's life and hopes."[12]

> The reason Orlo says "nuts to books" is because practically every book that he is able to read is far beneath his intellectual capacity. . . . When he twists the knob of his television set he meets everyone from Wyatt Earp to Governor Faubus. He attends the launchings of intercontinental ballistic missiles. He observes the building of the pyramids, flies across the South Pole and he knows what tools you have to use if you want to defang a cobra. Orlo, at 6, has seen more of life than his great-grandfather had seen when he died at the age of 90. Yet, if you go out to get Orlo a good book he can read . . . you can bring all the available books back home in a paper bag and still have room in the . . . bag for three oranges and a can of tuna.[13]

At the conference, and later as president of Beginner Books, Ted railed against "cute" books, which he called "bunny-bunny books." He gave a lecture entitled "Mrs. Mulvaney and the Billion-Dollar Bunny," which was a satirical account of the origin and subsequent swift acclaim of an imaginary children's book called "Bunny, Bunny, Bunny, Bunny, Bunny, Bunny, Bunny."[14]

Ted's model was most likely the Fuzzy Wuzzy Bunny books from the Whitman Publishing Company in Racine, Wisconsin.[15] Ted saw these bunny books, first published in 1943, multiplying like, well, rabbits. Ted appears to have perceived book after book called "Fuzzy Wuzzy Bunny" as one long book called "Bunny, Bunny, Bunny, Bunny, Bunny, Bunny, Bunny."

Although his ideas drastically changed the landscape of children's literature, not every one of Ted's theories was universally regarded as a work of genius. He proposed a teachers' textbook to Random House, which the publisher declined, believing that readers preferred to enjoy the fruits of his theories rather than having to read about them.

Another idea that he regarded very highly was not pursued:

> The funniest book I've ever written was never published. It's "I Don't Spelk Very Welk," and my publisher insisted that if that book came out no kid would ever learn to spell. Still, I like it. And I thought it would force children to look at words. It goes along for a couple of pages with maybe only a word or two misspelled and then—whoops—a page that reads like Chinese. Maybe one day I'll dust it off and give it another try.[16]

He dusted off Bartholomew Cubbins again. A year after the tale of his run-in with King Grimalken's wishbones was published, Bartholomew returned to face an even more challenging predicament, this time with oobleck. The story goes back in time to when King Derwin, rather than Grimalken, was still the ruler of Didd.

A little more than a year after *Bartholomew and the Oobleck* was published, Ted cited an incident from his time in Europe during World War II as the impetus for this story. In France, "it had been raining for weeks and everyone in the whole army was soaked to the skin. Out of the dark splashed two American soldiers. 'Rain! Always rain comes down!' one soldier muttered.

'Why can't we have something different for a change?'"[17] The king, like those soldiers, wishes to have something *different* come down from the skies, and he lives to rue his wish when the oobleck starts falling.

In early 1950, three months after the publication of *Bartholomew and the Oobleck,* Ted used his trustworthy character for the fourth time in "The Royal Housefly and Bartholomew Cubbins." This story began in earnest the period of his "lost stories," and these pieces serve as the missing link between Ted's pre- and postwar work—the turning point in his literary career. In "The Royal Housefly," Bartholomew finds the easily irascible King Derwin annoyed at a fly that is buzzing around him on his throne and offers to swat the fly for him. "You may swat all you wish from the noses of *common people.* But no one in the world may swat flies from the nose of the king! . . . When a king has a fly on the end of his royal nose, *that,* Bartholomew, is a very serious matter. I must talk to someone who knows more about flies than you do. . . ."[18]

The shaggy-dog story that follows is essentially Ted's version of the traditional ditty "I Know an Old Lady Who Swallowed a Fly."[19] Bartholomew first fetches the Royal Gardener, who suggests that they employ a special bird to frighten the fly into stopping its buzzing. That works, but the bird's "KLOOK-KLOOK-KLOOK!" is just as distracting and, if they take away the bird, the fly will no longer be frightened and will start buzzing again. So the king sits with the fly on his nose and the bird on his crown. The Royal Huntsman brings in a wildcat called a Bobtailed Linnix to frighten the bird. The Linnix, with long orange tassels on the ends of its floppy ears, perches on the king's shoulder and quiets the bird. But the Linnix makes its own "purrunking" noise.

As was the case with Bartholomew's 500 hats and the missing wishbones, the wise Sir Nadd is summoned. He explains that a special animal is required to stop a Linnix from purrunking—"a frightening creature . . . that no one but me has ever seen. This creature is called a Hippocras. . . ."[20]

In 1950, another periodical piece featured some old friends and some new ones—a beleaguered King Derwin comes face to face with a Linnix and a Hippocras (top) and then hand to face with Bartholomew (bottom).

The Hippocras landed with a crash in his majesty's royal lap.

It was the hardest, sharpest, loudest swat that had ever been swatted in the kingdom.

The animal leaps into the king's lap and lets out a terrifying "WAH-HOO-WAH-HOO-WAH!" Even Sir Nadd is not wise enough to determine how to stop the Hippocras's yowl. But if they remove the Hippocras from the king's lap, the Linnix will start purrunking again. As expected, it is up to Bartholomew to solve the problem with the very simple solution that the prideful king refused to heed in the first place.

As the United States entered the Korean War, Ted began a series of stories for various periodicals. In 1950, *Redbook* magazine carried "Gustav, the Goldfish," "If I Ran the Zoo," "Tadd and Todd," "Marco Comes Late," "How Officer Pat Saved the Whole Town," "Steak for Supper," and "The Big Brag." In a significantly altered form, *If I Ran the Zoo* became Ted's ninth book later that year. "Marco Comes Late" was subsequently anthologized,[21] and "The Big Brag" appeared eight years later in the book *Yertle the Turtle and Other Stories*.[22] But the rest of the stories were never reprinted.

"Gustav, the Goldfish," advertised as "An Amazing Adventure Story for Youngsters and Other People of Imagination," introduced the new series of stories as being "presented . . . with a technique that's new. To get the best results . . . read it aloud to your youngsters. . . ."[23]

Up to this point, Ted had published eight books, half of which rhymed and half of which did not. Having had the experience with the boy who was too young to read but who had memorized the sounds of the words in *Thidwick,* Ted was now planning to use the sound of his words to reach youngsters at an early age. "Rhyming . . . makes kids pronounce words correctly . . . [when] sounding [them] out . . ." he would later say.[24] A few months prior, the recording of *Gerald McBoing-Boing* was released; Ted did not illustrate an accompanying story—it was intended as a completely auditory experience. Although "Gustav, the Goldfish" remained in virtual obscurity for more than 50 years, it marks the beginning of Ted employing his theories to change the way that reading was taught in America.

It is a wonderful tale about a boy who receives a warning from Mr. VanBuss, the pet-shop owner who sells him a goldfish.

> The man who sold Gustav the Goldfish to us
> Had warned us, "*Take care!* When you feed this small cuss
> Just feed him a spot. If you feed him a lot
> Then something might happen! It's hard to say what."[25]

Unfortunately, "Gus" looks so thin that the boy overfeeds him, and soon:

> He was bursting the glass! He was big as a trout!
> I grabbed for the rose bowl. I yanked the rose out.
> My mother's best bowl, but I spilled Gustav in it.
> But what was the use? 'Cause the very next minute
> Gustav was bigger! As big as a shad!
> And he looked through the glass and he looked mighty mad!
> And he splashed and he thrashed, and he burped and he blew,
> As much as to tell me, "I blame this on you!"[26]

A child looking at the pictures of the ever-enlarging fish can easily follow the simple and funny story as Gustav is moved from bathtub to basement, while the rhyme and meter successfully ingrain the narrative into

the child's memory. The concept functions the same for this story as it did for *Mulberry Street,* but now it was something that Ted was doing consciously. Eleven years later, Helen reworked the story in *A Fish Out of Water.*

At first glance, the magazine version of "If I Ran the Zoo" appears simply to be a shorter version of the book that was published three months later. But the magazine version actually features drastically different illustrations of beasts like the It-Kutch, Preep, Proo, Nerd, Seersucker, and Fizza-ma-Wizza-ma-Dill. The book describes the last of these as the world's biggest bird, from the Island of Gwark, "who only eats pine trees and spits out the bark."[27] But in the magazine, that animal is *called* a Gwark, and it "eats Sassafras Berries and Bumble-Nut Bark!"[28] The magazine piece could not hope to contain the book's full menagerie, but it does have the Nerps, Fings, Snids, and Snides that the book lacks.

"Tadd and Todd" is the story of identical twins, one of whom (Todd) likes the idea and the other (Tadd) who hates it—and goes to extraordinary

Magazines were a sort of testing ground for Ted's book ideas. Often the periodical work looked and sounded quite different from the book form, as with *If I Ran the Zoo.*

TADD AND TODD

BY DR. SEUSS

1. *One twin was named Tadd*
And one twin was named Todd.
And they were alike
As two peas in a pod.

They were so much alike, from their hair to their feet
That people would stare when they walked down the street,
And no one, not even their own mother, knew
Which one was what one, and what one was who.

2. Now Todd (on the right) was the happier one.
He thought being twins was a whole lot of fun.
He liked it 'cause no one could tell him from Tadd.
But Tadd (on the left) . . . well, it made him quite sad,
So Tadd (on the left side) one day said to Todd,
"I *don't* want to be like two peas in a pod!

lengths to try to change the situation. Often passed on through faded photocopies, the story has developed a bit of a following among twins.

Marco, still trailing Bartholomew Cubbins's four appearances in Ted's stories, returned for the third time in "Marco Comes Late." He confabulates more strange occurrences on Mulberry Street but this time tells them to his teacher, Miss Block, who scolds him when he arrives more than two hours late for school.

Marco explains that he headed for school with the very best of intentions, but then "something happened on Mulberry Street." A bird laid an egg on his arithmetic book, and he was afraid to move for fear of dropping the egg. So he stood there while different animals debated the situation. Ted makes sure to differentiate between imaginative stories and outright lying, and the irrepressible Marco remains as admirably creative as ever. It's James Thurber's "The Secret Life of Walter Mitty" as applied to children—but Ted's Marco preceded Thurber's Mitty by four years.

Other denizens of Mulberry Street abound in "How Officer Pat Saved the Whole Town," in which the vigilant policeman manages to keep disaster from befalling the many characters—from Mrs. Minella with her umbrella to horn-tooter Fritz and dynamite-truck-driver Schmitz—while pounding a beat on Mulberry Street.

A portion of Ted's twin tale, "Tadd and Todd." It appeared as a magazine piece in 1950.

A boy resembling Marco appears in "Steak for Supper," another story set along Mulberry Street. In this one, he is overheard talking excitedly to himself about the steak his family serves for dinner every Saturday night. He is followed home by an Ikka, a Gritch, a Grickle, a Nupper, and two Wild Wheefs—more "lost" members of the Seussian bestiary. Any fan of the Sneetches will want to take note of the Wild Wheefs, whose bellies Ted adorned with stars before inventing the Sneetch.

Ted closed the year with "The Big Brag," and in 1951, he published seven more stories before he became consumed with *The 5000 Fingers of Dr. T* and his tenth book, *Scrambled Eggs Super!* Eleven years after hatching Mayzie's egg and three years before hearing Jo-Jo's "Yopp" emanating from Who-ville, Horton's faithfulness, good nature, and patience were tested in "Horton and the Kwuggerbug." Once again, he is suckered into helping a manipulative animal during the month of May. In this case:

> [A] Kwuggerbug dropped from a tree with a plunk
> And landed on Horton the Elephant's trunk!
> The Kwuggerbug leaned toward the elephant's ear.
> "Perhaps you are wondering," he said, "why I'm here.
> Well, I've got a secret!" he whispered. "I know
> Of a Beezlenut tree where some Beezlenuts grow!"[29]

The principled Horton being pestered by the Kwuggerbug in 1951.

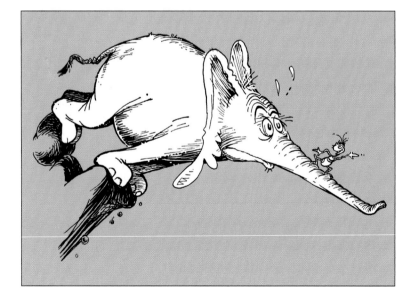

The Kwuggerbug offers to show Horton the way if the elephant will carry him there. When the path to the Beezlenut tree proves to be unnecessarily perilous, the Kwuggerbug reminds Horton that "a deal is a deal." Naturally, the ethical Horton is faithful to his word—one hundred percent—and is ultimately rewarded. But first he braves crocodiles to cross a lake and climbs a 9,000-foot-high mountain "while the Kwuggerbug perched on his trunk all the time /

And kept yelling, 'Climb! You dumb elephant, Climb!'"[30]

"The Rabbit, the Bear and the Zinniga-Zanniga"[31] might be familiar to some from Marvin Miller's dramatization on the phonograph album *Dr. Seuss Presents . . . Fox in Socks/Green Eggs and Ham* that was produced 14 years later. The story concerns a quick-thinking rabbit, in the style of Br'er or Bugs, outwitting a bear that threatens to eat him. The rabbit convinces the bear that his head is crooked because his right eye has one fewer eyelash than his left eye, and he recommends the bogus curative juices of the Zinniga-Zanniga Tree.

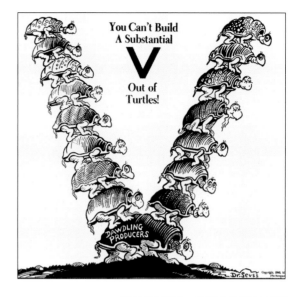

"Yertle the Turtle," first mentioned in the introduction to "Zinniga-Zanniga," was his next story, followed soon after by "Gertrude McFuzz," seven years before the book containing the stories was published. They differ only minimally from the more familiar versions.[32] It is interesting to watch the progression of stacking turtles in Ted's work over a nearly 25-year period. The turtle was the animal on which Ted focused his very first "Boids and Beasties" cartoon for *Judge* magazine. He began stacking them in May 1928 and repeated that image through the next two decades. Sixteen years before Yertle, it was a stack of turtles in "Hejji" that The Mighty One descended to get down from a tree—an early instance of a self-important ruler shaken when he finds himself too high. During his time with *PM,* Ted observed the inherent instability of a stack of turtles. In his cartoon criticizing "dawdling producers" who were providing the necessary war materials at a turtle's pace, thereby jeopardizing the chance of building toward victory, Ted noted that "You Can't Build A Substantial V Out of Turtles!"[33]

In "The Bippolo Seed," a duck named McKluck discovers a magical seed, which, if he plants it and makes a wish, will quickly sprout, bearing the object of the wish on the Bippolo Tree. The duck wishes for a week's worth of duck food, but a cat walking by suggests that he wish for a great deal more, like enough food so that they could go into business and make lots of money. Maybe duck food isn't even the best thing for which to wish. Perhaps the duck should wish for the tree to grow doughnuts and crullers, skates and umbrellas, bicycles made out of pearls, shirts made of kangaroo hair, olives

Turtle towers: Time and again, the image of stacked turtles found its way into Ted's work. These precariously perched fellows from World War II (top) would find another formation in a 1951 Redbook piece and, ultimately, in the classic book Yertle the Turtle (bottom).

stuffed with cherries, and buckets of purple ice cream. Greed gets the best of the pair in the end. As Bartholomew discovered in "King Grimalken and the Wishbones," one must be careful with one's wishes.

Ted began his first draft of the script for *The 5000 Fingers of Dr. T* in the summer of 1951. But before the movie claimed his complete attention, Ted published two more stories that year. "The Strange Shirt Spot" would later provide the basis for the bathtub-ring scene in *The Cat in the Hat Comes Back,* as a spot is transferred from one object to another. It is another tall tale that highlights the way children view the gap between their experiences, real or perceived, and the stories that they think their parents will believe.

In "The Great Henry McBride," Ted focuses on another wonderful aspect of childhood that is often overlooked—that magical time when one's responsibilities are very limited and daydreaming is considered an important job. Henry fantasizes about what he'd like to be when he grows up, but from his child's point of view, there are so many exciting careers he could pursue and he doesn't see the limitations that an adult would point out.

Consumed by *Dr. T* through its 1953 preview and *Scrambled Eggs Super!,* which was released two months later, Ted and Helen celebrated Ted's forty-ninth birthday and took a much-needed vacation for six weeks that spring, sailing to Japan. When they returned in May, Ted published "Wife Up a Tree," his first strictly adult story in 14 years, since the unsuccessful *The Seven Lady Godivas*. It is the story of a compulsive bird named Phoebe McPhee who is forever straightening the leaves that are hanging awry and tidying up the nest she shares with her husband, Gus. With Phoebe constantly polishing buds, washing twigs, scrubbing knotholes, and even dusting under-ground roots, Gus eventually flies off with another bird, named Ruth, who doesn't obsess about cleanliness—a side of the good Doctor's humor that friends knew but readers rarely saw.

In November 1952, on the same day that Lucy first held a football for Charlie Brown, Ted published the article ". . . But for Grown-Ups Laughing Isn't Any Fun," in which he took adults to task for the mean-spirited nature of their humor, making a public stand against racism and prejudice. He had done so at the Utah conference three years earlier, describing America as a country that "preaches equality but doesn't always practice it."[34] Curiously, in his first book written entirely after that conference, *If I Ran the Zoo,* there were still questionable depictions of Asians ("helpers who all wear their eyes at a slant")[35] and African tribe members,[36] even at a time when he was consciously trying to change the face of prejudice in America. The first real strike against bigotry in one of Ted's stories came in the summer of 1953 with the publication of the original version of "The Sneetches."

The roots of the story reach back almost 25 years to a cartoon Ted did for *Judge* in 1930, in which turtles and mock turtles resemble each other so closely that "no one has the slightest idea whom he is fighting."[37] The magazine version of "The Sneetches" differs significantly from the book version that followed eight years later, when Ted expanded marvelously on the original brief three-paragraph piece. In the original, there is no Sylvester McMonkey McBean and no Star-Off or Star-On Machine. The social stratification is not as clearly defined either. In the lone illustration, both the Star-Belly and Plain-Belly Sneetches are equally haughty to one another. When the Star-Belly Sneetches don't ask the Plain-Belly Sneetches to their celebrations and events, the latter don't stand around feeling dejected as they do in the book—"they throw dreadful things at the Star Bellies' heads . . . like oysters and clams and the springs of old beds."[38] And unlike the book, there is no resolution of the prejudice. But Ted distilled the issue of intolerance down to a final rhymed couplet:

> (And, really, it's sort of a terrible shame,
> For, except for those stars, every Sneetch is the same.)[39]

Unflustered by the simple brilliance of his most recent story, Ted continued to create new characters for his stable, including Flustards. Ted described them in "The Flustards"[40] as being strange, dumb beings that don't *do* anything and never have any fun, living a very unfulfilling existence. Instead of playing and enjoying themselves, they stand with their fingers

A terrible shame: Ted's feelings about prejudice had been percolating for years, and in 1953, he offered "The Sneetches," his groundbreaking diatribe against bigotry, as a magazine piece (top). Eight years later, it found its way to book form (bottom).

clasped and wait to see impossible things like two-inch-high elephants, apple trees with steering wheels, and roller skates made from cheese.

Ted's first Christmas-themed story was not *How the Grinch Stole Christmas!* He concluded 1953 with "Perfect Present." Like "The Sneetches" and "The Flustards," it is poem-length rather than story-length. In it, Ted recommends a Fluff-footed, Frizzle-topped, Three-fingered Zifft as the perfect Christmas gift, for reasons ranging from the fact that he doesn't talk in his sleep to the observation that he is friendly with eagles and doesn't pick fights with neighborhood beagles. Plus, he doesn't smell too bad when wet.

The following year, Ted continued his magazine work with installments about "The Munkits," "The Zaks," and "The Ruckus." In the first piece, two Munkits demonstrate the fallacy of the grass always being greener on the other side. They spend their time running back and forth between two rocks on the Desert of Dreer in the blazing sun, never stopping to enjoy either rock because the one that they are *not* on looks more inviting.

Ted reworked "The Zaks," which was published the month of his fiftieth birthday, as "The Zax," in *The Sneetches and Other Stories,* seven years later. The stories are essentially the same, although the book ends with the Zax remaining "un-budged," while in the "lost story," the two Zaks stand in each other's way until they are both dead. Nearly a quarter-century earlier, Ted had drawn a man named Xax Zakkx—an inventor. "Anyone can invent something complicated, but the real inventor is one who invents something simple," Ted wrote. "Ages ago, for instance, people stood up all the time . . . simply because no one had yet invented sitting down."[41] Ironically, while the Zaks/Zax are remembered for stubbornly standing in perpetuity, Xax Zakkx was the inventor of sitting down.

The title character in "The Ruckus," as would be expected, is a very noisy bird who works for a year to develop a colossal noise. Then he produces "a mouthful of shrieks . . . like ten thousand elephants blowing trombones" and declares himself a success. But a worm puts the feat in perspective when he says, "But I have a question to ask, if I may . . . / You made yourself heard . . . but just what did you say?"[42]

Making a Ruckus: Another example of Ted's magazine work featured a feathered fellow who liked to bellow.

The Ruckus

BY DR. SEUSS

On the top of a hill on the Island of Zort
Lived a bird called the Ruckus, whose favorite sport
Was making loud noises. It gave him a thrill
To be known as the loudest-mouthed bird on the hill.
Then, one day, he thought, "I can be louder still!

Of course, the most famous sound in Ted's oeuvre was not the Ruckus's enormous bellow but the very faint "YOPP!" issued by a Who named Jo-Jo in *Horton Hears a Who!,* which was published the very next month. In relation to very small things like the Whos, it is interesting to note that Ted focused the attention of the nation's children on the importance of items too small to be seen with the naked eye at a time when Americans were preoccupied with the polio virus's effects on children.[43] In April 1954, a massive trial of the polio vaccine began, ultimately involving more than 650,000 children.[44] In August, *Horton Hears a Who!* was published—Ted's eleventh book.

Like *The Sneetches* the previous year, *Horton Hears a Who!* promoted the treatment of all creatures as equals (viruses being an obvious exception). The beasts who senselessly torment Horton and keep him from his noble duty are the Wickersham Brothers, named after the Wickersham Report, which, in 1931, reviewed and evaluated police enforcement of Prohibition (which Ted's family felt had senselessly tormented them and kept them from their noble brewing business). When Vlad Vlad-i-koff, the black-bottomed eagle, takes Horton's clover and drops it into a clover patch, the piles he makes when sorting through the patch have been compared to the landscaping of the walkways and shrubbery of lily ponds Ted saw in Springfield's Forest Park as a child.[45]

Ted's concentration on the way his words sounded—and their ability to interest and entertain children even too young to read—began to win him recognition within the field of children's literature. One enthusiast wrote, "Sound! It's a tantalizing trickster when Seuss manipulates it. It's as if the words so neatly pinned down to the pages by clean, clear type were just on tip-toe with excitement to be turned loose by being read aloud. . . . Read aloud a Seuss book once to a young audience and there is a . . . big-eyed quiet, but read the book through twice and . . . everybody gets into the act and recites the yarn."[46]

Once again, a childhood vista influenced Ted's work. Horton's clover field with its meandering path (top) brings to mind a popular Springfield garden near Ted's home (bottom).

Ted next did a series of stories for *Children's Activities* magazine. In "Latest News from Mulberry Street," a Marco-like boy continues to see marvels, like a Galla-ma-Gook juggling a radish, a blue fish, a sock, three nuts and a bolt, and a one-handed clock (that looks suspiciously like a Telechron).

"THE SUPER-COW OF TOMORROW"

The head eats . . .
. . . the rest gets milked

Seuss fans are probably familiar with the image of the Umbus from the book *On Beyond Zebra!* The stretch-limousine-like cow appears to be the progeny of a delirious affair between a centipede and a Holstein—another member of the stable of chimerical beasts tended in the mind of Ted Geisel. However, Ted had been concocting, modifying, and improving this "extend-a-cow" in various venues since 1928, when he decided to construct a better cow, rendering the ordinary one obsolete. It was the American way, after all, to improve products scientifically to make them more efficient. From the "individual cow," which had a head-to-udder ratio of 1:1, Ted invented the "Vache Triplex," which had one mouth to feed but three sets of udders to milk. From there, he postulated the production of the "Super-Cow of Tomorrow," a ten-mile-long cow

312

that Amalgamated Milk, Inc., soon planned to complete.

The idea resurfaced 13 years later in *PM* with a new interpretation. Instead of focusing on the convenience of having to feed only one mouth, the new cartoon concentrated on the fact that regardless of how many udders there were to produce products, they all had to go wherever that head led them. That image made for an excellent commentary on the countries subsumed by Hitler's Germany.

The germ of this idea lay dormant for another 14 years. Five months before *On Beyond Zebra!,* in "The Great McGrew Milk Farm," Gerald revived the outlandish beast to improve his business, explaining to his sister the problem with the old-fashioned cow:

"Now the *old* kind of cow . . . well, I'm telling you, Liz,
The old-fashioned cow is not right as she is.
Take a look at a cow and you'll see what I mean . . .
Only *half* of each cow has a milking machine.
It's the half that's in back that gives all of the juice
And the half that's in front . . . well, the front half's no use.
'Cause the half that's in front has a big hungry head
And that big hungry head always has to be fed
And to feed that big head is a lot of expense.
That isn't smart business. That doesn't make sense."[47]

This wasn't the only addition to Gerald's collection of crazy creatures. If you thought that you were familiar with all the residents of Gerald's zoo, it's important to know that the animal that was the hardest for him to catch was the Ram-Tazzled Filla-ma-Zokk, which he got to follow him to his zoo by playing music on an immense and expensive instrument called an o'Grunth in "How Gerald McGrew Caught the Filla-ma-Zokk."

The bovine line: **The multi-uddered cow from *On Beyond Zebra!* (opposite page, top left) had many predecessors, including the 1928 Vache Triplex and the Super-Cow of Tomorrow (opposite page, top right and middle left) and the goose-stepping, swastika-emblazoned cow from a 1941 *PM* cartoon (opposite page, bottom). And five months before *Zebra,* "The Great McGrew Milk Farm" (this page) appeared in a popular children's magazine.**

Speedy Boy

By Dr. Seuss

THE most talked about bird in the town of East Lynn
Was a fast-flying blue jay called Zip-Around Flynn.
Young Zip flew so fast when he streaked through the skies,
The other birds all would get dust in their eyes.
Young Zip flew so fast he could fly from his nest
To a faraway church steeple ninety miles west
And back to East Lynn again *all in one day!*
This worried his friends. They would wonder and say,
"Yes, you really *are* fast. It's a rather good trick.
But what is the purpose of flying so quick?"

Then Zip would start boasting, "I like being speedy.
What's more, I'll fly faster! I will! Yes, indeedy!"
And, somehow or other, this fast-flying feller
Managed to grow, on his nose, a propeller!
(Don't ask how he did it. I really don't know.)
But he grew that propeller. And then! *Did he go!*
He took off one morning and flew all the way
To England and back in just half of a day!
Then his friends said, "So what? We just can't see the need
Of a bird flying round at such neck-breaking speed."

Speedy Boy (this page and opposite page), a fresh new addition to the Seuss aviary, was the focus of a March 1955 magazine spread.

Likewise, if you thought that Gertrude McFuzz was the only vain bird in Ted's repertoire to grow desired appendages that ultimately caused problems, you obviously haven't read about Speedy Boy.

Catching up with Bartholomew Cubbins and Marco, Gerald McGrew made his fourth appearance in five years in the magazine version of "If I Ran the Circus," which preceded the book version by seven months. The original

But Zip-Around bragged as he threw out his chest,
"I'm the fastest young bird in the world. I'm the best.
But I'll fly even faster! I shall. And I can.
I'll fly even faster than rockets and man!"
And, somehow or other, he managed to grow . . .
(Don't ask how he did it. I really don't know.)
But, somehow or other, young Zip-Around grew it.
A jet on his back! And one morning he flew it.
He flew from East Lynn, and he steered for the moon.
And he zipped past the moon just before it was noon.
Then he zipped along quicker. He zipped past the sun
Precisely, I've heard, at a quarter to one.
Then he yelled, "Faster! Faster! I've only begun!
I'm just warming up! This is only a start!"
But then something went wrong,
And he blew all apart!
And his friends watched his pieces come tumbling down
And land in the dump in their slow little town.
And today he is talked of as Zip-*No-More* Flynn,
While his friends sing and fly in the sky of East Lynn.

piece concerns the World's Greatest Stunt—the Gerald McGrew Super-Balancing Act—involving a precarious pyramid of animals towering above an elephant standing on his trunk on a high wire, at the peak of which Gerald swings his aunt Gussie by her teeth. Ted used the concept for his next book (*On Beyond Zebra!* was already at the publisher) but replaced Gerald McGrew with Morris McGurk[48] and eliminated Gerald's big trick.

In 1955, Dartmouth bestowed upon Ted the honorary title of Doctor (this page, top).

Most people stop with the Z . . . but not Ted! Instead, he encouraged children to use their imagination and discover a Yuzz-a-ma-Tuzz (this page, bottom) or some Nutches in Nitches (opposite page).

After 27 years of referring to himself as "Dr. Seuss," the month that the first "If I Ran the Circus" was published, the "Doctor" became official when his alma mater, Dartmouth College, awarded Ted a "Doctorate of Humane Letters" as an honorary degree. He was now Dr. Seuss *and* Dr. Geisel.

In September 1955, Ted's wife, Helen, was recuperating from her struggle with Guillain-Barré syndrome and its associated paralysis in their hilltop La Jolla home, where Ted tried to enjoy the publication of *On Beyond Zebra!* The story of the boy whose philosophy is "most people stop with the Z *but not me!*" encapsulates all that has made Dr. Seuss so important and endearing. Fundamentally, the book posits the empowerment of children through the use of their imagination. Instead of rote memorization of that which has been given to them, there is excitement to be found in what has come to be known as "thinking outside the box." There are new worlds without limits to be discovered by people who can think creatively. But that did not have to entail trips to exotic locales to discover uncharted territories. Rather than accepting the standard 26-letter alphabet as it has been handed down and taught to countless children, what if a kid were to explore what comes after *Z*? Fantastic things could be found right under your nose.

This kind of thinking was, for the times, downright radical. From the beginning, Ted's children's books had encouraged readers not to settle for the routine. In his first book, the daily walk home from school could be an adventure for a creative mind. By his sixth book, it wasn't enough for Marco to show readers giraffes and elephants in a parade along Mulberry Street; when Marco ponders what types of fish might be found in the unknown waters connected to McElligot's Pool, he creates new and wild species. In Ted's ninth book, new species presented the need for new names, and Ted continued to stretch young readers' imaginations to consider the varieties of animals that could be found for Gerald's zoo in the far reaches of the world, like Joats, Nerkles, and tizzle-topped Tufted Mazurkas. In his twelfth book, he was now suggesting that children be willing to question the very alphabet from which these names and words are made.

Animals like the giraffe and the elephant from Mulberry Street are made to seem mundane on the first page of *On Beyond*

Zebra!, where Conrad Cornelius o'Donald o'Dell intones, "The A is for Ape. And the B is for Bear. The C is for Camel. The H is for Hare."[49] Those animals (and that alphabet) are for people who stop at Z. After all, those animals and letters are the ones that adults teach to children. In Dr. Seuss's world, another child tells Conrad:

> "In the places I go there are things that I see
> That I *never* could spell if I stopped with the Z.
> I'm telling you this 'cause you're one of my friends.
> *My* alphabet starts where *your* alphabet ends!"[50]

In conspiratorial tones, Ted gets the young reader to want to join the mysterious club, to be invited into the hidden clubhouse and be given the secret decoder ring. "I'm telling you this 'cause you're one of my friends"— children aren't accustomed to the trust implicit in adults' confiding in them like that. The advertising man knows how to interest people in his products. Ted's new products were imagination and literacy, and he got children interested in them in ways that few authors have been able to match. Turn the page, and immediately you find out just what kind of things you'll see if you'll just follow him down this path—animals like a Yuzz-a-ma-Tuzz.[51] The reader knows for certain that the boy is telling the truth when he says, "You'll be sort of surprised what there is to be found / Once you go beyond Z and start poking around!"[52]

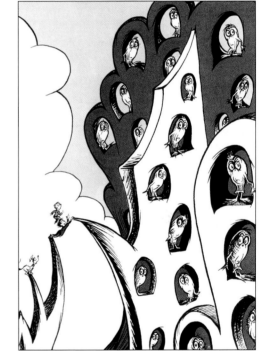

That expectation is rewarded repeatedly with inspired and rollicking language, like Ted's explanation of the concerns of the odd little animal known as a Nutch and the archway-like caves they inhabit called Nitches.

> These Nutches have troubles, the biggest of which is
> The fact there are many more Nutches than Nitches.
> Each Nutch in a Nitch knows that some other Nutch
> Would like to move into his Nitch very much.[53]

In the mid-1950s, Ted's last hurrah in the ad biz came in the form of a two-year stint for Holly Sugar.

In the month that Martin Luther King, Jr., led a boycott of the Montgomery, Alabama, bus system, Ted published "A Prayer for a Child," in which he uncharacteristically addressed God. Although he had published pieces in the *Junior Catholic Messenger,* his stories had no religious connotations, just as his Christmas-related cartoons and stories avoided the subject of religion. But in this short poem that accompanied an equally unusual view of a house on Earth from space, Ted wishes that God would "Tell all men / That Peace is Good. / That's all / That need be understood."[54]

On a less solemn note, Ted humorously addressed the issue of indecision in "Did I Ever Tell You How Lucky You Are?" In that story, a creature called a Zode comes to a fork in the road and cannot make up his mind which way to go, deciding in the end to try to take both roads at the same time.

A bird named McGruff learns a lesson about greed in "The Kindly Snather." The shade provided by the Snather's beak is not enough for McGruff and he tries to take advantage of the Thidwick-like bird, eventually outsmarting himself.

In the final "lost story," Ted returned to Phoebe McPhee, last seen driving away her husband, Gus, with her incessant cleaning in Ted's adult story "Wife Up a Tree." In "Tree Number 3," Phoebe is living with Phillip McPhee and nattering on about wanting a bigger nest in a better neighborhood—a place where they have room to store worm chops and entertain friends without crumpling their feathers. Besides, she distinctly remembers that in his proposal, Phillip had promised her an Eggshell Disposal. Phillip just wants to relax and enjoy the view from their nest after a hard day's work in the Worm Fields and can't afford a new nest on his pay anyway. Those who thought that *The Seven Lady Godivas* was Ted's only story for adults will enjoy the two "lost" Phoebe McPhee stories.

From 1954 to 1956, Ted worked on an advertising campaign for Holly Sugar, designing billboards, subway cards, and posters through the agency Mogge-Privett, Inc., under the art direction of David Rose. It proved to be the last of his great advertising projects, with a cast of colorful characters.

In the spring of 1956, Ted created, gratis, an eight-page booklet called

Signs of Civilization! for the La Jolla Town Council as his contribution to the local movement to ban billboards. In the booklet, Ted's advertising everyman Gus—or in this prehistoric case, Guss—invents a product called a Guss-ma-Tuss that he advertises with a small carved sign on the rockface outside his cave. But Zaxx, the inventor of the Zaxx-ma-Taxx, erects a larger sign next to Guss's simple one in order to sell more of his product. The competition and the resulting signage escalate furiously.

> And, thus between them, with impunity
> They loused up the entire community.
> Sign after sign, after sign, until
> Their property values slumped to nil. . . .[55]

The Holly Sugar Corporation, which had been using Ted's artwork on billboards for the last three years, neither missed, nor appreciated, the irony of Ted's latest publication. Bill Tara's work replaced Ted's when they terminated his contract.

Also "lost" from this time period are many of Ted's songs, the unpublished lyrics for which remain in the University of California at San Diego's Mandeville Collection. During his work on *The 5000 Fingers of Dr. T,* Ted wrote many lyrics and interacted with several top-notch composers and musicians. Two years after the movie was released, "Kids Song" was already being covered on Lucy Reed's album *Singing Reed* (as "Because We're Kids"), and it would continue to be performed by artists ranging from Jerry Lewis (1963)[56] to Tony Bennett (1998). Just as he had experimented with a career in moviemaking, Ted dabbled in songwriting as well, working with Leigh Harline—an eight-time Academy Award nominee and two-time winner—to cut a master for the song "Searching," and consulting on "Doggone It, I've Done It Again!" with Frederick Hollander, whose work with Ted on *The 5000 Fingers of Dr. T* resulted in the last of Hollander's four Academy Award nominations.

Ted tried a variety of musical styles in songs like the playful "Mama Take Your Thimble Off," the comical "Bald-Headed Love Song," the linguistically clever "Just Name Your Game," and the narrative show tune "Trees Stay

Whether intended or not, Ted's 1956 pro bono work in support of a local drive to ban billboards coincided with his final foray into advertising.

Put." His facility for rhythm and rhyme imbued his lyrics with musicality, as if reading them aloud were akin to hearing them sung. For instance, he obviously had a jazzy tune in his head when he penned the virtually self-orchestrating "Bimba-Lotta Bam."

> Don't you listen to Joe!
> Don't you listen to Sam!
> Don't you listen to the flobbing
> Of the flib-flub-flam!
> Don't you listen to Gus!
> No, Sir!
> No, Mam!
> Listen only to the gorma-lotta-bimba-lotta bam![57]

Children's literature alone could never have provided sufficient outlet for all of Ted's imaginative energy. But children's books had become his primary focus. Much of his work during this period has been overlooked or forgotten, but whether he wrote scripts, stories, or songs—for children or adults—this decade shaped Ted's literary future. He stopped cartooning. He abandoned advertising. He gave up on Hollywood. He set his sights on changing the field of children's literature. Already heralded as a children's author, he spent the decade after the writers' conference honing his ideas and craft before taking the industry by storm in 1957.

CHAPTER 21
A Very Big Year

A timeline of Ted's career places *The Cat* and *The Grinch* at the exact midpoint.

Ted's step-daughter, Lark Dimond-Cates, has said, "I always thought the Cat . . . was Ted on his good days, and the Grinch was Ted on his bad days."[1] Many people are not aware that Ted did not create these two characters, with which he is most readily identified, until halfway into his career, or that both remarkable books—*The Cat in the Hat* and *How the Grinch Stole Christmas!*—were published in the same year! But that monumental year, 1957, is the exact midpoint in Ted's career between the time he took over editorship of the *Jack-O-Lantern* in 1924 and the publication of his final book, *Oh, the Places You'll Go!*, in 1990.

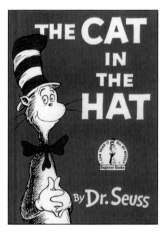

After John Hersey's 1954 article "Why Do Students Bog Down on the First R?" appeared in *Life*, Ted felt as if he had been shoved to the forefront of the debate on how to teach children to read. He reflected, "Hersey . . . casually suggested in *Life* that I was the type of writer who should write a first-grade reader. So, with innocent conceit, I said, 'Why not?'"[2] For his most entertaining explanation of the problem, he drew upon his friend Orlo:

> Every year, just a moment before Christmas, millions of Americans named Uncle George race into a book store on their only trip of the year.
>
> "I want a book . . . that my nephew Orlo can read. He's in the first grade. Wants to be a rhinosaurus hunter."
> "Sorry," said the salesman. "We have nothing about

rhinosauri that Orlo could possibly read."

"O.K.," say the millions of Uncle Georges. "Gimme something he can read about some other kind of animal." And on Christmas morning, under millions of Christmas trees, millions of Orlos unwrap millions of books . . . all of them titled, approximately, "Bunny, Bunny, Bunny."

This causes the rhinosaurus hunters to snort, "Books stink!" And this, in turn, causes philosophers to get all het up, and to write essays entitled "Why Can't Orlo Read.". . .

So . . . one day I got so distressed about Orlo's plight, that I put on my Don Quixote suit and went on a crusade. I announced loudly to all those within earshot, "Within two short weeks, with one hand tied behind me, I will knock out a story that will thrill the pants right off all Orlos!"

My ensuing experience can best be described as not dissimilar to that of being lost with a witch in a tunnel of love. . . .

In writing for kids of the middle first grade, the writer gets his first ghastly shock when he learns about a diabolical little thing known as "The List." School book publishing houses all have . . . lists . . . of words that kids can be expected to read, at various stages in their progress through the elementary grades. How they compile these lists is still a mystery to me. But somehow or other . . . with divining rods or something . . . they've figured out the number of words that a teacher can ram into the average child's noodle. (Also the approximate dates on which these rammings should take place.)

Poor Orlo! At the age of 6½, his noodle has scarcely been rammed at all!

He can, of course, recognize some 1,500 *spoken* words when they enter his head through the holes in his ears. But . . . he can recognize only about 300 when they try to get into his head through his eyes. All the other printed words in the world all look, to Orlo, like Appomatox [*sic*]. And there I was, in my shining armor, with my feet nailed down to a pathetic little vocabulary that I swear my Irish setter could master.

. . . After the first few weeks, I was still looking for a subject to write about. Then, suddenly one night, I dreamed the answer. . . . I rushed for my typewriter. Even before I got there, my happy fingers were already typing in the air. "The Queen Zebra" was the title of my story!

I had dashed off thirty-two red hot pages when, suddenly, I felt sort of all-over-queasy. Out of the corners of my eyes, I snuck a look at the Word List. *Queen* and *Zebra* weren't there after all! . . .

At the end of the first four months . . . I was now trying to sweat out a story about a bird . . . at the same time refraining from using the word *bird*. . . .

But *wing* was on the list. And *thing* was on the list. So I COULD write about a bird IF I called the bird a WING THING! And then I discovered that I could use the word *fly!* . . . After six weeks of trying . . . I had to give up. . . . My *wing thing* couldn't have *legs* or a *beak* or a *tail*. . . . And she couldn't lay *eggs*. . . .

I solved my problem by writing "The Cat in the Hat." How I did it is no trade secret. The method is the same method you use when you sit down to make apple stroodle without the stroodles. . . .

Since "The Cat" I've been trying to invent some easier method. But I am afraid the above procedure will always be par for the course . . . as long as the course is laid out on a word list.[3]

True to form, Ted had told a different anecdote several months earlier, in which his first attempt involved neither a queen zebra nor a wing thing. "All I needed, I figured, was to find a whale of an exciting subject which would make the average six-year-old want to read like crazy. . . . None of the old dull stuff: Dick has a ball. Dick likes the ball. The ball is red, red, red, red."[4] He claimed to have offered his publisher a book about scaling Mount Everest in 60-degree-below-zero weather, which received the response, "Truly

See Ted soar: In one fell swoop, Dick and Jane's stilted world (this page, top) was upended when Ted told the tale of Sally and her brother (this page, bottom) and their encounter with the silly, subversive Cat in the Hat.

Perhaps the Krazy Kat of comics (opposite page, top) and movies (opposite page, bottom) inspired the appearance of Ted's own cat (opposite page, middle).

exciting. . . . However, you can't use the word 'scaling,' you can't use the word 'peaks,' you can't use 'Everest,' you can't use 'sixty' and you can't use 'degrees.'"[5] Instead of the queen zebra yarn, he told the interviewer that he'd tried a story about a king and queen cat until he realized that "queen" wasn't on the list. In any case, the book, which proved to be a catalyst for his career, was published ten days after his fifty-third birthday.

Ted communicated with children in a different way than the authors of previous primers had done. In part, that was due to his understanding that "the trick is to imply with your illustrations what you're not allowed to say in words."[6] He also avoided mechanically well-mannered characters. "I think a youngster likes to read about someone who is bad for a change—then he realizes that he's not the only one who gets into trouble, messes up the house when mother is away. The other thing that's new in *The Cat* is humor. Kids respond to a little humor, to a crazy situation instead of that solemn old stuff, 'See my dog, Spot. Run, Spot, run.'"[7]

By now the story is familiar to nearly everyone—Sally and her brother are at home on a rainy afternoon. With their mother gone for the day, their only moral guidance when the Cat in the Hat arrives comes from their pet fish in his bowl, which the Cat immediately begins balancing atop his umbrella. To entertain the bored children, the Cat releases Thing One and Thing Two from a box. The Things rampage through the house, making an enormous mess. Just when it appears that they'll never be able to straighten things up before the imminent return of their mother, the Cat fixes everything with a ride through the house aboard a machine with hands that clean and pick up all of his "playthings," leaving behind only the question of what the kids should tell their mother about the incident.

The Cat would return one year later in *The Cat in the Hat Comes Back.* As the identifying logo of Beginner Books, the Cat's image would become synonymous with learning to read. But where did this Cat come from? Ted had been drawing cats since his very first college publication, 36 years earlier. Although they never chased mice, they were relatively normal cats—always fun but mostly unremarkable. Throughout the 1930s and 1940s, a cat appeared in the background of Dr. Seuss illustrations the way that Hitchcock appeared in his films—not in every one but often enough to be noticed. So how did Ted build this better mousetrap—this Cat?[8]

When Ted was a child, the predominant animated cat was Krazy Kat, a character Ted followed through the comics. Krazy Kat first appeared in "Krazy Kat and I. Mouse," a comic strip that ran briefly while "The Dingbats" was on vacation in July 1912. It became an independent strip in October 1913, when Ted was nine years old. Three years later, Krazy Kat became the world's first animated-cartoon-film cat, and in 1922, the comic was even made into a ballet. During this same period, Ted apparently was aware of the Uncle Wiggily books and games as well and, although Wiggily was a rabbit, Ted appears to have carried over Wiggily elements to his Cat.

A cursory consideration of these two characters from Ted's childhood would not lead directly to the Cat in the Hat. Krazy Kat was a meek animal that was always put upon by the smarter and more forceful Ignatz Mouse. Uncle Wiggily was hampered by rheumatism. However, much as his memory separated the text of Hilaire Belloc's books from their illustrations by Basil T. Blackwood, Ted selectively retained some of the physical attributes in his visual memory but not the personalities. What Ted seems to have kept of Krazy Kat was the image of a bipedal cat wearing a bow tie. Even before Krazy appeared in color starting in June 1935, movie posters from the 1920s showed Krazy's bowtie to be *red*. Uncle Wiggily reinforced the characteristic of walking erect and wearing a red bow tie and added the element of a crutch or cane, which Ted transformed into the Cat's umbrella. On the covers of many books, such as *Uncle Wiggily's Automobile* (1913) and *Uncle Wiggily at the Seashore* (1915), Wiggily also wears a top hat.

The feline predecessor whose personality most resembles the Cat in the Hat is Felix the Cat. He too was confident enough to go anywhere and do anything, but he tended to bungle things along the way. Felix began with a different name, first appearing in the November 1919 movie *Feline Follies* as Master Tom. Two

The Cat's Own

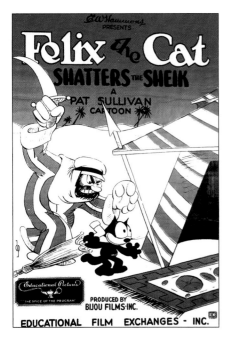

films later, Tom became "Felix" in *The Adventures of Felix*. After more than 50 movies, Felix debuted as a comic strip in Great Britain's *Daily Sketch* in August 1923. The strip first appeared in the United States later in August in the *Boston American,* the same paper in which Ted had followed Krazy Kat as a child.

For almost a decade, until Mickey Mouse debuted in 1928, Felix the Cat was the world's most popular cartoon character. The influence of a particular Felix movie on *The King's Stilts* was demonstrated earlier, but there are elements of other Felix movies that bear a strong resemblance to *The Cat in the Hat.* In *Felix Minds the Kid* (1922), Felix ends up in a home alone with a child and proves to be the world's worst babysitter. At one point, he uses a white ball, decorated with one thick, dark band, in a balancing routine, as Ted's Cat would do 35 years later. In *Polly-Tics* (1928), Felix is given the run of a house, much to the chagrin of the pet goldfish in his bowl, whom Felix antagonizes until the goldfish is left shaking his fist at the cat. Felix was another upright-standing cat, and he may have been the impetus for Ted to change the Uncle Wiggily crutch into an umbrella.

By May 1924, 73 Felix cartoons had been released. That month, in the first issue after Ted had been elected editor-in-chief of the *Jack-O-Lantern*, he used "Felix" as one of his first pseudonyms. But at that age, before he had developed his idiosyncratic style, Ted's cats looked as much like regular cats as he could manage. Cats continued to populate the backgrounds of an extraordinary number of his illustrations over the years. They became more stylized as his technique improved, but Ted's cats from the 1920s and 1930s conformed to the traditional feline look and behavior.

In May 1936, Ub Iwerks's cartoon production of *Dick Whittington's Cat* was released. The poster for that movie bears a remarkable resemblance to the Cat in the Hat and is clearly another link in the catenation. This cat holds a cane in his right hand instead of an umbrella. But the pinkie of that hand is jauntily raised within a puffy glove. His left hand is waving, palm up. He wears a two-color top hat. And as he walks

through the door, his feet and tail look much like those of the Cat in the Hat entering Sally and her brother's home.

Two years later, Ted's transitional cat appeared in the May 14, 1938, issue of *Liberty*. Ted illustrated several characters for an article by bandleader Benny Goodman entitled "What Swing Really Does to People." In one illus-

tration, a horn-blowing cat, though crouching, stands on its hind legs—a first for Ted.

Goodman's article explains the language of swing music, whose "musicians are 'cats' who *send, ride,* and *go out of the world*"[9] and whose dancers, known as "jitterbugs," do a step called the "flittercut." Ted illustrated these characters literally, with Who-like jitterbugs and a cat that bears the face that would become the Cat in the Hat. Not only had Ted found the face for his Cat, but he had also formulated his personality. He'd be a hepcat, for, as Goodman wrote, "with a *swinging cat sending,* you can never tell where he's going . . . or . . . when he'll stop. . . . And the listeners don't care where he goes, but that they are going with him 'out of the world.'"[10]

All that Cat needed now was a hat!

In November 1907, Harry Conway "Bud" Fisher had started the comic strip "Mutt and Jeff." By the 1930s, he had allowed it to be handled predominantly by assistants like Al Smith. In the comic,

In the 1920s, Ted was still drawing ordinary cats (opposite page, top), but in all likelihood, he was filing away some personality traits of the confident, fearless Felix and his umbrella (opposite page, second from top). Felix even incurred the ire of a fist-shaking fish (opposite page, third from top), a character Ted would echo memorably in *The Cat in the Hat* (opposite page, bottom).

Ted may have looked to Uncle Wiggily (this page, top left) and *Dick Whittington's Cat* (this page, top middle) for sartorial inspiration when concocting the Cat (this page, top right).

Ted's illustrations for a 1938 *Liberty* article by Benny Goodman (this page, middle left) featured an upright-standing cat, some Who-like jitterbugs, and a feline whose expression (this page, second from bottom left) would become very familiar in 1957 (this page, bottom left).

Augustus Mutt's son, Cicero, had a cat, which Smith spun off in 1933 into a new strip called "Cicero's Cat" (although the strip was published under Fisher's name).[11] The May 22, 1949, installment, "The Cat Didn't Want the Hat for Easter Anyway," was devoted exclusively to the cat trying on different hats. Interestingly, at that same time, Ted was working on *Bartholomew and the Oobleck,* in which he drew a small cat standing erect and wearing a hat that mimicked those of King Derwin's Royal Magicians. The cat and the hat were finally put together, and the hat is shaped very much like the one the Cat in the Hat would eventually wear, although this one does not have stripes. But stripes appeared soon afterward.

Enter a carefree Ormie in festive mood.

Sometime between May and December of 1949, Ted created the Cat in the Hat's most direct predecessor—the carefree Ormie—to advertise Ford Motor Company. The stripes might have been blue and white, but the rest of the Ormie will look familiar to any fan. He has white gloves, something red around his neck, and that placid, closed-eyed smile. In his right hand, he's carrying something—it's not yet an umbrella, but it's close. En route from Ormie to Cat, Ted made one more brief stop to further refine the look and the character when he produced the meddlesome cat in "The Bippolo Seed."

Many of the scenes from *The Cat in the Hat Comes Back* were also developed over time. One example is the image of little cats A through Z stacked upon one another's heads. The theme first turned up in a 1924 college illustration featuring a stack of teddy bears, inspired by Ted's childhood teddy bear. In it, one of the bears tips a top hat. Ted changed species when he refined the image for one of his 1949 Ford commercials, this time putting the smaller character under a top hat. Finally, he adapted the image to fit the Cat in *The Cat in the Hat Comes Back.*

And so the Cat evolved over half a career to become the iconic and iconoclastic figure he is today. Despite its ultimate popularity, *The Cat in the Hat* was, in its way, a heretical book that did not immediately have universal appeal. "London literary agent, Elaine Greene, did her best to interest the British public in *The Cat in the Hat,* but almost gave up in the face of disapproval from 'those genteel spinster

THESE SEVEN new films are the finest set of service trailers ever offered

ladies in their twin sets and pearls who edited children's books' and who thought Ted's Cat too vulgar for words." By 1965, when Ted's books had begun to catch on in Britain, it was because "the English don't so much regard Ted's books as children's books. They're just bloody good fun and never condescending."[12] It was precisely because he didn't catechize that Ted was able to build a better mousetrap.

How the Grinch Stole Christmas! is another fascinating candidate for literary forensics. In 1954, the Whos won popularity when Horton saved them from destruction. Horton had championed the Whos with the catchphrase "A person's a person, no matter how small." But when Helen reviewed Ted's new book in progress, she said, "You've got the papa Who too big. Now he looks like a bug." Betraying a bit of Wickersham, Ted replied, "Well, they are bugs. . . ." Fortunately, Helen kept him on track, retorting, "They are not bugs. . . . Those Whos are just small people."[13] Perhaps children enjoyed reading about creatures smaller than themselves, toward whom they, like Horton, could feel nurturing, much as they felt about their dolls and stuffed toys. So Ted returned to Who-ville and paired the Whos with a character who was every bit as dastardly as Horton was faithful—the Grinch.

An interesting thing happened during the 1957 holiday season. Random House published Dr. Seuss's *How the Grinch Stole Christmas!* But its theme of a Christmas that might not happen was not as unique as readers today might imagine. That fall, bookstore shelves were groaning with books about ill-fated yuletides. Little, Brown & Co. published Ogden Nash's *The Christmas That Almost Wasn't,* in which seven-year-old Nicholas Knock (aided by King

Ted first put a hat on a cat in 1949's *Bartholomew and the Oobleck* (opposite page, top). That same year, he created a festive-looking carefree Ormie (opposite page, middle) for a Ford ad. With its striped hat, gloves, and red ruffle, it is a virtual prototype for the Cat (opposite page, bottom).

Two teddy bears from a college piece (this page, left) and a balancing act from a 1949 Ford commercial (this page, middle) are visual forerunners to Ted's stacked alphabet cats (this page, right).

A little self-
reflection about
Ted's own yuletide
attitude (this page,
top) gave birth to
the Grinch (this
page, bottom).

From Dachs-Deer
to reindeer-stork
to dax-deer to . . .
Max-deer (opposite
page, from top to
bottom)!

Wenceslaus) saves Christmas for the citizens of Lullapat. J.B. Lippincott & Co. published Phyllis McGinley's *The Year Without a Santa Claus*. Since her story was first published in a women's magazine in 1956, it is possible that it planted the seed in the minds of the other two authors.

All three proved to be very successful. In 1966, movie adaptations of both Nash's and Ted's stories were released, and McGinley's tale became a 1974 stop-motion animated film. But as popular as these other books were, few today joke about Evilard outlawing Christmas or Mr. Prune evicting Santa. Clearly the Grinch has been the most memorable Christmas villain to undergo redemption since Ebenezer Scrooge.

To some degree, Ted identified with the Grinch. Later in life, Ted's car sported a GRINCH license plate. When asked why he wrote the book, Ted replied, "I was brushing my teeth on the morning of the 26th of last December when I noted a very Grinch-ish countenance in the mirror. It was Seuss! So I wrote the story about my sour friend, the Grinch, to see if I could rediscover something about Christmas that obviously I'd lost."[14] It was no coincidence that, when the book appeared in 1957, the Grinch complained, "For fifty-three years I've put up with it now! I MUST stop this Christmas from coming! . . . *But HOW?*"[15] Ted, of course, was born in 1904—53 years earlier.

Seuss looking like a Grinch

Ted's distaste for the materialism of Christmas dated back to his college years. For the 1924 Christmas issue of the *Jack-O-Lantern,* Ted penned a piece called "Santy Claus Be Hanged," in which he explained that "on Christmas morning everyone feels disappointed. . . . Sister wanted silk unmentionables and she gets burlap unpronounceables; brother wanted a case of Scotch and he gets a bowl of goldfish. Jacko . . . suggests . . . [the establishment of] an Exchange for Christmas presents. He expects to have several good neckties which he will exchange for an accordion."[16]

For Christmas 1930, Ted had another suggestion as to how to "Make Christmas More Meaningful."

Among his proposals was "Rolling Five into One":

> It is estimated that the average mother spends half her time telling her kiddies about our five complicated traditional characters—Santa, his Reindeer, the Sand-Man, the Boogey-Man and the Stork. If ever a merger was needed, here it is! By merging Santa with the Sand- and Boogey-Man and amalgamating the Reindeer with the Stork, we'd have something twice as poetical and something their little minds could grasp in a jiffy.[17]

A cross between Santa and the boogeyman certainly sounds like a reasonable description of the Grinch. This sort of amalgamation also brings to mind one of the most enjoyable treats in *How the Grinch Stole Christmas!* A reindeer-stork was not Ted's first experiment with reindeer hybridization. For the 1927 Christmas issue of *Judge,* Ted had invented the Dachs-Deer, an animal "that out-Luthers Mr. Burbank

1,647,829 B.C. Experiments between reindeer and dachshund result in fiasco.

himself. . . . It is no everyday feat . . . to cross a reindeer with a dachshund!"[18] He revisited the idea seven years later in an issue of *Life.* Ted began spelling "Dachs-Deer" as "dax-deer," which the Grinch eventually transformed into the Max-deer.

Just as Ted's mind returned to the noisy Wild Tones (from his booklet for Stromberg-Carlson radios) when creating Thing One and Thing Two, the same publication stuck in his mind when conjuring up the noisy revelry of the

Who children on Christmas morning. In a fascinating example of visual memory, he fused two Wild Tones that appeared on the same page into one Who for *How the Grinch Stole Christmas!* In the earlier booklet, one spiky-haired Wild Tone is suspended horizontally in midair. With a round mitt on the end of his thin arm, the second one bangs a bass drum bordered by a series of Y-shaped hooks. Ted fused these two images into one spiky-haired Who, beating a bass drum with the same Y-shaped filigree, with a thin-handled drumstick topped by a round, fuzzy striking end. It's hard to believe that these images—right down to the cloud puffs of sound emanating from the drums in both illustrations—were separated by 20 years.

The first mention of a Grinch by name came in 1953 in *Scrambled Eggs Super!* One of the birds that Peter T. Hooper passes because they aren't laying eggs is the Beagle-Beaked-Bald-Headed Grinch. The name next arose two years later in the short story "The Hoobub and the Grinch," in which Grinches are a group of beings that con you into buying things you don't need. In the story, a Hoobub is relaxing peacefully in the sun when a Grinch approaches him and tries to sell him a piece of green string, successfully convincing him that it is much more reliable than the sun that the Hoobub enjoys so much since it remains available to him day and night.

Ted's sense of irony makes this scenario even funnier when one realizes that, at the same time as he published this story, he was using the Grinch to sell Holly Sugar. The character in that advertisement might not have been named Grinch, but the sour puss, the gaunt figure, and the pointy fingers are unmistakably Grinch-ish.

After *The Cat* and *The Grinch,* Ted's reputation grew exponentially. Sales of his other books were already up. *Horton Hatches the Egg* had sold 15,000 copies in 1956—three times as many as in its first year. But that was nothing compared to the 200,000 copies of *The Cat in the Hat* that were sold in its first year. And after *The Cat* and *The Grinch,* sales of *Horton Hatches the Egg* spiked to 27,463 in 1958. Even Ted's slowest-selling children's book, *The King's Stilts,* sold two and a half times as many books in 1958 as it had in its first year of sales. In its second year, *Stilts* sold only 394 copies,

whereas *The Cat in the Hat* sold 500 copies per *day* in its second year![19] In less than three years, *The Cat in the Hat* had sold a million copies. The number of actual readers, of course, was far greater, as sales figures didn't account for books withdrawn from libraries, which invariably had waiting lists for Dr. Seuss books.

As his reputation flourished, Ted's sense of responsibility to the field of children's literature grew as well. The month that *How the Grinch Stole Christmas!* was launched, so was the Soviet satellite *Sputnik I.* In case Hersey's 1954 article hadn't already caused enough concern, it was followed the next year by Rudolf Flesch's book *Why Johnny Can't Read.* Americans were worried that their children were falling behind the rest of the world in education. Ted made the following observation:

> In Japan, awhile back, I saw something I have never seen anywhere else. Every bookshop in every Japanese city seemed to be crammed with Japanese school kids. Reading. Standing up. Hour after hour. . . . They were all gobbling up knowledge like mad. . . .
>
> I asked a friend . . . a Japanese educator . . . "How do you make your children WANT to read?"
>
> "We don't have to make them," he said. "The Necessity of Reading is something they feel in the air all around them. They realize from their earliest days, from the atmosphere in their homes and on the streets, that . . . the problem of being better housed and better fed will only be solved by More and More Knowledge. So our children read with the grim determination of pioneers.
>
> "Maybe," he added, "your American Civilization

Ted first used the word "Grinch" in 1953's *Scrambled Eggs Super!* with the introduction of the Beagle-Beaked-Bald-Headed Grinch (opposite page, bottom right).

Although he went unnamed in a 1957 Holly Sugar ad (this page, top), there's no denying this sourpuss's striking likeness to a certain Christmas curmudgeon (this page, bottom).

The cover of an early edition of *The Cat in the Hat* from Houghton-Mifflin (this page, bottom left) for the educational market became, with a color change, the title page for the Random House edition (this page, bottom right) for the trade market.

Not surprisingly, the form letter for Ted's fan mail showed a funny mail-carrying beast (opposite page, left), whose predecessor appeared almost 30 years earlier in *Judge* (opposite page, top right). Ted would create yet another form letter (opposite page, bottom right) for those fans who wrote Dr. Seuss again and again.

has become a bit too comfortable for your children to feel much urgency to tackle the hard job of reading."

. . . But that's something about which an author-illustrator can do little. What an author-illustrator *can* do, however . . . (and altogether too few of them do) . . . is to improve the quality and improve the techniques of the books we give our beginning readers to read. By just plain giving them stuff that is more interesting to read.[20]

Despite the popularity of Dr. Seuss's previous works and these two new mammoth successes, Ted's face was still unknown. When he appeared with two impostors on the popular television show *To Tell the Truth* in 1958, three of the four celebrity judges believed that one of the other men was Ted Geisel. In fact, the rumor that began in 1933—which held that Ted was an armless artist who drew with his toes—was still around as late as 1951.

In January 1954, he wrote the script for a half-hour television episode of the Ford Foundation's *Excursions* called "Modern Art on Horseback." The segment featured Ted with Burgess Meredith and Hans Conried. Conried had worked with Ted previously, having narrated the Japanese-accented parts in *Design for Death* (1947) and starred in the title role of *The 5000 Fingers of Dr. T* (1953). *Excursions,* aimed at children, examined how six different abstract painters represented the same horse. Two years later, in March 1956, Ted wrote a segment for the Omnibus TV-Radio Workshop of the Ford Foundation, in which he discussed the Boston Science Museum and his ideas for enlivening the museum experience for children. He also participated in a November 1958 book-signing tour and a segment of *The Fran Allison Show* the following month. These public appearances would eventually squelch the armless artist rumor.

As his books drew more attention and his position in the field of children's literature became increasingly influential, it was speculated that Ted's plan in 1957 to launch Beginner Books, his own early-reader imprint at Random House, might result in "the biggest

thing that has happened to the American classroom since the advent of William Holmes McGuffey's Readers in 1836."[21] Another writer lauded Dr. Seuss as "single-handedly changing the reading habits of hundreds of thousands of American children."[22] Ted even had to create a form letter to deal with the amount of fan mail he was receiving. Random House screened his mail, sending Ted letters from "teachers, librarians, sick or crippled children, and entire school classes,"[23] and replying with his form letter to the rest. It explained that Dr. Seuss's mail service was unreliable because he lived on a steep precipice that could be accessed only by an animal called a Budget, ridden by a Nudget. At this point, it should come as no surprise that the Budget was a beast Ted had imagined three decades earlier, in a cartoon that punned on the concept of traveling on a budget. "At the end of 1957, Random House announced that in the previous twelve months, he had received nine thousand two hundred and sixty-seven pounds"[24] of fan mail. By late 1960, he was receiving thousands of letters each week—so many that he had to create yet another form letter, this time involving a Three-Muffed Apfel Moose, because fans were complaining that Dr. Seuss always wrote about the Budget and the Nudget.

It was entirely possible that Dr. Seuss had become more popular than anyone realized. . . .

For Economy, Travel on a Budget!

This summer, hundreds of American families will be cantering through Europe on reliable Budgets furnished by Seuss. You, too, may enjoy the Old World's wonders on Budgetback! Drop in at our kennels and have a trial spin!

Your letter came today while I was in my studio painting a Three-Muffed Apfel Moose.

It was just about the nicest letter my Three-Muffed Apfel Moose and I have ever read.

Thank you very, very much.

Your friend,

Dr. Seuss

CHAPTER 22

Misunderstanding Dr. Seuss

Celebrity is its own reward and punishment. The better his books sold, the higher Ted's profile rose. Many became interested in him as a personality, and he had to turn down requests to speak at all manner of events, particularly as his stage fright became more pronounced. Others focused on his work and began to analyze it. Early on, Ted became the subject of graduate theses—at least "four M.A.s were written on Geisel in 1957 alone."[1] The attention and analyses led to many misunderstandings about Ted and his work.

In 1958, Ted published *The Cat in the Hat Comes Back*. He remained the same old stickler for detail. "After more than a hundred thousand copies of 'The Cat in the Hat Comes Back' had been sold, he decided that a single black line on the original jacket was too black, and a new jacket was made up."[2] As keen as Ted's own sight was when it came to a detail on the cover, others believed that they saw even more in the book itself. For example, several analyses have been made concerning the bathtub ring left behind by the Cat, which is subsequently spread around the house. The discourses compare the Cat's spreading ring to the spread of communism and suggest that the story was an allegory for Ted's fear of the expanding Red Menace (if the color struck the analyst as red)[3] or the problem of communist-sympathizing "pinkos" (if the color struck the critic as pink).[4]

The arguments are similar. Both begin by hypothesizing, for example, that *The Cat in the Hat Comes Back*'s representation of the "spreading red stain across the landscape certainly echoes the fears of the times."[5] With that mind-set, the argument leads to the conclusion that, to purge the stain, Voom "arrives like an atomic bomb to clean away the threat of subversion,"[6] or that "the association with nuclear holocaust and its sterilizing fallout, wiping the planet clean of pinkness and pinkos, is impossible to ignore."[7]

When the Russians announced their first intercontinental ballistic missile and the launch of two *Sputnik* satellites the same year *How the Grinch Stole Christmas!* was published, one might have just as easily argued that the pink-eyed, red-suited Grinch, trying to keep a religious holiday from coming, represented the Red Menace. But such analyses focus on superficial details and fail to examine Ted's actual feelings on the subject. He worked in Hollywood and spent most of his time in the army surrounded by Hollywood personnel. When these people were called before the House Un-American Activities Committee, Ted's sympathies lay with the accused. He addressed this subject directly in a 1947 cartoon in which "Uncle Sam peers down in horror at a community reduced through its mutual suspicions to chaos. Babies name their mothers as communists. A little boy denounces a run-down horse pulling a wagon. Another man suspects a passing bird of leftist sympathies."[8] This cartoon was not drawn by someone who felt threatened by the indomitable spread of communism, but rather by someone who urged tolerance.

In fact, the scene with the spreading spot was devised before 1958. It was a revision of a story Ted had published seven years earlier, called "The Strange Shirt Spot." The spreading spot in that story was blue-green and spread just the same as in the book, making stops on a cat, a bathtub, and the mother's dress. Red was just a color choice; perhaps Ted thought blue-green was too similar to oobleck to use again in a book. Most likely, it was just the ultra-critical author at work—if he could correct the thickness of a black line on the cover, he could certainly have decided to change the color of the spot within. These facts put the Voom that cleans the stain in a completely different light. The explosive "Voom" was most likely added to make the story more exciting for young readers, replacing the "broom" in "The Strange Shirt Spot." Ted was adamant that his stories could start with one outrageous element, but everything thereafter had to follow logically. Trying to clean up with a broom was the natural progression. If the stain spread too far, you'd need a super-broom, which then needed a name—and Voom worked nicely.

When asked about Ph.D. theses based on his work that made this kind

True colors:
To understand Ted's feelings on communism, there's no need to suss out hidden messages in his children's books. Instead, a 1947 *Judge* cartoon showing his unequivocal call for tolerance in the face of the Red Scare says it all.

of analysis, Ted responded, "I think they're a waste of time. . . . For example, they'll take a book of mine that has one color in it and talk about my great sensitivity in handling that color, and why I chose that color, when the fact is that Bennett Cerf called me up one morning and said, 'We're having a bit of a financial problem, so cut down your colors.'"[9]

Another misapprehension that has developed concerns the marketing of items based on Dr. Seuss stories. Just as the public often attributes to an actor the traits of one of his characters, the anti-consumerist message imparted in *How the Grinch Stole Christmas!* has led many people to believe that Ted was opposed to turning his characters into consumer goods. The opinion has been expressed that Ted "was wary of anything—product franchising most of all—that might cheapen the Dr. Seuss image."[10] Another source claimed: "During his life, Geisel restricted the marketing of his work to books and a few television specials. . . . [One] time Geisel 'set up a sculpting studio next to the pool house in La Jolla and created the Cat, Horton and four "Seuss multi-beasts" to be marketed as self-assembly polyethylene kits for the March toy show in 1959. But no one's version of a Dr. Seuss creature satisfied Ted,' and so the creatures were never made."[11]

It is true that Ted was a demon for detail and often did not like the results when others tried to portray his creations. But, like much of the information circulated about Ted without the substantiation of firsthand sources, the conclusions are inaccurate. *How the Grinch Stole Christmas!* was written out of Ted's specific "annoyance with the tradition of Christmas [being] turned into a mercantilistic holiday,"[12] but Ted had nothing against making money in principle. He was not averse to marketing items based on his work—from coasters to sculptures—provided that the quality of the product was acceptable to him.

But that level of quality was not nearly as impossible to reach as is often suggested. It just entailed Ted's being intimately involved in the production of the items, just as he insisted on being involved in the production of his books. In both situations, he needed to ensure that his vision was not lost in the translation. The polyethylene kits cited as substantiating Ted's singular "wariness" about merchandising his work serve to prove this point. The kits *were* produced and marketed by Revell, Inc. In fact, Ted liked the ones from 1959 enough to put out a second set in 1960.

Critics contend that following Ted's death, "Dr. Seuss" has become a brand name that has been marketed in the Disney mode, from figurines to films and from theater plays to theme parks. So where did the merchandising of Dr. Seuss begin, and is it really incompatible with the messages against rampant consumerism and anti-environmental industrialization found in such works as *How the Grinch Stole Christmas!* and *The Lorax?*

After the publication of *Horton Hears a Who!* in 1954, an article appeared that, in the process of describing the wild gizmos Ted created in some of his stories, unwittingly hit upon a critical point. The author observed, "This creator of tales extraordinary also qualifies as a tool and die maker, although the products of his own fertile imagination have not—as yet—flooded the market!"[13] Unbeknownst to Ted, others were working on that very idea.

Ted's reputation for creating strange beasts had grown to the point that the San Diego Fine Arts Gallery honored his work by holding an exhibition of his book illustrations in 1956. His menagerie had also come to the attention of people with more selfish designs—people who had seen the merchandising potential in his work. Around this time, the Kreiss Company produced a line of ceramic figurines called Moon Beings. Over the years, collectors noticed that these figures looked "vaguely Seussian," but many discounted the Moon Beings as not being directly connected to Ted's work. Dr. Seuss was not mentioned in promoting the Kreiss Moon Beings, and Ted does not appear to have known anything about them. As late as 2002, Dr. Seuss Enterprises was unaware of their existence.

But the Kreiss Moon Beings were, in fact, the first mass-produced figures based on Dr. Seuss characters—a distinction rendered dubious by the fact that they were unlicensed, and therefore illegal, reproductions. These figures did not merely resemble Ted's style. They were ceramic renderings of characters from three of the last four books he had published—*If I Ran the Zoo* (1950), *Scrambled Eggs Super!* (1953), and *On Beyond Zebra!* (1955). The figures are undated, but several factors help to place their production in approximately 1956.[14]

At least 11 different Moon Beings based on Seuss characters have been identified—five each from *If I Ran the Zoo* and *Scrambled Eggs Super!* and one from *On Beyond Zebra!* Ironically, in the late 1950s, Ted was visiting with first- and second-grade students at the La Jolla Day School and sketched an impromptu beast for them, saying:

. . . the first thing is to figure out what color spinach to put at the end of his tail. . . . Do you think his topknot should be noodley? Should we put a nose on the end of his nose? Now, what'll we call it? That's good— a MOON MONSTER![15]

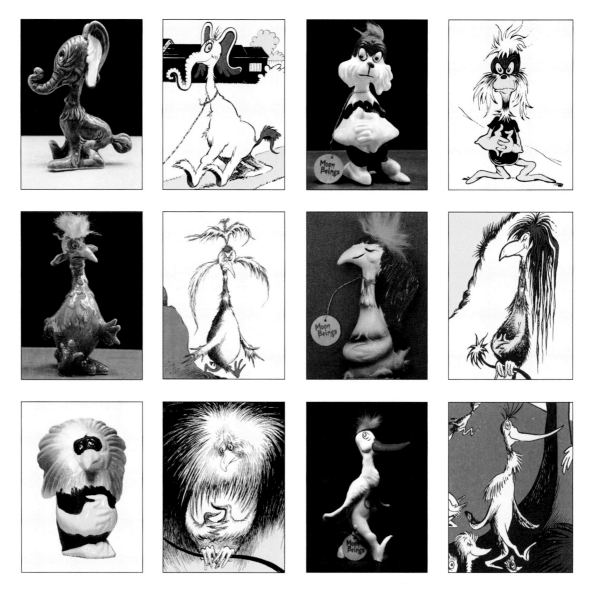

Even though Ted was not involved in their creation, the Moon Beings produced by Kreiss bore an uncanny resemblance to creatures from *If I Ran the Zoo, Scrambled Eggs Super!*, and *On Beyond Zebra!*

As the decade drew to a close, Ted's popularity was enormous. By 1959, five million Dr. Seuss books had been sold, and the push to make official toys based on the characters in those books was great. One interviewer related, "Over the years, many companies . . . besought Geisel to let them manufacture Dr. Seuss products of one kind or another. He has . . . steered clear of by-products that he cannot personally create. Two years ago, though, he was persuaded by Revell, Inc. . . . to authorize, and help design, a series of Dr. Seuss toys and games."[16] The Venice, California, toy company, run by Lew and Royle Glaser, allowed Ted to work intimately on the project and keep the number of creatures relatively small so that he could vigilantly oversee their production. Revell's Dr. Seuss Zoo initially consisted of only five figures. However, the zoo could be expanded. Ted explained, "My animals all have a way of looking somewhat drunk. . . . I've designed an articulated four-in-one animal I call the multi-beast, which is made up of Norval the Bashful Blinket, Gowdy the Dowdy Grackle, Chingo the Noodle-topped Stroodle, and Roscoe the Many-footed Lion."[17] He later changed Chingo's name to Tingo. Revell estimated that "by changing legs, bodies, heads, etc., some 14,000,000 combinations can be created."[18]

This first successful foray into merchandising Dr. Seuss characters was anything but mercenary. Ted had formulated his books to reach beginning readers, and his model of the Cat in the Hat was announced as the first "hobby kit for beginners." In an ad brochure, Revell claimed that "even a six-year-old can easily cement together the 25 big, colorful styrene pieces and create a whimsical figure almost a foot tall."

Many collectors feel that the Revell pieces come closer to translating Dr. Seuss's two-dimensional characters into three dimensions than any items crafted since, regardless of advances in technology. Ted worked with two sculptors for many months to capture that unnameable "something" that makes a character Seussian. Ted said, "None of my animals have joints and none of them balance . . . none of them are animals. They're all people, sort of."[19] But he paid meticulous attention to detail and maintained his exacting standards to the point that one interviewer noted, "Mrs. Glaser, who calls herself Vice-President in Charge of Geisel, keeps a notebook containing reminders like 'Test shots of eye decorations to T.G. for approval.'"[20]

In keeping with Ted's philosophy, the interchangeable parts allowed children to use their imaginations to be creative. Two more interchangeable models were added the next year—Busby the tasselated afghan spaniel yak and Grickily the gractus. Models of Horton, the Cat with Things One and Two, and the Birthday Bird joined the other Beginner Kits, intended to be easy enough for a preschooler to assemble. A balancing game based on "Yertle the Turtle" was produced, but sculpted models of the Grinch and a bust of

Horton intended for a plastic hand puppet were abandoned.

Meanwhile, Ted's legacy in children's books continued to grow. Five of the 16 best-selling children's books in the spring of 1960 were Dr. Seuss books.[21] That November, Ted's books occupied three of the top four positions on that list.[22] With Ted as president, Phyllis Cerf as chief executive officer, and an editorial board that included Ted's wife, Helen, the upstart Beginner Books became a division of Random House, Inc., in August 1960 and continued to produce books aimed at getting children to read at an early age. During the 1960s alone, Ted wrote and published 16 more books. Among these, Beginner Books issued "some books that

Seuss says come from 'the vast trunk of unfinished material' he has collected. They are in no way 'second-rate Seuss books,' he says. 'These stories often call for more human characters than animals, and I've always been more comfortable with animals . . .' so these books are illustrated by others,"[23] to be published under the pseudonym Theo. LeSieg.

By the end of 2000, 18 of Ted's books had sold more than a million copies each, the most popular being *Green Eggs and Ham*, which had sold 8,143,088 hardcover copies in the United States—excluding book-club sales—making it the fourth-highest-selling children's book by those parameters.[24] After the August 1960 publication of *Green Eggs and Ham*, Ted's stature had grown to the point that he merited a profile in the December issue of the *New Yorker,* covering everything from his publications to his pets—from a current tidbit about Cluny ("an aging, wheezy Irish setter") to the fact that the Geisels "once kept twenty-five or thirty cats."[25]

After *The Cat in the Hat Comes Back* was published, the next item to be fabricated from Ted's work was the very first Dr. Seuss plush doll. Random House had a stuffed version of the Cat made by Impulse Items, Inc. At least two versions were made, differentiated most easily by their hats, one of which is white cloth with dyed red stripes, while the other hat has red felt strips instead of dye. They also differ in size and body markings. Although neither carries any information about the date of manufacture, pictures of Ted with the dolls suggest that they may have been made in 1961. Impulse may have made a Thing One doll, or at least a prototype; in the documentary *In Search of Dr. Seuss* (1994), a Thing One doll strongly resembling Impulse's Cat sits on the shelf of Ted's workroom.

Through 1956, Ted never published a book without some other source of income.[26] "As late as 1954 he asked his agent, Phyllis Jackson, if he might count on $5,000 a year from royalties,"[27] one interviewer revealed, explaining that "finances have always been rather bewildering to Ted. . . . When he turned to writing and illustrating books . . . Geisel was not certain whether he could make a full-time living in this way."[28] But after *The Cat* and *The Grinch,* his popularity grew so immense that he no longer had the same financial concerns, and he created no more large advertising campaigns. In 1959, he received book royalties of almost $200,000.[29] Despite an increased initial print run of 100,000 copies, when *Happy Birthday to You!* was released in August that year, "within a few weeks, stocks of the book were exhausted, and fifty thousand additional copies were run off."[30] Released the following month, the Revell figures had retail sales of $1.5 million in the first four months—and that was at a time when they sold for $1.98 apiece!

And yet, from 1959 through 1969, the Revell models and the Impulse dolls, along with records made from his books, were the only licensed merchandising of Dr. Seuss that occurred. Given his increasing prestige, it certainly was a paltry amount. And, until then, the marketing of Dr. Seuss characters into different media was not so much merchandising as it was experimentation and expansion of Ted's ideas into new fields. But in 1970, Ted

Revell's Dr. Seuss Zoo collectibles had Ted's backing and involvement every step of the way. They included (opposite page, clockwise from lower left) Horton; the Cat in the Hat and Things One and Two; Tingo, Gowdy, Norval, and Roscoe; Grickily and Busby; and the Birthday Bird.

The interchangeable parts allowed children to make up their own creatures (opposite page, bottom right).

In the early 1960s, the first plush Seuss character appeared. Predictably, it was the Cat, albeit in two slightly different versions (this page).

licensed an enormous number of products. "Dr. Seuss" hit the market in everything from wicker tables to washcloths, which easily could have led to the impression that he had given in to temptation and greed. But that was unquestionably not the case. To the contrary, in 1964, Ted had rejected one such opportunity to cash in on some of his old material. It turned out to be the beginning of the worst period of his professional life.

It began back in September 1949, when Broadway producer Lorraine Lester had negotiated an option for her production company to develop short stories from *Liberty* magazine for use in radio, TV, and film. A year later, upon learning that the magazine would cease to publish, her company, Lester-Fields Productions, Inc., purchased *Liberty*'s "copyright library," which gave them the rights to all of the stories and articles published in *Liberty* magazine from May 1924 through July 1950—approximately 17,000 literary properties, including Ted's 1932 cartoons.

In 1964, Robert Whiteman visited Lester concerning a film project and became interested in the *Liberty* holdings. When Lester's group assigned the original agreement to the Liberty Library Corporation later that year, Whiteman entered into an exclusive agreement with the corporation to exploit the material from *Liberty* magazine. Among his other plans for the material (the *Mister Ed* television show stemmed from one of these properties), Whiteman showed the early Dr. Seuss cartoons to Ted's agent, Phyllis Jackson, and offered her the opportunity to join the Liberty Library Corporation in exploiting the material or to repurchase the rights to the work. Jackson contacted Ted, who rejected the offers.

In December of that year, Whiteman wrote Jackson to tell her that he had received an offer for reprint rights to Ted's cartoons. Ted contacted his attorney, Frank Kockritz, requesting that he dispute Liberty Library Corporation's right to the cartoons and try to prevent the company from using them. In May 1965, while Ted was busy making preparations for his fortieth reunion at Dartmouth, Whiteman contracted with Universal Publishing & Distributing Corporation to permit them to publish a paperback book consisting of Ted's contributions to *Liberty* magazine, believing that the corporation did indeed own the rights to do so. In June 1966, Universal Publishing wrote to Ted and requested that he retitle and revise his cartoons. But Ted, who was deeply enmeshed in the animated television production of *How the Grinch Stole Christmas!*, rejected the proposal. Against Ted's protests, the book, *Dr. Seuss's Lost World Revisited*, was published in 1967.

After the book was published, the Liberty Library Corporation tried one last time to sell the rights to the cartoons back to Ted, but he would have none of it. So Whiteman began to explore the possibility of selling merchandising rights to the cartoons, and the idea of turning them into toys was broached. In a June 24, 1967, letter to Charles D. Webster, who had contacted Ted about a memorial for Mike McClintock—the man who got *Mulberry Street* published for Ted when no one else was interested—Ted wrote that he and McClintock had "ended what was once a very warm friendship in two very unpleasant explosions that blew us miles apart. One had to do with the toy business."[31] In September 1967, Robert Whiteman executed a licensing agreement with Donald B. Poynter to manufacture dolls based on Ted's cartoons.

Adding to Ted's frustration, the recently published *The Cat in the Hat Songbook* was not well received. Sales were so poor that it became the only Dr. Seuss book besides *The Seven Lady Godivas* to be allowed to go out of print.[32] If 1957–58 was the acme of Ted's career, 1967–68 would prove to be its nadir. The book was dedicated to "Lark and Lea of Ludington Lane." They were the daughters of Ted and Helen's close friends Dr. E. Grey Dimond and his wife, Audrey.

Ted's wife had been stricken ill in 1954. Helen had been pretty much everything to Ted—mate and manager, accomplice and editor, companion and critic, bookkeeper and business partner. Ted dedicated *On Beyond Zebra!* to her while she was recuperating from the paralysis caused by her illness. The next year, she was well enough for them to travel to Ireland. During what was, for Ted, an otherwise delightful year, she fell ill again in 1957. The following year, she was able to answer his fan mail and join him in the business of launching Beginner Books. But by 1967, Helen again fell ill. Six years older than Ted, she turned 69 that September. Their fortieth wedding anniversary was only two months away. Sadly, Helen would not live to celebrate the occasion. During the night of October 22, 1967, perhaps thinking about her only sibling, Robert Judson Palmer, who had died the previous year, Helen wrote a note to Ted. The note expressed her sense that she was caught in a downward spiral from which she could not escape. Despite the four books she had written and the success of Beginner Books, she felt surrounded by the echoes of "failure, failure, failure." "I love you so much," she wrote. "I am too old and enmeshed in everything you do and are, that I cannot conceive of life without you."[33] She signed her suicide note "Grimalken, Drouberhannus, Knabler and Fepp."

As if Helen's death was not enough to bring Ted's life crashing down around him, the man who didn't even keep his own checkbook had to discuss the tax liabilities engendered by gains from Helen's portion of their community property. Memorial services were held for Helen in the second week of November. That month, Robert Whiteman held a meeting with Don Poynter, to which Poynter brought a hand-sculpted Styrofoam and papier-mâché model he had made of one of Ted's *Liberty* characters. Poynter then spent six weeks in Japan working on the dolls and choosing a manufacturer. In December, he sent prototypes of the planned hangtags to his lawyer. Finally, in January 1968, Poynter sent a letter authorizing the manufacture in Japan of 12 small vinyl dolls from wax models he had sculpted—six different vinyl characters, each in two different colors, although advertisements later showed a thirteenth. In February, Whiteman approved the dolls and the advertising materials. The Poynter figures went on sale on February 16.

Taking liberty: **Ted lost the legal battle to remove these products (loosely based on his *Liberty* characters) from the marketplace.**

Two weeks later, Ted's sixty-fourth birthday arrived, bringing with it, in all likelihood, thoughts of his own mortality. Six days afterward, he filed a complaint against four parties, including the manufacturer (Poynter), distributor (Alabe), and licensor (Liberty Library Corporation), as well as the New York group that sold the toys to retailers (Linder et al.), alleging that the toys were being advertised "as 'Dr. Seuss' creations . . . and that the dolls are 'tasteless, unattractive and of inferior quality.'"[34] He sought compensatory and punitive damages and an injunction to prevent the defendants from using "Dr. Seuss" in any connection with their product. He did so on the basis of five different points of law, including defamation of character and unfair competition. The court saw enough validity in Ted's claims to issue a temporary restraining order on March 12, after which time no more of the product was shipped for sale.

Perhaps he had reached his lowest ebb and was witnessing the turn of the tide. Ted and Audrey Dimond had fallen in love. That spring, Audrey told her husband that she intended to marry Ted. But the world would continue to intrude on them. On April 4, James Earl Ray assassinated Martin Luther King, Jr. Five days later, at the preliminary injunction hearing, the hangtags, display boxes, advertising literature, and oral and written sales presentations used by Poynter were deemed to convey the impression that Dr. Seuss had designed, manufactured, or authorized the Poynter dolls. An injunction was issued, preventing the company from making such statements. The many other points of law were to be decided in a hearing set for April 22, 1968, but the case was not heard until December.

The case seemed to be going in Ted's favor. However, the preliminary injunction said nothing about who owned the rights to Ted's original cartoons. So Poynter simply revised labels to conform to the ruling. The copy on one side of the original hangtag read, THIS IS MY (YOU NAME IT) FROM DR. SEUSS' MERRY MENAGERIE, and, on the other, FROM THE WONDERFUL WORLD OF DR. SEUSS— AN ORIGINAL MERRY MENAGERIE. After the preliminary injunction, the copy on both sides was changed to diminish the emphasis on Dr. Seuss.

The print on the plug on the bottom of the figures presented a different problem. The tags could be reprinted, but the cost of changing the figures would have been prohibitive. The plugs already had information about the 1932 copyright by Liberty Publishing Company and the renewal in 1968 by Poynter Productions. And there was information that the figures were FROM ORIGINAL ILLUSTRATIONS BY DR. SEUSS. However, that name was printed in the logo style derived from Ted's printed signature, which the court would not allow. Poynter's simple solution was to scratch or melt off the Dr. Seuss logo. The existing figures could then be sold with the new advertising, in compliance with the court.

Ted expressed his situation that miserable year in a painting. In "Fooling Nobody," a taciturn bird, with hands clasped like those of the Cat in the Hat, walks with a ridiculously huge hat fastened to its head. The hat is

actually a mask with leonine features but, with its dazed stare and down-turned mouth, it looks no happier than the bird. Ted, who thought of his aquiline nose as a beak and often represented himself as a bird, did so here—morose and contemplative. Although he wears a big mask—"a face to meet the faces that you'll meet"[35]—the mask looks just as depressed as he does. Even the background—intended to be bright with yellows and rose—is rendered sad, mottled with greens. Ted was aware that his own facade was "fooling nobody" and that the mask was just a lot of unnecessary baggage. In yet another example of Ted's peculiar memory, the image of the oversized mask first appeared in the October 1, 1932, issue of *Liberty*, in a cartoon that had been used as the basis for one of the Poynter figures—the cat with the d.t.'s mask. Ted also used the image twice for *PM* newspaper.[36]

Ted was aware also that he and Audrey were "fooling nobody." So on June 21, a couple of weeks after Sirhan Sirhan assassinated Robert F. Kennedy and only eight months after Helen's death, Audrey Dimond and Ted Geisel moved into a hotel in Reno for the requisite six-week waiting period before her divorce would become legal. As Ted explained it, "My best friend is being divorced and I'm going to Reno to comfort his wife."[37] He told some friends in a letter, "This is an inevitable, inescapable conclusion to five years of four people's frustration."[38] Audrey was the only bright beacon in the darkest period of Ted's life. His budding relationship with her was surely the stabilizing force for him during this extremely unbalanced time.

Less than two weeks after Pope Paul VI published his papal encyclical, *Humanae Vitae,* which forbade Catholics the use of artificial birth control,[39] Ted had his first children. In the first week of August, he married Audrey, 17 years his junior, and became stepfather to Lark and Lea. (Thirty-four summers later, in 2002, Audrey and Lark, the elder of the two daughters, would honor Ted's memory when Lark's sculptures of him and his creatures were unveiled at the Dr. Seuss National Memorial in Springfield.) Outside of his happiness with his new family, everything else was a mess—even his La Jolla home, which workmen were remodeling to accommodate Ted's larger family. Bringing the dismal year to a close, on December 9, 1968, Ted's father died in a

Ted's 1968 painting "Fooling Nobody" (this page) was a window into his troubled mind. This painting was not the first time Ted employed the mask motif. He also used it in a 1941 *PM* cartoon (opposite page, left) and in one from *Liberty* (opposite page, right) on which one of the disputed Poynter figures was based (opposite page, middle).

nursing home in Agawam, Massachusetts. Ted's court case against Poynter Productions and the other defendants began the next day.

The court judged the altered marketing materials sufficient to ensure that no one was deceived into thinking that the toys were made or authorized by Dr. Seuss. To Ted's dismay, despite testimony from Chuck Jones, it also found that the models were reasonable reproductions of his work, so his contention that they were aesthetically unpleasing was dismissed. Furthermore, the court found that "Dr. Seuss" was an assumed name, not a surname, and was therefore not protected under the right to privacy. Similar findings left only the key remaining issue, which was to determine whether Ted or the Liberty Library Corporation owned the original copyright to Ted's cartoons from *Liberty*. Even the testimony of his friend Bennett Cerf could not help Ted here—he lost that point too. If Ted had claimed that the copyrights had not belonged to *Liberty* originally, the cartoons would have already fallen into public domain, since Ted had never renewed them. So he had to claim that *Liberty* was holding the rights in trust for him since 1932. The court believed the arguments that Ted had created the pieces at *Liberty*'s request, and when he was paid $300 per installment, the magazine retained all rights, according to custom. One person testified, all rights meant "dramatic, movie, television, skywriting on Mars, anything you want to say—everything."[40] The court found that since Ted had not obtained a separate copyright for his work in *Liberty*, as he had for the Flit cartoons that appeared in the magazine, the magazine retained all rights. Other than confirming that the figures and their advertising could not reproduce the name "Dr. Seuss" in his particular logo style, the case was a total loss for Ted. His legal

fees were over $100,000.

As far as Ted knew, that was the end of the story. The point has not been made until now, but the fate of those cartoons didn't end there. In February 1968, the S. Rosenberg Company signed papers to change its company name to Fun World, Inc. That year, the company courted controversy

by making knockoffs of Ideal's line of Flatsys dolls. It appears that about a month after filing for the name change, the company also began selling Huggles Zee Zoo plush dolls. Like the Kreiss figurines, they were not advertised as Dr. Seuss dolls and thus eluded detection. But they are clearly "stuffed doll versions" of Ted's characters from the same *Liberty* cartoons that spawned the Poynter figures. Court documents specify that "Poynter made and rejected a stuffed doll version of the figures."[41] It is not yet known whether there was a connection between Don Poynter and Fun World, Inc., or if the similarity between the Poynter and Zee Zoo characters was anything more than a remarkable coincidence.

As a result of the Poynter case, Ted went on to approve the largest production of Seussiana in his lifetime, and a flood of Dr. Seuss toys hit the market as the new decade began.[42] Nabisco produced an inflatable white elephant during their promotion of the animated *Horton Hears a Who!*, which was telecast on March 19, 1970.

Aladdin Industries put out both metal and vinyl lunch boxes and a thermos covered with Seuss characters. Decades before there were rides at Universal's Seuss Landing, there was the Seuss House (or, as it was marketed, the "Seuss Hoos")—a jungle gym with a slide, steering wheel, bell, bucket on a string (the Seuss Hoos Heister), magnetic goldfish, and various games to play, plus "secret messages and other stuff."

In November, Mattel, Inc., released "Color Neats" coloring boards, a Dr. Seuss Mattel-O-Phone, and a Dr. Seuss Fish-A-Ma-Jigger game, in which players used a hook to fish out whale-shaped cards that instructed them how to move around the playing board. The Cat in the Hat Geetar and jack-in-the-box both played crank-turned tunes. Mattel produced a line of educational "See 'n Say" talking toys. In the days before microcircuitry and minuscule computer chips, such pull-string talking toys were more of a novelty than they are today, and Mattel produced a line of pull-string plush dolls, including two sizes of the Cat in the Hat, Hedwig the nonsense-talking bird, Yertle the Turtle, and Horton the elephant, each of which spoke eight or nine different phrases—from the big Cat's delightfully pleased "I've got the tallest hat in the world!"

and Hedwig's gibberishy, fun "Hey—Toodle-Hoofer-Noodle-Doover!" to Yertle's humorous "You say you like turtle soup?" and the little Cat's spooky "Does your mother know I'm here?"

That same month, in preparation for the holidays, Sears Roebuck sold complete Seuss-themed bedroom and bathroom sets. The former included everything for the bed—sheets, pillowcases, shams, bedspreads, throw pillows, and a canopy, mostly covered with green, yellow, white, and red stripes or images of the Cat in the Hat. Furniture included primary-colored beanbag chairs, a cabinet, a hamper-and-storage chest displaying a cavalcade of Dr. Seuss characters, and even a wicker Yertle the Turtle table. For the windows, there was a choice of curtains, drapes, valances, curtain rods, and shades, most heavy on the stripes and Cats. The doors and walls could be decorated with letter and number placards, a door mirror, a "wall measurer" for keeping track of a child's height, framed pictures of the Cat and of Horton, wallpaper with more striping—the monotony of which was to be broken up by a five-foot-ten-inch-tall image of the Cat on a nine-foot wallpaper graphic—and interior latex enamel paints in "Bloopy Blue," "Grinch Green," "Overly Orange," "Quite White," "Yertle Yellow," "Blink Black," and "Multi-Mix-Upps." Other appointments included a wastebasket with a character parade and even a Cat in the Hat radio. For the bathroom, there were rugs in either an ABC animal print or more of the stripes, animal-parade bath and hand towels, and a circular Yertle wash mitt. Anyone who thought that Ted severely limited Dr. Seuss products during his lifetime, or that the merchandising of Dr. Seuss began after his death, surely missed the beginning of the 1970s.

That year, the *National Lampoon* published a bawdy parody called "I, a Splurch." Like *Mad*'s "The Cats Are All Bats" three years earlier and "A Very Wrong Turn" in the superhero *Defenders* comic book 13 years later,[43] it was one of many spoofs that Ted's work spawned. Seymour the Splurch was a bird in the midst of discovering his sexuality. The notion of the children's author writing about sex must have seemed hilarious to the satirists, but that was another misunderstanding based on their unidimensional vision of Ted.

Ironically, in March 1969, the year before the *Lampoon*'s sex parody, Ted engaged in a similar stunt of his own. Indulging his penchant for practical

Fun World's Zee Zoo plush toys had the look of the Poynter figures and are clearly tied to Ted's hotly contested *Liberty* cartoons (opposite page).

After his legal woes were over, Ted went on to approve the largest merchandising push of his career, of which this thermos and these lunch boxes are a mere sampling (this page).

A cornucopia of collectibles: **Contrary to popular belief, Ted did not reject the concept of merchandising, as is evidenced by this array of toys, games, home furnishings, watches, dolls, puppets, and even paint—all produced with his approval throughout the 1970s (this page and opposite page).**

jokes, he "wrote a five-page outline for a dirty book. He sent it to Robert Bernstein, successor to Bennett Cerf, and Seuss' own editor at Random House. . . . Dr. Seuss stayed home . . . didn't answer the phone, and laughed himself sick."[44] Asked to describe the proposed book, Ted said, "It was awful. . . . Outrageous. The worst thing you can imagine."[45]

The next year, Seuss characters blew up—literally! There was an inflatable backrest, and Nabisco offered premiums including inflatable character chairs and a blow-up pink Horton. That year, Mattel made the art-oriented Jigsaw Draw toy with Seuss characters. In 1972, Lafayette produced two styles of Cat in the Hat "Time Teller" watches, which were intended to teach a child how to tell time through color association, with the blue-gloved hour hand pointing to blue-numbered hours and the red-gloved minute hand pointing to red-numbered minute increments. (Ted also had a contract with R. Gsell & Co. for a "Time Teacher" Cat watch, which may have been related.) Charlie's Girls produced a line of "kidswear" character shirts. In 1973, Milton Bradley made the second Cat in the Hat plush doll. The following year, the same doll, with a slightly altered structure, was produced by Douglas in a couple of different versions, along

with two kinds of Cat hand puppet. Lafayette released a digital Cat watch. Douglas continued the Cat in the Hat plush in 1975 and 1976, adding two versions of a Sam-I-am puppet as well. In 1977, Random House created a Cat in the Hat grow chart. RCA released a boxed set of Dr. Seuss story recordings. A Cat in the Hat alarm clock with the old-fashioned striker and bells was sold in 1978, as were Fisher-Price Talk-to-Me book versions of "Yertle the Turtle" and "Gertrude McFuzz." Ted turned 75 in 1979, the year that Eden Toys released the first full complement of Dr. Seuss plush figures, including four varieties of the Cat, a two-faced Grinch with a happy and a mean side, and Lorax, Sam-I-am, and Star-Bellied Sneetch plush dolls. The Cat came back for Eden in 1980.

The next big boom in Seussiana came in February 1983, when Ted signed a deal with Coleco Industries for a reported $10 million. This event was not just a significant leap forward in the merchandising of Dr. Seuss products but was apparently a deal that was regarded as enormous for the merchandising of any cartoon character—

"an all-encompassing contract . . . to produce toys, games, dolls, board games, ride-on toys, and . . . video games and computer software. . . . He has approval of the designs and the packaging, very extensive approvals. . . . A deal like this is certainly groundbreaking, going way, way beyond the Kliban T-shirts and Garfield lunchboxes."[46] In 1984, the toys were ready and Coleco rolled out a Cat in the Hat infant rocker and a Cat rider for toddlers. There was also a line of plush dolls in boxes that included the Cat, Horton, the Grinch, a Star-Bellied Sneetch, the Lorax, Thidwick, and Yertle. Several styles of Cat prototypes with a wire framework were abandoned, but a

55-inch Cat was produced. For promotional purposes, some eight-foot Cats were made as well.

In the early days of home computer games (Tetris wasn't developed until the following year), Coleco Family Learning Software included the Dr. Seuss Fix-Up the Mix-Up Puzzler. Ted worked with Coleco on The Dr. Seuss Story Factory, which was later renamed the Coleco Word Bird Game—in which a child flies a Swumee swan to the Truffula trees and selects words to write a sentence or eventually a short story. Into his eightieth year, Ted worked on details like placing the words in the past tense to avoid syntactic problems.[47] In retrospect, this turns out to have been a large commitment of time for Ted at his age. He would publish only three more books in his lifetime, but despite all his efforts, Coleco killed the Word Bird in July 1984.[48]

The following year, Hallmark created a Cat in the Hat party set that included invitations, a paper tablecloth, dessert plates, napkins, cups, and even a centerpiece. For Christmas, Hallmark crafted the first Seuss tree ornament, based on the animated *How the Grinch Stole Christmas!*

Television was the other area into which Ted's characters expanded. He was aware of television's influence, as he'd been battling it for children's attention. Ted was approached by Chuck Jones, with whom he had worked on the Private SNAFU cartoons. Jones thought a television production could help Ted financially:

"I knew Ted was writing children's books and he wasn't making very much money from them. He told me one evening that if he could only earn $5,000 or $6,000 a

year from his books' royalties then he'd never have to worry about finances."

. . . Jones continued in the movie business. . . . He wasn't aware that old buddy was a multi-millionaire many times over from these children's books. . . .

"I figured maybe he could use some extra money, by letting me produce one of his children's books for television."

After the phone call, during which Jones learned that his pal didn't exactly need extra loot, negotiations still continued. It seems Geisel had been offered countless deals to let his characters move into television, and had turned them down regularly.

"I wanted creative control over what happened to my characters," says Geisel. "And most of the offers just were that: offers of a lot of money and kindly stay home and let us tend to the TV business. With Chuck, I knew I could work actively with him on the Grinch."[49]

"I decided . . . that if I was going to go on TV I'd better do it before I am 70,"[50] Ted explained. He also enjoyed productions like this one and the ones that would follow because they were the only chance the frustrated song-writer got to write lyrics. In those pre-Poynter days, it certainly wasn't just for the money—the pressbook for the production noted, "If sales are any measure of success, Dr. Seuss is at the top. His books are second in sales throughout the world only to the Bible."[51] At the time, Ted's collaboration with Jones resulted in "what is reported to be the most expensive half-hour animated cartoon ever created for television."[52] When it premiered for CBS on December 18, 1966, color broadcasts were not a completely new technology, but they were not routine either, since NBC had become the first network to broadcast completely in color just the previous month.

Few can argue with the results. Jones's image of the Grinch may even have supplanted Ted's original. Who, for example, doesn't think of the Grinch as green? Ted enjoyed the production enough to begin plans with Chuck Jones for a similar treatment of *Horton Hears a Who!* Originally intended for Thanksgiving the following year, it was another of the projects that didn't pan

A really big deal: Ted's comprehensive contract with Coleco brought his merchandising of Seuss to a whole new level. Even in his advancing years, he was deeply involved with all aspects of creating these inventive products (opposite page, top and middle).

In 1985, Hallmark offered *The Cat in the Hat* party products (opposite page, bottom).

out for Ted in 1967–68, and the film wasn't completed and broadcast until 1970. That year, "The Dr. Seuss Programs" won a Peabody Award, with specific mention that "*Horton Hatches the Egg* is a superb example of how an inspired children's book can be translated into an equally entrancing television show—IF the author is allowed to work on the script himself and pick the right people to help him with the job."[53]

Ted continued to produce children's television specials at the rate of one each year. The following March, *The Cat in the Hat* was broadcast. Ted explained that, originally, "the *Cat* was written for six-year-olds. What we had to do was present it on television in a way suitable for the whole family. Well, I've turned it into an opera. It's stuffed with songs. There were three songs in the *Grinch* and six in *Horton*. But there are eight or nine in the *Cat*."[54] Chuck Jones and Maurice Noble brought the Cat to life as they had done for the Grinch and Horton, but it was the last of Ted's productions with them. In 1972, Ted worked with another SNAFU compatriot, Friz Freleng, and together they adapted *The Lorax* with great success. Freleng also co-produced the next television special with Ted—*Dr. Seuss on the Loose,* a three-part production released in 1973 that included *The Sneetches, The Zax,* and *Green Eggs and Ham* (later released as *Green Eggs and Ham and Other Stories*).

Production then slowed to allow for a new film every other year, as Ted began writing new material—creating the Emmy-nominated *The Hoober-Bloob Highway* (1975), the Emmy-winning *Halloween Is Grinch Night* (1977), and the Emmy-nominated *Pontoffel Pock, Where Are You?* (1979). The 74-year-old Ted gave his acceptance speech for the Emmy as a limerick:

> In our studio out in Van Nuys,
> There are so many great gals and great guys.
> If I thanked them all,
> We'd be here until fall,
> And I don't think that would be wise.[55]

Although Freleng continued as executive producer on these films, the new pieces looked different, largely due to new director Gerard Baldwin. Ted also had a new look. In the hirsute of happiness, he'd grown the beard with which most fans now picture him. For his last production, Ted paired two of his best-known characters in the Emmy-winning *The Grinch Grinches the Cat in the Hat* (1982, retitled in later releases *The Cat in the Hat Gets Grinched*). Freleng co-produced the film, and a new director, Bill Perez, took the helm.

All of this celebrity came with certain expectations. But even later in life, despite living "in the upper-crust La Jolla hierarchy, which includes an astonishing total of at least one hundred bona-fide millionaires,"[56] Ted remained a Groucho Marx among a community full of Margaret Dumonts.

> Shortly after moving to La Jolla, Geisel called on the registrar of voters. Automatically, a dowager type at the desk handed him the Republican book to sign. Geisel smiled. "Thanks," he said, "but I'm a Democrat." The La Jolla lady laughed until her jewels rattled. "Oh, Mr. Geisel," she said, "you cartoonists say the funniest things!" Recalling the incident, Geisel says, "Even after I signed the Democratic book, she still thought I was joking."[57]

Ted called such ladies "Birdwomen"; he satirized them and their society functions often in his artwork from this period. "It is a proud boast of the Geisels that they have never given a cocktail party. 'A cocktail party,' says Ted, 'is something you invite people to that you don't like well enough to invite to dinner.' . . . At least once a week, the Geisels entertain at a sit-down dinner with from eight to twenty guests."[58] Later in life, when Ted's position forced him to attend such functions, he maintained the attitude of a child forced to attend religious services when he'd rather be playing ball. The programs from various charity auctions and balls contain telltale doodles and sketches Ted made to save himself from boredom.

He kept his usual sense of humor about his own artwork and about modern art in general. After the Escorobus episode, in which Ted fooled a friend by painting the fictional artist's oeuvre, Ted had commented, "That experience made me suspect that a lot of modern art is malarkey. . . . If I can do it myself, it can't be any good."[59] Continuing in that vein, Ted even contributed some humorous commentary on Giorgio de Chirico's 1917 painting "Hector and Andromache," claiming that "as a fledgling art student in Paris in the early 1920s, he did indeed have an 'association' with the enchanting Ms. Andro, the model for this painting." Ted wrote of the robotic model:

She drank a lot.
But I didn't much mind.
That merely made her eyes blank.
What I did mind
Was the sloppy rivet job
That made her lovely thighs klank.[60]

Ted also lent his artistic efforts to local political concerns. In 1972, the former executive vice president of San Diegans, Inc., John E. Hirten, was predicting that "by 1980 . . . eight out of ten Americans will be living in cities and their surrounding metropolitan areas."[61] Ted drew a cover for *San Diego Magazine* in which a lone green tree remains under the city's smog. Only a small orange area of earth can be seen amid the buildings of the urban sprawl. In 1990, this image was resurrected on flyers in San Diego (without the orange ground) when Proposition E, a park and open-space bond measure, was debated. Ted also did an anti-drug poster for the *San Diego Tribune*—which was used in schools and by the navy—depicting a boy with a large hole through his head, fittingly captioned, "Dope! You need it like a hole in the head!"

A retrospective of Ted's work started in San Diego in 1986 and toured the country for a few years, giving the larger world its first inkling of the breadth and variety of Dr. Seuss's genius, to complement the affection already accorded to his children's books. Of those books, Ted contended, "There is no particular message . . . unless it's one of eternal hope."[62] Testament to that sentiment can be found in the comments of his younger readers, like the one who wrote, "Dear Dr. Seuss, I love your books because they are so funny. I wish every book in the library were your book. Do you have any pets? If you do, I'll bet he is the craziest pet on earth."[63]

Despite his failing health, Ted continued to write those books and garner awards. Although he never won the Randolph Caldecott Medal for the "artist of the most distinguished American picture book for children,"[64] he was one of the five honored nominees in 1948, 1950, and 1951, for

McElligot's Pool, Bartholomew and the Oobleck, and *If I Ran the Zoo,* respectively. A vote of confidence from the readers themselves was also given to *McElligot's Pool* when it won a Young Reader's Choice Award.[65] The Laura Ingalls Wilder Medal is given sporadically to "recognize an author or illustrator whose books, published in the United States, have over a period of years made a substantial and lasting contribution to literature for children."[66] Ted received the award in 1980, 43 years after he first started publishing children's books. The year he published *The Butter Battle Book,* Ted received similar recognition of his life's work when he was awarded a special Pulitzer citation in 1984 "for his special contribution over nearly half a century to the education and enjoyment of America's children and their parents."[67]

These awards were well deserved. For the ten years between 1947 and 1956, Ted put out a book per year except when he was working on *The 5000 Fingers of Dr. T.* For the next 20 years, from 1957 through 1976, Ted published two or three books every year except for the year that he was working on the animated version of *How the Grinch Stole Christmas!* After that time, he began to slow down again, publishing a book a year through 1981. In the later years of his life, Ted suffered from several different afflictions. He grew weary, and the frequency of his books trailed off to one book every other year from 1982 through 1986. The last of those, *You're Only Old Once!,* was published on Ted's eighty-second birthday. It was the only book he illustrated in the period from 1985 through 1990. That book famously addressed his experiences with the medical community as he aged.

The only book published under his "Dr. Seuss" pseudonym for which he did not do the illustrations, *I Am NOT Going to Get Up Today!,* came out the following year. James Stevenson's illustrations portray a boy who does not want to get out of bed. "Please let me be. Please go away. . . . My bed is warm. My pillow's deep. Today's the day I'm going to sleep." Surely these are expressions of the author's own bone weariness.

Oh, the Places You'll Go! (1990), the last book of new work published in his lifetime, proved to be as beloved as his first book, *And to Think That I Saw It on Mulberry Street,* published more than 50 years earlier. Tempering hopefulness with the reality that life will not always be easy, it became a staple graduation gift, and by the end of 2000, it was already one of the top-20 best-selling children's hardcover books of all time, selling in excess of 250,000 more copies than *The Sneetches and Other Stories, Yertle the Turtle and*

Later in life, Ted became a reluctant fixture at more and more social events, where he would wile away the hours scribbling (opposite page, top and middle). In 1990, Ted's art adorned a flyer (opposite page, bottom) that dealt with local politics.

Other Stories, Horton Hatches the Egg, Dr. Seuss's Sleep Book, and *Happy Birthday to You!* combined.

Ted's first book began with the optimistic uncertainty of never knowing what one might find, even on the way to school. Marco's father tells him to "keep your eyelids up and see what you can see." His last book ended with that same positive yet uncertain future, as Ted assured readers, "You're off to Great Places! Today is your day! Your mountain is waiting. So . . . get on your way!"

From start to finish, Ted's book career encouraged readers to maintain a sense of wonder and adventure, to use their imaginations and be willing to participate in the strange experiences life has to offer, to be one of the people who don't stop at the Z. Fifty-four autumns after his first book was published, on the morning of September 24, 1991, Theodor Seuss Geisel died at the age of 87.

Bennett Cerf—who brought Ted to Random House—once described him as "a genius, pure and simple. . . . Ted is the nicest, most dignified, unassuming, soul-satisfying person I've ever met in my entire life—and this goes for his wife, Helen, as well."[68] Of course, Cerf also once described a scene in which Ted and Helen were eating at a restaurant in Mexico City, where Ted was told that if he could grab one of the koi in the fish tank with his bare hands and bring it to the bartender, the drinks would be on the house. "He had experimented with just enough tequila to swallow the tale whole. He succeeded in catching the very largest goldfish and conveyed it, flapping wildly, over to the bar, where he deposited it. 'Drinks for everybody!' he ordered." The look on the bartender's face communicated to Ted very quickly that he'd been hoodwinked. So he grabbed the fish off of the bar and "tossed it back over his head. It landed in a platter that had just been served to a dashing Mexican senor. Furthermore, the senor was equipped with firearms. Fortunately, cooler heads prevented bloodshed—which is another way of saying that Mr. Geisel paid for a new suit and dinner for six for the senor."[69]

Misunderstanding Ted as a person was, well, understandable. He did live that double life of Ted Geisel and Dr. Seuss. He was an unusual man, particularly with respect to his memory and vision, and his penchant for storytelling and practical jokes often led people astray from the facts. Those who knew him only as the author of children's books would never have suspected what a complex man he really was.

Misunderstanding Ted's work stems more from the sheer amount of it and the small percentage to which people have been exposed. The final word here, fittingly, is the advice Ted gave to the graduating class at Lake Forest College in 1977:

> My uncle ordered popovers
> from the restaurant's bill of fare.
> And, when they were served, he regarded them
> with a penetrating stare. . . .
> Then he spoke great Words of Wisdom
> as he sat there on that chair:
> "To eat these things," said my uncle,
> "you must exercise great care.
> You may swallow down what's solid . . .
> BUT . . . you must spit out the air!"
> And . . . as you partake of the world's bill of fare,
> that's darned good advice to follow.
> Do a lot of spitting out the hot air.
> And be careful what you swallow.[70]

In *Oh, the Places You'll Go!* (opposite page), Ted exhorted the reader to "soar to high heights." His parting paean? "KID, YOU'LL MOVE MOUNTAINS!"

Ted at the drawing board in his La Jolla studio (this page).

ON BEYOND Z
Endnotes

Wherever possible, Theodor S. Geisel has been identified as the author. In those cases where attribution is unconfirmable, no author has been listed.

Charles Cohen has catalogued his extensive collection of Seussiana. Some endnotes include a reference number that corresponds to pieces in that collection. These reference numbers appear in brackets and are placed at the end of the note, where applicable.

Chapter 1: An Elephant's Faithful . . . Sometimes

1. Cynthia Lindsay, "Who's News: The Miracle of Dr. Seuss," *Good Housekeeping,* December 1960, 37 [CC19601200001]; Donald Freeman, "The Nonsensical World of Dr. Seuss," *McCall's* 92, no. 2 (November 1, 1964): 201 [CC19641100000]; Don Bell, "It's Dr. Seuss, by Zeus, and He's on the Loose," *Chicago Tribune Magazine,* June 6, 1970, 19 [CC19700607000]; Donald Freeman, "Dr. Seuss at 72—Going Like 60," *The Saturday Evening Post* 249, no. 2 (March 1977): 104 [CC19770300000].

2. Dr. Seuss, public interview in San Diego Museum of Art's Copley Auditorium, December 8, 1982 [CC19821208000]. As quoted in "A Conversation with Maurice Sendak and Dr. Seuss," *Carver: An Interdisciplinary Journal Published at Bloomsburg University* 8, no. 1 (spring 1990): 30 [CC199004z000]. The article appeared previously in "Maurice Sendak and Dr. Seuss: A Conversation," *The Horn Book Magazine* 65, no. 5 (Sept.–Oct. 1989): 582–88 [CC19890900000], and later in "Afterword: A Conversation with Maurice Sendak and Dr. Seuss," *Teaching Children's Literature: Issues, Pedagogy, Resources,* 1992, 241–50 [CC19920000035].

3. Stephen King, "Dr. Seuss and the Two Faces of Fantasy," *Fantasy* 7, no. 5 (June 1984): 10 [CC19840600000]. "I have a standard speech that I give—it's light, has a few laughs, and ends up saying remarkably little about what I do for a living. But I have discovered . . . that if you amuse people enough, they'll leave you alone—it's as if they never really wanted to know what makes one write all those crazy things at all. . . . Alfred Hitchcock . . . gave a great many interviews over his lifetime, but . . . [I] am amazed by how little of substance he actually had to say about his chosen field . . . and how often he told the same anecdotes over and over."

4. Robert Cahn, "The Wonderful World of Dr. Seuss," *The Saturday Evening Post* 230, no. 1 (July 6, 1957): 46 [CC19570706000].

5. See note 1.

6. E. J. Kahn, Jr., "Profiles: Children's Friend," *The New Yorker* 36, no. 44 (December 17, 1960): 82 [CC19601217000].

7. Ibid.

8. Ibid.

9. Arthur Gordon, "The Wonderful Wizard of Soledad Hill," *Woman's Day* 28, no. 12 (September 1965): 99 [CC19650900000].

10. James Stewart-Gordon, "Dr. Seuss: Fanciful Sage of Children," *Reader's Digest* 100, no. 600 (April 1972): 143 [CC19720400000].

11. The same story appears later that year in Digby Diehl, "Q&A 'Dr. Seuss,'" *Los Angeles Times West,* September 17, 1972, 37 [CC19720917000].

12. Claudia Glenn Dowling, "Dr. Seuss," *Life* 12, no. 8 (July 1989): 107 [CC19890701000]. "Once . . . a piece of tracing paper with an elephant sketched on it blew on top of a drawing of a tree." Struck by the image, he says, "All I had to do was figure out what the hell that elephant was doing in that tree, and I had a book."

13. Judith and Neil Morgan, *Dr. Seuss and Mr. Geisel* (New York: Random House, 1995), 96–97 [CC19950421000].

14. The January 3, 1940, edition of the *New York Times* in its Weather Reports cited a range of 16°F to 30°F, nine degrees below normal. Temperatures on the street outside of Ted's window probably ranged from -15°F to 8°F with the wind chill, with a mean of -5°F.

Chapter 2: Forensics—Stalking the Elephant

1. Theodor S. Geisel, "Who Is This Morose Little Rascal?" *Judge* 93, no. 2403 (November 11, 1927): 14 [CC19271126000].

2. Theodor S. Geisel, "Hieronomo Is Drunk Again!" *Life* 93, no. 2408 (July 19, 1929): 10 [CC19271224000].

3. Theodor S. Geisel, "Life's Little Educational Charts: The German Language at a Glance," *Life* 94, no. 2437 (July 19, 1929): 10 [CC19290719000].

4. Theodor S. Geisel, "The Truly-Dumb Animal Shoppe," *Judge* 100, no. 2587 (May 30, 1931): 21 [CC19310530000].

5. John Riddell, "The Science of Everything," *Vanity Fair* 36, no. 4 (June 1, 1931): 76 [CC19310600003].

6. Theodor S. Geisel, "The Facts of Life: Or How Should I Tell My Child? Part 1," *Life* 101, no. 2587 (February 1934): 22 [CC19340200000].

7. Albert Deane, *Spelling Bees: The Oldest and the Newest Rage* (New York: Frederick A. Stokes, 1937) [CC19370000001].

8. Theodor S. Geisel, "Matilda, the Elephant with a Mother Complex," *Judge* 114, no. 2713 (April 1938): 17 [CC19380400001].

9. NBC Radio advertisement, "Shux! And They Told Me This Was a Big Game Jungle!" *Broadcasting* 16, no. 4 (February 15, 1939): 49 [CC19390215000].

Chapter 3: My Book About Me

1. "Mülhausen" is variously anglicized as "Muhlhausen," "Muelhausen," and "Mulhausen."

2. Theodor S. Geisel, "Cripes! And she promised to marry me after the very first thaw!" *Judge* 101, no. 2616 (December 19, 1931): 6 [CC19311219000].

3. Theodor S. Geisel, "To My Grandmother, My 'Buddy,'" *Judge* 94, no. 2425 (April 21, 1928): 17 [CC19280421000].

4. Belloc and B.T.B. also had an influence on rock band Pink Floyd's Syd Barrett, inspiring lyrics and song titles like "Matilda Mother," from *The Piper at the Gates of Dawn* album (1967).

5. Dr. Seuss, *Dr. Seuss's ABC* (New York: Random House, 1963), 28–29 [CC19631000000].

6. Dr. Seuss, *If I Ran the Zoo* (New York: Random House, 1950), 3–7 [CC19501012000].

7. A "parvenu" is defined as a newly rich person who doesn't yet have the prestige or social qualifications associated with the position.

8. Theodor S. Geisel, "Our Own Natural History: The Woozle Bird," *Jack-O-Lantern* 16, no. 10 (June 2, 1924): 30 [CC19240602001].

Chapter 4: I Can Write!

1. Theodor S. Geisel [credited Theodore Geisel, '20], "O Latin," *Central Recorder* 2, no. 12 (February 7, 1919): 8 [CC19190207001].
2. Walt Whitman, "O Captain! My Captain!" *When Lilacs Last in the Door-Yard Bloom'd* (1865–6) [CC18650000000].
3. Theodor S. Geisel, "Banjo Club!" *Central Recorder* 3, no. 4 (October 24, 1919): 1 [CC19191024000].
4. Theodor S. Geisel [credited T.S.G.], "It'll be just our luck to be in Latin Class when they turn back the clocks," *Central Recorder* 3, no. 4 (October 24, 1919): 2 [CC19191024002].
5. "It's a fake!" *Central Recorder* 3, no. 12 (January 9, 1920): 4 [CC19200109001].
6. "History tells us that a few words from Caesar . . . ," *Central Recorder* 3, no. 12 (January 9, 1920): 3 [CC19200109000].
7. Theodor S. Geisel [credited T.S.G.], "A Pupil's Union," *Central Recorder* 3, no. 9 (November 26, 1919): 4 [CC19191126001].
8. Theodor S. Geisel [credited T.S.G.], "A Play—In One Gulp," *Central Recorder* 3, no. 14 (January 21, 1920): 16 [CC19200121001].
9. The Varnum Hotel, designed by Clement A. Didden, Jr., and located at New Jersey Avenue and C Street, SE, was a part of Washington, D.C., history from 1796 through 1929.
10. Theodor S. Geisel [credited T. S. Lesieg], "A Pupil's Nightmare," *Central Recorder* 3, no. 14 (January 21, 1920): 14 [CC19200121000].
11. Theodor S. Geisel [credited T. S. Geisel], "Prophecy on the Prophets," *Central High School Yearbook,* October 1920, 48 [CC19210100000].
12. "The Ideal Boy at Central Must Have," *Central Recorder* 4, no. 11 (January 7, 1921): 8 [CC19210107000].

Chapter 5: "I Am a Fellow o' th' Strangest Mind i' th' World . . ."

1. William Shakespeare, *Twelfth Night,* act 1, sc. 3 [CC16010100000]. The knight Sir Andrew Aguecheek to Sir Toby Belch . . .
2. "Freshmen, Welcome," *The Dartmouth*, September 22, 1921, 2 [CC19210922001].
3. Ted Geisel played Sir Andrew Aguecheek in his senior-year production of *Twelfth Night,* performed on January 21 and 22, 1921, and spoke this phrase to Sir Toby Belch.
4. Alfred Tennyson, "The Passing of Arthur," *Idylls of the King* (London: Strahan, 1869), lines 408–411 [CC18690000000].
5. "Advertising: As It Is Done by the Greeks," *Jack-O-Lantern* 15, no. 5 (February 8, 1923): 21 [CC19230208000].
6. "The B. and M. Timetable—A Book Review," *Jack-O-Lantern* 16, no. 10 (June 2, 1924): 33 [CC19240602001].
7. "Dartmouth Defeats Jacko Eleven, 13–7," *The Dartmouth* 46, no. 40 (November 1, 1924): 3 [CC19241101000].
8. Theodor S. Geisel, "All for the Love," *Jack-O-Lantern* 17, no. 5 (January 20, 1925): 22 [CC19250120000].
9. Theodor S. Geisel, "Helpful Hints for Textbook Writers," *Jack-O-Lantern* 16, no. 9 (May 8, 1924): 26 [CC19240508000].
10. Theodor S. Geisel, "A Note on Morality," *Jack-O-Lantern* 17, no. 3 (November 24, 1924): 21 [CC19241124000]. Ted would go on to write many cartoons for *Liberty* magazine entitled "A Note On . . ." one thing or another.
11. Theodor S. Geisel, "Jacko's Additions to 'Etiquette,'" *Jack-O-Lantern* 17, no. 3 (November 24, 1924): 28 [CC19241124000].
12. Theodor S. Geisel, "The Old Chivalric Faith—," *Jack-O-Lantern* 17, no. 4 (December 15, 1924): 23 [CC19241215000].
13. *The Cocoanuts,* directed by Robert Florey and Joseph Santley (Paramount, 1929).
14. Theodor S. Geisel, "The Lexicographer's Speak Easy," *Jack-O-Lantern* 17, no. 4 (December 15, 1924): 35 [CC19241215000].
15. Theodor S. Geisel, "Having no one to elect to the board this month . . . ," *Jack-O-Lantern* 17, no. 5 (January 20, 1925): 21 [CC19250120000].

Chapter 6: Theodor Grows a Welt

1. "This Generation of Ours," *The Dartmouth* 46, no. 138 (April 9, 1925): 2 [CC19250409000].
2. Max Rudin, "Beer and America," *American Heritage* 53, no. 3 (July 2002): 35.

3. Letter to Ted from his father, April 22, 1925, property of the Mandeville Special Collections Library at the University of California, San Diego [CC19250422001].
4. "C. H. Frankenberg '26 to Edit Jack-O-Lantern in 1925–1926," *The Dartmouth* 46, no. 155 (April 27, 1925) [CC19250429000].
5. "With Other Editors," *The Dartmouth* 46, no. 153 (April 27, 1925): 2 [CC19250427000].
6. Ibid., 3.
7. Theodor S. Geisel [credited L. Burbank], "Who's Who in Bo-Bo," *Jack-O-Lantern* 16, no. 3 (November 26, 1923): 24–25 [CC19231126000].
8. "An Invocation," *Jack-O-Lantern* 17, no. 9 (May 7, 1925): 22 [CC19250507000].
9. Theodor S. Geisel, "Sans Mens in Sano Pumpkin," *Jack-O-Lantern* 17, no. 7 (March 24, 1925): 25 [CC19250324000].

Chapter 7: "From There to Here and Here to There"

1. R.P.M., On the Firing Line, *Springfield Union,* July 6, 1925, 6 [CC19250706000].
2. Theodor S. Geisel, "No Cause for Celebration," On the Firing Line, *Springfield Union,* July 7, 1925, 10 [CC19250707000].
3. Theodor S. Geisel, "How can chewing gum be removed from a carpet?" On the Firing Line, *Springfield Union,* July 14, 1925, 10 [CC19250714000].
4. Theodor S. Geisel, "A correspondent to the *Detroit Free Press* . . . ," On the Firing Line, *Springfield Union,* July 11, 1925, 10 [CC19250711000].
5. Theodor S. Geisel, "Extending Felicitations," On the Firing Line, *Springfield Union,* July 9, 1925, 10 [CC19250709000].
6. Theodor S. Geisel, "Note to Executors," On the Firing Line, *Springfield Union,* July 10, 1925, 10 [CC19250710000].
7. Theodor S. Geisel, "Maxwell Bodenheim was arraigned Tuesday . . . ," On the Firing Line, *Springfield Union,* July 9, 1925, 10 [CC19250709000].
8. Ibid. "Santa Barbara Quake 24 Hours of Hades . . ."
9. Theodor S. Geisel, "For the purpose of eliminating street noises . . . ," On the Firing Line, *Springfield Union,* July 10, 1925, 10 [CC19250710000].
10. Theodor S. Geisel, "The curriculum of this university . . . ," On the Firing Line, *Springfield Union,* July 18, 1925, 10 [CC19250718000].
11. Theodor S. Geisel, "All in the Directions," *Springfield Sunday Republican,* July 26, 1925, 7 [CC19250726000].
12. Dr. Seuss, *If I Ran the Zoo* (New York: Random House, 1950), 34 [CC19501012000].

Chapter 8: Destiny Blinx

1. Letter from Theodor S. Geisel to Alexander Laing, property of the Rauner Special Collections Library, Dartmouth College [CC19270500000].
2. Ibid.
3. Ibid.
4. Ibid.
5. Ibid.
6. Ibid.
7. Ibid.
8. Theodor S. Geisel, "The Waiting Room at Dang-Dang," *Judge* 95, no. 2446 (September 15, 1928): 9 [CC19280915000].
9. Letter from Theodor S. Geisel to Alexander Laing, property of the Rauner Special Collections Library, Dartmouth College [CC19270500000].
10. In 1924, in Rochdale, England, home of Turner Brothers asbestos factory since 1880, the first inquest and pathological examination of an asbestos worker's death occurred, in which Nellie Kershaw's death was attributed to asbestos poisoning by Dr. Joss and corroborated by Dr. W. E. Cooke. Cooke published an article that year in the *British Medical Journal.* By December 3, 1927, Cooke would be the first to describe "asbestosis," a scarring of lung tissue from inhaling asbestos ("Pulmonary Asbestos," *British Medical Journal* 2, no. 1024–1025).
11. Judith and Neil Morgan, *Dr. Seuss and Mr. Geisel* (New York: Random House, 1995), 68 [CC19950421000].
12. "The Origin of Contract Bridge," *Judge* 94, no. 2415 (February 11, 1928): 8 [CC19280211000].
13. "Sir Galahad's Reforms," *Judge* 94, no. 2423 (April 7, 1928): 14 [CC19280407000].
14. Theodor S. Geisel [credited Doctor Theophrastus Seuss], "How Launcelot Did Pull a Fast One on the Kyng," *Judge* 94, no. 2424 (April 7, 1928): 15 [CC19280414000].
15. Ibid.

16. Theodor S. Geisel, "To My Grandmother, My 'Buddy,'" *Judge* 94, no. 2425 (April 21, 1928): 17 [CC19280421000].

17. Judith and Neil Morgan, *Dr. Seuss and Mr. Geisel* (New York: Random House, 1995), 65 [CC19950421000].

18. Bob Warren, "Dr. Seuss, Former *Jacko* Editor, Tells How Boredom May Lead . . . ," *The Dartmouth,* May 10, 1934, 2 [CC19340510000].

Chapter 9: You Can Book a *Judge* by Its Cover

1. Theodor S. Geisel, "The Cutting of the Wedding Cnouth, or Divorce Among the Druids," *Judge* 94, no. 2433 (June 16, 1928): 14 [CC19280616000].

2. André Breton, *Manifeste du surréalisme et poisson soluble* (Paris: Éditions du Sagittaire, chez Simon Kra, 1924).

3. Ibid.

4. Ibid.

5. Ibid.

6. Theodor S. Geisel, "Sex and the Sea God," *Judge* 95, no. 2441 (April 21, 1928): 15, 25 [CC19280811000].

7. Arthur Conan Doyle, *When the World Screamed, Strand,* April 1928.

8. Ibid.

9. Ibid.

10. Theodor S. Geisel, "The Great Diet Derby," *Judge* 95, no. 2445 (September 8, 1928): 16 [CC19280908000].

11. Theodor S. Geisel [credited Dr. Seuss], "A Few Subtle Pleasures Devised for Those Who Have Wearied of the Commonplace," *Judge* 95, no. 2455 (November 17, 1928): 6 [CC19281117000].

12. Theodor S. Geisel [credited Dr. Seuss], "Life's Little Educational Charts: A Critical Survey of the Custom of Hat-Doffing . . . ," *Life* 95, no. 2463 (January 17, 1930): 14 [CC19300117000]. "Young men appearing socially for the first time are always harassed by the problem, 'How high shall I doff my hat?'"

13. Theodor S. Geisel, "Ough! Ough! Or Why I Believe in Simplified Spelling," *Judge* 96, no. 2476 (April 13, 1929): 18 [CC19290413000].

14. Theodor S. Geisel, "Our Lamentable Misuse of Certain Fine Old Terms . . . ," *Judge* 96, no. 2472 (March 16, 1929): 16 [CC19290316000].

15. Ibid.

16. "'Left in the Lurch' and Just What Does It Mean?" *Judge* 96, no. 2481 (May 18, 1929): 22 [CC19290518000].

17. Ibid.

18. Judith and Neil Morgan, *Dr. Seuss and Mr. Geisel* (New York: Random House, 1995), 69–70 [CC19950421000]. The Morgans' biography states that "the cover of the March 23, 1929, issue of *Judge* was inhabited by ancestors of some of the most beloved Dr. Seuss animals. . . . At about the same time, Ted's work was on the cover of *Life*. Any magazine cover gave an artist a boost, and this double triumph brought him a measure of fame." The *Life* cover was actually his tenth magazine cover, and it appeared in May 1934, more than five years after this first one for *Judge*. As such, the concept of a "double triumph" overstates this historic event and may mislead readers into thinking that March 1929 was a sudden boon in recognition for Ted due to his cover work. His second cover illustration was not published until nearly two years later (in the January 3, 1931, issue of *Judge*).

Chapter 10: "Time, a Maniac Scattering Dust"

1. Alfred Tennyson, *In Memoriam* (1850), part L, stanza 2. "And Time, a maniac scattering dust, / And Life, a Fury slinging flame."

2. Titus Livy's *The History of Early Rome,* written sometime between the late first century BC and the early first century AD, discusses the legend (I.8–13). Ovid and Cicero covered the subject. Virgil's *Aeneid* includes the topic in book VIII. Plutarch wrote about it in *Lives* (II.14, 19). Charles Christian Nahl's "The Rape of the Sabines: The Abduction" (1871) depicts a single abductor and his captive, like Ted's version. Pablo Picasso did a version in 1962–63.

3. Letter from Ted Geisel to Harold Goddard Rugg, October 5, 1930, property of the Rauner Special Collections Library, Dartmouth College [CC19301005000].

4. Alexander Laing, review of *The King's Stilts, Dartmouth Alumni Magazine,* January 1940 [CC19400100001]. Laing refers to "The Rape of the Sabine Woman" as "the first great Seuss mural."

5. Ibid.

6. Letter from H. Allan Dingwall to the *Dartmouth Alumni Magazine,*

January 7, 1992, regarding "The Rape of the Sabine Woman," property of the Rauner Special Collections Library, Dartmouth College [CC19920107000].

7. Ogden Edwards, in a telephone conversation with the author, November 22, 2002.

8. See note 3.

9. When the title page of the original volume of *Boners* was being prepared for the printer, the manufacturing manager of Viking Press asked for the name of an editor. No name was forthcoming since the entire work of editing the book had been done by the editorial staff of this publishing house. Then came the problem of an introduction by a "big name." Several prominent authors were thought of and discarded: Herbert Hoover, Frank Sullivan, Bernard Shaw, and others. Time drew nearer and nearer for the book to be printed. Finally, desperate and tired of waiting, the manufacturing manager wrote the name of Alexander Abingdon on the title page, sent it to the printer, and made a mental reservation to substitute the correct name (or if no name were hit upon, to cut it out altogether) when the proofs came in. Time passed, and with its passing the mental reservation lapsed. Thus Abingdon entered history and became a byword in American homes.

10. *Boners* was the fourth-best-selling nonfiction book of 1931. www.caderbooks.com/best30.html.

11. See note 9.

12. Letter from Ted Geisel to Harold Goddard Rugg, circa January 1, 1933, property of the Rauner Special Collections Library, Dartmouth College [CC19330101z00].

13. Letter from Ted Geisel to Harold Goddard Rugg, circa January 15, 1933, property of the Rauner Special Collections Library, Dartmouth College [CC19330115z00].

Chapter 11: Standard Was Automatic

1. Examples of Black Flag advertising pamphlets include *The Hornet and Bumble Bee* (circa 1883), *Rhymes and Riddles to Please and Tease You* (1918), and *Black Flag Rhymes for Old and Young* (1921).

2. *Rhymes and Riddles to Please and Tease You* (Gilpin, Langdon, & Co., 1918), 13. "This is old Wiggly Puckaroo, He feeds on onions, beans and glue" [CC19180000000].

3. Howard W. Dickinson, *Printers' Ink,* October 11, 1928, 10, 12 [CC19281011000].

4. The other two Flit booklets of Seuss cartoons are: *Flit Cartoons as They Have Appeared in Magazines and Newspapers Throughout the Country* (New York: Stanco, 1930) [CC193008z0000] and *Adventures with a Flit Gun* (New York: Stanco, 1932) [CC193207z0000].

5. Among the newspapers closest to Ted's former home in Massachusetts, the Flit ads were reported to have appeared in the *Springfield Republican* and *Union,* the *Pittsfield Eagle,* the *Holyoke Transcript Telegram,* the *Northampton Gazette,* and the *Worcester Telegram and Gazette* in 1930.

6. *Catalog of Copyright Entries, Cumulative Series: Motion Pictures 1912–1939* (Library of Congress Copyright Office, 1951): 580, "'Neath the Bababa Tree (MP2689) and 688, "*Put on the Spout* (MP2737).

7. On June 24, 1931, Warner Bros.' short-subject subsidiary Vitagraph, Inc., applied for a license to be able to show those films in New York. The two films were reviewed, and four copies (one original and three duplicates) of each film were "approved without eliminations" by the censors.

8. In the application for licensure, Warner Bros.' representative Albert Howson described *Put on the Spout* as "synchronized" (which the application noted as "Musical Instruments Only") in one section of the form and further specified that it did not have dialogue elsewhere on the application. However, J. T. Donnelly, who examined the film for the State of New York Education Department's Motion Picture Division, noted it as having both synchronized sound and dialogue. Accordingly, the licenses that were granted (L62659–L62662) made note of "synchronization and dialogue." The *Film Daily*'s review confirms that a human voice speaks the "Quick, Henry, the Flit!" line, which probably accounts for the conflicting views of whether or not the film contained "dialogue."

9. "Put on the Spot," Reviews of Sound Shorts, *Film Daily* 56, no. 34 (August 9, 1931): 11 [CC19310809000].

10. The lack of dialogue is confirmed in Warner Bros.' application for licensure and by reviews by examiners M. D. Farrell and H. H. Kellogg.

'Neath the Bababa Tree was granted New York state licenses L62637–L62640.

11. Audio Cinema Studios were among the pioneers of sound in motion-picture production. Formed in 1923 as the Carpenter-Goldman Laboratories, in Long Island City, they worked as engineering consultants and were the first independent producers on the East Coast to be granted a license by Western Electric. Warner Bros. had also been trying to increase their work on industrial films and, in January 1931, Liggett & Myers Tobacco Company contracted with Warner Bros. to produce a series of 12 industrial sponsored shorts advertising Chesterfield cigarettes. *Film Daily* 55, no. 22 (January 27, 1931): 1, 8 [CC19310127000].

12. *Film Daily* 55, no. 21 (January 26,1931): 6 [CC19310126000].

13. *Film Daily* 55, no. 32 (February 8, 1931): 5 [CC19310208000].

14. *Film Daily* 55, no. 34 (February 10, 1931): 1 [CC19310210000].

15. *Film Daily* 55, no. 37 (February 13, 1931): 2 [CC19310213001].

16. On May 9, 1931, Warner Bros.' Vitaphone group completed its 1930–31 program of shorts, and the Brooklyn studio went on a skeleton crew until July 27.

17. *Film Daily* 55, no. 77 (April 2, 1931): 1–2 [CC19310402000].

18. *Film Daily* 55, no. 125 (May 28, 1931): 1 [CC19310528000].

19. *Film Daily* 55, no. 123 (May 26, 1931): 8 [CC19310526000]. One of the three shorts for Standard Oil was a scenic one shot in Pennsylvania by cameraman Frank Zukor, directed by Ben Blake, according to the May 27, 1931, issue of the *Film Daily* (5). The other two were either similar "sponsored" films or they were the two Flit films, which might have been presented as sponsored films rather than as "straight ad films," in which the whole film is an ad, as opposed to a film that is subsidized by a company.

20. Paul Terry owned 10 percent of Fables Pictures, Inc., with 90-percent partner The Keith-Albee Theater. In 1928, the latter sold its interest in Fables Studio to Amadee J. Van Beuren. Terry and Van Beuren disagreed about the incorporation of sound, a new phenomenon in the movies, into their cartoons. Terry favored silent cartoons with simple, separately recorded sound tracks, while Van Beuren preferred to stay current with the more expensive and modern technology of synchronized sound.

Terry left Fables Studio and founded TerryToons, best known for its later characters like Mighty Mouse and Heckle and Jeckle. Educational Pictures struck a deal with Audio Cinema whereby a new series of animated sound cartoons called *Terry-Toons* were released every two weeks, starting on February 23, 1931. TerryToons released their cartoons through Educational Pictures, which distributed them through the short-subject department of 20th Century–Fox. Terry was fond of saying, "Disney is the Tiffany's in this business . . . and I am the Woolworth's" (www.toonopedia.com/terrytoo.htm). Because of his resistance to technological advancements, he apparently did not release a color cartoon until 1938, under "encouragement" from Educational Pictures and 20th Century–Fox.

If a business like Penola, Inc./Standard Oil had utilized TerryToons, known as the industry's "bargain basement," to do a commercial venture like these Flit shorts, both of the films would almost certainly have been black-and-white reels with Philip A. Scheib's score recorded separately. Although some sources have cited Ted's Flit films as *Terry-Toons*, it is unlikely, since all accounts are that both films had synchronized sound, and since Warner Bros. was not the traditional distributor for *Terry-Toons*. It appears that Warner Bros. produced the films through Audio Cinema and that the relationship between TerryToons and Audio Cinema caused the confusion.

21. *Film Daily* 55, no. 6 (January 8, 1931): 15 [CC19310108000].

22. *Film Daily* 55, no. 7 (January 9, 1931): 6 [CC19310109000].

23. *Film Daily* 55, no. 80 (April 6, 1931): 4 [CC19310406000].

24. Graham Webb, in a letter to the author on July 12, 2002.

25. Lillian Friedman, interview with Harvey Deneroff, June 17, 1985, as reported in personal correspondence with Mr. Deneroff, August 14, 2002.

26. See note 6.

27. Graham Webb, *The Animated Film Encyclopedia: A Complete Guide to American Shorts, Features, and Sequences, 1900–1979* (Jefferson, NC: McFarland & Company, Inc., 2000).

28. Giovanna Righini, in correspondence with the author in July 2002. Ms. Righini's reference also cites the films as *Terry-Toons* and reports that the films are still distributed by Warner Bros. However, Warner Bros.

archivist Richard May contends, "We would not have any of this type of material in our possession, as the WB pre-1950 films were sold in 1955, and United Artists, who eventually came into ownership, donated all of the negatives to the Library of Congress, where they presently are stored" (personal correspondence, June 26, 2002). The Library of Congress has no record of either film in its holdings.

29. Jeff Lenburg, *The Encyclopedia of Animated Cartoons* (New York: Checkmark Books, 1999), 73.

30. See note 27.

31. Flit advertisement, "Now it's an hypothetical case, I know . . ." *Life* 97, no. 2516 (January 23, 1931) [CC19310123000]. During the appropriate window of time, Ted did a Flit print advertisement that could have been adapted to take place beneath a "Bababa" tree. One insect sitting on a small plant asks a second insect perched on a mushroom the hypothetical question, "If you were up to your neck in Flit and someone heaved a brick at your head, . . . would you duck?" Even without dialogue, it might have presented visual possibilities worthy of adaptation in cartoon form, but that is mere speculation.

32. Concerning his relationship with Ted Geisel, John Bransby has been described as "a motion picture producer for Standard Oil of New Jersey. . . . The two collaborated there on animated film projects." *Illustration House: Art Auction Catalog,* November 6, 1999, 26 [CC19991106000].

33. See note 9.

34. Rex Halfpenny, "Michigan Homebrewing During Prohibition," *Michigan Beer Guide* 7, no. 65 (Mar.–Apr. 2003) [CC200303z000]. "In the years leading up to 1933, home-brewing had become increasingly popular—so much so that the state of Michigan, for example, had already decided to tax the illegal booze traffic, specifically, the home brewer."

35. "Quick, Heinrich Das Flit," *Flit Advertising Booklet for 1933,* circa June 1933, 3 [CC193306z0000].

36. Esso products were apparently made by Penola, Inc. (probably specifically for Standard Oil, since it has been pointed out that "Esso" is the pronunciation of "S.O."—for Standard Oil). In any case, Esso products were distributed through major oil companies represented by the "baby Standards." When Ted was working for Essomarine in 1935, Essomarine ads were listed in the advertisers' index under Penola, Inc.

Chapter 12: Secrets of the Deep

1. Essomarine advertisement, "Anchors Aweigh for the Big Show!" *Yachting* 57, no. 1 (January 1935): 73 [CC19350100022].

2. Essomarine advertisement, "My name's Neptune—call me Nep. I'm King around here so watch your step . . . ," *Yachting* 58, no. 6 (December 1935): 67 [CC19351200002].

3. "Dr. Seuss' SS *Essomarine* on Her Annual Cruise," *Motor Boating* 57, no. 2 (February 1936): 306 [CC19360200001].

4. E. J. Kahn, Jr., "Profiles: Children's Friend," *The New Yorker* 36, no. 44 (December 17, 1960): 82 [CC19601217000].

5. "Essomarine Features Weird Creatures of the Deep," *Yachting* 61, no. 1 (January 1937): 122 [CC19370100003].

6. Ibid., 121.

7. *Vanguard Press Booklet,* spring 1938, 10 [CC19380400000].

8. Barbara Richardson, "Dr. Seuss: Creator of 'The Cat in the Hat,'" *Book and Magazine Collector,* no. 202 (January 2001): 45 [CC20010100000].

9. Judith and Neil Morgan, *Dr. Seuss and Mr. Geisel* (New York: Random House, 1995), 22 [CC19950421000].

10. Ibid., 84.

11. "Gay Menagerie of Queer Animals Fills the Apartment of Dr Seuss," *Springfield Union-News,* November 28, 1937, 5E [CC19371128001].

12. "Both Sides," *The Brooklyn Eagle,* January 6, 1940 [CC19400106000].

13. Theodor S. Geisel, "Essie, the Mermaid," *Motor Boating* 67, no. 1 (January 1941): 194 [CC19410100020].

14. See note 12.

15. Edward Connery Lathem, "Words and Pictures Married: The Beginnings of Dr. Seuss," *Dartmouth Alumni Magazine,* April 1976, 20 [CC19760400000].

16. "Rise of the Titans," *EXPO,* January 1997, www.expoweb.com/expomag/backissues/1997/0197_titans.htm [CC19970100000]. Harry A. Bruno appears to have had the drive, creativity, and practicality to make for a good pairing with Ted. Although Ted's career path would eventually change completely,

Bruno remained in the publicity field, and by the 1990s, his firm had grown so large that, after two mergers, it became part of the Miller Freeman, Inc., management group, one of the world's largest show producers.

17. See note 15.

Chapter 13: What Else Can This Ted Guy Sell?

1. Theodor S. Geisel, "Square-Dance for an Amateur Echo-Eater," *Jack-O-Lantern,* January 1936, 19 [CC19360101000].

2. Ted used "Square-Dance for an Amateur Echo-Eater" again the following year in "The Phantom of El Morocco," *Stage* 14, no. 7 (April 1937): 64 [CC19370400000]. It was equally nonsensical in that context.

3. Theodor S. Geisel, *The Strange Case of Adlebert Blump, The G-E Merchandiser* 20, no. 5 (November 1930) [CC193011z0000]. *The Strange Case of Adlebert Blump* appeared once in its full form, which included ten illustrations, in this issue. It was published again a year and a half later in a truncated form that reduced the number of illustrations to five in *G-E Appliance Merchandiser* 2, no. 7 (July 1932) [CC19320700000].

4. *The Strange Case of Adlebert Blump, G-E Appliance Merchandiser* 2, no. 7 (July 1932): 2 [CC19320700000].

5. Ibid.

6. Ibid., 3.

7. Ibid.

8. Ibid.

9. Ibid.

10. "With this issue *Telechronicle* presents Dr. Seuss (Theodor Geisel to you) . . . ," *Telechronicle* 3, no. 11 (February 1931): inside front cover [CC19320200001].

11. Bob Warren, "Dr. Seuss, Former *Jacko* Editor, Tells How Boredom May Lead . . . ," *The Dartmouth,* May 10, 1934, 2 [CC19340510000].

12. Although it is often cited that the American Can Company patented their "Keglined" technology in 1934, a patent search did not substantiate that claim. On November 23, 1933, the American Can Company applied for a patent for a can design that could withstand the necessary pressure of pasteurization. The patent for that can structure was granted on December 15, 1936, and the American Can Company applied to patent the Keglined process on January 7, 1937, including a special provision for lining the inside seam, which other processes might miss. Three months later—long before the patent was granted on November 7, 1939—the company ran an ad utilizing one of Ted's illustrations to promote their Keglined cans.

13. "It's a Real Pen Name Now," *Printers' Ink,* October 14, 1937, 24 [CC19371014002].

14. Paul Jerman, "Brief Biographies, 1925: Theodor Seuss Geisel," *Dartmouth Alumni Magazine,* March 1938 [CC19380300000].

15. "Gay Menagerie of Queer Animals Fills the Apartment of Dr. Seuss," *Springfield Union-News,* November, 28, 1937, 5E [CC19371128001].

16. Theodor S. Geisel, "Hankey Bird," *Printers' Ink,* February 1939, 46 [CC19390200004].

17. Theodor S. Geisel, "Nut Stuff," *Sales Management,* January 1939 [CC19390101000].

18. Ibid.

19. Ibid.

20. Examples of nineteenth-century Snyder & Black products include maps of the New York and New Haven Railroad in 1845; stock certificates for the Cleveland and Toledo Railroad in 1854 and Empresa Del Ferro-Carril de Guantánamo in Guantánamo, Cuba, in 1882; and mining-company certificates for the Arizona Butte Mining Company and Central City–Black Hawk Empress Mining Company in the late 1870s and early 1880s.

21. One such printing project for Snyder & Black in 1925 was a four-page school atlas for the Dominion of Canada and Newfoundland.

22. Snyder & Black advertisement, "Following the Barrage . . . with a POP-GUN," circa 1939 [CC1939z000000].

Chapter 14: *Life*, *Liberty*, and the Pursuit of Happiness

1. Theodor S. Geisel, "Man Being Carried Away by His Emotions," *College Humor* 17, no. 4 (July 1929): 24 [CC19290700000].

2. Theodor S. Geisel, "Everyone Laughed When I Stepped Up to the Piano," *College Humor* 19, no. 1 (December 1929): 27 [CC19291200000].

3. Theodor S. Geisel, "Daguerreotype of Three Seniors on a Spree,"

College Humor, no. 120 (February 1934): 46 [CC19340200001].

4. Theodor S. Geisel, "Quick, Henry! The Flit!" *Ballyhoo* 1, no. 3 (November 1931): inside front cover [CC19311000000].

5. Theodor S. Geisel, "Quick Herbie!" *Ballyhoo* 1, no. 4 (December 1931): 8 [CC19311200000].

6. "With Apologies to Dr. Seuss," *Razzberries* 1, no. 2 (September 1933): centerfold [CC19330900001].

7. Theodor S. Geisel, "Sherwood Bundshue, a constant reader . . . ," *College Humor,* no. 95 (November 1931): 33 [CC19311100002].

8. Theodor S. Geisel, "Unsung Animals Who Made Great Historical Events Possible," *Life* 95, no. 2483 (June 6, 1930): 15 [CC19300606000].

9. Theodor S. Geisel, "Unsung Animals Who Made Great Historical Events Possible," *Life* 95, no. 2484 (June 13, 1930): 15 [CC19300613000].

10. John Riddell, "The Science of Everything," *Vanity Fair* 36, no. 4 (June 1, 1931): 77 [CC19310600003].

11. Woody Allen, "If the Impressionists Had Been Dentists," *Without Feathers* (New York: Random House, 1975), 189.

12. Letter from Ted Geisel to Harold Goddard Rugg, January 20, 1932, property of the Rauner Special Collections Library, Dartmouth College [CC19320120000].

13. "Hundreds Are Sleeping Out Nightly in Chicago, Official Reports," *The New York Times,* September 20, 1931 [CC19310920000].

14. "Czar of the Insect World," *Vanity Fair* 37, no. 4 (December 1931): 29 [CC19311200002].

15. Although the banner on the building of Ted's third cover might appear to be the herald of a university sorority, W.C.T.U. was understood at the time to refer to the Women's Christian Temperance Union.

16. Franklin D. Roosevelt, "Our Political Racketeers," *Liberty* 9, no. 29 (July 16, 1932): 37 [CC19320716000].

17. A typical example of the difference between the sizes of Ted's original work and their magazine appearances reveals a reduction to 28.5 percent of the original.

18. Even full-page illustrations were greatly reduced in size. For example, "Forgotten Events of History: Noah's Dissolute Brother, Goah, Preserves the D.T. Beasts of His Day for Posterity" (July 1930) was reduced from its original dimensions of approximately 22.8" x 18.5" to approximately 9.1" x 6.3" when it was printed in *Life* 96, no. 2487 (July 4, 1930): 9 [CC19300704000].

19. Theodor S. Geisel, "New New Jersey: The Great New Jersey Rehabilitation Plan," *Life* 100, no. 2576 (March 1933): 24 [CC19330300001].

20. Ibid.

21. Ibid.

22. Ibid., 25.

23. Frank Sullivan, *In One Ear . . .* (New York: Viking Press, 1933), back cover [CC19330000002].

24. Ibid.

25. Bob Warren, "Dr. Seuss, Former *Jacko* Editor, Tells How Boredom May Lead . . . ," *The Dartmouth,* May 10, 1934, 2 [CC19340510000].

26. Judith and Neil Morgan, *Dr. Seuss and Mr. Geisel* (New York: Random House, 1995), 75 [CC19950421000].

27. Theodor S. Geisel, "Peru 4 (Angry Pig)," *The Secret Art of Dr. Seuss* (New York: Random House, 1995), 13 [CC19951026000].

28. *The American Press,* January 1934, 3 [CC19340100002].

29. See note 25.

30. "Gay Menagerie of Queer Animals Fills the Apartment of Dr. Seuss," *Springfield Union-News,* November 28, 1937, 5E [CC19371128001].

31. The color separations in Ted's "Seein' Things" series were presented in two booklets of six images each, with color proofs taken at each printing stage showing each color printed singly and then either superimposed on the preceding color or printed together in various combinations [CC19360000013, CC19360000014].

32. Theodor S. Geisel, "I've a Darned Good Mind to Get Caught—Just to Go Up and See the Argument," *This Week* (magazine), *New York Herald Tribune* 94, no. 32249, sec. 8 (March 3, 1935): 31 [CC19350303001] and "Even If She Does Lay an Egg, What Sort of Meal Is That?" *This Week* (magazine), *New York Herald Tribune* 94, no. 32256, sec. 8 (March 10, 1935): 16 [CC19350310000].

33. Mary Stofflet, *Dr. Seuss from Then to Now: A Catalogue of the Retrospective Exhibition* (New York: Random House, 1988), 35 [CC19880915000].

34. "See Dr. Seuss for Social Publicity!" *New York Woman* 1, no. 5 (October 7, 1936): 40 [CC19361007000].

35. Fantastic Art, Dada, Surrealism, MoMA Exhibit #55, December 7, 1936, through January 17, 1937.

36. "'Twas a Gay, Wet New Year's Eve . . . But War Clouds Hung Over It," *PM* 1, no. 179 (February 24, 1941): 17 [CC19410224000]. In the next few years, the fashionable scene on New York City's East Side would include such notable nightspots as the Stork, Versailles, Copacabana, Monte Carlo, Armando's, and Bill's Gay Nineties.

37. Club El Morocco was owned by John Perona, a character in Ted's piece.

38. The El Morocco was also mentioned in J. D. Salinger's 1951 book *The Catcher in the Rye*. In another coincidence, Ted Geisel traveled on the MS *Kungsholm* immediately prior to writing *And to Think That I Saw It on Mulberry Street*, and J. D. Salinger worked as an entertainer on that ship a few years after Ted took his trip.

39. The definition of "gusseteer" comes from Cat Howell's Book of Naughty Nomenclature, www.geocities.com/SouthBeach/Wharf/1292/catsbookc.htm.

40. Theodor S. Geisel, "The Phantom of El Morocco," *Stage* 14, no. 7 (April 1937): 64 [CC19370400000].

Chapter 15: The Annual Brat-Books

1. Swedish American Line brochure, circa April 1936, 28 [CC193604z0000].

2. Judith Martin, "Springfield's Dr. Seuss Stumbled into Success," *Springfield Republican,* November 28, 1971 [CC19711128000].

3. See note 1.

4. *The New York Times,* August 8, 1915, www.twainquotes.com/19150808.html. "Punch in the Presence of the Passenjare" was apparently composed by Isaac Bromley, Noah Brooks, W. C. Wyckoff, and Moses W. Handy.

5. Mark Twain, "Punch, Brothers, Punch," *The Stolen White Elephant, Etc.* (Boston: James R. Osgood & Co., 1882).

6. E. J. Kahn, Jr., "Profiles: Children's Friend," *The New Yorker* 36, no. 44 (December 17, 1960): 64 [CC19601217000].

7. Just how many publishers rejected Ted's first book? It depends upon whom you ask:
   (20) E. J. Kahn, Jr., "Profiles: Children's Friend," *The New Yorker* 36, no. 44 (December 17, 1960): 64 [CC19601217000].
   (25) "He Makes C-A-T Spell Big Money," *BusinessWeek,* July 18, 1964, 73 [CC19640718000].
   (26) *Publishers Weekly,* December 17, 1962, 11–14 [CC19621217000].
   (26) Arthur Gordon, "The Wonderful Wizard of Soledad Hill," *Woman's Day* 28, no. 12 (September 1965): 74 [CC19650900000].
   (27) Clifton Fadiman, "Party of One," *Holiday* 25, no. 4 (April 15, 1959): 16 [CC19590415000].
   (27) Betsy Marden Silverman, "Dr. Seuss Talks to Parents About Learning to Read and What Makes Children Want to Do It," *Parents* 35, no. 11 (November 1960): 44 [CC19601100000].
   (28) Cynthia Lindsay, "The Miracle of Dr. Seuss," *Good Housekeeping,* December 1960, 34 [CC19601200000].
   (29) Glenn Edward Sadler, "Maurice Sendak and Dr. Seuss: A Conversation," *The Horn Book Magazine* 65, no. 5 (September 1989): 586 [CC19890900000]. "By December 1982, even Ted could no longer recall how many publishers had rejected his first book: 'Twenty-seven or twenty-nine, I forget which. The excuse I got for all those rejections was that there was nothing on the market quite like it, so they didn't know whether it would sell.'"
   (43) Jill C. Wheeler, *Dr. Seuss: A Tribute to the Young at Heart* (Minnesota: Abdo & Daughters, 1992), 10 [CC19920000032].

8. Clifton Fadiman, "Party of One," *Holiday* 25, no. 4 (April 15, 1959): 16 [CC19590415000].

9. Judith and Neil Morgan, *Dr. Seuss and Mr. Geisel* (New York: Random House, 1995), 82 [CC19950421000].

10. Herbert Morrison, eyewitness radio broadcast of the Hindenburg explosion, May 6, 1937 (four months before the publication of *Mulberry Street*).

11. Although the *Booklist* review of *Mulberry Street* was negative, there were plenty of positive ones:
   "Highly original and entertaining. . . . It is a masterly interpretation."—*The New York Times*
   "Truly fresh and original."—*The Horn Book Magazine*
   "Introduces a rich new talent to picture books."
   —*National Parent-Teacher Magazine*
   "They say it's for children but . . . get a copy for yourself."
   —*The New Yorker*
   Quotes taken from *Vanguard Press Booklet,* spring 1938, 12 [CC19380400000].
   And Anne Carroll Moore, in the September 1937 issue of *Atlantic Monthly* [CC19370900004], hailed *Mulberry Street* as "so completely spontaneous that the American child can take it to his heart on sight . . . as original in conception, as spontaneous in the rendering as it is true to the imagination of a small boy."

12. Theodor S. Geisel, "Quality," *Judge* 114, no. 2712 (March 1938): 14 [CC19380300001].

13. Ford Motor Company television commercial, circa May 1949 [CC19490509z005].

14. Dr. Seuss, *And to Think That I Saw It on Mulberry Street* (New York: Vanguard, 1937) [CC19370900001].

15. Dr. Seuss Zoo (Dr. Seuss School of Unorthodox Taxidermy) advertisement, "The Blue-Green Abelard," *Judge* 114, no. 2713 (April 1938): inside back cover [CC19380400021].

16. Theodor S. Geisel, "Life's Little Educational Charts: Some Unusual Substitutes for Mistletoe," *Life* 94, no. 2457 (December 6, 1929): 35 [CC19291206000].

17. Theodor S. Geisel, "Some Recent Inventions in the Offspring Field," *Liberty* 9, no. 30 (July 23, 1932): 23 [CC19320723000].

18. Theodor S. Geisel, "The Facts of Life: Or How Should I Tell My Child? Part I, Chap. I," *Life* 101, no. 2587 (February 1934): 46 [CC19340200000].

19. *Publishers Weekly* 176, no. 8 (August 24, 1959): 23, 31 [CC19590824000].

20. See note 13.

21. Essomarine advertisement, "Are You on the Horns of a Sea-Going Dilemma?" *Yachting* 61, no. 1 (January 1937): 156–57 [CC19370100003].

22. Walter Anthony, "Unusual Occupations," *Dialogue Continuity* L 1–1 (Jan.–Feb. 1941) [CC194101–02000].

23. Ibid.

24. Regarding the Wolghast, the name may well have derived from lightweight boxer Adolph "Ad" Wolgast. It is very likely that Ted, a boxing fan, was aware of fellow German American Wolgast and read about Wolgast's bouts with Oscar "Battling" Nelson and Freddy Welsh around the time he was working on his sculptures and Essolube characters.

25. Ted's other sculptures included ones like the Anthony Drexel Goldfarb piece [CC19380400013] pictured in *The Secret Art of Dr. Seuss* (New York: Random House, 1955), 38 [CC19951026000].

26. "The Dr. Seuss School of Unorthodox Taxidermy," *Vanguard Press Booklet,* spring 1938, 11 [CC19380400000].

27. Barbara Bayler, personal correspondence with the author, April 30, 2002.

28. Lending some potential support to this timeline for Ted's marionette prototypes is the fact that in 1940, Ted's marionette partner, Sue Hastings, published her book *How to Produce Plays* with co-author Dorcas Ruthenburg. The previous year, Ted named one of his seven Lady Godivas "Dorcas." The timing suggests that Hastings and Seuss discussed the marionette project after the publication of *The 500 Hats of Bartholomew Cubbins* in July 1938, during which time Ted presumably met Dorcas Ruthenburg.

29. "Gay Menagerie of Queer Animals Fills the Apartment of Dr. Seuss," *Springfield Union-News,* November, 28, 1937, 5E [CC19371128001].

30. Sources indicate some of the earliest Uncle Wiggily books, published while Ted was six to ten years old, were *Uncle Wiggily and Sammie and Susie Littletail* (1910), *Uncle Wiggily and Jackie and Peetie Bow Wow* (1912), *Uncle Wiggily's Fortune* (1913), *Uncle Wiggily and Baby Bunty* (1913), and *Uncle Wiggily and Charlie and Arabella Chick* (1914).

31. Judith and Neil Morgan, *Dr. Seuss and Mr. Geisel* (New York: Random House, 1995), 87 [CC19950421000].

32. Dr. Seuss, *The 500 Hats of Bartholomew Cubbins* (New York: Vanguard, 1938), 17 [CC19380700000].

33. "Dr. Seuss," *Wilson Library Bulletin* 14, no. 3 (November 1939) [CC19391100002].

34. Carolyn See, "Dr. Seuss and the Naked Ladies," *Esquire* 81, no. 6 (June 1974): 118 [CC19740600000].

35. Ted spent one part of his life feeling that his job as an "advertising man" was inferior to that of an author, and later feeling that his job as a

children's book author was inferior to that of a "serious writer" of novels. In 1941, even with four children's books published, Ted described himself, or at least allowed himself to be described, in the following manner: "A doctor of literature, he writes nonsense books for a living and illustrates them for fun." Walter Anthony, "Unusual Occupations" *Dialogue Continuity* L 1–1 (Jan.–Feb. 1941) [CC194101–02000].

36. Alexander Laing, review of *The King's Stilts, Dartmouth Alumni Magazine,* January 1940 [CC19400100001].

37. Ibid.

38. E. J. Kahn, Jr., "Profiles: Children's Friend," *The New Yorker* 36, no. 44 (December 17, 1960): 93 [CC19601217000].

39. Carolyn See, "Dr. Seuss and the Naked Ladies," *Esquire* 81, no. 6 (June 1974): 176 [CC19740600000].

40. Countess Godiva is also referred to as "Godgifu," "Godgiva," or "Godwa" in various sources, all of which mean "God's gift." Depending upon the source, Lady Godiva's ride is alleged to have taken place on either May 31, 1057, or on a Thursday in August at noon. If it were the latter, it is interesting to note that Leofric died August 31, 1057.

41. J. A. Giles, trans., *Roger of Wendover's Flowers of History, Comprising the History of England from the Descent of the Saxons to A.D. 1235,* 2 vols. (1849; reprinted Lampeter, 1993).

42. Theodor S. Geisel, "A Hitherto Unpublished Fact," *Judge* 94, no. 2421 (March 24, 1928): 14 [CC19280324000].

43. Stephen Vincent Benét, "The Sobbin' Women," *Argosy* 24, no. 150 (November 1938): 61 [CC19381100005].

44. The 1939 World's Fair opened in Flushing Meadows, Queens, New York, on April 30, 1939, and closed its initial season on October 31, 1939. It reopened for its second season on May 11, 1940, and closed again on October 27, 1940.

45. Theodor Seuss Geisel and Ralph Warren, United States Patent 2,150,853 (camera), filed May 19, 1938, and issued March 14, 1939 [CC19390314000].

46. Examples of Conan O'Brien's "If They Mated" photographs can be found on the show's Web site, www.nbc.com/nbc/Late_Night_with_Conan_O'Brien/iftheymated.

47. Robert Cahn, "The Wonderful World of Dr. Seuss," *The Saturday Evening Post* 230, no. 1 (July 6, 1957): 42 [CC19570706000].

48. Ibid.

49. Pat Sullivan, *Felix Revolts* (Burbank, CA: M. J. Winkler, May 1, 1923) [CC19230501000].

50. Bennett Cerf, *At Random* (New York: Random House, 1977), 154 (February 24, 1941, royalty statement).

51. "The King's Stilts . . . ," *New York Herald Tribune Books* 99, no. 33964, sec. 9 (November 12, 1939): 22 [CC19391112000].

52. E. J. Kahn, Jr., "Profiles: Children's Friend," *The New Yorker* 36, no. 44 (December 17, 1960): 48 [CC19601217000].

53. Dr. Seuss, *Horton Hatches the Egg* (New York: Random House, 1940), 3, 6 [CC19401012000].

54. Judith and Neil Morgan, *Dr. Seuss and Mr. Geisel* (New York: Random House, 1995), 97 [CC19950421000].

55. Barbara Richardson, "Dr. Seuss: Creator of 'The Cat in the Hat,'" *Book and Magazine Collector,* no. 202 (January 2001): 50 [CC20010100000].

56. Response by Theodor S. Geisel to a hypothetical question from his character Americus Vesputius Fepp regarding Ted's work for *PM* newspaper, personal papers from the Mandeville Special Collections Library at the University of California, San Diego.

Chapter 16: Shunning His Frumious Brand of Sneetch

1. Theodor S. Geisel [credited: Dr. Seuss] ". . . But for Grown-Ups Laughing Isn't Any Fun," *The New York Times Book Review,* November 16, 1952, 2 [CC19521116000].

2. Theodor S. Geisel, "Explanation of an Ancient Joke," *Jack-O-Lantern* 17, no. 6 (February 5, 1925): 32 [CC19250205000]. Sigmund Freud's theory was that there are three ways to access the unconscious mind—through dreams, through slips of the tongue that he termed "parapraxes," and through jokes. Jokes, he felt, were always related to repressed wishes and, for Freud, sex was at the bottom of most unconscious wishes.

3. See note 1.

4. Theodor S. Geisel, "Joe seems rather tight," *Jack-O-Lantern* 17, no. 4 (December 15, 1924): 35 [CC19241215000].

5. Letter from Valentine & Sons, Ltd., to Theodor S. Geisel, September 30, 1929, property of the Mandeville Special Collections Library at the University of California, San Diego [CC19290930000].

6. Theodor S. Geisel, "The Wearing Out of the Green," *Jack-O-Lantern* 16, no. 4 (December 18, 1923): 33 [CC19231218000].

7. Theodor S. Geisel, "Unsung Heroes of the Gridiron (A Unique Signal System)," *Judge* 95, no. 2454 (November 10, 1928): 6 [CC19281110000].

8. Theodor S. Geisel, On the Firing Line, *Springfield Union,* July 10, 1925, 10 [CC19250710000].

9. www.cyberboxingzone.com/boxing/sikibio.htm

10. Judith and Neil Morgan, *Dr. Seuss and Mr. Geisel* (New York: Random House, 1995), 16 [CC19950421000].

11. "In January 1928, three months after the debut of 'The Jazz Singer,' only 157 of the estimated 20,000 movie theaters in the nation were wired for sound. By the end of 1929—after 'The Singing Fool'—some 8,741 movie theaters were able to show sound movies." Neil A. Grauer, "Al of Two Cities," *The Washington Post,* August 17, 1997, G4, www.jolson.org/works/film/js/washpost/al2city.html.

12. Theodor S. Geisel, "H. L. Mencken, writing of the people of Dayton . . . ," On the Firing Line, *Springfield Union,* July 20, 1925, 6 [CC19250720000].

13. Theodor S. Geisel, "New New Jersey: The Great New Jersey Rehabilitation Plan," *Life* 100, no. 2576 (March 933): 24 [CC19330300001].

14. *The Dartmouth,* May 10, 1934, 2 [CC19340510000] "In a couple of months I'm going to Africa with my wife to study the animal situation there."

15. "Negroes' Rights on Trains Won," *PM* 1, no. 225, complete edition (April 29, 1941): 4 [CC19410429002].

16. "Race Discrimination in Defense Plants Charged by 60 Prominent Americans," *PM* 1, no. 231, complete edition (May 7, 1941): 11 [CC19410507001].

17. "If Bigger Wasn't Black and If He Had Money and If They'd Let Him Go to Aviation School, He Could Fly," *PM* 1, no. 231, complete edition (May 7, 1941): 12 [CC19410507001].

18. Tom O'Connor, editorial, *PM* 1, no. 231, complete edition (May 7, 1941): 19 [CC19410507001].

19. www2.gasou.edu/special_collections/exhibits/msp/1942con.htm

20. Randall Kennedy, *Nigger: The Strange Career of a Troublesome Word* (New York: Pantheon, 2001).

21. A. Philip Randolph, "Why Should We March?" (1942), http://occawlonline.pearsoned.com/bookbind/pubbooks/divine5e/chapter27/medialib/primarysources1_27_2.html.

22. In contrast to Talmadge's Georgia, in Ted's home state of Massachusetts, segregation had been banned since 1855.

23. Dr. Seuss, "The Sneetches," *Redbook* 101, no. 3 (July 1953): 77 [CC19530700000].

24. *Brown* v. *Board of Education,* 347 U.S. 483 (1954).

25. Dr. Seuss, *Horton Hears a Who!* (New York: Random House, 1954), 6 [CC19540812000].

26. Ibid.

27. Theodor S. Geisel, "Japan's Young Dreams," *Life,* March 29, 1954, 89–95. Ted returned from Japan in April 1953 and "Japan's Young Dreams" was expected to appear that summer. However, it was hatcheted in the editing process and delayed almost a year before being published in *Life.* "His piece was rewritten, Ted grumbled, 'almost entirely, substituting conclusions of their [own] not warranted by the facts. . . . They raped the article.'" Judith and Neil Morgan, *Dr. Seuss and Mr. Geisel* (New York: Random House, 1995), 137 [CC19950421000].

28. Judith and Neil Morgan, *Dr. Seuss and Mr. Geisel* (New York: Random House, 1995), 276) [CC19950421000].

Chapter 17: Changing Views

1. Richard H. Minear, *Dr. Seuss Goes to War* (New York: The New Press, 1999), 10 [CC19991000000].

2. Gareth Jones, *The Western Mail,* April 11, 1931, www.colley.co.uk/garethjones/soviet_articles/how_it_is_working.htm.

3. Nikolay Dolgorukov, "Full speed ahead for the fourth and final year of the Five-Year Plan!" (Moscow/Leningrad: Ogiz-Izogiz, 1931), lithograph poster, www.iisg.nl/exhibitions/chairman/sov19.html.

4. Theodor S. Geisel, "Holding the Bag: A Projected Monument to the

Great American Public," *Judge* 102, no. 2629 (March 19, 1932): 4 [CC19320319000]. Ted's cartoon, "Holding the Bag: A Projected Monument to the Great American Public," depicts average citizens and their pets staring either vacantly or angrily at their empty bags, or looking up hopefully, all waiting for the "trickle-down" of money from above.

5. Edward Connery Lathem, "Words and Pictures Married: The Beginnings of Dr. Seuss," *Dartmouth Alumni Magazine,* April 1976, 19 [CC19760400000].

6. Ted's cartoon, "'Dropping the Pilot.' *Puck*'s Famous Cartoon Which Started the Astor House Riots," is an intentionally garbled mess, starting with its title. The reference is to a cartoon published in *Punch*—not *Puck*—in 1890, 41 years *after* the Astor Place Opera House Riot took place, so it is clear that, in keeping with the John Riddell story "Mr. Sullivan's Times," which it accompanied, Ted was not taking his own political prowess completely seriously.

7. Information on the prices of meat around 1937 was gathered from www.nber.org/databases/macrohistory/rectdata/04/m04166.dat and www.nber.org/databases/macrohistory/contents/chapter04.html.

8. Franklin D. Roosevelt, "Fireside Chat #10" radio broadcast, October 12, 1937 [CC19371012000].

9. *New York Journal and American,* no. 18691 (February 14, 1939): 1 [CC19390214000].

10. Wannsee Protocol, January 20, 1942, conference, based on the official U.S. government translation prepared for evidence in trials at Nuremberg, as reproduced in John Mendelsohn, ed., *The Holocaust: Selected Documents in Eighteen Volumes,* vol. 11: *The Wannsee Protocol and a 1944 Report on Auschwitz by the Office of Strategic Services* (New York: Garland, 1982), 18–32.

11. Japan's Kwangtung Army faced the Russian Red Army along the Soviet-Manchurian border, with Japanese imperialism leading to almost daily border clashes from 1932 to 1939.

12. Theodor S. Geisel, "Check Your Brains, Sir?" *New York Journal and American,* September 13, 1939, 18 [CC19390913000].

13. Theodor S. Geisel, "Fashion Note: Earmuffs Are Back Again," *New York Journal and American,* October 4, 1939, 20 [CC19391004000].

14. *New York Journal and American,* October 10, 1939, 16 [CC19391010000].

15. Narragansett Brewing Company advertisement, "Gangway for Gansett," *Boston Globe,* "Beverage Edition," November 1940 [CC19401100000].

16. When reviewing Ted's work with *PM,* it is important to eliminate one of the aspects that is bound to lead to confusion. Just as there were different editions of the *New Yorker*—one of which carried Ted's Chilton Pen ads and one of which did not—there were also several different editions of *PM* newspaper. The weekday issues were known as *PM Daily,* of which there were several types—the complete, national, mail, and last editions. In most cases, one of Ted's cartoons would appear one day in the complete edition and in the next day's national edition/mail edition, but that was not always the case. Sometimes a cartoon would appear in one edition and not in the corresponding edition. This variety accounts for the difference among dates found in diverse sources.

17. Theodor S. Geisel, "—And From Berlin:" *PM* 2, no. 63, complete edition (September 12, 1941): 14 [CC19410912000].

18. "Lindbergh's Dirtiest Speech: Attack on Jews," *PM* 2, no. 63, complete edition (September 12, 1941): 14 [CC19410912000].

19. "Senator Nye Joins Lindbergh . . . Anti-Semitism Comes Above Ground," *PM* 2, no. 67, complete edition (September 18, 1941): 8 [CC19410918000].

20. "Japanese Government Resigns," *PM* 2, no. 87, complete edition (October 16, 1941): 2 [CC19411016000].

21. Sutherland Denlinger, "Japan Assails U.S.A., Insists on 'New Order' in Asia," *PM* 2, no. 109, complete edition (November 17, 1941): 3 [CC19411117000].

22. Kenneth G. Crawford, "Japan Told Bluntly That We Won't Sell Out China to Keep Peace . . . Last of Marines Leave Shanghai," *PM* 2, no. 117, complete edition (November 27, 1941): 3 [CC19411127000].

23. Response by Theodor S. Geisel to a hypothetical question from his character Americus Vesputius Fepp regarding Ted's work for *PM* newspaper, personal papers from the Mandeville Special Collections Library at the University of California, San Diego.

Ted's description of his involvement with *PM* comes from biographical sketches he made by answering questions theoretically posed to him by his fictional character Americus Vesputius Fepp. In Americus Vesputius Fepp, Ted had not chosen a random fun-sounding name. Amerigo Vespucci (1454–1512) was an Italian explorer who realized the land discovered by Columbus was a new continent, not India as was claimed. "America" is the Latin feminine form of "Americus." Thus Ted used the man for which our country is named to represent the average American, or the collective American spirit, and it is to that fictitious figure that he explains himself in his informal biographical notes. Ted also used the name Fepp to reinforce the point. Fepp is a name that he had often used to represent the average citizen since the December 6, 1929, issue of *Life.* It has been illustrated that Fepp, along with Drouberhannus, Grimalken, and Nalbner, was a favorite name of Ted's to utilize. One of Ted's best representations of Fepp was the Staten Island Fepps (including son, Albermarle) in the February 1934 issue of *Life.*

24. Judith and Neil Morgan, *Dr. Seuss and Mr. Geisel* (New York: Random House, 1995), 103 [CC19950421000].

25. *Junk (A Sharing America Leaflet),* circa October 1942, 12 [CC19421000000].

26. See note 10.

27. See note 10.

28. Ernest Hemingway's only play, written in Madrid in the latter half of 1937, was called *The Fifth Column.* He has explained, "The title refers to the Spanish statement in the fall of 1936 that they had four columns advancing on Madrid and a fifth column of sympathizers inside the city to attack the defenders of the city from the rear." www2.uol.com.br/speakup/collection/183_hemingway_wartime.shtml.

29. Regarding the internment camps, after President Franklin D. Roosevelt issued Executive Order 9066 on February 19, 1942, Congress implemented the order on March 21, 1942, passing Public Law 503. Japanese Canadians faced a similar fate.

30. Richard H. Minear, *Dr. Seuss Goes to War* (New York: The New Press, 1999), 25 [CC19991000000].

31. Ralph Ingersoll, "An Editorial Answer to the 'Saturday Evening Post,'" *PM* 2, no. 202, national edition (March 27, 1942): 3 [CC19420327000]. While Ingersoll's response appears to have impassioned Ted, Milton Mayer's article, "The Case Against the Jew," was a bit more complex than Ingersoll's description suggests. It was the third of a series of articles that the *Saturday Evening Post* published, following Judge Jerome Frank's "Red-White-and-Blue Herring" and Waldo Frank's "The Jews Are Different." Mayer's article portrayed American Jews as being so desperate to assimilate that "they tried to lose themselves in the crowd, like men who have picked a pocket on a busy street. They resorted to every dodge known to fugitive criminals, from changing their names to changing their faces." Milton Mayer, "The Case Against the Jew," *The Saturday Evening Post* 214, no. 39 (May 28, 1942): 19 [CC19420528000].

32. Harold Lavine, "Profile of a Man Who Plans to Keep Talking for a Month," *PM* 3, no. 130, complete edition (November 16, 1942): 12 [CC19421116000].

33. The Southern Electoral Reform League cited editorials in Virginia newspapers that claimed "poll taxes are paid en bloc and . . . elections are largely a matter of buying and selling poll-tax receipts and absentee voter ballots." Nathan Robertson, "Virginia Press Slams Poll Tax," *PM* 3, no. 119, complete edition (November 3, 1942): 12 [CC19421103000].

34. See note 32. Bilbo apparently accepted money to vote a particular way and, when investigated by a grand jury, claimed that he did so in order to prove there was bribery going on. A vote to expel him from the legislature failed by one vote and a subsequent resolution requesting that Bilbo resign passed 25-1, but he refused to do so and was elected lieutenant governor anyway.

35. "An Odor of Skunk," *PM* 3, no. 157, complete edition (December 17, 1942): 11 [CC19421117000]. Ted's image of Laval crawling from the cave brings to mind J.R.R. Tolkien's Gollum, who had appeared in *The Hobbit, or There and Back Again* five years earlier.

Chapter 18: Taxing the Axis

1. *Why We Fight: War Comes to America,* (834th Signal Service Photographic Detachment, Special Services Division, U.S. Army, 1945).

2. On June 6, 1942, the 834th Signal Service Photographic Detachment, Special Services Division, Film Production Section was created, and

Major Frank Capra was put in charge. By the summer of 1943, the detachment received a commendation from Brigadier General Frederick H. Osborn, complimenting the group on successfully completing films for the orientation of the soldier that were "universally acclaimed as the ablest films in this field produced in this or any other country." However, on September 1, 1943, the unit was brought back into the Signal Corps' Army Pictorial Service, where it was originally. Ted remained in Hollywood at "Fort Fox" while most of the unit moved to the East Coast. For more, see Joseph McBride, *Frank Capra: The Catastrophe of Success* (New York: Simon & Schuster, 1992), 457, 470, 485.

3. Judith and Neil Morgan, *Dr. Seuss and Mr. Geisel* (New York: Random House, 1995), 109 [CC19950421000].

4. Ibid.

5. Joseph McBride, *Frank Capra: The Catastrophe of Success* (New York: Simon & Schuster, 1992), 470. *Army-Navy Screen Magazine* was initially called *The War* (June–Oct. 1942), then retitled through its final 1946 installments.

6. Ibid., 453.

7. Ibid., 474.

8. Ruth and Roger Whiter, "A Chat with Ray Harryhausen," *Animation World Magazine* 4, no. 11 (February 2000) [CC20000200000].

9. *PRIVATE SNAFU: "Gripes"* was directed by Isadore "Friz" Freleng. Among the "in" jokes, you can find Freleng's nickname at the beginning of the fourth line of the eye chart at SNAFU's physical.

10. Letter from Theodor S. Geisel to Harold Goddard Rugg, November 23, 1943, property of the Rauner Special Collections Library, Dartmouth College [CC19431123000].

11. Some examples of Ted's recurring usage of the image of a man riding the waves with his feet on two fish can be found in Theodor S. Geisel, "Advice to Wager Makers," *Judge* 95, no. 2453 (November 3, 1928): 6 [CC19281103000]; Theodor S. Geisel, "Sea Travel for All!" *Liberty* 9, no. 44 (October 29, 1932): 45 [CC19321029000]; and Theodor S. Geisel, "Hejji," no. 3 (April 21, 1935): panel 6 [CC19350421000].

12. "We Must Prevent Useless Spending for Scarce Consumer Goods," *Starve the Squander Bug* advertising brochure (U.S. Treasury Department, War Finance Division, Press Section, circa November 1943), 2 [CC19431100001]. In addition to the 18 Squander Bug ad samples, there was an ad mat featuring a close-up of the Squander Bug ingesting some income that was proposed as a daily or regular feature, in which that same image would be accompanied with different economic hints each time (15 examples of which were supplied). The horizontal fold-out version in the centerfold of this brochure was 30 percent larger than the other version that was distributed.

13. See note 10.

14. Theodor S. Geisel, *Memorandum: Report on Two Months' Work in ETO*, February 5, 1945, 2 [CC19450205000]. "My First Specific Assignment in the theatre was to . . . secure the theatre acceptance of *Your Job in Germany*."

   There are many similarities between the text of the *Pocket Guide to Germany* and the narrative portion of *Your Job in Germany*. Early in the booklet, the warnings about how to behave in Germany echo Ted's film almost verbatim. The first chapter of the booklet is, in fact, titled "Your Job in Germany." That chapter deals with non-fraternization and bears Ted's usual admonition that "we don't like to kick people when they are down." *Pocket Guide to Germany* (U.S. Government Printing Office 592037, November 1944), 2 [CC194411z0000].

15. Carolyn See, "Dr. Seuss and the Naked Ladies," *Esquire* 81, no. 6 (June 1974): 176 [CC19740600000].

16. See note 10.

17. Even the SNAFU cartoons done without much of Ted's help are interesting as odd period pieces. In the May 1944 *PRIVATE SNAFU: A LECTURE ON CAMOUFLAGE*, directed by Chuck Jones, one can see what Warner Bros. animators could do when they were allowed to draw bare-breasted mermaids, for example, without censorship. Later that month, in Jones's *PRIVATE SNAFU: Gas*, SNAFU pulls Bugs Bunny out of his knapsack. While Ted was otherwise engaged, Jones may have taken over even greater responsibility in this cartoon. A few weeks earlier, Warner Bros. had released the twenty-second Bugs Bunny cartoon for theatrical release, "Bugs Bunny Nips the Nips," which Jones had directed. There is also a character, who reports SNAFU's absence from the gas-mask drill, that looks a bit like a possible caricature of Ted,

lending more evidence that other personnel may have been having some fun with Ted while he was busy working on the first of his documentaries.

18. Judith and Neil Morgan, *Dr. Seuss and Mr. Geisel* (New York: Random House, 1995), 115 [CC19950421000].

19. Ibid.

20. Ibid., 115–16.

21. While Ted worked on *Your Job in Germany*, the SNAFU series continued. Friz Freleng's October release, *PRIVATE SNAFU: TARGET SNAFU*, was an anti-malaria piece but took a different approach than the one Ted had utilized. In November, the first of the pieces done outside of Warner Bros. was released. For UPA, Osmond Evans directed *PRIVATE SNAFU: A Few Quick Facts* (about inflation), which explained how Americans' buying up a foreign country's stock of a product left less of that product available to the locals, causing merchants to raise prices on the remaining stock. GIs were warned not to spend so much money overseas. Back at Warner Bros., Bugs Bunny made another appearance when Friz Freleng directed the December 1944 release of *PRIVATE SNAFU: THREE BROTHERS*, in which SNAFU's brothers, TARFU and FUBAR, were introduced. TARFU worked in the message center at the mercy of temperamental and pushy carrier pigeons ("nursemaid to a flock of feather dusters"), and FUBAR worked in the K-9 training center, where he was attacked by dogs while wearing a Japanese mask. FUBAR (Fucked Up Beyond All Repair/Recognition) did not appear again in the series, but under Ted's guidance, TARFU (Things Are Really Fucked Up) was reconfigured as SNAFU's equivalent in the navy.

22. In July 1944, the lone facet of Ted's influence was that the archways of the Trans-Iranian Express train in Friz Freleng's *PRIVATE SNAFU: HOT SPOT* bear the Seuss imprint. Later that month, Freleng's *PRIVATE SNAFU: OPERATION SNAFU*, in which SNAFU finally looks semi-competent in stealing Japanese war plans, shows none of Ted's touches. It would be three months until the next installment, Chuck Jones's *PRIVATE SNAFU: NO BUDDY ATOLL*, would arrive in October. Again, even the bumbling SNAFU is able to defeat the dedicated but ineffectual Japanese enemy, and again, there is little evidence that Ted had much to do with the episode.

23. Theodor S. Geisel, *Memorandum: Information Program for the Army of Occupation*, December 25, 1944, 4 [CC19441225000], property of the Mandeville Special Collections Library at the University of California, San Diego. "The first problem is not with the army. It is with us, and with our attitude toward this army."

24. Ibid. Although many of the projects Ted proposed in this memorandum were not pursued, others were begun but not necessarily completed. The situation is made more confusing by misinformation that continues to be spread. Descriptions of the supposed film *Coming Home* turn out to be identical to the plot of *PRIVATE SNAFU: GOING HOME*. For example, "Private SNAFU comes home and tells Army secrets to everyone in town. Because of his loose lips, his troop is ambushed." www.tultw.com/bios/snafu.htm.

25. Joseph McBride, *Frank Capra: The Catastrophe of Success* (New York: Simon & Schuster, 1992), 458.

26. Ibid., 471.

27. *Your Job in Germany* (Army Pictorial Services, Information and Education Division, U.S. Armed Forces, April 13, 1945) [CC19450413000].

28. Ibid.

29. Ibid.

30. Ibid.

31. Ephraim Katz, *The Film Encyclopedia* (New York: Putnam, 1982), 952.

32. Joseph McBride, *Frank Capra: The Catastrophe of Success* (New York: Simon & Schuster, 1992), 496.

33. Other sources list Dana Andrews as the narrator of *Your Job in Germany*, but Ted specified that it was John Beal.

34. SHAEF was established on February 13, 1944. Its headquarters had moved from London, England, to Versailles, France, by the time Ted visited in December 1944.

35. Lieutenant General Walter Bedell Smith, Chief of Staff, SHAEF, was assisted by Lieutenant General Sir Humfrey Gale, Deputy Chief of Staff and Chief Administrative Officer, SHAEF, 1942–45, and Ray W. Barker, Assistant Chief of Staff, G-1, SHAEF, 1944–45, but Ted's notes specify that the film was approved by Chief of Staff Smith.

36. In December 1944, no one could know exactly when V-E Day would

come. As it happens, *Your Job in Germany* was shipped to troops on April 13, 1945, a few weeks before V-E Day occurred on May 8, 1945.

37. See note 23.

38. See note 32.

39. "Hitler Lives?" *Picture News* 1, no. 8 (Sept.–Oct. 1946): 41 [CC19460900000].

40. Digby Diehl, "Q&A: 'Dr. Seuss,'" *Los Angeles Times West,* September 17, 1972, 39 [CC19720917000].

41. Saul Elkins, *Hitler Lives?* (Warner Bros. Pictures, 1945) [CC194510z00000].

42. U.S. involvement in the liberation of the various concentration camps did not begin until early in April 1945, according to information culled from http://library.ushmm.org/research.htm, as summarized at www.sdwwiimemorial.com/subpages/testimonies/liberator_units.htm.

    On April 2, 1945, the U.S. Army 95th Infantry Division began the liberation of the Werl prison and civilian labor camp. Other liberations that first week included the Dinslaken civilian labor camp and the Buchenwald subcamp Ohrdruf by the U.S. Army 29th and 89th Infantry Divisions, respectively. These successes continued throughout April, with the camps at Dachau being freed at the end of the month. In the first week of May, the army's 11th Armored Division liberated Mauthausen, with subcamps Ebensee and Gunskirchen falling to the army's 80th Infantry Division and 71st Infantry Division, respectively.

43. Ted was not the only person in his unit who was incredulous about Nazi atrocities. "Though the Allies had learned of the extermination of the Jews as early as August 1942 and the existence of the death camps was widely known by 1943, when Capra's film *The Nazi Strike* showed a concentration camp and stated that Hitler's plan was to 'exterminate all those he considers "inferior races,"' Capra told Bill Moyers in 1982 that he (like many others) did not believe those reports until he saw the photographic evidence at the end of the war." Joseph McBride, *Frank Capra: The Catastrophe of Success* (New York: Simon & Schuster: 1992), 497.

44. Theodor S. Geisel, "Atrocities," believed to be from *Memorandum: Report on Two Months' Work in ETO,* February 5, 1945 [CC19450205000].

45. One example of the "cleansing" of the Natzweiler-Struthof camps before Ted's arrival involved Léonce Vieljeux, who was mayor of La Rochelle in France from 1930 to 1940 before becoming a Resistance hero and being arrested and moved through several prison camps, ending up in Schirmeck. On September 1, 1944, the 80-year-old Vieljeux was one of 300 men and 92 women who were shot to death there. The camp was liberated two months later. www.vieljeux-larochelle.com/en/lvieljeux.htm.

46. Regarding the gas chamber to which Ted alluded, it has since been learned that "a gas chamber was installed in August 1943, although the camp remained primarily a labor camp. Victims of the gas chamber had their remains scattered in the surrounding area. Records indicate that the bill for the gas chamber was paid by the Strasbourg University Institute of Anatomy. Professor Hirt, director of the institute, wanted a skeleton collection. One hundred thirty people, mostly Jews, were shipped out of Auschwitz into the gas chamber for this purpose. Explicit reference to the gas chamber was made in this invoice. This was unusual because official Reich policy did not encourage open reference to gas chambers in documents." Beth Weiss, "Natzweiler-Struthof," www.us-israel.org/jsource/Holocaust/natzwieler.html.

47. Regarding the grisly "torture table" that Ted believed to have been used for routine embalming of deceased prisoners, he failed to address the question of who he thought was embalmed, since he contended that prisoners who died of natural causes were likely cremated.

    Despite his misapprehension concerning these events at the camps, Ted did garner some information about what the experience had been like for some of the people who had been imprisoned there. He made notes about a 17-year-old boy who was imprisoned for refusing to join the German army. The boy "witnessed prisoners being jumped upon by the guards after doing push-ups to the point of exhaustion." Theodor S. Geisel, "Disjointed Notes on Concentration Camp," (believed to be from about the same time as "General Observation," *Memorandum: Report on Two Months' Work in ETO,* February 5, 1945 [CC19450205000].

48. Theodor S. Geisel, "General Observation," *Memorandum: Report on Two Months' Work in ETO,* February 5, 1945, 1 [CC19450205000].

49. Ibid.

50. Initial screenwriter Warren Duff's script for *Know Your Enemy—Japan* set up some of the general principles for the depiction of the Japanese people as having a violent history and a fanatical devotion to their emperor, but it didn't work stylistically. For a year, the project was not pursued further. In the spring of 1943, while Ted was first beginning work on the Private SNAFU cartoons, Capra appointed Dutch documentarian Joris Ivens as the supervisor. The Joris Ivens Archives has artifacts, including outlines and synopses by editor Helen van Dongen and screenwriter Corporal Carl Foreman, from the six months that he worked to make a preliminary cut of the film. In September 1943, they were joined by Army Air Force Sergeant Irving Wallace, who was brought in to help with the script. He was the only person to work on the film who had firsthand knowledge of Japan.

    That team tried to portray the Japanese people as good people who has been bullied by their leaders. In the fall, the army reviewed the 20-minute piece and took exception to their analogy that Emperor Hirohito was to Japan what Adolf Hitler was to Germany. They instructed Capra to tell Ivens to stop work on the project and leave the unit. The government wanted the blame to be placed on the Japanese people, not their leadership, which Ivens took to mean that the U.S. intended to maintain a relationship with Hirohito after the war, so the movie could not refer to him as a war criminal. By February 1944, the film had been temporarily discontinued.

    Capra later hired Frances Goodrich and Albert Hackett, who finished a script in May 1944. Irving Wallace worked on drafts with production assistant Edgar Ardis Peterson until January 1945, at which time John Huston replaced Peterson. A script followed and a rough cut of the film was made in February. But the army still wanted further revisions. Somewhere along the way, Allen Rivkin apparently also worked on the script.

    As a result, much of the direction and the bulk of the script had already been formed when Frank Capra and Ted Geisel took over to write the final draft. The final shooting script is cited as the one from April 21, 1945, but there are references at the end of the film to events that took place as late as June 22, 1945, when the Japanese resistance on Okinawa was ended by their capture at the hands of the U.S. 10th Army. Since Capra was discharged from the army a week earlier, these additions were almost certainly Ted's work. Joseph McBride, *Frank Capra: The Catastrophe of Success* (New York: Simon & Schuster: 1992), 480.

51. William J. Blakefield, "A War Within: The Making of *Know Your Enemy—Japan,*" *Sight and Sound* 52, no. 2 (spring 1983): 130 [CC198304z0000].

52. Ibid., 131.

53. *Know Your Enemy—Japan* (Army Pictorial Service, Signal Corps Photographic Division, U.S. Army, August 9, 1945) [CC19450809001].

54. Much of the historical perspective in *Know Your Enemy—Japan* is credited to John Huston's version of the script.

55. See note 51.

56. See note 53.

57. See note 27.

58. *Know Your Enemy—Japan.*

59. Ibid.

60. Ibid.

61. Ibid.

62. See note 27.

63. *Know Your Enemy—Japan.*

64. Dr. T. Komaki, Kyoto University, February 22, 1942, as identified in *Know Your Enemy—Japan.*

65. *Know Your Enemy—Japan.*

66. Ibid.

67. Ibid.

68. Colonel Hideo Ohira, Japanese Army Press Section, August 1942, as identified in *Know Your Enemy—Japan.*

69. After it was pulled from release in August 1945, *Know Your Enemy—Japan* was not screened for the public until 1977 as part of PBS's *Films of Persuasion.* Joseph McBride, *Frank Capra: The Catastrophe of Success* (New York: Simon & Schuster, 1992), 727.

70. *Our Job in Japan* (Army Pictorial Service, Signal Corps Photographic Division, U.S. Army, March 1946) [CC19460300000].

71. Judith and Neil Morgan, *Dr. Seuss and Mr. Geisel* (New York: Random

House, 1995), 120 [CC19950421000]. Referring to *Hitler Lives?* and *Design for Death,* biographers Judith and Neil Morgan wrote that "neither film would survive. As the years passed, prints disappeared—withdrawn, Ted was convinced, under government order."

Similar claims have been made about Ted's wartime documentary work, but the notion that they, and the Hollywood movies based on them, no longer exist is, fortunately, a misconception. Virtually all of the Private SNAFU cartoons are available on a variety of DVD and VHS collections. In addition to copies that survive in private collections, *Your Job in Germany* can be found on the VHS tape *Federal Follies, volume 3.* Revamped in Hollywood as *Hitler Lives?,* it is shown occasionally on the Turner Classic Movies station and, in the past, was viewable as a streaming video on their Web site. *Know Your Enemy—Japan* has been released as part of the Frank Capra's War Years VHS tape series. *Our Job in Japan* can be found on the VHS tape *Federal Follies, volume 2.* Ted and Helen reworked that film for Hollywood as *Design for Death.* The Library of Congress has a copy of that film, and appointments can be made to view it. So none of them has really disappeared.

Chapter 19: Moving Pictures

1. "Brief Biographies, 1925—Number 2," *Dartmouth Alumni Magazine,* March 1938 [CC19380300000].
2. Donald D. Markstein, *Toonopedia,* www.toonopedia.com/horton.htm.
3. Theodor S. Geisel, "No Strings Attached," *Coronet* 15, no. 6 (April 1944): 113 [CC19440400000].
4. Ibid.
5. Theodor S. Geisel and Helen Palmer, *Design for Death* (RKO, December 1947) [CC19471200000].
6. Judith and Neil Morgan, *Dr. Seuss and Mr. Geisel* (New York: Random House, 1995), 120 [CC19950421000].
7. Letter from Theodor S. Geisel at Columbia Pictures Corporation to *Dartmouth Alumni Magazine,* circa December 1940, property of the Rauner Special Collections Library, Dartmouth College [CC194712z0000].
8. See note 6.
9. See note 7.
10. *Dartmouth Alumni Magazine,* January 1948, 57 [CC19480100000].
11. Theodor S. Geisel, script for Ford Motor Company advertisement, "Fast super-salesmanship," May–Dec. 1949 [CC19490509–194912 2].
12. Theodor S. Geisel, script for Ford Motor Company advertisement, "Weight Lifter," May–Dec. 1949 [CC19490509-194912 3].
13. Ted's artwork for the phonograph record that started the Gerald McBoing Boing franchise hyphenated Gerald's last name. Covers to the movies and book that followed omitted the hyphen, although VHS tapes of those movies reinserted it. The comic books didn't hyphenate the name, but the television show did in the opening credits.
14. Judith and Neil Morgan, *Dr. Seuss and Mr. Geisel* (New York: Random House, 1995), 133 [CC19950421000].
15. Ibid., 134–135.
16. Ibid., 137.
17. "The occasion was to promote a screening of *The 5000 Fingers of Dr. T,* which was being held at Maxwell's, in Hoboken, as a fundraiser for Projected Images of Hudson County." Tommy Rettig, telephone interview with Irwin Chusid of WFMU Radio in New Jersey, circa 1987, as transcribed by Dawn Eden, members.aol.com/seivadj18/other2.html.
18. Dr. Seuss, *The 5000 Fingers of Dr. T* screenplay (first draft), July 20, 1951, 24 [CC19510720000].
19. Ibid., 40.
20. Dr. Seuss and Allan Scott, *The 5000 Fingers of Dr. T* screenplay (revised final draft), February 25, 1952, 39 [CC19520225000].
21. The predecessors to *Dr. T's* stairways and portals can be found in the ladders and stairways Bartholomew Cubbins ascends in *Bartholomew and the Oobleck.*
22. Titles for the songs in *Dr. T* differ depending upon the various sources from which they are taken. For the hardcore fans, the 22 musical numbers known to have been associated with the film are: 1. "Mound Country Ballet Routine": Instrumental that plays during the dream sequence in which Terwilliker's henchmen try to catch Bart with butterfly nets. As a result, it has also been referred to as "Butterfly Ballet." 2. "Ten Happy Fingers": Mrs. Collins sings while Bart practices piano exercises. Called "Ten Little Fingers" in the first draft, it is called "Happy Fingers" in the final draft, but it is called "Ten Happy Fingers"
on the LP master demo. 3. "Happy Fingers": Instrumental variation on "Ten Happy Fingers" that Bart plays for Terwilliker upon his arrival at the institute. Consequently referred to as the "Piano Concerto—Ten Happy Fingers Variation" on the unofficial sound track album. 4. "Dream Stuff": Zabladowski sings to Bart after their pretend fishing adventure. 5. "Hypnotic Duel": Instrumental that accompanies Dr. T and Zabladowski trying to hypnotize each other. This is the name used in the final script and the LP master demo. 6. "Get-Together Weather": Sung by Zabladowski with Mrs. Collins and Terwilliker after they convince him that Terwilliker is not such a bad guy. 7. "Kids Song": Sung by Bart after Zabladowski refuses to believe that Terwilliker has ordered the plumber to be disintegrated. This was probably originally the "Boy's Song" for which the LP master demo was made. 8. "Schlim-Schlam Ballet": According to the final draft of the script, this is the song "in which Bart, seeking escape, is blocked by more and more musicians" in the non–piano player dungeon. It has become known as the "Dungeon Ballet." 9. "Skating Duel Routine": Instrumental that accompanies Zabladowski's battle with the roller-skating twins. 10. "Victory Procession": In the first draft, this song was called "March of the Crooks," under which title the LP master demo was cut. It is the song that Sgt. Lunk and Dr. T's other henchmen sing as they recapture Zabladowski, Bart, and Mrs. Collins. 11. "Dungeon Elevator": Sung in a bass voice by the elevator operator, the song relates the floors as the elevator descends through the different dungeons. Although it is untitled in the final script, the LP master demo uses the name "Dungeon Elevator." The unofficial sound track album calls it "Elevator Song." 12. "Terwilliker's Dressing Song": Sung to his henchmen as they prepare him for his big performance. It has been recorded by other artists as "Dress Me" and "The Dressing Song." The unofficial sound track album dubs it "Dressing Song—Do-Me-Do Duds." 13. "'Chopsticks' Number'": This is the derivation of the ubiquitous piano ditty as it is played by the child pianists, under Bart's mock direction, after they are freed by Terwilliker.

Ted's songs that were left out of the movie include: 14. "Freckle on a Pigmy": Sung by Zabladowski to divert Lunk and his soldiers' attention while they look for Bart. This song may have been recorded on an LP master demo as "Valse Triste." In the first version of the script, Zabladowski sings an untitled "slow dirge" in which he mentions "a freckle on a pigmy." In the final-draft version, the title of that song became "Freckle on a Pigmy." 15. "The Grindstone": Sung by Zabladowski as he works. LP master demos were cut for a song called "Plumber's Song" and "Zabladowski," either of which may be versions of this song, which is included on the outtakes portion of the unofficial sound track album simply as "Grindstone." 16. "I Will Not Get Involved": Sung by Zabladowski to Bart. This may be the song "Count Me Out" previously cut as an LP master demo. 17. "Many Questions Have No Answers": Sung by Mrs. Collins to Bart when he asks why he must grow up in Terwilliker's institute. This one is called "Many Questions" on the unofficial sound track album. 18. "Massage Opera": Performed with Terwilliker singing and Mrs. Collins speaking while she massages his arm with an electric vibrator. Although it appears in one of the lobby cards from the film, the scene and the song were edited out of the film before its release. The outtakes portion of the unofficial sound track album calls it "I Will Not Go to Sleep." 19. "Money, Money, Money": After Bart leaves to "borrow" money from Terwilliker's safe to pay Zabladowski to take out the sinks, Zabladowski sings this song, which is simply called "Money" on the unofficial sound track album. 20. "Terwilliker's Do-Ray-Me": A song that Terwilliker sings to Mrs. Collins, in which he explains that his favorite musical note is, appropriately enough, "Me." Hence the unofficial sound track album calls it "My Favorite Note." 21. "The Uncles' Roller-Skating Song": Sung by roller-skating guards about their Siamese beard. Although it was in both the initial and final versions of the script, the song was cut from the film. Taken from the first line of the song, the unofficial sound track album gives it the title "Oh! We Are the Guards." 22. "You Opened My Eyes": According to the initial version of the script, Ted envisioned this tune as the love theme for Mrs. Collins and Zabladowski. Based on a line from the song, the unofficial sound track album calls it "One Moment Ago."
23. Dr. Seuss and Allan Scott, *The 5000 Fingers of Dr. T* screenplay (revised final draft), February 25, 1952, 50 [CC19520225000].

24. Dr. Seuss, *The 5000 Fingers of Dr. T* screenplay (first draft), July 20, 1951, 3 [CC19510720000].

25. Ibid., 62.

26. Judith and Neil Morgan, *Dr. Seuss and Mr. Geisel* (New York: Random House: 1995), 14 [CC19950421000].

27. "5000 *Fantastic* Fingers," *Dixie Roto Magazine,* May 17, 1953, 19 [CC19530517002].

28. See note 17.

29. See note 17.

Chapter 20: The Missing Linnix

1. Ted's contemporary Salvador Dalí would address a similar question three years later in "Dali at the Age of Six When He Believed Himself to Be a Young Girl, Lifting with Extreme Precaution the Skin of the Water to Observe a Dog Sleeping in the Shadow of the Sea."

2. Henry Jenkins's article "'No Matter How Small': The Democratic Imagination of Dr. Seuss," presented at the Research in Childhood, Sociology, Culture, and History conference in October 1999 through the main campus of the University of Southern Denmark in Odense [CC19991000001], and the Mandeville Special Collections Library at the University of California, San Diego (where Ted's lecture notes reside), both cite this conference as taking place in July 1947. However, it appears to have taken place in July 1949. In the November 1949 *Dartmouth Alumni Magazine,* Ted wrote about traveling to Utah, where he was "doing some lecturing at the University in Salt Lake City." Conversely, while discussing his activities in a letter to the same magazine circa December 1947, he did not mention anything about Utah or the workshop.

3. Judith and Neil Morgan, *Dr. Seuss and Mr. Geisel* (New York: Random House, 1995), 124 [CC19950421000].

4. *Your Job in Germany* (Army Pictorial Services, Information and Education Division, U.S. Armed Forces, April 13, 1945) [CC19450413000].

5. Theodor S. Geisel, Mrs. Mulvaney and the Billion-Dollar Bunny lecture notes for the University of Utah writers' conference, July 1949.

6. Ibid.

7. John Hersey, "Why Do Students Bog Down on the First R?" *Life,* May 24, 1954, 147–48 [CC19540524000].

8. Ibid.

9. See note 5.

10. Judith and Neil Morgan, *Dr. Seuss and Mr. Geisel* (New York: Random House, 1995), 125 [CC19950421000].

11. Ibid.

12. "Teaching: The Logical Insanity of Dr. Seuss," *Time* 90, August 11, 1967, 59 [CC19670811000].

13. Dr. Seuss, "How Orlo Got His Book," *The New York Times Book Review,* November 17, 1957, 2 [CC19571117001].

14. E. J. Kahn, Jr., "Profiles: Children's Friend," *The New Yorker* 36, no. 44 (December 17, 1960): 86, 91 [CC19601217000].

15. The series started in 1943 with Louise Rowe's *Fuzzy Wuzzy Bunny.* The following year, Pat Sanchez published a book for Whitman with the same name. In 1946, Elsa Jane Werner produced *Patrick, the Fuzziest Bunny—A Fuzzy Wuzzy Book* for the same company. The next year, when Ted gave his presentation about Mrs. Mulvaney and the Billion-Dollar Bunny, Whitman published yet another *Fuzzy Wuzzy Bunny,* this time by an unspecified author (sometimes attributed to Anne Scheu Berry). That same year, Hazel Cederborg published *Bunny Polka Dot* with Saalfield, in Akron, Ohio.

16. "The Other Cool Cat," *Early Years,* April 1973, 24 [CC19730400000].

17. Dorothy Lou Dickey, "The Book Parade," *Raleigh Times,* January 6, 1951 [CC19510106000].

18. Dr. Seuss, "The Royal Housefly and Bartholomew Cubbins," *Junior Catholic Messenger* 16, no. 16 (January 13, 1950): 126B [CC19500113000].

19. Rose Bonne is often credited as the author of "I Know an Old Lady Who Swallowed a Fly." Canadian Alan Mills turned the children's verse into a song in 1952, which was popularized the following year by Burl Ives.

20. Dr. Seuss, "The Royal Housefly and Bartholomew Cubbins," *Junior Catholic Messenger* 16, no. 18 (January 27, 1950): 142B [CC19500127000]. In this incarnation, the Hippocras "was a sort of hound, but as wide as a horse. And his neck, when he stretched it, was as long as any camel's." Ted was characteristically inconsistent in the spelling of the word "Hippocras." In his 1927 sketches, he used "Hippocrass." In the

1949–50 "Wishbones" story, he used "Hippocras."

21. Dr. Seuss, "Marco Comes Late," in *Treat Shop,* sel. and ed. Eleanor M. Johnson and Leland B. Jacobs (Columbus, OH: Charles E. Merrill Books, 1954), 119–24 [CC19540000010].

22. "The Big Brag" appeared in *Yertle the Turtle and Other Stories* (New York: Random House, 1958) and was eventually translated into French, Polish, and Finnish, among other languages.

23. Dr. Seuss, "Gustav, the Goldfish," *Redbook* 95, no. 2 (June 1950): 48 [CC19500601000].

24. Betsy Marden Silverman, "Dr. Seuss Talks to Parents About Learning to Read and What Makes Children Want to Do It," *Parents* 35, no. 11 (November 1960): 136 [CC19601100000].

25. See note 23.

26. See note 23.

27. Dr. Seuss, *If I Ran the Zoo* (New York: Random House, 1950), 50 [CC19501012000].

28. Dr. Seuss, "If I Ran the Zoo," *Redbook* 95, no. 3 (July 1950): 58 [CC19500700000].

29. Dr. Seuss, "Horton and the Kwuggerbug," *Redbook* 96, no. 3 (January 1951): 46 [CC19510100000].

30. Ibid.

31. In the table of contents for the magazine and in the title of the story, the tree is referred to as the "Zinniga-Zinnaga," but the text specifies it as "Zinniga-Zanniga." When the album version was produced, the latter designation is used in the story and in the printed title. Since Ted is credited with having produced the album, the assumption is made that this latter spelling is the one that he intended.

32. In the original version of "Gertrude McFuzz," her uncle (Jake, rather than the book's Dake) more fully expresses his reservations about Gertrude's desire to increase the size of her tail. He also is less certain about the prescription he gives her and the results it will have. When her tail grows too big for her to fly, Jake solicits the help of Gertrude's family and relatives in the original. The corresponding illustration of Gertrude and her new tail being supported differs as well, with Gertrude looking more exhausted and embarrassed than shocked and confused. Dr. Seuss, "Gertrude McFuzz," *Redbook* 97, no. 3 (January 1951): 46 [CC19510700000]; Dr. Seuss, "Gertrude McFuzz," *Yertle the Turtle and Other Stories* (New York: Random House, 1958), 33 [CC19580412000].

33. Ted's cartoon "You Can't Build A Substantial V Out of Turtles!" was done at a time when there was a great deal of turmoil surrounding the movement to bring about the repeal of the 40-hour-workweek legislation. Nathan Robertson, "Lies About Labor Nailed with Facts," *PM* 2, no. 198, national edition (March 21, 1942): front cover [CC19420321000].

34. See note 5.

35. Dr. Seuss, *If I Ran the Zoo* (New York: Random House, 1950), 14–15 [CC19501012000].

36. Ibid., 35.

37. "Making the World Safe for Turtlery," Fish, Beast, and Bird: A Piscozooavistical Survey by Dr. Theophrastus Seuss, *Judge* 99, no. 2549 (September 6, 1930): 20 [CC19300906000].

38. Dr. Seuss, "The Sneetches," *Redbook* 101, no. 3 (July 1953): 77 [CC19530700000].

39. Ibid.

40. The Flustards in Ted's story "The Flustards" differ completely from the one he drew three years earlier in the book version of *If I Ran the Zoo.* That earlier version resembled an Asian lion and was described as a "very fine beast" from Zomba-ma-Tant that thrived on mustard with custard sauce.

41. "The Great Zakkx Pageant," *Judge* 100, no. 2571 (February 7, 1931): 8 [CC19310207000].

42. Dr. Seuss, "The Ruckus," *Redbook* 103, no. 3 (July 1954): 84 [CC19540700000].

43. Jonas Salk had first tried his polio vaccine in the summer of 1952. After presenting the results of testing his "killed virus" vaccine on 161 children to an advisory committee of the National Foundation for Infantile Paralysis in January 1953, preparations began for a larger field test. The subject was in the news while Ted was working on the book.

44. At the University of Michigan, on April 12, 1955, Dr. Thomas Francis announced the results of the massive field trial of Jonas Salk's polio vaccine, declaring it to be both safe and effective.

45. Several sources have compared scenes in Ted's Springfield, Massachusetts, hometown to elements of his books. For example, see Robert Sullivan, "The Boy Who Drew Wynnmphs," *Yankee* 59, no. 12 (December 1995): 54–59, 120–121 [CC19951200000)]. The comparison between the pathway among the mounds of clover in *Horton Hears a Who!* and the pathway among the bushes at the Lily Ponds in Forest Park near Ted's home was made, among other places, at the museum exhibition And to Think He Saw It in Springfield! at the Connecticut Valley Historical Museum in Springfield, Massachusetts (1995 through January 28, 1996).

46. Lorrene Love Ort, "Theodor Seuss Geisel—The Children's Dr. Seuss," *Elementary English: A Magazine of the Language Arts* 32, no. 3 (March 1955) [CC19550300000].

47. Dr. Seuss, "The Great McGrew Milk Farm," *Children's Activities* 21, no. 4 (April 1955): 13 [CC19550401000].

48. For those keeping track, Ted first used the name McGurk as a high school student in the fall of 1920, when he wrote of a "Big Sale at McGurk's Book Store," which had "just received a large shipment of vest pocket Ouija boards for use in examinations" for ten cents apiece. "Big Sale at McGurk's Book Store," *The Central Recorder* 4, no. 5 (October 29, 1920): 6 [CC19201029000)]. When Ted replaced Gerald McGrew with Morris McGurk in the book version of *If I Ran the Circus*, it had been 35 years since Ted wrote that joke.

49. Dr. Seuss, *On Beyond Zebra!* (New York: Random House, 1955), 1 [CC19550912000].

50. Ibid., 5.

51. In *On Beyond Zebra!*, Ted drew on some creatures from his past. The Wumbus, a whale that lives high on a hill and only comes down when it's time to refill, was based on Ted's July 1941 image of the isolationist whale who, in order to avoid fights among fish in the ocean, saves his own scalp by living high on an Alp. The Umbus, as was explained earlier, drew on a May 1941 image of a multi-footed cow that represented European nations following wherever the German head led them. The Quandry, a small symmetrical critter that worries whether his top-side is bottom or his bottom-side top, may have been one of those images that stuck in Ted's memory since childhood. Ted cited Peter Newell's *The Hole Book* as a particular favorite, so he may well have read other Newell creations, like his Topsys & Turvys books, which depicted scenes that differed in interpretation when they were viewed upside down. *Topsys & Turvys—No. 2* (1894) contained two images, involving fish and a Whang-bird, that are visually similar to the Quandry—both of which had to be considered top-side down and bottom-side up. Ted also drew on the Munkits to create the Itch-a-pods and delved into his private unpublished artwork to find Twin Heaslips from which to create the High Gargel-orum—a mode of transportation running from North Nubb to East Ounce, with seven stops in between.

52. Dr. Seuss, *On Beyond Zebra!* (New York: Random House, 1955), 7 [CC19550912000].

53. Ibid., 18.

54. Dr. Seuss, "A Prayer for a Child," *Collier's* 136, no. 13 (December 23, 1955): 86 [CC19551223000].

55. Dr. Seuss, *Signs of Civilization!* (La Jolla, CA: La Jolla Town Council, Inc., March 1956), 4–5 [CC19560300000].

56. Regarding the dating of the Jerry Lewis promotional single of the song, Liberty 55633 precedes Timi Yuro's "Gotta Travel On" (Liberty 55634), which charted on October 12, 1963, and Jan and Dean's "Drag City" (Liberty 55641), charting on December 17, 1963. (Hearty thanks to Curt Lundgren of Minnetonka, Minnesota, for supplying this information.)

57. Dr. Seuss, "Bimba-Lotta Bam," private papers in the Mandeville Special Collections Library at the University of California, San Diego.

Chapter 21: A Very Big Year

1. Lark Dimond-Cates, speech at the United States Postal Service's unveiling of the Theodor Seuss Geisel stamp, near the Dr. Seuss National Memorial Sculpture Garden, Springfield, Massachusetts, October 27, 2003.

2. Dr. Seuss, "My Hassle with the First-Grade Language," *Chicago Tribune*, November 17, 1957 [CC19571117000].

3. Dr. Seuss, "How Orlo Got His Book," *The New York Times Book Review*, November 17, 1957, 2, 60 [CC19571117001].

4. Robert Cahn, "The Wonderful World of Dr. Seuss," *The Saturday Evening Post* 230, no. 1 (July 6, 1957): 42 [CC19570706000].

5. Ibid.

6. David Dempsey, "The Significance of Dr. Seuss," *The New York Times Book Review*, May 11, 1958, 30 [CC19580511000].

7. Betsy Marden Silverman, "Dr. Seuss Talks to Parents About Learning to Read and What Makes Children Want to Do It," *Parents* 35, no. 11 (November 1960): 136–37 [CC19601100000].

8. Who were the familiar cats that came before the Cat in the Hat? One of the earliest was Dick Wittington's Cat. Richard Whittington, four-time mayor of London, was born in Pauntley, Gloucestershire, circa 1350, and died March 1423, so the legend of the feline that brought his owner from poverty to wealth by driving off all the rats in a kingdom, for which the ruler rewarded Dick Whittington handsomely, is likely to have stemmed from that time period. "Puss in Boots," according to the Penguin Young Readers Factsheets, originated as "*Le maistre chat, ou le chat botté . . .* written by Charles Perrault and first published in 1697." The Cheshire Cat was a character in Lewis Carroll's 1865 classic *Alice's Adventures in Wonderland*. Krazy Kat first appeared in "Krazy Kat and I. Mouse," a strip that lasted briefly while "The Dingbats" was on vacation in July 1912. Felix the Cat first appeared under the name Master Tom in the short film *Feline Follies*, which premiered on November 9, 1919. The June 5, 1931, *Film Daily* reported that "'Tom and Jerry,' the new series of animated cartoons being made by Van Beuren, for RKO, will be ready for release in August." Tom and his mouse companion debuted in *Wot a Night* on August 1, 1931. Al Smith spun off "Cicero's Cat" from "Mutt and Jeff" in 1933. Sylvester's nemesis—Tweety Bird—was created by Bob Clampett for Warner Bros. in 1942, but the cat himself (originally named Thomas) came later, premiering on March 24, 1945, in the Academy Award–nominated cartoon short, *Life with Feathers*, under the direction of Friz Freleng. Certainly there were other famous cats prior to the Cat in the Hat, but these were among the best known.

9. Benny Goodman, "What Swing Really Does to People," *Liberty* 15, no. 20 (May 14, 1938): 6 [CC19380514000].

10. Ibid.

11. For more information about "Mutt and Jeff," visit www.toonopedia.com/muttjeff.htm.

12. Barbara Richardson, "Dr. Seuss: Creator of 'The Cat in the Hat,'" *Book and Magazine Collector*, no. 202 (January 2001): 50 [CC20010100000].

13. Robert Cahn, "The Wonderful World of Dr. Seuss," *The Saturday Evening Post* 230, no. 1 (July 6, 1957): 46 [CC19570706000].

14. William B. Hart, "Between the Lines," *Redbook* 110, no. 2 (December 1957): 4 [CC19571200000].

15. Dr. Seuss, *How the Grinch Stole Christmas!* (New York: Random House, 1957), 11 [CC19571100000].

16. Theodor S. Geisel, "Santy Claus Be Hanged," *Jack-O-Lantern* 17, no. 4 (December 15, 1924): 23 [CC19241215000].

17. "Make Christmas More Meaningful," *Judge* 99, no. 2565 (December 27, 1930): 10 [CC19301227000].

18. "The Dachs-Deer," *Judge* 93, no. 2406 (December 10, 1927): 15 [CC19271210000].

19. See note 6.

20. Dr. Seuss, "Making Children Want to Read," *Book Chat* 9, no. 5 (fall 1958): 29 [CC19581000000].

21. See note 6.

22. Clifton Fadiman, "Party of One," *Holiday* 25, no. 4 (April 15, 1959): 17 [C19590415000].

23. E. J. Kahn, Jr., "Profiles: Children's Friend," *The New Yorker* 36, no. 44 (December 17, 1960): 82 [CC19601217000].

24. Ibid.

Chapter 22: Misunderstanding Dr. Seuss

1. David Dempsey, "The Significance of Dr. Seuss," *The New York Times Book Review*, May 11, 1958, 30 [CC19580511000].

2. E. J. Kahn, Jr., "Profiles: Children's Friend," *The New Yorker* 36, no. 44 (December 17, 1960): 84 [CC19601217000].

3. "Seuss seems to be representing but not critiquing anti-Communist paranoia." Philip Nel, "Dada Knows Best: Growing Up 'Surreal' with Dr. Seuss," *Children's Literature: Annual of the Modern Language Association Division on Children's Literature and the Children's Literature Association* (New Haven: Yale University Press, 1999), 171 [CC19990900005].

4. Louis Menand, "Cat People: What Dr. Seuss Really Taught Us," *The New Yorker,* December 23, 2002 [CC20021223000].

5. See note 3.

6. See note 3.

7. See note 4.

8. Henry Jenkins, "'No Matter How Small': The Democratic Imagination of Dr. Seuss," presented at the Research in Childhood, Sociology, Culture and History conference in October 1999, through the main campus of the University of Southern Denmark in Odense [CC19991000001].

9. Digby Diehl, "Q & A: 'Dr. Seuss,'" *Los Angeles Times West,* September 17, 1972, 39 [CC19720917000].

10. Judith and Neil Morgan, *Dr. Seuss and Mr. Geisel* (New York: Random House, 1995), 96–97 [CC19950421000].

11. Philip Nel, "Dada Knows Best: Growing up 'Surreal' with Dr. Seuss," *Children's Literature: Annual of the Modern Language Association Division on Children's Literature and the Children's Literature Association* (New Haven: Yale University Press, 1999), 173 [CC19990900005].

12. See note 9.

13. Lorrene Love Ort, "Theodor Seuss Geisel—The Children's Dr. Seuss," *Elementary English,* 1955, 33 [CC1955z000000].

14. The Kreiss Moon Beings are undated. Kreiss started stamping some of their figures (like Robin Hood) with copyright dates as early as 1955, but at least some of the figures must have been produced after the September 1955 publication of *On Beyond Zebra!,* since at least one character from that book is among the figures that were produced.

   Based on the characters used, production of some of the other figures theoretically could have started as early as December 1950, but it seems unlikely that Kreiss would have continued to produce the same illegal line for five or six years. On the other end of the timeline, the characters utilized by Kreiss do not appear to include any from books published after 1955, despite the many possibilities presented by the January 1956 publication of *If I Ran the Circus.* The most likely possible production times are for Christmas 1955 or the February/March toy shows in 1956. Kreiss did produce boy and girl figurines in space suits with 1957 copyrights stamped on them. It is presumed that the Moon Beings preceded these astronaut figures.

15. Peter Bunzel, "Wacky World of Dr. Seuss," *Life* 46, no. 14 (April 6, 1959): 108 [CC19590406000].

16. E. J. Kahn, Jr., "Profiles: Children's Friend," *The New Yorker* 36, no. 44 (December 17, 1960): 92 [CC19601217000].

17. See note 15.

18. *Publishers Weekly* 176, no. 8 (August 31, 1959): 53 [CC19590831000].

19. See note 16.

20. See note 16.

21. Cynthia Lindsay, "Who's News: The Miracle of Dr. Seuss," *Good Housekeeping,* December 1960, 32 [CC19601200001].

22. E. J. Kahn, Jr., "Profiles: Children's Friend," *The New Yorker* 36, no. 44 (December 17, 1960): 47 [CC19601217000].

23. Sybil S. Steinberg, "What Makes a Funny Children's Book?" *Publishers Weekly,* February 27, 1978, 87–90 [CC19780227000].

24. "All-Time Bestselling Children's Books," *Publishers Weekly,* December 17, 2001.

25. E. J. Kahn, Jr., "Profiles: Children's Friend," *The New Yorker* 36, no. 44 (December 17, 1960): 53 [CC19601217000].

26. Ted had taken one advertising campaign after another nearly continuously from 1928 to 1956. He sandwiched *Mulberry Street* between advertisements for Macy-Westchester Newspapers and Chilton Pens. *The 500 Hats* was immediately preceded by Ted's application for the Infantograph patent and was published amid Ted's Essomarine and Vico/Pep88 campaigns. He was devising marionettes and advertising NBC Radio spots just before *The Seven Lady Godivas,* and began selling political cartoons to Hearst newspapers shortly afterward. He was still pushing NBC and Essomarine and doing the political cartoons when *The King's Stilts* was published, and he continued those ads until *Horton Hatches the Egg* came out, after which he immediately began the Narragansett Brewery campaign. Even after the army, while working in Hollywood, *McElligot's Pool* was flanked by a new Essomarine campaign and an ad for New Departure ball bearings. Immediately after the publication of *Thidwick,* Ted expanded his children's stories from books into periodicals. *Bartholomew and the Oobleck* came amid Ford Motor Company ads. In the year between *Oobleck* and *If I Ran the Zoo,*

Ted published six stories in periodicals and wrote the story for the *Gerald McBoing-Boing* record. By the time *Scrambled Eggs Super!* was published, Ted had already finished *The 5000 Fingers of Dr. T. Horton Hears a Who!* was released between Holly Sugar advertisements.

27. Clifford L. Jordan, "Dr. Seuss," *Dartmouth Alumni Magazine,* October 1962, 26 [CC19621000000].

28. Ibid.

29. See note 22.

30. See note 22.

31. Letter from Theodor S. Geisel to Charles D. Webster, July 24, 1967, concerning the Mike McClintock Memorial [CC19670724000].

32. Barbara Richardson, "Dr. Seuss: Creator of 'The Cat in the Hat," *Book and Magazine Collector,* no. 202 (January 2001): 50 [CC20010100000].

33. Letter from Helen Palmer Geisel to Theodor S. Geisel, October 22, 1967, from the archives of the Office of the San Diego County Medical Examiner [CC19671022000], as quoted in Judith and Neil Morgan, *Dr. Seuss and Mr. Geisel* (New York: Random House, 1995), 195–96 [CC19950421000].

34. *Theodor S. Geisel, Plaintiff, v. Poynter Products, Inc., Alabe Crafts, Inc., Linder, Nathan & Heide, Inc., and Liberty Library Corporation, Defendants,* No. 68 Civ. 997, United States District Court for the Southern District of New York, 295 F. Supp. 331; 1968 U.S. Dist. LEXIS 10176; 160 U.S.P.Q. (BNA) 590; as amended December 23, 1968 [CC19681230000].

35. T. S. Eliot, "The Love Song of J. Alfred Prufrock," *Poetry* 6, no. 3 (June 1915): 130–35.

36. Interestingly, Ted's painting "Fooling Nobody" has also been interpreted as a reference to Ted's alleged concern about the cold war. One such opinion was based on an interpretation of the shape of the mask's eyes. "The 'atom' image that appears in each eye and the year of the painting—1968—suggest that nuclear arms are a likely subject." Philip Nel, "Dada Knows Best: Growing Up 'Surreal' with Dr. Seuss," 171 [CC19990900005].

37. Judith and Neil Morgan, *Dr. Seuss and Mr. Geisel* (New York: Random House, 1995), 201 [CC19950421000].

38. Letter from Theodor S. Geisel to Donald and Henri Bartlett, May 27, 1968 [CC19680527000], as quoted in Judith and Neil Morgan, *Dr. Seuss and Mr. Geisel* (New York: Random House, 1995), 201 [CC19950421000].

39. www.lfpress.com/millennium/timelines/default.htm

40. Testimony of Alden Norton in Ted's copyright-infringement lawsuit against toy manufacturers (see note 34).

41. See note 34.

42. In an April 14, 1969, letter to Phyllis Jackson, Ted wrote, "I had some spare paint lying around, so I made a few Offts, based on a character in the *Sleep Book.* Do you think there is anything in this for our toy line? I visualize them made out of goofer feathers, which are almost as soft as Offt feathers, which are, unfortunately, unavailable." Letter from Theodor S. Geisel to Phyllis Jackson, April 14, 1969 [CC19690414000]. These toys do not seem to have ever been produced. The court battle ended in December 1968. By April 1969, Ted appears to have been discussing toy possibilities with Random House. He can't have begun negotiations with Mattel and Sears too much later, because those product lines were in stores by December 1970.

43. In the January 1983 issue of *Defenders,* there is a segment called "A Very Wrong Turn" in which Gargoyle, Beast, Valkyrie, and Prince Namor materialize in a world full of Seussian creatures speaking in rhyme.

44. Carolyn See, "Dr. Seuss and the Naked Ladies," *Esquire* 81, no. 6 (June 1974): 118 [CC19740600000].

45. Ibid., 176.

46. Leonore Fleischer, "Horton Hatches a Deal," *Publishers Weekly,* March 4, 1983, 89 [CC19830304000].

47. Ted worked on the ill-fated Coleco Word Bird Game to simplify sentences for youngsters and to avoid errors of syntax. For example, in the present tense, clocks "bounce," but a box "bounces," but by putting everything in the past tense, Ted could ensure that either clocks or a box "bounced."

48. The Word Bird Game was never produced.

49. Isobel Ashe, "How a Grinch Stole Christmas, a Yule Video Special," television pullout, *Newport News Sunday Daily Press,* December 18, 1966, TV-2 [CC19661218002].

50. Hal Humphrey, "Special Visit with the Whos," *Los Angeles Times Mirror's TV Times* 7, no. 51 (December 18, 1966) [CC19661218001].

51. *Dr. Seuss's How the Grinch Stole Christmas!* press book (Culver City, CA: MGM Studios, 1966) [CC19661218010].

52. Leslie Raddatz, "Dr. Seuss Climbs Down from His Mountain . . . to Bring the Grinch to Television," *TV Guide* 14, no. 51, Chicago metropolitan edition (December 17, 1966): 13–14 [CC19661217000].

53. The Peabody Awards, www.peabody.uga.edu/archives. Contrary to other reports that list Ted as having won the award in 1972, this site specifies that he won the 1970 award and does not mention *How the Grinch Stole Christmas!*

54. Morton Moss, "Dr. Seuss Has the Cat Out of the Hat," *Los Angeles Herald-Examiner*'s *TV Weekly,* 5–6 [CC19710307000].

55. Editor's note in response to a letter from Virginia Casady, *The San Diego Union,* October 15, 1978, E-7 [CC19781015000].

56. Donald Freeman, "The Nonsensical World of Dr. Seuss," *McCall's* 92, no. 2 (November 1964): 201 [CC19641100000].

57. Ibid.

58. Ibid.

59. See note 25.

60. Dr. Seuss, "Giorgio de Chirico: Hector and Andromache," in *Lovers: 100 Works of Art Celebrating Romantic Love, with Commentaries by the Distinguished and the Great*, comp. Mary Lawrence (New York: Balance House, Ltd., 1982) [CC19820000000].

61. Herbert Fredman, "Why We Ought to Listen to John Hirten, the Planning Brain," *San Diego Magazine* 25, no. 2 (December 12, 1972): 77 [CC19721200000].

62. See note 1.

63. See note 21.

64. The American Library Association, presenters of the Caldecott Medal, www.ala.org/Content/NavigationMenu/ALSC/Awards_and_ Scholarships1/Literary_and_Related_Awards/Caldecott_Medal/ Caldecott_Medal.htm.

65. The Pacific Northwest Library Association's Young Reader's Choice Award, "the oldest children's choice award in the U.S. and Canada. . . . Nominations are taken only from the children, teachers, parents, and librarians of the Pacific Northwest—Washington, Oregon, Alaska, Idaho, Montana, British Columbia, and Alberta. Nominated titles were published three years previously, printed in the U.S. or Canada and are already favorites with the readers. Only 4th to 12th graders . . . are eligible to vote . . ." (www.pnla.org/yrca/). In accordance with the rules, *McElligot's Pool* (1947) won the award in 1950.

66. The American Library Association's Laura Ingalls Wilder Award, which is administered by one of its divisions—the Association for Library Service to Children, www.ala.org/Content/NavigationMenu/ALSC/ Awards_and_Scholarships1/Literary_and_Related_Awards/Wilder_ Medal/Wilder_Medal.htm.

67. The official Pulitzer Prize Web site, www.pulitzer.org/Archive/ archive.html.

68. See note 27.

69. Bennett Cerf, "Hilarity in Hollywood," *This Week Magazine,* November 27, 1960 [CC19601127000].

70. Theodor S. Geisel, "My Uncle Terwilliger on the Art of Eating Popovers," Lake Forest College commencement speech, June 4, 1977 [CC19770604000].

Index

Page numbers in *italics* refer to illustrations.

Credits

*Image details are listed by page number (in **bold**), from left to right, top to bottom.*

ii. Thomas D. Murphy calendar art (September 1935). **ix.** Dr. Seuss, pencil sketch (circa 1948). **1.** *The Saturday Evening Post* 230, no. 1 (July 6, 1957): 17. **2.** Dr. Seuss, *Horton Hatches the Egg* (Random House, 1940), title page. **3.** Dr. Seuss, *Horton Hatches the Egg* (Random House, 1940), 15. **4.** Motor Boat Show complimentary ticket, Essomarine (1940); Dr. Seuss. *Horton Hatches the Egg* (Random House, 1940), 23. **6.** *Judge* 93, no. 2404 (November 26, 1927): 14. **7.** *Judge* 93, no. 2408 (December 24, 1927): 7; *Judge* 100, no. 2587 (May 30, 1931): 21; *Life* 94, no. 2437 (July 19, 1929): 10. **8.** *Life* 96, no. 2487 (July 4, 1930): 9; *Vanity Fair* 36, no. 4 (June 1931): 76. **9.** *Life* 101, no. 2587 (February 1934): 22; *Spelling Bees: The Oldest and the Newest Rage* (Frederick A. Stokes Company, 1937), 29; Dr. Seuss, *Horton Hatches the Egg* (Random House, 1940), 55. **10.** *Judge* 114, no. 2713 (April 1938): 17. **11.** NBC advertisement, sampled in *Broadcasting* 16, no. 4 (February 15, 1939): 49; Dr. Seuss, *Horton Hatches the Egg* (Random House, 1940), 36; Dr. Seuss, *Horton Hatches the Egg* (Random House, 1940), 42; NBC advertisement, sampled in *Broadcasting* 16, no. 4 (February 15, 1939): 49. **13.** *Judge* 101, no. 2616 (December 19, 1931): 6. **14.** Kalmbach & Geisel beer bottles, style A (1876–1892) and style B (1892–1894) and Highland beer bottle (1895–1899); Springfield Breweries Co. Hampden Pale Ale bottle (1908); Springfield Breweries Co. Hampden Ale advertisement as it appeared in the Court Square Theatre program for *The Lilac Domino* (April 9, 1915): back cover; Liberty Brewing Company architectural drawing (the C. F. Hettinger Co., 1902); Liberty Brewing Company beer bottle (1901–1912). **15.** *Viewbook of Springfield, Massachusetts* (Springfield, MA: Johnson's Bookstore, 1910); photo of 74 Fairfield Street taken 2002; Gold Medal Tivoli label, Springfield Breweries Co. beer bottle (circa 1917–1920); Gold Medal Tivoli non-intoxicating label, Springfield Breweries Co. beer bottle (circa 1917–1920). **16.** Ted, age four, in 74 Fairfield Street yard (1908). **18.** Hilaire Belloc, *More Beasts for Worse Children* (Edward Arnold, 1897), 42; *Life* 94, no. 2447 (September 27, 1929): 15; *Jack-O-Lantern* 17, no. 8 (April 22, 1925): 24; *Jack-O-Lantern* 16, no. 3 (November 26, 1923): 25; *College Humor*, no. 86 (February 1931): 45; *Judge* 96, no. 2472 (March 16, 1929): 16; *Judge* 96, no. 2485 (June 15, 1929): 11. **19.** *More Boners* (Viking Press, 1931), 19; *Maple Leaves* 5, no. 2 (July 11, 1931): 7; *PM* 2, no. 191 (March 12, 1942): 21; Thomas D. Murphy calendar art (September 1935); *New York Sun* (October 13, 1937); Dr. Seuss, *Oh Say Can You Say?* (Yuan-Liou Publishing Co. Ltd., 1992), title page; Dr. Seuss, *I Can Draw It Myself* (Random House, 1970), 14. **20.** *Life* 95, no. 2467 (February 14, 1930): 23; Dr. Seuss, *Dr. Seuss's ABC* (Random House, 1963), 29; Dr. Seuss, *If I Ran the Zoo* (Random House, 1950), 13. **21.** Ted at the beach with father (circa 1914); Ted at the beach with father and sister, Marnie (circa 1907). **22.** *Telechronicle* 3, no. 11 (February 1932): inside front cover; *The 5000 Fingers of Dr. T* lobby card detail (Columbia Pictures, 1953). **24.** *Jack-O-Lantern* 16, no. 3 (November 26, 1923): 24; *The Tootle Bird* (Berger Publishing Company, 1907), frontispiece. **25.** Springfield Central High School postcard (Henry R. Johnson, publisher, 1908). **28.** Springfield Central High School calendar (1917). **29.** *Central Recorder* 3, no. 14 (January 21, 1920): 19. **30.** *Central Recorder* 3, no. 30 [misnumbered as 4, no. 16] (June 1920): 24; *Central Recorder* 4, no. 5 (October 29, 1920): 6. **31.** *The Brown and*

Gold Recorder (1921), 104. **34.** Ted's senior-yearbook portrait, *Pnalka*. **35.** *Jack-O-Lantern* 15, no. 1 (September 21, 1922): 25. **36.** *Judge* 94, no. 2410 (January 7, 1928): 20; *Jack-O-Lantern* 14, no. 1 (October 1, 1921): 24, 26, 20, 29. **37.** *Jack-O-Lantern* 14, no. 3 (December 14, 1921): 19. **38.** *Central Recorder* 3, no. 10 (December 12, 1919): 19; *Jack-O-Lantern* 14, no. 9 (June 8, 1922): 33; *Jack-O-Lantern* 14, no. 4 (January 24, 1922): 29; *Jack-O-Lantern* 14, no. 5 (February 9, 1922): 23. **39.** *Jack-O-Lantern* 15, no. 3 (November 13, 1922): 23; *Jack-O-Lantern* 15, no. 3 (November 13, 1922): 29; *Jack-O-Lantern* 16, no. 7 (March 20, 1924): 31. **40.** *Jack-O-Lantern* 17, no. 7 (March 24, 1925): 28; *Jack-O-Lantern* 15, no. 5 (February 8, 1923): 24; *Jack-O-Lantern* 16, no. 1 (September 26, 1923): 18; *Jack-O-Lantern* 16, no. 2 (October 25, 1923): 21. **41.** *Jack-O-Lantern* 17, no. 1 (September 30, 1924): 12; *Jack-O-Lantern* 17, no. 6 (February 5, 1925): 29; *Jack-O-Lantern* 16, no. 3 (November 26, 1923): 24–25 (Heumkia, Dingleblader, Bo, Blvgk, Pseukeh Snake). **42.** Rogers Peet advertisement in *The Dartmouth* 46, no. 17 (October 13, 1924): 2; *Jack-O-Lantern* 17, no. 3 (November 24, 1924): 17; *The Bad Child's Book of Beasts* (Simpkin, Marshall, Hamilton, Kent and Co., Ltd., 1896), 2; Dr. Seuss, *The Cat in the Hat Comes Back* (Random House, 1958), 37. **43.** *Jack-O-Lantern* 16, no. 2 (October 26, 1923): 28. **45.** *Jack-O-Lantern* 15, no. 5 (February 8, 1923): 21. **52.** "Noisiest Potty" sketch by Ted (March 17, 1985). **55.** *Dartmouth Freshman Green Book, Class of 1925* (December 13, 1921), 44. **57.** *Jack-O-Lantern* 17, no. 7 (March 24, 1925): 22. **58.** *Jack-O-Lantern* 17, no. 8 (April 22, 1925): 17, 21. **59.** *Jack-O-Lantern* 17, no. 8 (April 22, 1925): 33, 34. **61.** *Jack-O-Lantern* 17, no. 9 (May 7, 1925): 33. **62.** Dartmouth Pleiad(e) Class of 1925 membership list, 169. **66.** *Jack-O-Lantern* 17, no. 2 (October 22, 1924): 20. **67.** "Gobelin" (circa December 1926), from the Mandeville Special Collections Library at the University of California, San Diego. **68.** "Scene on the Forum" (circa December 1926), from the Mandeville Special Collections Library at the University of California, San Diego. **69.** "Enoch Arden" (circa December 1926), from the Mandeville Special Collections Library at the University of California, San Diego. **70.** "Emminent (sic) Europeans," Croupier Series: #1 (circa May 1927), property of the Rauner Special Collections Library, Dartmouth College. **71.** "Emminent (sic) Europeans," Croupier Series: #2 (circa May 1927), property of the Rauner Special Collections Library, Dartmouth College; "Emminent (sic) Europeans," Palace Tour Guide Series: #1 (circa May 1927), property of the Rauner Special Collections Library, Dartmouth College. **72.** "Emminent (sic) Europeans," Palace Tour Guide Series: #2" (circa May 1927), property of the Rauner Special Collections Library, Dartmouth College. **73.** *The Saturday Evening Post* 200, no. 3 (July 16, 1927): 28; *Judge* 93, no. 2399 (October 22, 1927): 5. **74.** *Jack-O-Lantern* 17, no. 5 (January 20, 1925): 22; *Judge* 93, no. 2400 (October 29, 1927): 3; *Judge* 93, no. 2403 (November 19, 1927): 9. **75.** Ted with Theophrastus (circa 1910); *Judge* 94, no. 2420 (March 17, 1928): 16, 17. **76–77.** Two images on p. 76 and five images on p. 77 from the unpublished "Hippocrass series" (circa March 1927), property of the Rauner Special Collections Library, Dartmouth College. **78.** *Judge* 93, no. 2405 (December 3, 1927); *Judge* 93, no. 2405 (December 3, 1927). **79.** *Judge* 94, no. 2415 (February 11, 1928): 8. **80–81.** *Judge* 94, no. 2422 (March 31, 1928): 16–17.

82. *Judge* 94, no. 2424 (April 14, 1928): 15; *Judge* 94, no. 2425 (April 21, 1928): 17. **83.** *Judge* 94, no. 2411 (January 14, 1928): 16; *Judge* 94, no. 2422 (March 31, 1928): 9. **84.** Flit advertisement, *Life* 91, no. 2378 (May 31, 1928): 30. **85.** Flit cartoon compilation (Stanco Incorporated, September 1929). **86.** *Judge* 94, no. 2426 (April 28, 1928): 15. **87.** *Judge* 94, no. 2429 (May 19, 1928): inside back cover; *Judge* 94, no. 2433 (June 16, 1928): 14. **88.** *Judge* 94, no. 2433 (June 16, 1928): 17. **89.** *Judge* 94, no. 2435 (June 30, 1928): 9; *Judge* 95, no. 2438 (July 21, 1928): 3. **90.** *Judge* 95, no. 2455 (November 17, 1928): 6; *Life* 95, no. 2463 (January 17, 1930): 14. **91.** *Judge* 95, no. 2455 (November 17, 1928): 6. **92.** *Judge* 96, no. 2481 (May 18, 1929); *Judge* 96, no. 2481 (May 18, 1929). **93.** *Life* 96, no. 2487 (July 4, 1930): 9. **94–95.** *College Humor*, no. 90 (June 1931): 38–39. **96.** *Life* 95, no. 2475 (April 11, 1930): 27. **97.** *Life* 92, no. 2384 (July 12, 1928): 36; *Life* 95, no. 2482 (May 30, 1930): 30; *Life* 95, no. 2479 (May 9, 1930): 31; *The New Yorker* (July 21, 1934): 50; *Life* 95, no. 2476 (April 18, 1930): 32. **98.** *Judge* 95, no. 2473 (March 23, 1929): front cover. **100.** "Rape of the Sabine Woman" (1930), Hood Museum of Art, Dartmouth College. **102.** Harkness Edwards mural, flamingos (1930). **103.** Harkness Edwards mural, doorway (1930). **104.** *Boners* (Viking Press, 1931), 7. **105.** *Boners* (Viking Press, 1931), 21. **106.** *Judge* 100, no. 1568 (January 17, 1931): 9; *Life* 95, no. 2477 (April 25, 1930): 13. **109.** *Rhymes and Riddles to Please and Tease You* (Gilpin, Langdon & Co., Inc., 1918), 3; Flit advertisement, *Life* 98, no. 2540 (July 10, 1931): 29; *Rhymes and Riddles to Please and Tease You* (Gilpin, Langdon & Co., Inc., 1918), 5; *Rhymes and Riddles to Please and Tease You* (Gilpin, Langdon & Co., Inc., 1918), 13. **110.** Flit advertisement, *Life* 95, no. 2484 (June 13, 1930): inside front cover. **112.** Flit advertisement, *Life* 97, no. 2525 (March 27, 1931): 31. **116.** Flit advertisement, *Boys' Life* 23, no. 7 (July 1933): inside back cover. **117.** Flit window display, matador (1933); Flit subway card, woman in hat with mosquitoes (1947). **118.** Standard Oil "Greet the Boys" poster (1932). **119.** "Foiled by Essolube" puzzle (1932); "Foiled by Essolube" puzzle bag (detail) (1932); Essolube newspaper advertisement, "Foil the Zero-doccus!" (December 1932). **120.** Essolube newspaper advertisement, "Foil the Moto-raspus!" (January 1933); Essolube poster card, "Foil the Karbo-nockus!" (January 1933); Essolube pamphlet, "Don't Feed These Animals" (1934). **121.** "Standard" Esso Topics pamphlet (circa 1933–34); Caterpillar Tractor Co. advertisement, *The Saturday Evening Post* (October 22, 1927): 105; Esso's "Happy Motoring" advertising campaign, "Meet Gus!" button (circa 1938); Ex-tane advertising display, "Take spots off a leopard?" (1934). **122.** *Secrets of the Deep* (June 1934): cover; *Secrets of the Deep* (June 1934): 15. **123.** *Secrets of the Deep* (June 1934): foreword page; *Secrets of the Deep* (June 1934): 22; *Secrets of the Deep* (June 1934): 11. **124.** Seuss Navy letter of acceptance (January 1936); Seuss Navy flag (January 1937); Admiral of the Seuss Navy certificate ("Esso" style) (January 1936). **125.** All three images from Essomarine pamphlet (1936). **126.** *Secrets of the Deep, Vol. II* (July 1936): front cover, back cover, 27. **127.** *Secrets of the Deep, Vol. II* (July 1936): 32, 25; *Little Dramas of the Deep* program (January 1938): cover, 1–2. **128.** Essomarine advertisement, *Yachting* 61, no. 1 (January 1937): 156–57; Essomarine advertisement, *Yachting* 61, no. 6 (June 1937): 87; Essomarine advertisement, *Yachting* 61, no. 5 (May 1937): 95. **129.** Seuss Navy Second Annual Manoeuvres' glass from 1938 Motor Boat Show (reproduced from the collection of Doug Striggow, with his permission); Seuss Navy Fourth Annual Manoeuvres' glass from 1940 Motor Boat Show; Seuss Navy Fifth Annual Manoeuvres' glass from 1941 Motor Boat Show. **130.** Seuss Navy matchbook (circa 1937); Seuss Navy "Nuzzlepuss" ashtray (1939). **131.** *The Sea Lawyer's Gazette* 1, no. 1 (January 11, 1940): masthead, 4, 1, 3. **132.** Ted at the National Motor Boat Show with Guy Lombardo (1940); Essomarine "Happy Cruising" passport (January 1941). **133.** Essomarine advertisement, *Yachting* 63, no. 5 (May 1938): 83; Essomarine advertisement, *Yachting* 63, no. 4 (April 1938): 89; Essomarine advertisement, *Yachting* 67, no. 3 (March 1940): 83. **134.** Essomarine advertisement, *Yachting* 63, no. 6 (June 1938): 81; Essomarine advertisement, *Yachting* 68, no. 4 (October 1940): 65; Essomarine advertisement, *Yachting* 67, no. 6 (June 1938): 75. **135.** *The Log of the Good Ship* (August 1947): cover. **136.** Seuss Navy "When Hen" glass set (January 1948). **137.** L.P.C. Co. Building Contractors advertising campaign postcards (March 1929–January 1930). **138.** *Jack-O-Lantern* 17, no. 6 (February 5, 1925): 30; Twentieth Annual Winter Carnival, Dartmouth Outing Club program (February 6, 1930): 5; Twenty-first Annual Winter Carnival, Dartmouth Outing Club program (February 5, 1931): 2, 5. **139.** Twenty-second Annual Winter Carnival, Dartmouth Outing Club program (February 5, 1932). **140.** Crosman rifle advertisement, *Science and Invention* 18, no. 1 (May 1930); Crosman rifle advertisement, *Life* 95, no. 2481 (May 23, 1930): 30; *The*

G.E. Merchandiser 20, no. 5 (June 1930): 1. **141.** *The G.E. Appliance Merchandiser* 2, no. 7 (July 1932): 2; *The G.E. Merchandiser* 20, no. 5 (June 1930): 5; *General Electric Merchandiser* 1, no. 2 (March 1931): 9; GE "bulbsnatching" advertisements, *Collier's* 106, no. 15 (October 11, 1941): 48. **142.** *Telechronicle* 3, no. 11 (Feb.–Mar. 1931): cover; *Telechronicle* 3, no. 12 (Apr.–May 1932): cover; *Telechronicle* 4, no. 1 (Sept.–Oct. 1932): cover; *Telechronicle* 4, no. 2 (Nov.–Dec. 1932): cover; *Telechronicle* 4, no. 3 (Jan.–Feb. 1933): cover. **143.** United States Envelope Co. Ajax Cups & Cabinets pamphlet (circa June 1933); Daggett & Ramsdell advertisement, *Your Magazine* (circa July 1933): 15; Daggett & Ramsdell advertisement, Lambs of St. Patrick's Dinner, Gambol, and Ball program (March 17, 1934): 16. **144.** Gilbert & Barker Manufacturing Company advertisement (April 22, 1936); Stromberg-Carlson advertising booklet (1937): 1, 3; Dr. Seuss, *The Cat in the Hat* (Random House, 1957), 48. **145.** Schaefer Bock Beer poster (March 1937); American Can Company advertisement, *Cincinnati Times-Star* (April 20, 1937): 11. **146.** Macy-Westchester Newspapers advertisement, *Advertising & Selling* (July 15, 1937): 51; Macy-Westchester Newspapers advertisement, *Advertising & Selling* (July 29, 1937): 47; Macy-Westchester Newspapers advertisement, *Advertising & Selling* (September 9, 1937): 63. **147.** Chilton Pen Co., Inc., advertisement, *The New Yorker* 13, no. 36, New York edition (October 23, 1937): 69; Chilton Pen Co., Inc., advertisement, *The New Yorker* 13, no. 37, New York edition (October 30, 1937): 101. **148.** Pep 88 gasoline billboard (circa December 1937); Pep 88 gasoline billboard (circa May 1938); Vico motor oil billboard (circa August 1938); Vico motor oil billboard (circa September 1938); Pep 88 motor oil billboard (circa November 1938). **149.** Hankey Bannister Scotch whisky advertisement, *Printers' Ink* (February 1939): 46; Twentieth Annual Winter Carnival program (February 6, 1930): 1; Hankey Bannister Scotch whisky advertisement (1939). **150.** Snyder & Black, Inc., point-of-sale advertising campaign (circa 1939); NBC Radio brochure (January 1939); NBC Radio brochure (March 1939); NBC Radio brochure (May 1939). **151.** NBC Radio brochure (1939); NBC Radio brochure (1939); NBC Radio advertisement, *Broadcasting* 17, no. 8 (October 15, 1939): 8; NBC Radio brochure (1939). **153.** *College Humor* 19, no. 1 (December 1929): 27; *Ballyhoo* 1, no. 3 (October 1931): inside front cover. **154.** *Life* 94, no. 2435 (July 5, 1929): 13; *Life* 94, no. 2442 (August 23, 1929): 19; *Life* 94, no. 2437 (July 19, 1929): 10; *Life* 94, no. 2444 (September 6, 1929): 18. **155.** *Jack-O-Lantern* 17, no. 3 (November 24, 1924): 17; *Judge* 94, no. 2423 (April 7, 1928): 8; *The G.E. Appliance Merchandiser* 2, no. 7 (July 1932): 3; Flit advertisement, *The New Yorker* (August 24, 1935): 45. **156.** *Life* 95, no. 2477 (April 25, 1930): 13; *Life* 94, no. 2464 (January 24, 1930): 16; *Life* 95, no. 2476 (April 18, 1930): 32; *Life* 95, no. 2478 (May 2, 1930): 23; *Life* 95, no. 2465 (January 31, 1930): 14; *College Humor*, no. 88 (April 1931): 45. **157.** *Judge* 100, no. 2566 (January 3, 1931): front cover. **158.** *Vanity Fair* 36, no. 4 (June 1931): 77; *Vanity Fair* 36, no. 6 (August 1931): 50. **159.** *Judge* 102, no. 2618 (January 2, 1932): 16–17. **160.** *Judge* 102, no. 2619 (January 9, 1932): front cover; coaster set advertisement, *Judge* 102, no. 2628 (March 12, 1932): 31; coaster set advertisement, *Judge* 102, no. 2629 (March 19, 1932): 26. **161.** *Liberty* 9, no. 28 (July 9, 1932): 47. **162.** *Liberty* 9, no. 26 (June 25, 1932): 29; *College Humor*, no. 104 (August 1932): 50–53. **163.** *Ballyhoo* 3, no. 2 (September 1932): 16. **164.** *Judge* 104, no. 2652 (March 1933): cover. **165.** *Life* 100, no. 2576 (March 1933): 24–25; *Judge* 104, no. 2655 (June 1933): cover; *Razzberries* 1, no. 2 (September 1933): center spread. **166.** *Are You a Genius? Second Series* (Frederick A. Stokes Company, 1933), dust jacket; *Who's the Genius? A Riotous Game for Parties* (Frederick A. Stokes Company, 1933), cover; *In One Ear . . .* (Viking Press, 1933), cover. **167.** *University* 1, no. 3 (October 1933): 47 (top two images); *Life* 101, no. 2590 (May 1934): cover; *Ballyhoo* 12, no. 6 (July 1937): back cover. **168.** "Blue-Green Abelard" sculpture (circa March 1931); ice sculpture outside Dartmouth College's Phi Gamma Delta house (circa February 5, 1931). **170.** 1935 calendar art series: "Seein' Things" (Jan.–Aug.). **171.** 1935 calendar art series: "Seein' Things" (Sept.–Dec.); 1937 calendar art series: "It's a Great World" (Jan.–Dec.). **172.** "Hejji," no. 1, *Sunday American* (April 7, 1935). **173.** "Hejji," no. 12, *Sunday American* (June 23, 1935). **175.** "The Advertising Business at a Glance" posters (1936). **176.** *So You Like Puzzles?* (Frederick A. Stokes, 1936), dust jacket; *Spelling Bees: The Oldest and the Newest Rage* (Frederick A. Stokes, 1937), dust jacket; *Mystery Puzzles* (Frederick A. Stokes, 1937), dust jacket, 29; *How's Tricks?* (Frederick A. Stokes, 1938), frontispiece. **177.** *The New York Woman* 1, no. 5 (October 7, 1936): 40; *The New York Woman* 1, no. 10 (November 11, 1936): 40. **178.** *University* 1, no. 5 (December 1933): 41. **179.** *Stage* 14, no. 7 (April 1937): 64. **180.** *Collier's* 100, no. 5 (July 31, 1937): 18. **181.** Swedish

American Line brochure (circa April 1936), 2. **183.** *Judge* 95, no. 2456 (November 24, 1928): 8; *Judge* 96, no. 2482 (May 25, 1929): 14; *Judge* 96, no. 2482 (May 25, 1929): 14. **185.** Postcard, Mason Bros. & Co., Boston (1910); *Judge* 96, no. 2478 (April 27, 1929): 20; *Life* 94, no. 2448 (October 4, 1929): 16; *Telechronicle* 4, no. 3 (Jan.–Feb. 1933): front cover; Dr. Seuss, *And to Think That I Saw It on Mulberry Street* (Vanguard, 1937), 9. **186.** "Hejji," no. 1, *Sunday American* (April 7, 1935); Dr. Seuss, *And to Think That I Saw It on Mulberry Street* (Vanguard, 1937), 19; Indian "V" Twin motorcycle from Hendee Manufacturing Co., Springfield, MA (1914); *And to Think That I Saw It on Mulberry Street* (Vanguard, 1937), 27. **187.** *Judge* 114, no. 2712 (March 1938): 11; *Judge* 114, no. 2712 (March 1938): 13; *Judge* 114, no. 2712 (March 1938): 14. **188.** *Judge* 114, no. 2713 (April 1938): inside back cover. **190.** Photos of Ted at work and "Goo-goo-eyed Tasmanian Wolghast" sculpture, *Look* 2, no. 12 (June 1938): 47–48; "Mulberry Street Unicorn" original sculpture (circa April 1938); "Mugglesmirt" sculpture, *Unusual Occupations*, Episode 1941-1 (October 3, 1941); "Kangaroo Bird" original sculpture (circa 1938); "Cruel Hack-Biter" sculpture (same as "Mugglesmirt"). **191.** Ceramic rabbit candleholder (1938). **192.** Seuss-Hastings marionettes, property of Barbara Bayler (circa 1938–39). **193.** Game envelope (Milton Bradley, 1919); Dr. Seuss, *The 500 Hats of Bartholomew Cubbins* (Vanguard, 1938), 18. **194.** "Hejji," *Sunday American* (April 14, 1935); Dr. Seuss, *The 500 Hats of Bartholomew Cubbins* (Vanguard, 1938), 36; NBC Radio brochure (May 1939). **196.** *Judge* 94, no. 2421 (March 24, 1928): 14. **197.** *Judge* 96, no. 2475 (April 6, 1929): 4; Dr. Seuss, *The Seven Lady Godivas* (Random House, 1939), cover, 44. **199.** Theodor Seuss Geisel and Ralph Warren. United States Patent #2,150,853 (camera) (patented: March 14, 1939). **200.** Dr. Seuss, *The King's Stilts* (Random House, 1939), 30, 49. **206.** *Judge* 96, no. 2481 (May 18, 1929): 8; *Life* 94, no. 2446 (September 20, 1929): 10; *Life* 94, no. 2446 (September 20, 1929): 10. **207.** *Life* 94, no. 2446 (September 20, 1929): 10; *Jack-O-Lantern* 15, no. 8 (April 26, 1923): 26; *Jack-O-Lantern* 15, no. 8 (April 26, 1923): 30; *Judge* 95, no. 2454 (November 10, 1928): 6. **208.** *Life* 95, no. 2475 (April 11, 1930): 16; *Judge* 95, no. 2456 (November 24, 1928): 8. **209.** *Jack-O-Lantern* 15, no. 5 (February 8, 1923): 24; *Judge* 94, no. 2426 (April 28, 1928): 15; *The Jazz Singer* lobby card (Warner Bros., 1927). **211.** Ted with pet bulldog, Rex (circa 1917). **212.** *Judge* 95, no. 2446 (September 15, 1928): 2; Griffords, *The Aggrevator* (as reproduced in *College Humor*, June 1927: 61); *Judge* 95, no. 2447 (September 22, 1928): 16. **213.** *Judge* 96, no. 2462 (January 5, 1929): 16; *Judge* 96, no. 2473 (March 23, 1929): 14; *Judge* 96, no. 2462 (January 5, 1929): 16; Old Gold cigarettes advertisement, *Judge* 96, no. 2467 (February 9, 1929): 25; *Judge* 96, no. 2463 (January 12, 1929): 2; *Life* 93, no. 2430 (May 31, 1929): 9; *Judge* 96, no. 2483 (June 1, 1929): 24. **214.** *Judge* 96, no. 2465 (January 26, 1929): 11; *Life* 95, no. 2466 (February 7, 1930): 21; *Life* 94, no. 2454 (November 15, 1929): 19. **215.** Flit advertisement, *Judge* 96, no. 2468 (February 16, 1929): 27; *Life* 100, no. 2576 (March 1933): 24; *Life* 101, no. 2592 (July 1934): 13. **217.** *PM* 2, no. 76 (October 1, 1941): 12. **218.** *PM* 2, no. 256 (June 11, 1942): 20; *PM* 3, no. 10 (June 30, 1942): 22; *PM* 3, no. 18 (July 9, 1942): 22; *PM* 3, no. 8 (July 20, 1942): 21. **219.** *PM* 3, no. 54 (August 19, 1942): 22. **220.** Dr. Seuss, *The Sneetches and Other Stories* (Random House, 1961), 4. **221.** *Life* 95, no. 2473 (March 14, 1930): 21; Dr. Seuss, *And to Think That I Saw It on Mulberry Street* (Vanguard, 1937), 32. **222.** *Judge* 12, no. 2624 (February 13, 1932): 8. **223.** *Vanity Fair* 39, no. 6 (February 1933): 39. **224.** "The State of the World in 1931" (circa 1933), property of Audrey Geisel. **225.** *The New York Sun* (circa October 1937); *The New York Sun* (October 13, 1937). **226.** *New York Journal and American* (February 15, 1939): 18; *New York Journal and American*, no. 18867 (August 11, 1939): 12. **227.** *New York Journal and American*, no. 18694 (February 17, 1939): 16. **228.** *New York Journal and American* (July 29, 1939): 8; *New York Journal and American*, no. 18879 (August 23, 1939): 2; *New York Journal and American* (September 19, 1939): 14. **229.** *New York Journal and American* (September 13, 1939): 18. **230.** Ted in Native American outfit (circa 1911); *Jack-O-Lantern* 17, no. 5 (January 20, 1925): 26; Narragansett Brewing Co. advertisement, *Boston Evening Globe* (October 22, 1940); Narragansett Brewing Co. advertisement, *Boston Evening Globe* (October 29, 1940); Narragansett Lager & Ale beer tray (circa 1941); Narragansett Brewing Co. advertisement (1941). **231.** Narragansett Brewing Co. advertisement, *Boston Daily Globe* (November 25, 1940); *PM* 1, no. 179 (February 24, 1941): 4; Narragansett Brewing Co. advertisement, *Boston Evening Globe* (March 18, 1941): 21; Narragansett coaster (circa March 1941); Narragansett Brewing Co. advertisement, *Boston Evening Globe* (April 15, 1941): 22; Narragansett Bock Beer poster (circa February 1942). **233.** *PM* 1, no. 224 (April 28, 1941): 22; *PM* 1, no. 46 (May 4, 1941): front cover; *PM* 1, no. 232 (May 8, 1941):

front cover; *PM* 1, no. 235 (May 13, 1941): 17; *PM* 1, no. 245 (May 27, 1941): 12; *PM* 1, no. 248 (June 2, 1941): 20. **234.** *PM* 2, no. 36 (August 6, 1941): front cover; *PM* 2, no. 41 (August 13, 1941): front cover. **235.** *PM* 2, no. 67 (September 18, 1941): 10; *PM* 2, no. 69 (September 22, 1941): cover; *PM* 2, no. 91 (October 22, 1941): 4. **236.** *PM* 2, no. 106 (November 22, 1941): cover; *PM* 2, no. 118 (November 28, 1941): 20; *PM* 2, no. 24 (November 30, 1941): cover. **237.** *PM* 2, no. 124 (December 8, 1941); *PM* 2, no. 125 (December 9, 1941): 14; *PM* 2, no. 129 (December 15, 1941): front cover; *PM* 2, no. 133 (December 19, 1941). **238.** *Victory: Official Weekly Bulletin of the Office of Emergency Management* 3, no. 17 (April 28, 1942): 5; *Victory: Official Weekly Bulletin of the Office of Emergency Management* 3, no. 20 (May 19, 1942): 17; U.S. Treasury Department's war savings bonds and stamps advertisement #5. **239.** *PM* 2, no. 210 (April 8, 1942): 21; *PM* 2, no. 155 (January 21, 1942): 22. **240.** *PM* 2, no. 165 (February 4, 1942): 21; *PM* 2, no. 172 (February 13, 1942): 21. **243.** *PM* 2, no. 206 (April 2, 1942): 21; *PM* 2, no. 215 (April 15, 1942): 21. **244.** *PM* 3, no. 36 (July 30, 1942): 22; *PM* 3, no. 109 (October 22, 1942): 21; *PM* 3, no. 130 (November 16, 1942): 13. **245.** *PM* 3, no. 148 (December 7, 1942): 21; *PM* 3, no. 156 (December 16, 1942): 18. **246.** *PM* 3, no. 157 (December 17, 1942): 18; unpublished *PM* cartoon from the Mandeville Special Collections Library at the University of California, San Diego (December 1942). **247.** Ted in military uniform (circa January 1943). **251.** "This Is Ann" malaria pamphlet (U.S. Government Printing Office, August 1943): cover, 4, 5, 15. **252.** Army cartoon by Ted, *Screen Magazine* (circa July 1943); Chuck Jones, *PRIVATE SNAFU: SPIES*—image of horse, image of moose heads (August 1943). **254.** *Judge* 95, no. 2453 (November 3, 1928): 6; *Liberty* 9, no. 44 (October 29, 1932): 45. **255.** "Cartoonists draw the Squander Bug" poster (detail of Squander Bug, British version), National Savings Committee (1943); "Don't Take the Squander Bug When You Go Shopping" poster, Great Britain (1943); *Schools at War: Fifth War Savings News Bulletin for Teachers* (U.S. Government Printing Office, no. 550855, December 1943): 20; *Art in the Service of Schools at War* booklet (Related Art Service, circa November 1943): back cover; *Starve the Squander Bug* advertising brochure [vertical poster] (U.S. Government Printing Office, no. 16-35253-1, circa November 1943): cover; *Starve the Squander Bug* brochure [horizontal poster] (U.S. Government Printing Office, no. 555548, circa November 1943). **256.** *Starve the Squander Bug* brochure (U.S. Government Printing Office, no. 560021, circa November 1943): center foldout poster [3 of 18 posters shown]; "This Is Ann" *NewsMap* poster, version A (U.S. Government Printing Office, no. 538110, November 8, 1943). **257.** United States war bonds and stamps envelope (December 1943). **258.** *PRIVATE SNAFU: RUMORS* bird with bugle beak and monster abed (December 1943); Dr. Seuss, *Hop on Pop* (Random House, 1963), 34. **259.** SNAFU matchbook covers (circa 1944). **260.** "Sunset House" army cartoon by Ted (circa September 1944) from the Mandeville Special Collections Library at the University of California, San Diego. **261.** "Coca Cola" sketch by Ted (circa 1944) from the Mandeville Special Collections Library at the University of California, San Diego. **263.** "Be calm, BE CALM! One way or another, I'll pull you through!" *PM* 3, 133 (November 19, 1942): 21; *PM* 3, no. 155 (December 15, 1942): 18. **266.** *Picture News* 1, no. 8 (Sept.–Oct. 1946): 4. **270.** "Having a Ball" ornament (December 1982). **280.** Half-sheet and one-sheet poster from *Design for Death* (RKO Radio Pictures, Inc., 1948). **281.** *The Ford Dealer* 4, no. 5 (August 1949): 14, back cover. **282.** "The Unicyclist" short film advertisement for Ford Motor Company—stopping car, chatting, and bird sequences (circa August 1949); "The Zither-Player" short film advertisement for Ford Motor Company—strumming sequence and moon still (circa August 1949); "The Squeak-Squeak" short film advertisement for Ford Motor Company—mustache sequence (August 16, 1949); storyboard sketch (man in bubble car) possibly for "Weightlifter" short film advertisement for Ford Motor Company (circa May–Dec. 1949); *The Ford Dealer* 4, no. 5 (August 1949): two images from back cover. **283.** Ford Motor Company short film, three storyboards (circa August 1949); Gerald McBoing-Boing (Capitol Records, 1950): cardboard cover sleeve. **284.** *Gerald McBoing Boing* (Simon & Schuster, 1952), front cover; *Gerald McBoing Boing and Mr. Magoo* comic book (Dell, Aug.–Oct. 1952): cover; *Gerald McBoing Boing and the Wonderful Kingdom of "Oop"* (Cricket Records, 1970); *Magoo Meets McBoing Boing* (United Arista, April 3, 1962); *Gerald McBoing Boing* (Columbia Pictures, 1973). **287.** *Crazy Music* lobby card 7 (Columbia Pictures, 1958); *The 5000 Fingers of Dr. T* window card (Columbia Pictures, 1952). **288.** Still photo [tuba] D-8064-238 from *The 5000 Fingers of Dr. T* (Columbia Pictures, 1952); still photo [standing bass] D-8064-243 from *The 5000 Fingers of Dr. T* (Columbia Pictures, 1952); still photo [stairway] D-8064-183K from *The 5000 Fingers of Dr. T* (Columbia Pictures, 1952); Dr. Seuss, *Bartholomew and the Oobleck* (Random House, 1949), 24. **290.** *Crazy Music* lobby card 4 (Columbia Pictures, 1958). **292.** *College Humor,* no. 96 (December 1931): 30; "Hejji" (April 7, 1935); *PM* 2, no. 15 (July 8, 1941): 20; still photo from *The 5000 Fingers of Dr. T* (Columbia Pictures, 1952). **293.** Still photo D-8064-254 from *The 5000 Fingers of Dr. T* (Columbia Pictures, 1952); Ford Motor Company advertisement (circa May 1949); Dr. Seuss, *Hunches in Bunches* (Random House, 1982), front cover, 17; "Hejji" no. 12, panel 2 (June 23, 1935); still photo D-8064-027 from *The 5000 Fingers of Dr. T* (Columbia Pictures, 1952). **294.** *The 5000 Fingers of Dr. T* merchandise—jewelry, instruments, and phonographs (circa 1953). **295.** Still photo D-8064-P38 of Tommy Rettig in Ted Geisel's lap during the making of *The 5000 Fingers of Dr. T; The 5000 Fingers of Dr. T* merchandise—instruments (circa 1953); *The 5000 Fingers of Dr. T* merchandise—roller skates (circa 1953); half-sheet poster of *The 5000 Fingers of Dr. T* (Columbia Pictures, 1952); Spanish herald (style B) poster *Los 5000 Dedos del Dr. T* (circa January 1953). **296.** Ted after fishing (circa 1919). **297.** *The Log of the Good Ship* (circa August 1947): 18; Dr. Seuss, *McElligot's Pool* (Random House, 1947), 36; *The Log of the Good Ship* (circa August 1947): 20; Dr. Seuss, *McElligot's Pool* (Random House, 1947), 41; *The Log of the Good Ship* (circa August 1947): 5; Dr. Seuss, *McElligot's Pool* (Random House, 1947), 52; New Departure ball bearings advertisement, *Farm Implement News* 69, no. 10 (May 1958): back cover; *Dartmouth Alumni Magazine* (December 1948): 58. **298.** "King Grimalken and the Wishbones," as it appeared in *Junior Catholic Messenger* (October 29, 1948): 55-B, 62-B. **302.** "The Royal Housefly and Bartholomew Cubbins," as it appeared in *Junior Catholic Messenger* 16, no. 18 (January 27, 1950): 142-B; *Junior Catholic Messenger* 16, no. 19 (February 3, 1950): 151-B. **304.** Dr. Seuss, *If I Ran the Zoo* (Random House, 1950), 55–56. **305.** "Tadd and Todd," as it appeared in *Redbook* 95, no. 4 (August 1950): 56. **306.** "Horton and the Kwuggerbug," as it appeared in *Redbook* 96, no. 1 (January 1951): 46–47. **307.** *PM* 2 no. 198 (March 21, 1942): 21; Dr. Seuss, *Yertle the Turtle and Other Stories* (Random House, 1958), 23. **309.** Dr. Seuss, "The Sneetches," as it appeared in *Redbook* 101, no. 3 (July 1954): 77; Dr. Seuss, *The Sneetches and Other Stories* (Random House, 1961), 5. **310.** "The Ruckus," as it appeared in *Redbook* 103, no. 3 (July 1954): 84. **311.** Dr. Seuss, *Horton Hears a Who!* (Random House, 1954), 31; postcard of Forest Park in Springfield, Massachusetts (Springfield News Company, 1907). **312.** Dr. Seuss, *On Beyond Zebra!* (Random House, 1955), 19; *Judge* 95, no. 2447 (September 22, 1928): 14; *Judge* 95, no. 2447 (September 22, 1928): 14; *PM* 1, no. 239 (May 19, 1941): 5. **313.** Dr. Seuss, "The Great McGrew Milk Farm," *Children's Activities* 21, no. 4 (April 1955): 13. **314–15.** Dr. Seuss, "Speedy Boy," *Children's Activities* 21, no. 3 (March 1955): 14–15. **316.** Ted receiving honorary title of Doctor, property of the Rauner Special Collections Library, Dartmouth College (1955); Dr. Seuss, *On Beyond Zebra!* (Random House, 1955), 7. **317.** Dr. Seuss, *On Beyond Zebra!* (Random House, 1955), 19. **318.** Holly Sugar advertising campaign (1954–56). **319.** *Signs of Civilization!* booklet for the La Jolla Town Council (March 1956): front cover. **321.** Dr. Seuss, *The Cat in the Hat* (Random House, 1957), cover; Dr. Seuss, *How the Grinch Stole Christmas!* (Random House, 1957), cover. **324.** *A Storybook Treasury of Dick and Jane* (Grosset & Dunlap, 1993), 61. **324.** Dr. Seuss, *The Cat in the Hat* (Random House, 1957), 55. **325.** Fourth panel of "Krazy Kat" comic strip, entitled "Ignatz Mouse: The Avenger!!" (July 16, 1912); Dr. Seuss, *The Cat in the Hat Comes Back* (Random House, 1958), 60. *For Crime's Sake* movie poster (Paramount Pictures, 1923). **326.** *Jack-O-Lantern* 15, no. 4 (January 8, 1923): 24; *Felix the Cat Shatters the Sheik* (Educational Pictures, 1926) [poster and close-up of fish in fishbowl]; Dr. Seuss, *The Cat in the Hat* (Random House, 1957), 11. **327.** Game poster (Milton Bradley, 1919); poster for *Dick Whittington's Cat* (Iwerks & Celebrity Productions, Inc., May 30, 1936); *The Cat in the Hat* (Random House, 1957), 7; *Liberty* 15, no. 20 (May 14, 1938): 6; Dr. Seuss, *The Cat in the Hat* (Random House, 1957), 26. **328.** Dr. Seuss, *Bartholomew and the Oobleck* (Random House, 1949), 18; Ford Motor Company short film storyboard (1949); Dr. Seuss, *The Cat in the Hat Comes Back* (Random House, 1958), 6. **329.** *Jack-O-Lantern* 17, no. 3 (November 24, 1924): 17; *The Ford Dealer* 4, no. 5 (August 1949): back cover; Dr. Seuss, *The Cat in the Hat Comes Back* (Random House, 1958), 37. **330.** *Redbook* 110, no. 2 (October 1957): table of contents; Dr. Seuss, *How the Grinch Stole Christmas!* (Random House, 1957), 24. **331.** *Judge* 93, no. 2406 (December 10, 1927): 25; *Judge* 99, no. 2565 (December 27, 1930): 10; *Life* 101, no. 2587 (February 1934): 22; Dr. Seuss, *How the Grinch Stole Christmas!* (Random House, 1957), 15. **332.** Stromberg-Carlson advertising booklet

(1937): 3; Dr. Seuss, *How the Grinch Stole Christmas!* (Random House, 1957), 17; Dr. Seuss, *Scrambled Eggs Super!* (Random House, 1953), 11. **333.** Holly Sugar advertisement (circa July 1955); Dr. Seuss, *How the Grinch Stole Christmas!* (Random House, 1957), 47. **334.** Dr. Seuss, *The Cat in the Hat,* educational market edition (Houghton Mifflin, 1957), cover; Dr. Seuss, *The Cat in the Hat* (Random House, 1957), title page. **335.** *Judge* 96, no. 2484 (June 8, 1929): 18; Dr. Seuss's stock fan-mail reply letters (1957, 1960). **337.** *New Republic* 117, no. 4 (July 28, 1947): 7. **340.** Elephant-Cat (Kreiss Moon Being, circa December 1955); Dr. Seuss, *If I Ran the Zoo* (Random House, 1950), 16; Nerd (Kreiss Moon Being, circa December 1955); Dr. Seuss, *If I Ran the Zoo* (Random House, 1950), 53; Grickily Gractus (Kreiss Moon Being, circa December 1955); Dr. Seuss, *Scrambled Eggs Super!* (Random House, 1953), 45; Mop-Noodled Finch (Kreiss Moon Being, circa December 1955); Dr. Seuss, *Scrambled Eggs Super!* (Random House, 1953), 17; Twiddler Owl (Kreiss Moon Being, circa December 1955); Dr. Seuss, *Scrambled Eggs Super!* (Random House, 1953), 20; Unnamed, white bird with neck tuft (Kreiss Moon Being, circa December 1955); Dr. Seuss, *Scrambled Eggs Super!* (Random House, 1953), 19. **342.** Dr. Seuss Zoo (clockwise from left within image): Gowdy the Dowdy Grackle, Tingo the Noodle-Topped Stroodle, Roscoe the Many-Footed Lion, Norval the Bashful Blinket (Revell, Inc., September 1959); Dr. Seuss Zoo: Grickily the Gractus and Busby the Tasseated Afghan Spaniel Yak (Revell, Inc., 1960); Dr. Seuss Zoo: Cat in the Hat with Things One and Two (Revell, Inc., 1960); Dr. Seuss Zoo: Birthday Bird (Revell, Inc., 1960); Dr. Seuss Zoo: Horton the Elephant with display box (Revell, Inc., 1960); Dr. Seuss Zoo: Revell interchangeable model example (Revell, Inc., September 1959). **343.** Cat in the Hat dolls (Impulse, circa 1961). **346.** Put-Your-Nose-Here Terrier (Poynter Products, Inc., March 1968); *Liberty* 9, no. 24 (June 11, 1932): 19; Stone Age Wild Gift Horse (Poynter Products, Inc., March 1968); *Liberty* 9, no. 41 (October 8, 1932): 54. **348.** Dr. Seuss, "Fooling Nobody" (1968), property of Audrey Geisel. **349.** *PM* 2, no. 48 (August 22, 1941): 20; Cat with "Handmade D.T.s" (Poynter Products, Inc., March 1968); *Liberty* 9, no. 40 (October 1, 1932): 47. **350.** *Liberty* 9, no. 24 (June 11, 1932): 19; Taper-Tailed Dingo (Fun World, Inc., circa March 1969); *Liberty* 9, no. 24 (June 11, 1932): 19; Rubber-Hating Grackle (Fun World, Inc., circa March 1969). **351.** Aladdin World of Dr. Seuss lunch boxes and thermos (Aladdin Industries, Inc., 1970). **352.** Mattel-O-Phone (Mattel, Inc., November 1970); toy box (Sears, Roebuck and Co., November 1970) with toys (Mattel, Inc., November 1970); Fish-A-Ma-Jigger game (Mattel, Inc., November 1970); two Cat in the Hat pull-string talkers (Mattel, Inc., November 1970); The Cat in the Hat in-the-Music-Box (Mattel, Inc., November 1970); Cat in the Hat, Hedwig, and Yertle the Turtle pull-string talkers (Mattel, Inc., November 1970); toy box, version 2, yellow (Sears, Roebuck and Co., November 1970), top view; Horton the Elephant pull-string talker (Mattel, Inc., 1970); Cat in the Hat radio cover (Sears, Roebuck and Co., November 1970); Yertle Yellow interior latex paint (Sears, Roebuck and Co., November 1970); bedroom set (Sears, Roebuck and Co., November 1970). **353.** Cat in the Hat alarm clock (unknown manufacturer, 1978); The Cat in the Hat Time Teller watches (Lafayette Watch Co., 1972–1974); Cat in the Hat plush dolls (Milton Bradley, 1973, and Douglas Co., Inc., 1974); Douglas puppets (Douglas Co., Inc., 1974–1976); Eden plush dolls (Eden Toys, Inc., 1979). **354.** Coleco toys (Coleco Industries, Inc., 1984); Coleco plush dolls (Coleco Industries, Inc., 1984); Hallmark Cat in the Hat party accessories (Hallmark Cards, Inc., 1985). **358.** Dr. Seuss, original sketch on Chaine des Rotisseurs menu and auction catalog (June 4, 1984); Dr. Seuss, original sketch on Bordeaux dinner menu: Bordeaux Toujours Bordeaux (March 17, 1985); park and open-space bond measure flyer (San Diegans for Parks and Open Space, October 1990). **360.** Dr. Seuss, *Oh, the Places You'll Go!* (Random House, 1990), 19, 51. **361.** Photo of Ted at drawing board (1984), © E. T. Masterson. **390.** Dr. Seuss, original artwork, "Un Chat dans Chapeau fume un mouchoire Blanc Elegant . . ." (January 1980).

Thank You

The Geisel and Seuss extended families for their warmth and generosity: Audrey Geisel, Peggy and Albert Owens, Ted Owens, and Barbara Bayler and family.

The folks at Dr. Seuss Enterprises for their assistance and encouragement in pursuing this project: Herb Cheyette for International Creative Management as agents for Dr. Seuss Enterprises, L.P.

The Mandeville Special Collections Library at the University of California, San Diego, for maintaining a marvelous archive and allowing serious research, with particular gratitude to Lynda Corey Claassen, Director.

The earnest and creative editors and assistants at Random House, Inc., for providing me with this opportunity, for their unwavering belief in this project through hard times, and for all of their incredible patience, wisdom, and guidance: Kate Klimo, Cathy Goldsmith, Suzy Capozzi, Judith Haut, Ken Sirulnick, and the special breed called Copy Editors.

For research assistance: Shirley A. Keech, WMRLS search specialist, for absolutely limitless resourcefulness in tracking and obtaining research materials; Richard West and Kayt Ehrmann of Periodyssey, *the* source for late-nineteenth- and early-twentieth-century periodicals; Elise Feeley and Moira Callahan at the Forbes Library research desk; Harkness Edwards II for the generous contribution of his memories about Ted's mural; Images of TDM for information regarding Ted's calendar series for the Thos. D. Murphy Company.

Dartmouth College for making available its research resources, with special appreciation to reading-room supervisor Sarah Hartwell and the staff at Dartmouth's Rauner Special Collections Library; Associate Registrar Kathleen P. O'Malley, Cynthia A. Gilliland, and the staff at Dartmouth's Hood Museum of Art.

Fellow Dr. Seuss enthusiasts for their help, encouragement, and shared information: Richard Michelson, Paul Gulla, and the expert staff at the wonderful R. Michelson Galleries;

Bill Dreyer and Bob Chase of The Chase Group, producer of glorious reproductions of Ted's Secret Art; original Dr. Seuss guru Dallas Poague, and supercollectors James Otis and Doug Striggow.

For Flit film research assistance and suggestions: animation experts Graham Webb, Harvey Deneroff, Michael Barrier, Jerry Beck, Keith Scott, Will Friedwald, Mark Kausler, and Donald Crafton; Ron Hutchinson with The Vitaphone Project, film critic Leonard Maltin, film research specialist Giovanna Righini, and Warner Bros. chief preservation officer Richard May.

For the sometimes herculean efforts of the Connecticut Valley Historical Museum staff and executives: Melanie Solomon, Steve Meunier, President Joseph Carvalho, Director Guy McLain, Sarah Orr, Laurie Darby, Susan Davison, Maggie Humbertson, and the rest of the CVHM staff.

The wizards at Audio-Visual Archives for their assistance in preserving and transferring footage across media: Steve Unkles and Patrick Rowan.

For book talk: Dr. Jonathan Pevsner for the many discussions between two neophytes in the publishing world; Herb Berman, for all of his wise insights and helpful suggestions; Oolong "Blue" Govinda Brautiga, my own Cat in the Hat.

Finally, the research, discovery, collection, and preservation of these Dr. Seuss materials would absolutely not have been possible without the Internet and the auction site eBay. Discovery and invention make the world smaller but the possibilities greater.

MERCI !

↑ Un Chat dans Chapeau
fume
un mouchoire Blanc
Elegat